Computer Science and Engineering

Computer Science and Engineering

Edited by Robert Henderson

CLANRYE
INTERNATIONAL
www.clanryeinternational.com

Clanrye International,
750 Third Avenue, 9th Floor,
New York, NY 10017, USA

ISBN: 978-1-63240-951-5

Cataloging-in-Publication Data

Computer science and engineering / edited by Robert Henderson.
p. cm.
Includes bibliographical references and index.
ISBN 978-1-63240-951-5
1. Computer science. 2. Computer engineering. 3. Computers. I. Henderson, Robert.
QA76 .C66 2020
004--dc23

For information on all Clanrye International publications
visit our website at www.clanryeinternational.com

Contents

Preface

I am honored to present to you this unique book which encompasses the most up-to-date data in the field. I was extremely pleased to get this opportunity of editing the work of experts from across the globe. I have also written papers in this field and researched the various aspects revolving around the progress of the discipline. I have tried to unify my knowledge along with that of stalwarts from every corner of the world, to produce a text which not only benefits the readers but also facilitates the growth of the field.

Computer science and engineering is a sub-field of electronic engineering that integrates the fields of computer science and computer engineering. It encompasses core areas like the design and analysis of algorithms, operating systems, data structures and database systems, computer architecture, high-performance computing, processor design, embedded systems, parallel processing, etc. The development, design and troubleshooting of computing devices, operating system design, digital system design, database management and software development are under the purview of this field. Computer science and engineering is an upcoming field of science that has undergone rapid development over the past few decades. This book includes contributions of experts and scientists, which will provide innovative insights into this field. For someone with an interest and eye for detail, it covers the most significant topics in this area of study.

Finally, I would like to thank all the contributing authors for their valuable time and contributions. This book would not have been possible without their efforts. I would also like to thank my friends and family for their constant support.

Editor

A Bit String Content Aware Chunking Strategy for Reduced CPU Energy on Cloud Storage

Bin Zhou,[1] ShuDao Zhang,[2] Ying Zhang,[3] and JiaHao Tan[1]

[1]*College of Computer Science, South-Central University for Nationalities, Wuhan, Hubei 430074, China*
[2]*School of Information Engineering, Wuhan Technology and Business University, Wuhan, Hubei 430065, China*
[3]*School of Foreign Languages, Huazhong University of Science and Technology, Wuhan, Hubei 430074, China*

Correspondence should be addressed to Bin Zhou; binzhou@mail.scuec.edu.cn

Academic Editor: Lu Liu

In order to achieve energy saving and reduce the total cost of ownership, green storage has become the first priority for data center. Detecting and deleting the redundant data are the key factors to the reduction of the energy consumption of CPU, while high performance stable chunking strategy provides the groundwork for detecting redundant data. The existing chunking algorithm greatly reduces the system performance when confronted with big data and it wastes a lot of energy. Factors affecting the chunking performance are analyzed and discussed in the paper and a new fingerprint signature calculation is implemented. Furthermore, a Bit String Content Aware Chunking Strategy (BCCS) is put forward. This strategy reduces the cost of signature computation in chunking process to improve the system performance and cuts down the energy consumption of the cloud storage data center. On the basis of relevant test scenarios and test data of this paper, the advantages of the chunking strategy are verified.

1. Introduction

Along with the development of the next generation of network computing technology, such as the application of Internet and cloud computing, the scale of the data center is showing the explosive growth in the past 10 years. The total amount of global information is double every 2 years. It was 1.8 ZB in 2011 and will reach 8 ZB in 2015. In the next 5 years (2020), the data will be 50 times higher than that of today [1].

According to the 2005 annual report of the international well-known consulting company Gartner [2], the total power consumption was 45,000,000,000 kwh of electricity for the whole data centers in USA in 2005. In its latest report about the data center efficiency the Natural Resources Defense Council (NRDC) [3] suggested that it was 91,000,000,000 kwh of electricity in 2013, which was more than double the total power for homes of New York. The annual electricity consumption will reach 140,000,000,000 kwh by 2020. Data center has developed into one of the great energy consumption industries rapidly.

How was electrical energy wasted in the data center? References [4–6] carried out experimental analysis and found out that the biggest power consumption was from first refrigeration system and the server, second IT infrastructure, such as storage and network air conditioning, and last air conditioning and lighting, and so forth. Among them, the storage system consumes about 14% electrical energy [7]. Construction of energy-efficient green data center is the future research and development tendency for the industry. Most businesses including IBM, Microsoft, HP, SUN, Cisco, Google, and other companies have launched a research on green data center.

Green storage technology refers to reduction of the data storage power consumption, electronic carbon compounds, the construction and operation cost, and improvement of the storage equipment performance in terms of the environment protection and energy saving. The study shows that there is a large amount of redundant data in the growing data. And the proportion of redundancy will be higher as time goes on, leading to a sharp decline in the utilization of storage space. The low utilization of storage space leads to a waste of both storage resources and lots of energy.

In order to improve the utilization of storage space, a large number of intelligent data management technologies, such as virtualization, thin provisioning, data deduplication, and hierarchical storage, have been widely applied in the cloud data center. Deduplication, now a hot research topic, meets the ends of energy conservation, efficiency of customers' investment and reduction of emission, and operation costs by saving lots of storage space, improving the performance of data read and write, and lessening the bandwidth consumption effectively.

Research shows that a large amount of data is duplication in the growing data. Therefore, the key for reducing the data in the system is to find and delete the redundant data. The basis of detecting it is the high-performance and stable chunking strategy.

It takes advantage of signature calculation to partition the data objects in the most existing literatures [8–10] on the variable length data chunking algorithms. The research on the optimization measure of time cost for data chunking algorithm is relatively few.

It is CPU intensive for detecting the chunk boundaries through signature calculation. For a 100 MB file, if the expected average length of chunk is 8 KB, the minimum length of chunk is 2 KB, and the file is expected to be divided into 12800 chunks. For each chunk boundary, 6144 times signature calculations and comparisons are required. $12800 * 9144$ times signature calculations and comparisons are required for a 100 MB file. In the heavy CPU operation, the ratio of the number of chunk to the total number of signature calculation is only $1 : 6144$, which is a difference of nearly three orders of magnitude. A lot of valuable CPU resources are consumed by invalid signature calculations and comparisons, which leads to more waste of energy.

The key problem of improving chunking performance lies in cutting down the consumption of CPU resources by reducing the number of invalid signature calculations and comparisons.

In this paper, we build the BCCS to a prototype of storage system. The primary contribution of our work is as follows. Firstly, as the deficiencies of total signature computations of Rabin fingerprinting algorithm are very huge, it is very CPU-demanded to divide the chunks that decrease the system performance. A new strategy, BCCS, is presented, reducing the overhead of generating fingerprints, as well as converting the question of files data partitioning stably to matching two binary bit strings. It samples a special bit from a text byte to constitute its data fingerprint, which converts the signature computation to binary string comparison. Only 1/8 of the text reads originally, and the bit operation is taking place of the traditional comparison. Secondly, by replacing the comparison operation, BCCS uses bitwise operation to optimize each matching process and exclude the unmatching positions as much as possible, getting the maximum jumping distance to quicken the matching process of binary string. It also reduces calculation and comparison costs by taking advantage of the bit feature information brought by failure matching every time. This measure reduces the cost of signature computation in chunking process and brings down CPU resource consumption to improve the system performance.

BCCS also divides the chunking process into two steps: the preprocessing step and the partitioning step. Then, BCCS adopts the parallel processing mode dealing with the preprocessing at a preprocessing node that synchronizes with partitioning at the front-end node. It saves the time of the preprocessing when the system is working. All of the measures minimize the total time consumption for data partitioning.

The rest of this paper provides the following. Section 2 introduces related works of traditional chunking algorithms. Section 3 studies BCCS algorithm in detail. In Section 4, we perform various experiments to measure the overhead of the data chunking, and Section 5 draws the conclusion.

2. Related Works

In order to solve the stability problem of chunking, Muthitacharoen et al. [11] adopted a variable length chunking algorithm named CDC based on content in the Low Bandwidth Network File System. It predetermined a piece of data as the boundary of the chunk in the pending data objects (called Marker in this paper) and determined the boundary of each chunk by finding the Marker. In actual practice, Rabin algorithm [12] is used to calculate the fingerprint of the data in the window to find the boundary of each chunk in the data objects. But the CDC algorithm remains inadequate. Firstly, for the chunk of different sizes, in some cases, since volatility is relatively large, it increases the difficulty of storage management. Secondly, the granularity settings will directly affect the precision and effect of duplicate. The higher the precision of deduplication, the smaller the granularity, but the chunk metadata overhead will increase to affect the overall performance of the system. Conversely, if the granularity is too large, reducing the metadata overhead, it is possible that the duplicate precision cannot reach the requirements. Thirdly, it is possible that the boundaries of chunks cannot be found, and hard chunking will be employed.

Eshghi and Tang [13] proposed double threshold algorithm TTTD (Two Thresholds Two Divisors) to get the stability for chunking, which regulated the size of chunk only in the upper and lower bounds ($min_C < length_C < max_C$, $length_C$ is the length of chunk). To a certain extent, TTTD alleviated the contradiction between chunking granularity and metadata overhead. However it did not completely solve the problem of hard chunking.

Bobbarjung et al. [14] put forward another chunking algorithm named FingerDiff based on variable length chunking. The main idea of this algorithm was merging multiple chunks that were not changed into a single SuperChunk as far as possible to reduce the amount of chunk metadata. To a certain extent, it could reduce the storage space and it accelerated the speed of query.

Research works on how to avoid long chunks, how to choose the optimal chunk size to achieve the optimal deduplication effect, and so on have been done a lot; nevertheless it is seldom mentioned in the literature how to reduce the overhead of fingerprint calculation for the data in the sliding window in the chunking process. When the amount of data becomes large, the calculation of the CPU overhead will be greatly increased; thus chunking algorithm will face enormous pressure on the performance.

3. The Bit String Content Aware Chunking Strategy

Most existing chunking strategies [15–17] had used Rabin algorithm in signature calculation in which the total amount of chunk and the total number of signature calculations were nearly 3 orders of magnitude. There still existed a lot of invalid signature calculations. And each signature calculation called for modulo operation which consumed a large amount of CPU resources.

Two key problems should be solved in order to reduce the signature calculation and save CPU resources. The first is to reduce the calculations of fingerprints as far as possible; the second is to minimize the number of signature computations.

According to binary string, BCCS borrows the incremental calculation method of fingerprint from the Rabin fingerprint algorithm to convert the problem of chunking file stably to the matching process of two binary strings, reducing the overhead of chunk fingerprints generation. BCCS also learns the leap-forward match from the BM [18, 19] to get the maximum length of jump through each match, reducing the middle overhead of calculation and comparison. All above bring down the cost of signature in the process of chunking to improve the efficiency of matching.

3.1. Fast Fingerprint Generation Based on Bitwise Operation. The Rabin algorithm is based on the principle that a pattern string whose length is m is mapped into a binary bit string (fingerprint) and each text string whose length is m is also mapped into binary bit string. Then the algorithm determines whether the two strings are equal by comparison.

The Rabin algorithm was more efficient, but it consumed a large amount of CPU resource for modulo operation. Therefore, the key to reduce CPU overhead is improving algorithm to minimize modulo operation.

The basic comparison unit is byte in the Rabin algorithm. The new algorithm can be considered to select on binary bit to represent the basic comparison unit to accelerate the algorithm speed. The process can be completed by bitwise operation instruction without modulo operation and greatly reduces the CPU overhead of generated fingerprints.

Therefore, the new algorithm selects the low order bit of each basic comparison unit to form its fingerprint. If the fingerprint $f(T_s)$ of string T_s ($T_s = [b_s, b_{s+1}, \ldots, b_{s+m-1}]$) is known, the $f(T_{s+1})$ can be got by the following bitwise operations.

Let us assume that BX $= f(T_s)$ and AL $= T_{s+1}$ *(the next new substring)*:

SHR AL, 1;

SHL BX, 1.

Then, the data stored in the BX is the fingerprint of T_{s+1}, namely, $f(T_{s+1})$.

3.2. Implementation of BCCS. Assume that the length of the original pattern string is m basic units; the m bits pattern string fingerprint P is consisting of the low order bit of each basic unit. The BCCS prefetches n low order bit of the text

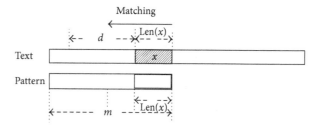

FIGURE 1: Matching the substring of text from pattern.

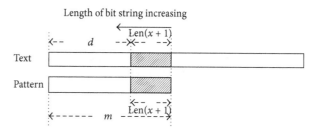

FIGURE 2: The perfect matching of text bit string.

basic units to storage in the bit array BT and then computes the text string fingerprints $f(T_s)$ by the fast fingerprint generation algorithm.

It considers the following two ways for pattern matching in this paper.

(I) BCCS Based on Pattern (BCCS-P). Similar to the BM algorithm, BCCS-P uses the scanning mode from left to right to pattern match. As shown in Figure 1, in order to reduce the matching computation, the pattern and text should be left-justified and then a substring at the tail of text in alignment with the pattern whose length is $\text{len}(x)$ should be selected; the BCCS-P will search the match substring from the right of pattern, but not matching the whole pattern at first.

As bit string comparison, BCCS-P is slightly different from BM, each time comparing a substring through a bitwise operation. Two cases are considered separately in this paper.

(i) The Perfect Matching of Text Bit String

Definition 1. As shown in Figure 2, the perfect matching of text bit string is that that the length of the bit substring of the text will increase by 1 if the match is successful. And then it matches the corresponding bit substring at the tail in the pattern until the length increases to m whose matching direction is from right to left.

The good suffix match of text bit string should be working if there is a failure of matching.

As shown in Figure 3, it suggests that the perfect matching of text bit string is successful if the string matches with substring of text in the pattern successfully $(m - x) + 1$ times. The further accurate comparison is done at this time that is the actual string comparison. If the string does not match, then BCCS-P continues to match the substring x; otherwise the chunk boundary should be marked, and pattern skips

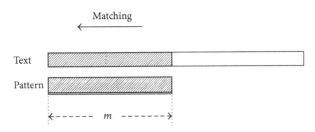

FIGURE 3: Success of perfect matching of text bit string.

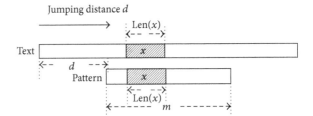

FIGURE 5: d-jumping distance from right ($d \leq m$).

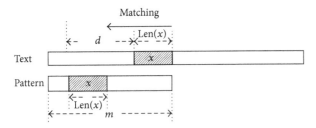

FIGURE 4: The good suffix matching of text bit string.

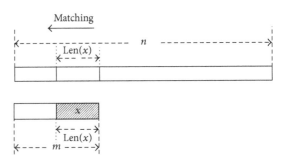

FIGURE 6: Matching the substring of pattern from text.

2 KB; namely, $d = d + 2048$. Then BCCS-P goes to the next round of comparison (the minimum chunk length is 2 KB).

(ii) The Good Suffix Matching of Text Bit String

Definition 2. As shown in Figure 4, the good suffix matching of text bit string happens when the bit substring of text whose length is len(x) matches with a corresponding bit substring of pattern. If the match is not successful, the pattern slides to the left one bit and reselects another bit substring of pattern to match until it finds the matching substring in the pattern in the match process.

The jumping distance to right for the pattern is d when the good suffix matching of text bit string is successful. It should obtain maximum jumping distance in order to reduce the amount of matching computation in the matching process. As shown in Figure 5, the biggest jumping distance is the length of pattern that the pattern jumps to right for m bits if no substring matched in pattern.

(II) BCCS Based on Text, BBCS-T. As shown in Figure 6, similar to (I), BBCS-T uses the scanning mode from right to left to pattern match and pattern and text should be left-justified at first in order to reduce the matching computation; different from (I), BBCS-T selects the bit substring whose length is len(x) at the right-most position in pattern and searches the matching bit substring in text from m-len(x) position.

The following two cases are attached importance in this paper.

(i) The Perfect Matching of Pattern Bit String

Definition 3. As shown in Figure 7, the perfect matching of pattern bit string is that the length of the bit substring of the pattern increases by 1 if the match is successful. And then it

matches the corresponding bit substring at the tail in the text until the length increases to m.

The good suffix match of pattern bit string is working once the matching fails.

It suggests that the perfect matching of pattern bit string is successful if the string matches with substring of pattern in the text successfully $(m - x) + 1$ times.

Similar to Figure 3, the further accurate comparison is done at this time that is the actual string comparison. If the string does not match, then BCCS-T continues to match the substring x; otherwise the chunk boundary is marked, and pattern skips 2 KB; namely, $d = d + 2048$. Thus BCCS-T goes to the next round of comparison (the minimum chunk length is 2 KB).

(ii) The Good Suffix Matching of Pattern Bit String

Definition 4. As shown in Figure 8, the good suffix matching of pattern bit string when the length of bit substring is len(x) matches with a corresponding bit substring of text; the text slides to right one bit and reselects another bit substring of text to match until finding the matching substring in the text in the matching process.

The jumping distance for pattern to right is still d when the good suffix matching is successful. But as shown in Figure 9, the jumping distance d can be far greater than the length of pattern and the maximum reaches $n - $ len(x) due to the scanning from left to right.

3.3. Performance Analysis. Through the above analysis we know that, in order to reduce the comparison cost, BCCS obtains the maximum jumping distance d and accelerates the speed of matching. In actual operation, being aimed at

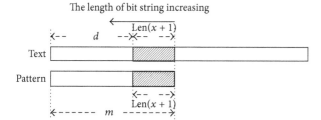

FIGURE 7: The perfect matching of pattern bit string.

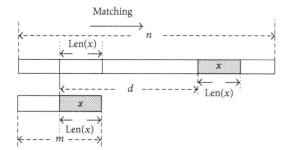

FIGURE 8: The good suffix matching of pattern bit string.

the bit string comparison, BCCS obtains the matching results quickly through the bitwise operation XOR which greatly reduces the CPU overhead compared to modulo operation in the Rabin algorithm.

The following items are on the range of d in detail.

3.3.1. BCCS-P. BBCS-P selects a bit substring whose length is len(x) in the text and searches the matching bit substring in the pattern from right to left. In this case, the biggest jumping distance is m by the good suffix matching of text bit string; that is, $1 \leq d \leq m$, for the length of pattern is m.

3.3.2. BCCS-T. Compared with BCCS-P, BCCS-T selects the bit substring whose length is len(x) in the pattern and searches the matching substring in text by changing the scanning mode as from left to right, which changes the main matching body in this way. The biggest jumping distance d of BCCS-T is far greater than m; the length of pattern, for the biggest length of text, is n ($n \gg m$). It saves the intermediate data comparisons overhead to the most degree.

The detailed discussion of the values range of the jumping distance d in BCCS-T is as follows.

Assuming that $\overline{d}$ is the average jumping distance for matching,

$$\overline{d} = \sum_{i=0}^{n-\text{len}(x)} i \times \text{prob}. \tag{1}$$

The len(x) is the length of the bit substring pattern containing x binary bit; prob is the matching probability of failure for pattern whose length is len(x) and text matching i times, so the prob is prob = $q^i * r$; r is the matching probability of success: $r = (1/2)^{\text{len}(x)}$. q is the matching probability of failure: $q = 1 - r = 1 - (1/2)^{\text{len}(x)}$.

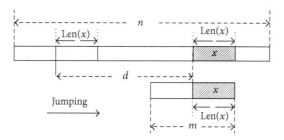

FIGURE 9: d-jumping distance from right ($1 < d < (n - x)$).

From [20],

$$\sum_{i=0}^{n} i \times q^i = q \times (1-q)^{-2} - (n+1) \times q^{n+1} \times (1-q)^{-1} \tag{2}$$
$$- q^{n+2} \times (1-q)^{-2}.$$

Here, $(1/2) \leq q < 1$, n is a great number, and (2) can be simplified to

$$\sum_{i=1}^{n} i \times q^i \approx q (1-q)^{-2}. \tag{3}$$

Equation (1) can be

$$\overline{d} \approx \frac{q}{r} = 2^{\text{len}(x)} - 1. \tag{4}$$

Compared with the traditional pattern matching algorithm, the speedup of f is written as

$$f = \frac{\overline{d}}{m} = \frac{2^{\text{len}(x)} - 1}{m}. \tag{5}$$

Through the above analysis, the bigger $\overline{d}$, the lower hit rate for the x in pattern matching in text, while the setting of the length of bit substring x, that is, len(x), is the key problem. When len(x) is smaller, the hit probability is higher and $\overline{d}$ is relatively smaller, which does not jump enough distance and leads to smaller speedup. On the contrary, if the len(x) is bigger, and $\overline{d}$ and f are bigger, it also affects the efficiency of the matching because of the increasing text units.

4. Performance Evaluation

This paper establishes a prototype system for big data storage based on deduplication technology. It does the performance evaluation of the Bit String Content Aware Chunking Strategy, and the effects of the different length of the target bit string on chunking speed, chunk size, and chunk compression ratio are analyzed.

4.1. The Experimental Environment Settings. The prototype system consists of two server nodes. The CPU of each server node is 2-way quad-core Xeon E5420 with 8 GB DDR RAM, whose frequency is 2 GHz. And the cache of each core is 6114 KB. The chunks are stored in RAID 0 with two disks

TABLE 1: Chunking test data set.

Data set	File type	Set size (MB)	File number	Average length of files (B)	Minimum length of files (B)	Maximum length of files (B)
Modified	Linux source codes 2.6.32, 2.6.34, 2.5.36	999	76432	13,083	6	145,793
Unmodified	rmvb	883	2	464,507,195	439,263,182	489,751,207

(Seagate Barracuda 7200 RPM, 2 TB capacity of each one). While each node is equipped with an Intel 80003ES2LAN Gigabit card connecting to the Gigabit Ethernet, one of the nodes is the main server and another is the mirror server.

4.2. Performance Test. Four different chunking algorithms, Rabin algorithm, FSP algorithm, BCCS-P, and BCCS-T, are compared in the experiment.

Two different test data sets are set up to test the influence of chunking speed of different file types by different chunking algorithms. As shown in Table 1, the first test data set contains 3 different versions of the Linux kernel source code files, with a total of 76432 documents, 999 M bytes. This test data set is modified data set for the files in the set are modified frequently. The second test data set is unmodified data set. This one contains two RMVB files. These two files are different versions of the same movie, shorter RMVB files from the RMVB file by RealMedia long and Editor Clip. The overall capacity of the second data set is 883 MB. The files in the second data set are modified rarely.

An adaptive control scheme on chunking for the two different test data sets is proposed. The prototype system automatically chooses the optimal algorithm according to different test set types.

The prototype system determines the type of the file by the suffix of file name. The multimedia files and compressed files are classified as unmodified file type, and system establishes a static text file, containing suffix name of unmodified file. Other types of documents are classified as modified file. When the files belong to the unmodified the system analyses the suffix of a file name at first and then chooses FSP algorithm or BCCS algorithm to chunk according to the different conditions whether the given parameters need faster duplicate speed or higher duplicate rate. Otherwise the system uses BCCS algorithm directly when the files belong to the modified data set.

The chunking is divided into two steps by BCCS: the first is preprocessing and the second step is a binary string matching, namely, chunking.

The preprocessing is that the system processes the input text data, extracting one bit of each text byte to generate fingerprints, providing support for the following chunking before calling the chunking module.

The experiment first compares the time of the preprocessing time and chunking time by BCCS-T and BCCS-P for the modified data set. The time overhead ratio is as shown in Figures 10 and 11.

X-axis and Y-axis in the figures indicate the length of the target pattern and the percentage of the processing time

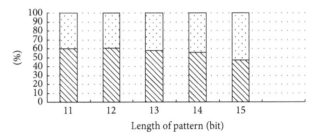

Chunking time for modified data set of BCCS-T
Preprocessing time for modified data set of BCCS-T

FIGURE 10: Ratio of chunking time and preprocessing time for modified data set of BCCS-T.

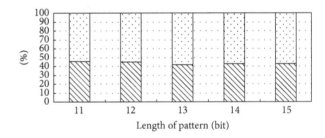

Chunking time for modified data set of BCCS-P
Preprocessing time for modified data set of BCCS-P

FIGURE 11: Ratio of chunking time and preprocessing time for modified data set of BCCS-P.

accounting for the total processing time, respectively. In fact, for the same test data set, preprocessing time of BCCS-T and BCCS-P is the same, but the chunking times are different. It is shown as in Figures 10 and 11 that the preprocessing time of BCCS-T accounts for the total processing time between 45% and 60% and that of BCCS-P accounts for about 42% and 45%, according to the different lengths of the pattern. It is a great time overhead. Therefore, the preprocessing operations are processed in a processing node and chunking operations are processed in the front-end server node to achieve similarly the pipeline operation mode through the parallel operation by BCCS. It just needs a startup time of preprocessing for the big data and the actual data processing time is the time of chunking when the pipeline works normally, thus greatly reducing the actual time overhead.

The minimum chunk size is proposed as 2 KB by BCCS to avoid too many short chunks, which reduces the overhead of metadata and decreases the unnecessary computation.

TABLE 2: Comparison of BCCS-T and FSP algorithms for unmodified data set.

Chunking algorithm	Total time cost (ms)	Chunking time cost (ms)	Saving time (ms)	Deduplication rate
BCCS-T-11	16453	5218	10642	1.2061
BCCS-T-12	18303	5503	11588	1.2050
BCCS-T-13	19336	6485	11851	1.0952
BCCS-T-14	19627	5743	13942	1.0920
BCCS-T-15	20045	7956	13920	1.0920
FSP	16167	686	15456	0.9771

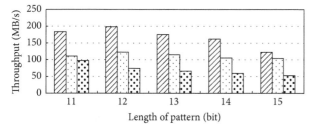

☑ BCCS-T of modified data set
☐ BCCS-P of modified data set
⊡ Rabin of modified data set

FIGURE 12: The comparison of chunking throughput of modified data set.

As shown in Figure 12, it is the chunking throughput for BCCS-T, BCCS-P, and Rabin to modified test set when the different lengths of pattern are set. The X-axis represents the length of pattern; the Y-axis represents the chunking throughput. Rabin algorithm reaches its maximum throughput rate of about 98 MB/s when its length of pattern is 11; BCCS-T and BCCS-P reach maximum chunking throughput, about 198 MB/S and 123 MB/S, respectively, when the length of pattern is 12; the three algorithms reach the minimum chunking throughout, about 122 MB/S, 105 MB/S, and 52.5 MB/S, respectively, when the length of pattern is 15. Different matching modes by BCCS-T, BCCS-P, and BCCS-T reduce more intermediate matching overhead through the good suffix matching of pattern bit string rule. Therefore, the chunking throughput of BCCS-T is almost 1.63 times as that of BCCS-P when the length of pattern is the same. For modified data set, with 12-bit target pattern, the BCCS-T chunking speed is raised to be close to 160% compared to that of the Rabin algorithm or so; with 15-bit target pattern, it is 80%. The length of pattern greatly affects the chunking throughput rate.

The unmodified test data sets are chunked by FSP and BCCS-T algorithms, respectively. It is shown in Table 2 that it only takes 686 ms to chunk the RMVB files with 883 MB by FSP algorithm, and the deduplication rate is only 0.9771 because it does not find any similar chunks and spends extra metadata cost. Furthermore, the storing time of chunks by FSP algorithm is far longer than that by BCCS-T algorithm. But by BCCS-T algorithm, with 11-bit pattern, the chunking time is 5218 ms, and the total processing time is 16453, just 1.8% over FSP with the deduplication rate 1.2061. Therefore, for the unmodified files, the prototype system provides

a flexible method to select the chunking algorithm in the light of actual conditions.

5. Conclusion

It is an essential prerequisite for finding redundant data and improving deduplication rate to rapidly and stably divide the data objects into suitable size chunks. Most existing chunking algorithms obtain the fingerprints in the sliding window by Rabin algorithm to determine the chunk boundary. It consumes a large amount of CPU computing resources on fingerprint computing. The CPU cost of fingerprints computing is greatly increased when the processed data becomes huge, and the chunking algorithm faces plenty of pressure on the performance.

This paper proposes a novel chunking strategy, namely, the Bit String Content Aware Chunking Strategy (BCCS), through researching and analyzing the advantages of Rabin algorithm and BM algorithm.

The primary contributions of our work are as follows: first, according to characteristics of the binary bit string, it simplifies the fingerprint calculation requiring a lot of CPU computing resources into the simple shift operation with reference to calculation methods of Rabin incremental fingerprint algorithm; secondly, it converts the problem of data objects chunking stability into the process of two binary bits' string matching.

According to the different matching subjects, this paper proposes two kinds of chunking strategies based on Bit String Content Aware Chunking Strategy, namely, BCCS-P and BCCS-T, with the bad character matching rule and the good suffix matching rule in BM. BCCS-P is pattern matching centered when the jumping distance for unmatching is limited every time. The maximum jumping distance does not exceed the length of pattern; thus the benefits are limited. BCCS-T is text-matching centered that rules out the unmatching positions and gets the maximum jumping distance to reduce intermediate calculation and comparison costs by making best use of the bit feature information brought by failure matching every time. This measure reduces the cost of signature computation in chunking process to improve the system performance.

To a certain extent in the large data center using the deduplication technology to store the data, it reduces the storage system reliability and also has some limitations in storage overhead and system performance with multiple files sharing data objects or chunks. It is also one of the problems that needs to be further studied in the future regarding how to make up for this defect, ensure the safety and reliability of big data storage, and provide the QoS.

Conflict of Interests

The authors declare that there is no conflict of interests regarding the publication of this paper.

Acknowledgment

This research was supported by Natural Science Foundation of Hubei Province (no. 2013CFB447).

References

[1] J. Gantz and D. Reinsel, "Extracting value from chaos," IDC IVIEW, 2011, http://www.emc.com/collateral/analyst-reports/idc-extracting-value-from-chaos-ar.pdf.

[2] Gartner, *Meeting the DC Power and Cooling Challenges*, 2008.

[3] NRDC, "Report to congress on server and data center energy efficiency," 2013, http://www.nrdc.org/.

[4] J. Sweeney, "Reducing data centers power and energy consumption: saving money and go green," 2008.

[5] W. Tschudi, T. Xu, D. Sartor et al., *Energy Efficient Data Center*, California Energy Commission, Berkeley, Calif, USA, 2004.

[6] J. Hamilton, "Cooperative expendable micro-slice servers (CEMS): low cost, low power servers for internet-scale services," in *Proceedings of the 4th Biennial Conference on Innovative Data Systems Research (CIDR '09)*, pp. 1–8, Asilomar, Calif, USA, 2009.

[7] S. Y. Jin, *Research on some key issues for resource management in green virtualized data center [Ph.D. thesis]*, University of Electronic Science and Technology of China, Chengdu, China, 2012.

[8] G. Lu, Y. Jin, and D. H. C. Du, "Frequency based chunking for data de-duplication," in *Proceedings of the 18th Annual IEEE/ACM International Symposium on Modeling, Analysis and Simulation of Computer and Telecommunication Systems (MASCOTS '10)*, pp. 287–296, IEEE, August 2010.

[9] H. M. Jung, S. Y. Park, J. G. Lee, and Y. W. Ko, "Efficient data deduplication system considering file modification pattern," *International Journal of Security and Its Applications*, vol. 6, no. 2, pp. 421–426, 2012.

[10] Y. Wang, C. C. Tan, and N. Mi, "Using elasticity to improve inline data deduplication storage systems," in *Proceedings of the 7th IEEE International Conference on Cloud Computing (CLOUD '14)*, pp. 785–792, IEEE, Anchorage, Alaska, USA, June-July 2014.

[11] A. Muthitacharoen, B. Chen, and D. Mazières, "A low-bandwidth network files system," in *Proceedings of the Symposium on Operating Systems Principles (SOSP '01)*, pp. 174–187, ACM Press, 2001.

[12] M. O. Rabin, *Fingerprinting by Random Polynomials*, Center for Research in Computing Technology, Aiken Computation Laboratory, Harvard University, Cambridge, Mass, USA, 1981.

[13] K. Eshghi and H. K. Tang, "A framework for analyzing and improving content based chunking algorithms," Tech. Rep. HPL-2005-30R1, Hewlett-Packard Labs, 2005.

[14] D. R. Bobbarjung, S. Jagannathan, and C. Dubnicki, "Improving duplicate elimination in storage systems," *ACM Transactions on Storage*, vol. 2, no. 4, pp. 424–448, 2006.

[15] Y. Liu, X. Ge, D. H. C. Du, and X. X. Huang, "Par-BF: a parallel partitioned Bloom filter for dynamic data sets," in *Proceedings of the International Workshop on Data Intensive Scalable Computing Systems (DISCS '14)*, pp. 1–8, IEEE Press, 2014.

[16] N. Jain, M. Dahlin, and R. Tewari, "Taper: tiered approach for eliminating redundancy in replica synchronization," in *Proceedings of the 4th USENIX Conference on File and Storage Technologies (FAST '05)*, p. 21, USENIX Association Press, Berkeley, Calif, USA, 2005.

[17] J. B. Wang, Z. G. Zhao, Z. G. Xu, H. Zhang, L. Li, and Y. Guo, "I-sieve: an inline high performance deduplication system used in cloud storage," *Tsinghua Science and Technology*, vol. 20, no. 1, Article ID 7040510, pp. 17–27, 2015.

[18] S. Robert, J. Boyer, and S. Moore, "A fast string searching algorithm," *Communications of the ACM*, vol. 20, no. 10, pp. 762–772, 1977.

[19] Z. Galil and T. Aviv, "On improving the worst case running time of the Boyer-Moore string matching algorithm," in *Automata, Languages and Programming: Fifth Colloquium, Udine, Italy, July 17–21, 1978*, vol. 62 of *Lecture Notes in Computer Science*, pp. 241–250, Springer, Berlin, Germany, 1978.

[20] A. N. M. E. Rafiq, M. W. El-Kharashi, and F. Gebali, "A fast string search algorithm for deep packet classification," *Computer Communications*, vol. 27, no. 15, pp. 1524–1538, 2004.

A Privacy-Preserving Outsourcing Data Storage Scheme with Fragile Digital Watermarking-Based Data Auditing

Xinyue Cao,[1] Zhangjie Fu,[1,2] and Xingming Sun[1,2]

[1]*School of Computer and Software, Nanjing University of Information Science and Technology, Nanjing 210044, China*
[2]*Jiangsu Engineering Centre of Network Monitor, Nanjing University of Information Science and Technology, Nanjing 210044, China*

Correspondence should be addressed to Xingming Sun; sunnudt@163.com

Academic Editor: Isao Echizen

Cloud storage has been recognized as the popular solution to solve the problems of the rising storage costs of IT enterprises for users. However, outsourcing data to the cloud service providers (CSPs) may leak some sensitive privacy information, as the data is out of user's control. So how to ensure the integrity and privacy of outsourced data has become a big challenge. Encryption and data auditing provide a solution toward the challenge. In this paper, we propose a privacy-preserving and auditing-supporting outsourcing data storage scheme by using encryption and digital watermarking. Logistic map-based chaotic cryptography algorithm is used to preserve the privacy of outsourcing data, which has a fast operation speed and a good effect of encryption. Local histogram shifting digital watermark algorithm is used to protect the data integrity which has high payload and makes the original image restored losslessly if the data is verified to be integrated. Experiments show that our scheme is secure and feasible.

1. Introduction

With the development of cloud computing, outsourcing data to cloud storage servers has become a popular way for firms and individuals. Cloud storage reduces data storage and maintenance costs. And cloud storage can provide a flexible and convenient way for users to access their data anywhere. However, the cloud service providers (CSPs) may not be honest and the data should not be disclosed to the CSPs. So the data must be encrypted before it is uploaded to the cloud. Encryption is a fundamental method to preserve data confidentiality. For privacy preserving concerned, data owner can encrypt the data before outsourcing it to CSPs. Many problems of querying over encrypted domain are discussed in research literatures [1–3]. In addition, data owners worry whether the outsourcing data is modified or revealed by the CSPs. It is necessary to add the data auditing service in outsourcing data storage scheme.

In the existing outsourcing data storage schemes, the data auditing methods can be classified into three categories: message authentication code- (MAC-) based methods, RSA-based homomorphic methods, and Boneh-Lynn-Shacham

signature- (BLS-) based homomorphic methods [4]. In these methods, the data is calculated using MAC or digital signature and the verification information needs to be attached to the original data. If the data is digitally signed, any change in the data after signature invalidates the signature. Furthermore, these methods increase the data sizes and the time to sign, which is inconvenient in digital media (images, video, audio, etc.). So we use digital watermarking technology to offset the deficiency. Digital watermarking technology hides watermark information in the digital media without affecting data utilization. And it reduces the communication and computation costs. This means digital watermarking technology can provide a more effective auditing method than other cryptographic protocols for auditing.

Many works on outsourcing data storage schemes with digital watermarking are proposed. N. Singh and S. Singh [5] point out that collaboration of digital watermarking and cloud computing can significantly increase the robust of system as well as security of user's data. Boopathy and Sundaresan [6] propose a model of data storage and access process with digital watermarking technology in the cloud. Though they do not give concrete realization, it shows the broad prospects of applying digital watermarking technology into the cloud environment. In addition, digital watermarking technology is used for data auditing in cloud environment. Wang and Lian [7] focus on the application scenarios of multiwatermarking in cloud environment by investigating the secure media distribution models. Ren et al. [8] propose a provable data possession scheme based on self-embedded digital watermark for auditing service. However, they do not provide privacy preserving with encryption methods. It is believed that supporting privacy preserving is of vital importance to outsourcing data storage.

In this paper, logistic map-based chaotic cryptography algorithm is used to preserve the privacy of outsourcing data, which has a fast operation speed and a good effect of encryption. Traditional encryption techniques such as AES, DES, and RSA have low speed to encrypt media data. And they are not suitable for high real time in media data transmission. Chaotic cryptography has many good characteristics such as sensitivity to initial value, pseudorandom properties, and ergodicity. Logistic map-based chaotic cryptography is a simple nonlinear model, but it has complex dynamics, which is widely used in image encryption. In this paper, logistic map-based chaotic cryptography method is used to permute the positions of the image pixels in the spatial domain. It is suitable for embedding watermark information with local histogram shifting digital watermark algorithm later. Local histogram shifting digital watermark algorithm is utilized to protect the data integrity. It has high payload and makes the original image restored losslessly if the data is verified to be integrated.

We propose an outsourcing data storage scheme supporting auditing service by using fragile digital watermarking technology. Meanwhile, the scheme uses encryption methods to preserve privacy. In this scheme, digital watermarking technology and encryption methods are used to enhance the integrity and privacy of outsourcing data storage. Our contributions are as follows.

(i) We propose an outsourcing data storage scheme supporting privacy-preserving and auditing service. In this scheme, we use the scrambling encryption algorithm based on logistic chaotic map, which has a fast operation speed and a good effect of encryption. Besides, local histogram shifting digital watermark algorithm [9] is used to embed the watermark, which has high payload and makes the original image restored losslessly if the data is verified to be integrated.

(ii) To reduce data owners' overhead cost, a third-party auditor (TPA) is used to verify the integrity of data in cloud. And TPA verifies the data integrity in encryption domain, which ensures the data confidentiality in the auditing process.

The rest of this paper is organized as follows. Section 2 summarizes the related work. Section 3 introduces the proposed scheme. Experiment results are given in Section 4. Section 5 concludes the paper and the future work.

2. Related Work

Many secure outsourcing data storage schemes are proposed these years. The privacy and integrity of data in cloud are the most concerns of data owners. Outsourcing data is often distributed geographically in different locations. CPSs can access the stored data if it is stored in plain format. Data owners have lost control over their data after it is uploaded to the cloud. So data privacy information [10] or sensitivity information [11] causes the outsourcing data to be encrypted in the data storage schemes.

To verify the data integrity, data auditing is considered in outsourcing data storage schemes. Ateniese et al. [12] first define the provable data possession (PDP) model for auditing service in untrusted storages. Juels and Kaliski Jr. [13] describe a proof of retrievability (POR) model, which ensures both "possession" and "retrievability" of data files. Sravan Kumar and Saxena [14] propose a proof of data integrity in the cloud, which could be agreed upon by both clients and the server via the Service Level Agreement (SLA). Hao et al. [15] propose the first protocol that provides public verifiability without TPA. Lu et al. [16] exploit the secure provenance model, which consists of the following modules: system setup, key generation, anonymous authentication, authorized access, and provenance tracking. Their scheme is based on the bilinear pairing techniques. And it records the ownership and the process history of data objects to increase the trust from public users. But all these methods have additional data to verify the data integrity and are not suitable for multimedia file. Digital watermarking technology can offset the deficiency, which is an effective method for data auditing. Digital watermarking can be divided into spatial domain and frequency domain [17]. Spatial domain digital watermark directly embeds watermark information into the image pixels. Frequency domain [18] algorithm embeds watermark information into coefficients of transform domain.

Encryption is a fundamental method to preserve data confidentiality in outsourcing data storage schemes. Digital watermarking technology is an effective method for data auditing. The methods of embedding digital watermark in encryption domain are proposed [6, 19, 20]. In medical domain, many healthcare information systems (HISs) [21] are proposed. Haas et al. [22] propose a privacy-protecting information system for controlled disclosure of personal data to third parties. This scheme uses authentic log files to check the completeness of data. And digital watermarking is used for tracing nonauthorized data disclosure. In the field of information hiding, Zhang [19] uses the simple encryption algorithm of exclusive-OR operation by a stream cipher and embedded watermark information by flipping the 3 LSBs of each encrypted pixel. Zhang [20] further proposes a scheme which makes watermark extraction independent from image decryption. That means a user can extract data from the encrypted image directly. Yin et al. [9] propose a scheme with the multigranularity encryption algorithm and local histogram shifting digital watermark algorithm, which ensures larger embedding capacity and better embedding quality. But chaotic-based scrambling encryption is widely used in

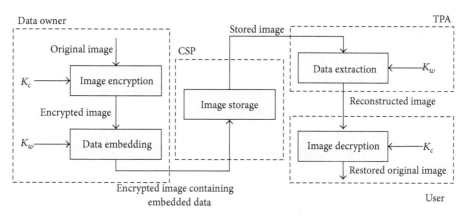

FIGURE 1: Sketch of the proposed scheme.

image encryption. The common encryption algorithms are one-dimensional logistic map, two-dimensional Smale and Henon map, and three-dimensional Lorenz map. The logistic map-based chaotic cryptography is a simple nonlinear model, but it has complex dynamics, which has good effect and fast speed.

In our scheme, we combine encryption technology with watermark technology. Data owner encrypts the image before transmission. CSP embeds some additional message into the encrypted image without knowing the original image content. TPA is required to extract the watermark from the encrypted image. A user can first decrypt the encrypted image containing watermark information with the decryption key and then extract the embedded watermark from the decrypted version with the extraction key. The transmission of encryption keys is assumed to be secure and is not discussed here. Here the logistic map-based chaotic cryptography method is used to permute the positions of the image pixels in the spatial domain. So the histogram of the encryption version is the same as the original image. The histogram statistical property makes the encryption method suitable for embedding watermark information with local histogram shifting digital watermark algorithm [9]. And this is a blind fragile watermark algorithm. The extraction of the watermark does not need the original image and original watermark information. Its error-free decryption can be used for military, remote sensing, and medicine data.

3. Proposed Scheme

In this section, we first analyze the framework of the system and then give the main steps of our scheme.

3.1. System Model. We first give the sketch of the proposed scheme in Figure 1. Then four parties in the scheme are described as follows.

(i) Data owner encrypts an original image with an encryption key K_c, computes a verification information as watermark information W for the encrypted image, embeds W to the encrypted image with

the embedding key K_w, and upload the encrypted image to CSP.

(ii) CSP stores the watermark-embedded encrypted image.

(iii) TPA extract the watermarking information W' with K_w in the encrypted domain to verify the integrity and reconstructed the image if it is integrated.

(iv) Data user receives the reconstructed image from TPA and exactly decrypts the data to the original image with the decryption key K_c.

3.2. Main Steps of Proposed Scheme. The proposed scheme contains four modules: image encryption, watermarking embedding, watermarking extraction, and image decryption. The main steps of the proposed scheme are shown as follows.

3.2.1. Image Encryption. Data owner creates an original image I. Assume I is a gray image sized $M \times M$ pixels in uncompressed format.

The process of image encryption is as follows.

(i) Connect the jth row to the $(j - 1)$th row, where $j = 2, 3, \ldots, M$, and generate the sequence of length $M \times M$.

(ii) Generate a chaotic sequence of length $M \times M$ with

$$x_{n+1} = x_n \times \mu \times (1 - x_n), \tag{1}$$

where $x_n \in (0, 1)$, $n = 0, 1, 2, \ldots$, $\mu \in (0, 4]$. x_0 is the initial value. n is the number of iterations. μ is growth parameter and when $\mu \in [3.5699456, 4]$, the generated sequence is in the state of pseudorandom distribution.

(iii) Sort the chaotic sequence and record the location set.

(iv) Scramble the sequence of image with the same location set.

The encryption key K_c consists of x_0 and μ. The encrypted image E is generated. This algorithm is simple and has good performance. The algorithm keeps the image histogram statistical properties.

3.2.2. Watermarking Embedding. The embedded watermarking information should be unpredictable and random. Arnold transforming or chaotic-based encryption can be used in this paper to improve the security of image watermarking algorithm. The above-mentioned encryption algorithm preserves the same image histogram statistical properties. Therefore, local histogram shifting watermarking algorithm is suitable for embedding data into the encrypted image [6].

When data owner embeds watermarking information W into the encrypted image E, the steps are as follows.

(i) Divide the encrypted image E into blocks $\{B_i\}_{i=1}^{N}$ of pixels in the size of $m \times m$. Two basic pixels $b_{i,L}$ and $b_{i,R}$ are randomly selected in each block B_i with the seed of random permutation k.

(ii) Calculate the difference $d_i = |b_{i,L} - b_{i,R}|$ to estimate the smoothness of each block. Blocks with smaller d_i are smoother than blocks with larger d_i. Blocks with smaller d_i have higher priority to be chosen for carrying data.

(iii) Determine the two peaks $(p_{i,L}, p_{i,R})$ in each block with

$$
\begin{aligned}
p_{i,L} &= \min(b_{i,L}, b_{i,R}) \\
p_{i,R} &= \max(b_{i,L}, b_{i,R}).
\end{aligned}
\tag{2}
$$

If $p_{i,L} = p_{i,R}$, $p_{i,R} = p_{i,R} + 1$.

(iv) Saturated pixels q ($q = 0$ or $q = 255$) have to be preprocessed by modifying one grayscale unit. Then they will be recorded in a location map L to avoid saturated pixels from overflow or underflow during embedding process. Scan the pixels block by block and append bit "1" to L when $q \in \{1, 254\}$. Then append bit "0" to L when $q \in \{0, 255\}$ and modify q to q' using

$$
q' = \begin{cases} 1, & q = 0 \\ 254, & q = 255 \\ q, & \text{otherwise.} \end{cases}
\tag{3}
$$

The embedding capacity of each block is the number of pixels whose values are equal to peak points in each block.

(v) Embedded information S consists of the location map L and the histogram information H of the image. Scan the nonbasic pixels in each block. If the scanned pixel r is valued $p_{i,L}$ or $p_{i,R}$, a bit $s \in \{0, 1\}$ from S will be embedded. Modify r to r' as

$$
r' = \begin{cases} r - 1, & r < p_{i,L} \\ r - s, & r = p_{i,L} \\ r, & p_{i,L} < r < p_{i,R} \\ r + s, & r = p_{i,R} \\ r + 1, & r > p_{i,R}. \end{cases}
\tag{4}
$$

The encrypted image $\widehat{E}$ with embedded data is obtained. The embedding key K_w consists of the parameter m, $|L|$, $|H|$, and the seed k. The data owner outsources the encrypted image $\widehat{E}$ with embedded watermarking information to the cloud. Then the watermark embedding key K_w is transferred to TPA and the decryption key K_c is shared with the legal users.

3.2.3. Watermarking Extraction and Data Auditing. TPA extracts the watermarking information W' with the extraction key K_w before the user downloads the data from the cloud. The watermarking information can only be extracted from the encrypted domain by TPA that ensures data privacy. This blind extracting algorithm is shown as follows.

(i) Divide the image $\widehat{E}$ into blocks $\{B_i'\}_{i=1}^{N}$ of pixels in size $m \times m$. Determine the basic pixels $b_{i,L}'$ and $b_{i,R}'$ in each block B_i'.

(ii) The difference $d_i' = |b_{i,L}' - b_{i,R}'|$ is calculated to estimate the smoothness of each block. Blocks with smaller d_i' have higher priority to be chosen for extracting data.

(iii) Determine the two peaks $(p_{i,L}', p_{i,R}')$ in each block with

$$
\begin{aligned}
p_{i,L}' &= \min(b_{i,L}', b_{i,R}'), \\
p_{i,R}' &= \max(b_{i,L}', b_{i,R}').
\end{aligned}
\tag{5}
$$

If $p_{i,L}' = p_{i,R}'$, $p_{i,R}' = p_{i,R}' + 1$.

(iv) Scan nonbasic pixels in each block B_i'. If the scanned pixel is r', embedding information S will be extracted according to

$$
s = \begin{cases} 0, & r' = p_{i,L}' \text{ or } r' = p_{i,R}' \\ 1, & r' = p_{i,L}' - 1 \text{ or } r' = p_{i,R}' + 1. \end{cases}
\tag{6}
$$

The extracted $|S|$ bits consist of location map L and histogram information H.

TPA verifies the data integrity after extracting the watermark information W'.

The auditing process is as follows.

(i) Scan nonbasic pixels in each block B_i'. If the scanned pixel is r', the restored pixel r can be computed by

$$
r = \begin{cases} r' - 1, & r' > p_{i,R} \\ r', & p_{i,L} < r' < p_{i,R} \\ r' + 1, & r' < p_{i,L}. \end{cases}
\tag{7}
$$

FIGURE 2: (a) Original image; (b) encrypted image; (c) encrypted image containing watermark; (d) reconstructed image; (e) decrypted image.

(ii) Restore the saturated pixels q with the location map L. If the pixel $q' \in \{1, 254\}$, extract a bit l from L. q is computed by

$$q = \begin{cases} 0, & l = 0, \ q' = 1 \\ 1, & l = 1, \ q' = 1 \\ 255, & l = 0, \ q' = 254 \\ 254, & l = 1, \ q' = 254. \end{cases} \quad (8)$$

The reconstructed encrypted image E' is generated.

(iii) Compute the histogram information H' of the image E'. Then compute the Euclidean distance by (9) and compare the value with the preset threshold θ:

$$D\left(H, H'\right) = \text{sqrt}\left(\sum_{i=1}^{n}\left(H[i] - H'[i]\right)^2\right), \quad (9)$$

where $H = (H(1), H(2), \ldots, H(N))$, $H' = (H'(1), H'(2), \ldots, H'(N))$.

If the value $D(H, H') < \theta$, the watermark information is correct and the data is verified to be integrated.

3.2.4. *Image Decryption.* The legal users can decrypt the reconstructed encrypted image E' using the decryption key K_c and can also obtain the original image I. The decryption process is as follows.

(i) Generate a chaotic sequence of length $M \times M$ with the decryption key K_c.

(ii) Sort the chaotic sequence and record the location set.

(iii) Scramble the sequence of image and restore a decrypted image with the location set.

Then the original image I is obtained by the legal users.

4. Experimental Results

To study the performance of the proposed scheme, MATLAB software 7 is used. The test image Lena of 8-bit gray level sized 512×512 pixels is selected as original image and it is shown in Figure 2(a). We use logistic map-based chaotic cryptography algorithm to generate an encrypted image ($x_0 = 0.5$, $\mu = 3.7$), which is shown in Figure 2(b). The encrypted image containing watermarking information is shown in Figure 2(c). After the watermarking information is extracted by TPA, a reconstructed image is shown in Figure 2(d). Then the legal user can decrypt the reconstructed image. The decrypted image is shown in Figure 2(e).

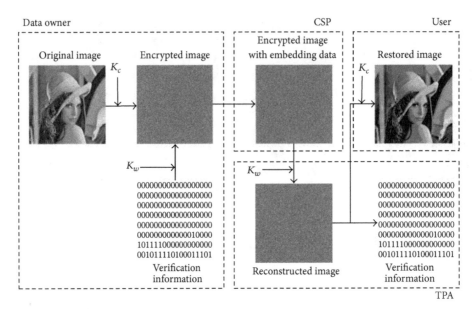

FIGURE 3: Experimental results of the proposed scheme.

TABLE 1: Payload bits and MSE.

Image	Payload bits (dB)	Payload bpp	MSE
Lena	2892	0.0110	0
Bridge	8234	0.0314	0
Aerial	4252	0.0162	0
Dollar	2892	0.0110	0

The experimental results of proposed scheme are shown in Figure 3.

The quality of encrypted image can be evaluated by Peak Signal-to-Noise Ratio (PSNR):

$$\text{PSNR} = 10 \times \log_{10}\left(\frac{255^2}{\text{MSE}}\right),$$

$$\text{MSE} = \frac{1}{M \times M}\sum_{i=1}^{M}\sum_{j=1}^{M}\left(I(i,j) - I'(i,j)\right)^2,$$

(10)

where I is the original image and I' is the image with watermark information. The size of image I is $M \times M$ pixels. The mean square error (MSE) can evaluate the error between the original image and decrypted image.

Table 1 lists the embedding payloads and MSEs for image Lena, bridge, aerial, and dollar without any attacks.

From Table 1, the MSEs between the decrypted version and the original image are 0. This means the encrypted image will be reconstructed error-free during watermark extraction and data auditing process if the data in cloud is not attacked. The payload is enough for embedding verification information.

In this paper, the watermark algorithm is fragile, which cannot resist any attacks. This can be used in military, remote sensing, and medicine images.

5. Conclusion and Future Work

In this paper, we propose a privacy-preserving and auditing-supporting outsourcing data storage scheme by using encryption and digital watermarking. The proposed scheme combines digital watermark technology with encryption methods for outsourcing data storage. And the scheme supports auditing service and privacy preserving. We adopt the logistic map-based chaotic cryptography algorithm for image encryption and local histogram shifting watermarking algorithm [6] for embedding data integrity verification information. This scheme has high authentication precision which can be used in high quality images.

In the future, we will add semifragile watermark to verify the integrity of images, which can resist some good image operations, such as JPEG compression. We can also apply some algorithms for the sake of supporting tamper localization and recovery.

Competing Interests

The authors declare that they have no competing interests.

Acknowledgments

This work is supported by the NSFC (U1536206, 61232016, U1405254, 61373133, and 61502242), BK20150925, and PAPD fund.

References

[1] N. Cao, C. Wang, M. Li, K. Ren, and W. Lou, "Privacy-preserving multi-keyword ranked search over encrypted cloud data," in Proceedings of the IEEE INFOCOM, pp. 829–837, Shanghai, China, April 2011.

[2] Z. Xia, X. Wang, X. Sun, and Q. Wang, "A secure and dynamic multi-keyword ranked search scheme over encrypted cloud data," *IEEE Transactions on Parallel and Distributed Systems*, vol. 27, no. 2, pp. 340–352, 2015.

[3] Z. Fu, X. Sun, Q. Liu, L. Zhou, and J. Shu, "Achieving efficient cloud search services: multi-keyword ranked search over encrypted cloud data supporting parallel computing," *IEICE Transactions on Communications*, vol. E98B, no. 1, pp. 190–200, 2015.

[4] K. Yang and X. Jia, "Data storage auditing service in cloud computing: challenges, methods and opportunities," *World Wide Web-Internet & Web Information Systems*, vol. 15, no. 4, pp. 409–428, 2012.

[5] N. Singh and S. Singh, "The amalgamation of digital watermarking & cloud watermarking for security enhancement in cloud computing," *International Journal of Computer Science and Mobile Computing*, vol. 2, no. 4, pp. 333–339, 2013.

[6] D. Boopathy and M. Sundaresan, "Data encryption framework model with watermark security for data storage in public cloud model," in *Proceedings of the 8th International Conference on Computing for Sustainable Global Development (INDIACom '14)*, pp. 903–907, New Delhi, India, March 2014.

[7] J. Wang and S. Lian, "On multiwatermarking in cloud environment," *Concurrency Computation Practice and Experience*, vol. 24, no. 17, pp. 2151–2164, 2012.

[8] Y. Ren, J. Shen, J. Wang, J. Xu, and L. Fang, "Security data auditing based on multifunction digital watermark for multimedia file in cloud storage," *International Journal of Multimedia and Ubiquitous Engineering*, vol. 9, no. 9, pp. 231–240, 2014.

[9] Z. Yin, B. Luo, and W. Hong, "Separable and error-free reversible data hiding in encrypted image with high payload," *The Scientific World Journal*, vol. 2014, Article ID 604876, 8 pages, 2014.

[10] N. Thiranant, M. Sain, and H. J. Lee, "A design of security framework for data privacy in e-health system using web service," in *Proceedings of the 16th International Conference on Advanced Communication Technology (ICACT '14)*, pp. 40–43, PyeongChang, South Korea, February 2014.

[11] R. L. de Souza, H. V. Netto, L. C. Lung et al., "SSICC: sharing sensitive information in a cloud-of-clouds," in *Proceedings of the 9th International Conference on Systems (ICONS '14)*, pp. 185–191, Nice, France, February 2014.

[12] G. Ateniese, R. Burns, R. Curtmola et al., "Provable data possession at untrusted stores," in *Proceedings of the 14th ACM Conference on Computer and Communications Security (CCS '07)*, pp. 598–610, November 2007.

[13] A. Juels and B. S. Kaliski Jr., "Pors: proofs of retrievability for large files," in *Proceedings of the 14th ACM Conference on Computer and Communications Security (CCS '07)*, pp. 584–597, November 2007.

[14] R. Sravan Kumar and A. Saxena, "Data integrity proofs in cloud storage," in *Proceedings of the 3rd International Conference on Communication Systems and Networks (COMSNETS '11)*, pp. 1–4, Bangalore, India, January 2011.

[15] Z. Hao, S. Zhong, and N. Yu, "A privacy-preserving remote data integrity checking protocol with data dynamics and public verifiability," *IEEE Transactions on Knowledge and Data Engineering*, vol. 23, no. 9, pp. 1432–1437, 2011.

[16] R. Lu, X. Lin, X. Liang, and X. Shen, "Secure provenance: the essential of bread and butter of data forensics in cloud computing," in *Proceedings of the 5th ACM Symposium on Information, Computer and Communication Security (ASIACCS '10)*, pp. 282–292, Beijing, China, April 2010.

[17] W. N. Cheung, "Digital image watermarking in spatial and transform domains," in *Proceedings (TENCON '00)*, vol. 3, pp. 374–378, IEEE, Kuala Lumpur, Malaysia, 2000.

[18] S.-H. Wang and Y.-P. Lin, "Wavelet tree quantization for copyright protection watermarking," *IEEE Transactions on Image Processing*, vol. 13, no. 2, pp. 154–165, 2004.

[19] X. Zhang, "Reversible data hiding in encrypted image," *IEEE Signal Processing Letters*, vol. 18, no. 4, pp. 255–258, 2011.

[20] X. Zhang, "Separable reversible data hiding in encrypted image," *IEEE Transactions on Information Forensics and Security*, vol. 7, no. 2, pp. 826–832, 2012.

[21] C.-L. Hsu, M.-R. Lee, and C.-H. Su, "The role of privacy protection in healthcare information systems adoption," *Journal of Medical Systems*, vol. 37, no. 5, article 9966, 2013.

[22] S. Haas, S. Wohlgemuth, I. Echizen, N. Sonehara, and G. Müller, "Aspects of privacy for electronic health records," *International Journal of Medical Informatics*, vol. 80, no. 2, pp. e26–e31, 2011.

3

An Online Causal Inference Framework for Modeling and Designing Systems Involving User Preferences

Ibrahim Delibalta,[1] Lemi Baruh,[1] and Suleyman Serdar Kozat[2]

[1]*Koc University, Istanbul, Turkey*
[2]*Bilkent University, Ankara, Turkey*

Correspondence should be addressed to Ibrahim Delibalta; idelibalta13@ku.edu.tr

Academic Editor: Zhixin Yang

We provide a causal inference framework to model the effects of machine learning algorithms on user preferences. We then use this mathematical model to prove that the overall system can be tuned to alter those preferences in a desired manner. A user can be an online shopper or a social media user, exposed to digital interventions produced by machine learning algorithms. A user preference can be anything from inclination towards a product to a political party affiliation. Our framework uses a state-space model to represent user preferences as latent system parameters which can only be observed indirectly via online user actions such as a purchase activity or social media status updates, shares, blogs, or tweets. Based on these observations, machine learning algorithms produce digital interventions such as targeted advertisements or tweets. We model the effects of these interventions through a causal feedback loop, which alters the corresponding preferences of the user. We then introduce algorithms in order to estimate and later tune the user preferences to a particular desired form. We demonstrate the effectiveness of our algorithms through experiments in different scenarios.

1. Introduction

Recent innovations in communication technologies, coupled with the increased use of Internet and smartphones, greatly enhanced institutions' ability to gather and process an enormous amount of information on individual users on social networks or consumers in different platforms [1–4]. Today, many sources of information from shares on social networks to blogs, from intelligent device activities to security camera recordings are easily collectable. Efficient and effective processing of this "big data" can significantly improve the quality of many real life applications or products, since this data can be used to accurately profile and then target particular users [5–7]. In this sense, abundance of new sources of information and previously unimaginable ways of access to consumer data have the potential to substantially change the classical machine learning approaches that are tailored to extract information with rather limited access to data using relatively complex algorithms [8–11].

Furthermore, unlike applications where the machine learning algorithms are used as mere tools for processing and inferring using the available data such as predicting the best movie for a particular user [12], the new generation of machine learning systems employed by enormously large and powerful data companies and institutions have the potential to change the underlying problem framework, that is, the user itself, by design [8, 13]. Consider the Google search engine platform and its effects on user preferences. The Google search platform not only provides the most relevant search results but also gathers information on users and provides well-tuned and targeted content (from carefully selected advertisements to specifically selected news) that may be used to change user behavior, inclinations, or preferences [14].

Online users are exposed to persuasive technologies and are continually immersed in digital content and interventions in various forms such as advertisements, news feeds, and recommendations [15]. User decisions and preferences are affected by these interventions [16]. We define a feedback

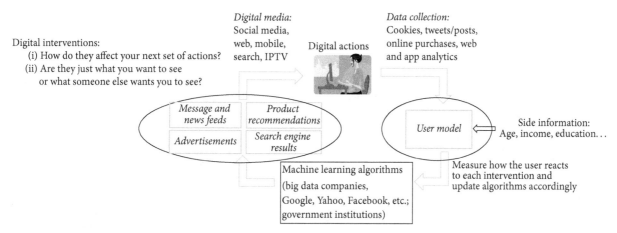

Digital interventions:
  (i) How do they affect your next set of actions?
  (ii) Are they just what you want to see
       or what someone else wants you to see?

Digital media: Social media, web, mobile, search, IPTV

Digital actions

Data collection: Cookies, tweets/posts, online purchases, web and app analytics

Message and news feeds

Product recommendations

Advertisements

Search engine results

User model

Side information: Age, income, education. . .

Machine learning algorithms (big data companies, Google, Yahoo, Facebook, etc.; government institutions)

Measure how the user reacts to each intervention and update algorithms accordingly

FIGURE 1: The Digital Feedback Loop.

framework in which these interventions can be selected in a systematic way to steer users in a desired manner. In Figure 1, we introduce "The Digital Feedback Loop" on which we base our model.

To this end, in this paper, we are particularly interested in the causal effects of machine learning algorithms on users [17, 18]. Specifically, we introduce causal feedback loops to accurately describe effects of machine learning algorithms on users in order to design more functional and effective machine learning systems [18, 19]. We model the latent preferences and/or inclinations of a user, as an unknown state in a real life causal system, and build novel algorithms to estimate and, then, alter this underlying unobservable state in an intentional and preferred manner. In particular, we model the underlying evolution of this state using a state-space model, where the latent state is only observed through the behavior of the user such as his/her tweets and Facebook status shares. The internal state is causally affected by the outputs of the algorithm (or the actions of the company), which can be derived from the past observations on the user or outputs of the system. The purpose of the machine learning algorithm can be, for example, (i) to drive the internal system state towards a desired final state, for example, trying to change the opinion of the population towards a newly introduced product; (ii) to maximize some utility function associated with the system, for example, enticing the users to a new and more profitable product; or (iii) to minimize some regret associated with the disclosed information, for example, minimizing the effects of unknown system parameters. Alternatively, the machine learning system may try to achieve a combination of these objectives.

This problem framework readily models a wide range of real life applications and scenarios [18, 19]. As an example, an advertiser may aim to direct the preferences of his/her target audience towards a desired product, by designing advertisement using data collected by consumer behavior surveys [18]. This framework is substantially different from the classical problem of targeted advertisement based on user profiling. In the case of targeted advertising, the goal is to match the best advertisement to the current user, based on the user's

profile. Another part of the classical problem is to measure the true impact of an ad (a "treatment" or an "intervention" in the general case) and thus find its effectiveness to help the ad selection for the next time or the next user as well as for billing purposes. Here, we assume that the underlying state, that is, the preferences of the consumers, are not only used to recommend a particular product but also intentionally altered by our algorithm. As in some of the earlier works [12, 17, 20], we use a causal framework to do our modeling. We then take it a step further to mathematically prove that the impact of a treatment can be predesigned and the user can, in theory, be swayed in accordance with the designer's intent. To the best of our knowledge, this is unique to our work. We can further articulate the difference between our work and some of the earlier works using an example in the context of news recommendation. The classical approach tries to show the user news articles he/she might be interested in reading, based on their profile and possibly some other contextual data. A separate process collects information on whether the user clicked on a particular news item and what that item's context is. This collected data is then used to augment the user's profile so that the recommendation part of the process makes a better decision the next time or for the next user. The connection between separate decisions is mainly the enhanced user profile. In reality, the recommended news articles have impacted the user's news preferences to some degree. This is a classical counterfactual problem [8]. While the user preferences themselves are latent and cannot be directly measured, the impact manifests itself in a number of ways that are observable. For instance, the user might tweet about that news with a particular sentiment or buy a book online which is related to the topic in the news item. What we prove with our framework is that, using the observable data and our model, one can produce a sequence of actions which will influence and steer the user's preferences in a pattern that is intended by the recommender system. These actions can be in the form of content served to the user such as news articles, social media feeds, and search results.

In different applications the preferences can be the state and the advertisements (content, the medium of the advertisement, the frequency, etc.) are the actions or output of the machine learning algorithm. In a different context, the opinions of the social network users on Facebook of a particular event or a new product can be represented as a state. Our model is comprehensive such that the relevant information on the user such as his/her age, gender, demographics, and residency is collectively represented by a side information vector since the advertiser collects data on the consumer such as the spending patterns, demographics, age, gender, and polls.

A summary of our work in this paper is as follows, with the last bullet being our key contribution:

(i) We model the effects of machine learning algorithms such as recommendation engines on users through a causal feedback loop. We introduce a complete state-space formulation modeling: (1) evolution of preferences vectors, (2) observations generated by users, and (3) causal feedback effects of the actions of algorithms on the system. All these parameters are jointly optimized through an Extended Kalman Filtering framework.

(ii) We introduce algorithms to estimate the unknown system parameters with and without feedback. In both cases, all the parameters are estimated jointly. We emphasize that we provide a complete set of equations covering all the possible scenarios.

(iii) To tune the preferences of users towards a desired sequence, we also introduce a linear regression algorithm and introduce an optimization framework using stochastic gradient descent algorithm. Unlike all the previous works that only use the observations to predict certain desired quantities, as the first time in the literature, we specifically design outputs to "update" the internal state of the system in a desired manner.

The rest of the paper is organized as follows. In the next section, we present a comprehensive state-space model that includes the evolution of the latent state vector, underlying observation model and side information. In the same section, we also introduce the causal feedback loop and possible variations to model different real life applications. We then introduce the Extended Kalman Filtering framework to estimate the unknown system parameters. We investigate different real life scenarios including the system with and without the feedback. We present all update and estimation equations. In the following section, we introduce an online learning algorithm to tune the underlying state vector, that is, preferences vector, towards a desired vector sequence through a linear regression and causal feedback loop. We then demonstrate the validity of our introduced algorithms under different scenarios via simulations. We include our simulation results to show that we are able to converge on unknown parameters in designing a system which can steer user preferences. The final section includes conclusions and scope of future work.

2. A Mathematical Model for User Preferences with Causal Feedback Effects

In this paper, all vectors are column vectors and denoted by lower case letters. Matrices are represented by uppercase letters. For a vector $\mathbf{u}$,

$$\|\mathbf{u}\| = \sqrt{\mathbf{u}^T \mathbf{u}} \tag{1}$$

is the l^2-norm, where $\mathbf{u}^T$ is the ordinary transpose. For vectors $\mathbf{a} \in \mathbb{R}^m$ and $\mathbf{b} \in \mathbb{R}^n$, $\mathbf{a}^T$ is the transpose and $[\mathbf{a}; \mathbf{b}] \in \mathbb{R}^{m+n}$ is the concatenated vector. Here, $\mathbf{I}$ represents an identity matrix, $\mathbf{0}$ represents a vector or a matrix of all zeros, and $\mathbf{1}$ represents a vector or a matrix of all ones, where the size is determined from the context. The time index is given in the subscript; that is, $\mathbf{x}_t$ is the sample at time $\mathbf{t}$. δ_t is the Kronecker delta functions.

We represent preferences of a user as a state vector $\mathbf{p}_t$, where this state vector is latent; that is, its entries are unknown by the system designer. The state vector can represent affinity or opinions of the underlying social network user for different products or for controversial issues like privacy. The actual length and values of the preferences depend on the application and context. As an example for the mood of a person in a context of 6 feelings (happy, excited, angry, scared, tender, and sad), the preference vector might be $[0, 1, 0, 0, 0, 0]^T$.

The relevant information on the user such as his/her age, gender, demographics, and residency is collectively represented by a side information vector $\mathbf{s}_t$. The side information on users on the social networks can be collected based on their profiles or their friendship networks. We assume that the side information is known to the designer and, naturally, change slowly so that $\mathbf{s}_t = \mathbf{s}$ is constant in time.

The machine learning system collects data on the user, say $\mathbf{x}_t$, such as Facebook shares, comments, status updates, and spending patterns, which is a function of his/her preferences $\mathbf{p}_t$ and the side information $\mathbf{s}$, given by

$$\mathbf{x}_t = F_t\left(\mathbf{p}_t, \mathbf{s}\right), \tag{2}$$

where the functional relationship $F(\cdot)$ will be clear in the following. Since the information collection process may be prone to errors or misinformation, for example, untruthful answers in surveys, we extend (2) to include these effects as

$$\mathbf{x}_t = F_t\left(\mathbf{p}_t, \mathbf{s}\right) + \mathbf{n}_t, \tag{3}$$

where $\mathbf{n}_t$ is a noise process independent of $\mathbf{p}_t$ and $\mathbf{s}$. We can use other approaches instead of an additive noise model; however, the additive noise model is found to accurately model unwanted observation noise effects [21]. We use a time varying linear state-space model to facilitate the analysis such that we have

$$\mathbf{x}_t = \mathbf{F}_t \mathbf{p}_t + \mathbf{n}_t, \tag{4}$$

where $\mathbf{F}_t$ is the observation matrix [22] corresponding to the particular user and $\mathbf{n}_t$ is i.i.d. with

$$E\left[\mathbf{n}_t \mathbf{n}_r^T\right] = \delta_{t-r} \mathbf{R}, \tag{5}$$

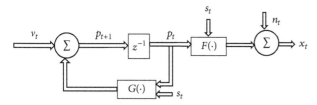

FIGURE 2: A state-space model to represent evaluation of the user preferences without feedback effects.

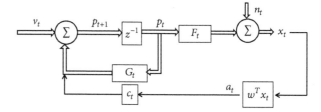

FIGURE 3: A complete state-space model of the system with action generation and feedback effects.

where $\mathbf{R}$ is the autocorrelation matrix. The autocorrelation matrix $\mathbf{R}$ is assumed to be known, since it can be readily estimated from the data [22] in a straightforward manner. We do not explicitly show the effect of $\mathbf{s}$ on $\mathbf{F}$ for notational simplicity.

Based on prior preferences, different user effects and trends, and the preferences of the user change, we represent this change as

$$\mathbf{p}_{t+1} = G_t(\mathbf{p}_t, \mathbf{s}) + \mathbf{n}_t, \qquad (6)$$

with an appropriate $G_t(\cdot)$ function. To facilitate the analysis, we also use a state-space model

$$\mathbf{p}_{t+1} = \mathbf{G}_t \mathbf{p}_t + \mathbf{v}_t, \qquad (7)$$

where $\mathbf{G}_t$ is the state update matrix, which is usually close to an identity matrix since the preferences of user cannot rapidly change [19, 20]. Here, $\mathbf{v}_t$ models the random fluctuations or independent changes in the preferences of users, where it is i.i.d. with

$$E\left[\mathbf{v}_t \mathbf{v}_r^T\right] = \delta_{t-r} \mathbf{Q} \qquad (8)$$

and $\mathbf{Q}$ is the autocorrelation matrix. The autocorrelation matrix $\mathbf{Q}$ is assumed to be known, since it can be readily estimated from the data [22] in a straightforward manner. The model without the feedback effects is shown in Figure 2.

Remark 1. To include local trends and seasonality effects, one can use $\mathbf{v}_t = \mathbf{B}_t \mathbf{u}_t$, where $\mathbf{B}_t$ may not be full rank when local trends exist (local trends can cause some data points to be derived from others). Also, $\mathbf{u}_t$ is an i.i.d. noise process. Our derivations in the next sections can be generalized to this case by considering an extended parameter set.

In the following, we model the effect of the actions of the machine learning algorithm in the "observation" (4) and "evolution" (7) equations.

2.1. Causal Inference through the Actions of the Machine Learning System. Based on the collected data $\mathbf{x}_t$, the algorithm takes an action represented by a_t. The action of the machine learning system or the platform can be either discrete or continuous valued depending on the application [21]. As an example, if the action represents a campaign advertisement to be sent to a particular Facebook user, then the set of campaign ads is finite. On the other hand, the action of the machine learning system can be continuous such as providing money

incentives to particular users to perform certain tasks such as filling questionnaires. We model the action as a function of the observations as

$$a_t = W_t^T(\mathbf{x}_t), \qquad (9)$$

where $W(\cdot)$ may correspond to different regression methods [21]. To facilitate the analysis, we model the action generation using a linear regression model as

$$a_t = W_t^T \mathbf{x}_t. \qquad (10)$$

If we have a finite set of actions, that is, $a_t \in \{1, \ldots, K\}$, we replace (10) by

$$a_t = Q\left(\mathbf{w}_t^T \mathbf{x}_t\right), \qquad (11)$$

which is similar to saturation or sigmoid models [23], where $Q(\cdot)$ is an appropriate quantizer. The linear model in (11) can be replaced by more complex models since $\mathbf{x}_t$ can contain discrete entries such as gender and age. However, we can closely approximate any such complex relations by piecewise linear models [24]. The piecewise linear extension of (11) is straightforward [24].

Based on the actions of the machine learning algorithm (and prior preferences), we assume that the preferences of the user changes in a linear state-space form with an additive model for the causal effect [18–20], which yields the following state model:

$$\mathbf{p}_{t+1} = \mathbf{G}_t \mathbf{p}_t + \mathbf{v}_t + \mathbf{c}_t a_t, \qquad (12)$$

where $\mathbf{c}_t$ is the unknown causal effect. The complete linear state-space model is illustrated in Figure 3. Although there exists other models for the feedback, apart from the linear feedback, the linear feedback was found to accurately model a wide range of real life scenarios provided that causal effects are moderate [19], which is typically the case for social networks; that is, advertisements usually do not have drastic effects on user preferences [19, 20]. Our linear feedback model can be extended to piecewise linear models to approximate smoothly varying nonlinear models in a straightforward manner.

Remark 2. We can also use a jump state model to represent the causal effects for the case where a_t is coming from a finite set. In this case, as an example, the causal effects will change the state behavior of the overall system through a jump state model as

$$\mathbf{p}_{t+1} = \mathbf{G}_{t, Q(\mathbf{w}^T \mathbf{x}_t)} \mathbf{p}_t + \mathbf{v}_t. \qquad (13)$$

Our estimation derivations in the following sections can also be extended to cover this case using a jump state model [22].

Remark 3. For certain causal inference problems, the actions sequence a_t may be required to be predictive of some reference sequence d_t, in a traffic prediction context, to sway driver preferences $\mathbf{p}_t$ in a certain direction by disclosing estimates a_t for a certain road d_t, using some publicly available data $\mathbf{x}_t$. To account for these types of scenarios, we complement the model in (12) by introducing

$$d_t = H_t(\mathbf{p}_t) + \boldsymbol{\sigma}_t, \tag{14}$$

where $\boldsymbol{\sigma}_t$ is i.i.d. In this case, the feedback loop will be designed in order to tune d_t to a particular value.

In the following, we introduce algorithms that optimize $\mathbf{w}_t$ so that the overall system behaves in a desired manner given the corresponding mathematical system. However, we emphasize the overall system parameters including the feedback loop parameters are not known and should be estimated only from the available observations $\mathbf{x}_t$. Hence, we carry out both the estimation and design procedures together for a complete system design.

3. Design of the Overall System with Causal Inference

We consider the problem of designing a sequence of actions $\{a_t\}_{t \geq 1}$ in order to influence users based on our observations $\{\mathbf{x}_t\}_{t \geq 1}$, where behavior of the user is governed by his/her hidden preference sequence $\{\mathbf{p}_t\}_{t \geq 1}$. The machine learning system is required to choose the sequence $\{\mathbf{w}_t\}_{t \geq 1}$ in order to accomplish its specific goal. The specific goal naturally depends on the application. As an example, in social networks, the goal can be to change the opinions of users about a new product by sending the most appropriate content such as news articles and/or targeted tweets. In its more general form, we can represent this goal as a utility function and optimize the cumulative gain:

$$\max_{\mathbf{w}_{t \geq 1}} \sum_{t=1}^{\infty} E[U_t], \tag{15}$$

where $U_t = U_t(\mathbf{p}_t)$ is an appropriate utility function for a specific application. To facilitate the analysis, we choose the utility function as the negative of the squared Euclidean distance between the actual consumer preference $\mathbf{p}_t$ and some desired state $\mathbf{q}_t$. We emphasize that, as shown later in the paper, our optimization framework can be used to optimize any utility function provided that it has continuous first-order derivatives due to the stochastic gradient update. In this case (15) can be written as

$$\min_{\mathbf{w}_{t \geq 1}} \sum_{t=1}^{\infty} E[\|\mathbf{p}_t - \mathbf{q}_t\|^2]. \tag{16}$$

The overall system parameters, $\{\mathbf{F}, \mathbf{G}, \mathbf{c}\}$, are not known and should be estimated from our observations. We introduce an Extended Kalman Filtering (EKF) approach to estimate the unknown parameters of the system. We separately consider the estimation framework without the feedback loop, that is, $\mathbf{w} = \mathbf{0}$, and with the feedback loop, that is, $\mathbf{w} \neq \mathbf{0}$. Clearly the estimation task for $\{\mathbf{F}, \mathbf{G}\}$ can be carried out before we produce our suggestions $\mathbf{w}$. In this case, we can estimate these parameters with a better accuracy without the feedback effects since we need to estimate a smaller number of parameters under less complicated noise processes. However, for certain scenarios where this feedback loop is already active, we also introduce a joint estimation framework for all parameters. A system with feedback is more general, realistic, and comprehensive. And feedback is needed in order to tune or influence the preferences of a user in a desired manner. However, a system with feedback is more complex to design and analyze. Therefore, we first provide the analysis for a system without feedback and build on it for an analysis of a system with feedback. After we get the estimated system parameters, we introduce online learning algorithms in order to tune the corresponding system to a particular target internal state sequence, which can be time varying, nonstationary, or even chaotic [23, 25].

3.1. Estimating the Unknown Parameters of the System without Feedback. Without the feedback loop, the system is described by

$$\mathbf{p}_{t+1} = \mathbf{G}_t \mathbf{p}_t + \mathbf{v}_t, \tag{17}$$

$$\mathbf{x}_t = \mathbf{F}_t \mathbf{p}_t + \mathbf{n}_t, \tag{18}$$

where $\mathbf{v}_t$ and $\mathbf{n}_t$ are assumed to be Gaussian with correlation matrices $\mathbf{Q}$ and $\mathbf{R}$, respectively. We then define

$$\boldsymbol{\theta}_t \triangleq [\mathbf{G}_t(:); \mathbf{F}_t(:)], \tag{19}$$

where $\mathbf{G}_t(:)$ is the vectorized $\mathbf{G}_t$; that is, the columns of $\mathbf{G}_t$ are stacked one after another to get a full column vector. To jointly estimate $\mathbf{p}_t$ and $\boldsymbol{\theta}_t$, we formulate an EKF framework by considering

$$\boldsymbol{\theta}_{t+1} = \boldsymbol{\theta}_t + \boldsymbol{\varepsilon}_t, \tag{20}$$

where $\boldsymbol{\varepsilon}_t$ is the noise in estimating $\boldsymbol{\theta}_t$ through the EKF. Then, using (17) and (20) and considering $\mathbf{p}_t$ and $\boldsymbol{\theta}_t$ as the joint state vector, we get

$$\mathbf{x}_t = f_1(\boldsymbol{\theta}_t, \mathbf{p}_t) + \mathbf{n}_t,$$

$$\begin{pmatrix} \mathbf{p}_{t+1} \\ \boldsymbol{\theta}_{t+1} \end{pmatrix} = \begin{pmatrix} f_2(\boldsymbol{\theta}_t, \mathbf{p}_t) \\ \boldsymbol{\theta}_t \end{pmatrix} + \begin{pmatrix} \mathbf{v}_t \\ \boldsymbol{\varepsilon}_t \end{pmatrix}, \tag{21}$$

where

$$f_1(\boldsymbol{\theta}_t, \mathbf{p}_t) \triangleq \mathbf{F}_t \mathbf{p}_t,$$

$$f_2(\boldsymbol{\theta}_t, \mathbf{p}_t) \triangleq \mathbf{G}_t \mathbf{p}_t \tag{22}$$

are the corresponding nonlinear equations so that we require the EKF framework. The corresponding EKF equations to estimate the augmented states are recursively given as

$$\begin{pmatrix} \mathbf{p}_{t|t} \\ \boldsymbol{\theta}_{t|t} \end{pmatrix} = \begin{pmatrix} \mathbf{p}_{t|t-1} \\ \boldsymbol{\theta}_{t|t-1} \end{pmatrix} + \mathbf{L}_t \left(\mathbf{x}_t - f_1 \left(\boldsymbol{\theta}_{t|t-1}, \mathbf{p}_{t|t-1} \right) \right),$$

$$\mathbf{p}_{t+1|t} = f_2 \left(\boldsymbol{\theta}_{t|t}, \mathbf{p}_{t|t} \right),$$

$$\boldsymbol{\theta}_{t+1|t} = \boldsymbol{\theta}_{t|t}, \tag{23}$$

$$\mathbf{L}_t = \mathbf{P}_{t|t-1} \mathbf{H}_t \left(\mathbf{H}_t^T \mathbf{P}_{t|t-1} \mathbf{H}_t + \mathbf{R} \right)^{-1},$$

$$\mathbf{P}_{t|t} = \mathbf{P}_{t|t-1} - \mathbf{L}_t \mathbf{H}_t^T \mathbf{P}_{t|t-1},$$

$$\mathbf{P}_{t+1|t} = \mathbf{D}_t \mathbf{P}_{t|t} \mathbf{D}_t^T + \mathbf{Q},$$

where

$$\mathbf{p}_{t|t} \triangleq \widetilde{E} \left[\mathbf{p}_t \mid \mathbf{x}_t, \mathbf{x}_{t-1}, \ldots \right],$$

$$\mathbf{p}_{t|t-1} \triangleq \widetilde{E} \left[\mathbf{p}_t \mid \mathbf{x}_{t-1}, \mathbf{x}_{t-2}, \ldots \right],$$

$$\boldsymbol{\theta}_{t|t} \triangleq \widetilde{E} \left[\boldsymbol{\theta}_t \mid \mathbf{x}_t, \mathbf{x}_{t-1}, \ldots \right], \tag{24}$$

$$\boldsymbol{\theta}_{t|t-1} \triangleq \widetilde{E} \left[\boldsymbol{\theta}_t \mid \mathbf{x}_{t-1}, \mathbf{x}_{t-2}, \ldots \right]$$

are EKF terms that approximate the optimal "linear" MSE estimated values in the linearized case and $\mathbf{H}_t$ and $\mathbf{D}_t$ are the gradients for the first-order Taylor expansion needed to linearize the nonlinear state equations in (21)

$$\mathbf{H}_t = \begin{pmatrix} \left(\nabla_{\mathbf{p}_t} f_1 \left(\boldsymbol{\theta}_{t|t-1}, \mathbf{p}_{t|t-1} \right) \right)^T \\ \left(\nabla_{\boldsymbol{\theta}_t} f_1 \left(\boldsymbol{\theta}_{t|t-1}, \mathbf{p}_{t|t-1} \right) \right)^T \end{pmatrix}, \tag{25}$$

$$\mathbf{D}_t = \begin{pmatrix} \nabla_{\mathbf{p}_t} f_2 \left(\boldsymbol{\theta}_{t|t}, \mathbf{p}_{t|t} \right) & \nabla_{\boldsymbol{\theta}_t} f_2 \left(\boldsymbol{\theta}_{t|t}, \mathbf{p}_{t|t} \right) \\ \mathbf{0} & \mathbf{I} \end{pmatrix}, \tag{26}$$

respectively. Here, $\mathbf{L}_t$ is the gain of the EKF and $\mathbf{P}_t$ is the error variance of the augmented state. The complete set of equations in (23) defines the EKF update on the parameter vectors. We next consider the case when there is feedback.

3.2. Estimating the Unknown Parameters of the System with Feedback.

For estimating the parameters of the feedback loop, that is, $\mathbf{c}_t$ (please see Figure 3), we have two different scenarios. In the first case, where we can control $\mathbf{w}$, we set $\mathbf{w} = \mathbf{0}$, estimate $\{\mathbf{F}, \mathbf{G}\}$, and then subsequently estimate $\mathbf{c}$ for fixed $\mathbf{w}$. For scenarios where the feedback loop is already present (or we cannot control it), that is, $\mathbf{w} \neq \mathbf{0}$, we need to estimate all the system parameters under the feedback loop. Naturally, in this case the estimation process is more prone to errors due to compounding effects of the feedback loop on the noise processes. We consider both cases separately.

Using (10) in (12), we get

$$\begin{aligned} \mathbf{p}_{t+1} &= \mathbf{G}_t \mathbf{p}_t + \mathbf{v}_t + \mathbf{c}_t \mathbf{w}_t^T \mathbf{x}_t \\ &= \mathbf{G}_t \mathbf{p}_t + \mathbf{v}_t + \mathbf{c}_t \mathbf{w}_t^T \mathbf{F}_t \mathbf{p}_t + \mathbf{c}_t \mathbf{w}_t^T \mathbf{n}_t. \end{aligned} \tag{27}$$

Hence, the complete state-space description with causal loop is given by

$$\mathbf{p}_{t+1} = \left(\mathbf{G}_t + \mathbf{c}_t \mathbf{w}_t^T \mathbf{F}_t \right) \mathbf{p}_t + \mathbf{v}_t + \mathbf{c}_t \mathbf{w}_t^T \mathbf{n}_t, \tag{28}$$

$$\mathbf{x}_t = \mathbf{F}_t \mathbf{p}_t + \mathbf{n}_t. \tag{29}$$

In (29), $\mathbf{w}_t$ is known; however, all the parameters including $\mathbf{c}$ are unknown. We have two cases.

Case 1. Since we can control $\mathbf{w}$, we set $\mathbf{w} = \mathbf{0}$ and estimate $\boldsymbol{\theta}$ as $\widetilde{\mathbf{F}}_t$ and $\widetilde{\mathbf{G}}_t$ as in the case without feedback. Then, use these estimated parameters in (29) yielding

$$\mathbf{p}_{t+1} = \left(\widetilde{\mathbf{G}}_t + \mathbf{c}_t \mathbf{w}_t^T \widetilde{\mathbf{F}}_t \right) \mathbf{p}_t + \mathbf{v}_t + \mathbf{c}_t \mathbf{w}_t^T \mathbf{n}_t,$$

$$\mathbf{x}_t = \widetilde{\mathbf{F}}_t \mathbf{p}_t + \mathbf{n}_t. \tag{30}$$

To estimate $\mathbf{c}_t$, we introduce an EKF framework by considering $\mathbf{c}_t$ as another state vector:

$$\mathbf{c}_{t+1} = \mathbf{c}_t + \boldsymbol{\rho}_t, \tag{31}$$

where $\boldsymbol{\rho}_t$ is the noise in the estimation process, yielding

$$\mathbf{x}_t = \widetilde{\mathbf{F}}_t \mathbf{p}_t + \mathbf{n}_t,$$

$$\begin{pmatrix} \mathbf{p}_{t+1} \\ \mathbf{c}_{t+1} \end{pmatrix} = \begin{pmatrix} f_3 \left(\mathbf{c}_t, \mathbf{p}_t \right) \\ \mathbf{c}_t \end{pmatrix} + \begin{pmatrix} \mathbf{v}_t \\ \boldsymbol{\rho}_t \end{pmatrix} + \begin{pmatrix} \mathbf{c}_t \mathbf{w}_t^T \\ \mathbf{0} \end{pmatrix} \mathbf{n}_t, \tag{32}$$

where

$$f_3 \left(\mathbf{c}_t, \mathbf{p}_t \right) \triangleq \left(\widetilde{\mathbf{G}}_t + \mathbf{c}_t \mathbf{w}^T \widetilde{\mathbf{F}}_t \right) \mathbf{p}_t \tag{33}$$

is the corresponding nonlinearity in the system.

In the state update equation (32), unlike the previous EKF formulation, the process noise depends on $\mathbf{c}_t$ as $\mathbf{c}_t \mathbf{w}_t^T \mathbf{n}_t$, which is unknown and part of the estimated state vector. Hence, the EKF formulation is more involved.

After several steps, we derive the EKF equations to estimate the augmented states for this case as

$$\begin{pmatrix} \mathbf{p}_{t|t} \\ \mathbf{c}_{t|t} \end{pmatrix} = \begin{pmatrix} \mathbf{p}_{t|t-1} \\ \mathbf{c}_{t|t-1} \end{pmatrix} + \mathbf{L}_t \left(\mathbf{x}_t - \widetilde{\mathbf{F}}_t \mathbf{p}_{t|t-1} \right),$$

$$\mathbf{p}_{t+1|t} = f_3 \left(\mathbf{c}_{t|t}, \mathbf{p}_{t|t} \right) + \mathbf{S}_t \boldsymbol{\Omega}_t^{-1} \left(\mathbf{x}_t - \widetilde{\mathbf{F}}_t \mathbf{p}_{t|t-1} \right),$$

$$\mathbf{c}_{t+1|t} = \mathbf{c}_{t|t},$$

$$\mathbf{L}_t = \mathbf{P}_{t|t-1} \mathbf{H}_t \boldsymbol{\Omega}_t^{-1},$$

$$\mathbf{S}_t = \mathbf{c}_{t|t-1} \mathbf{w}_t^T \mathbf{R}, \tag{34}$$

$$\boldsymbol{\Omega}_{t|t} = \mathbf{H}_t^T \mathbf{P}_{t|t-1} \mathbf{H}_t + \mathbf{R},$$

$$\mathbf{P}_{t|t} = \mathbf{P}_{t|t-1} - \mathbf{L}_t \mathbf{H}_t^T \mathbf{P}_{t|t-1},$$

$$\mathbf{P}_{t+1|t} = \mathbf{D}_t \mathbf{P}_{t|t-1} \mathbf{D}_t^T - \mathbf{B}_t \boldsymbol{\Omega}_t^{-1} \mathbf{B}_t^T + \widehat{\mathbf{Q}}_t,$$

$$\mathbf{B}_t = \mathbf{D}_t \mathbf{P}_{t|t-1} \mathbf{H}_t + \begin{pmatrix} \mathbf{S}_t \\ \mathbf{0} \end{pmatrix},$$

where

$$\mathbf{p}_{t|t} \triangleq \tilde{E}\left[\mathbf{p}_t \mid \mathbf{x}_t, \mathbf{x}_{t-1}, \ldots\right],$$

$$\mathbf{p}_{t|t-1} \triangleq \tilde{E}\left[\mathbf{p}_t \mid \mathbf{x}_{t-1}, \mathbf{x}_{t-2}, \ldots\right],$$

$$\mathbf{c}_{t|t} \triangleq \tilde{E}\left[\mathbf{c}_t \mid \mathbf{x}_t, \mathbf{x}_{t-1}, \ldots\right], \tag{35}$$

$$\mathbf{c}_{t|t-1} \triangleq \tilde{E}\left[\mathbf{c}_t \mid \mathbf{x}_{t-1}, \mathbf{x}_{t-2}, \ldots\right]$$

are EKF terms that approximate the optimal "linear" MSE estimated values in the linearized case and $\mathbf{H}_t$ and $\mathbf{D}_t$ are the gradients for the first-order Taylor expansion needed to linearize the nonlinear state equations in (32):

$$\mathbf{H}_t = \begin{pmatrix} \left(\nabla_{\mathbf{p}_t}\left(\tilde{\mathbf{F}}_t \mathbf{p}_t\right)\right)^T \\ \left(\nabla_{\mathbf{c}_t}\left(\tilde{\mathbf{F}}_t \mathbf{p}_t\right)\right)^T \end{pmatrix} = \begin{pmatrix} \tilde{\mathbf{F}}^T \\ 0 \end{pmatrix},$$

$$\mathbf{D}_t = \begin{pmatrix} \nabla_{\mathbf{p}_t} f_3\left(\mathbf{c}_{t|t}, \mathbf{p}_{t|t}\right) & \nabla_{\mathbf{c}_t} f_3\left(\mathbf{c}_{t|t}, \mathbf{p}_{t|t}\right) \\ 0 & \mathbf{I} \end{pmatrix}, \tag{36}$$

respectively. Here, $\mathbf{L}_t$ is the gain of the EKF and $\mathbf{P}_t$ is the error variance of the augmented state.

To obtain an expression for $\widehat{\mathbf{Q}}_t$ in terms of $\mathbf{w}_t$, we define the composite error vector $\mathbf{b}_t$ for the state update equation so that

$$\widehat{\mathbf{Q}}_t = E\left[\mathbf{b}_t \mathbf{b}_t^T \mid \mathbf{x}_{t-1}, \mathbf{x}_{t-2}, \ldots\right] \tag{37}$$

with

$$\mathbf{b}_t \triangleq \begin{pmatrix} \mathbf{v}_t \\ \boldsymbol{\rho}_t \end{pmatrix} + \begin{pmatrix} \mathbf{c}_t \mathbf{w}_t^T \\ 0 \end{pmatrix} \mathbf{n}_t. \tag{38}$$

After straightforward algebra, we get

$$\widehat{\mathbf{Q}}_t = \begin{pmatrix} \mathbf{Q} + \mathbf{w}_t^T \mathbf{R} \mathbf{w}_t \boldsymbol{\Gamma}_t & 0 \\ 0 & \mathbf{U} \end{pmatrix}, \tag{39}$$

where

$$\mathbf{U} = E\left[\boldsymbol{\rho}_t \boldsymbol{\rho}_t^T\right],$$

$$\boldsymbol{\Gamma}_t \triangleq \begin{pmatrix} 0 & \mathbf{I} \end{pmatrix} \mathbf{p}_{t|t-1} \begin{pmatrix} 0 \\ \mathbf{I} \end{pmatrix} + \mathbf{c}_{t|t-1} \mathbf{c}_{t|t-1}^T. \tag{40}$$

These updates provide the complete EKF formulation with feedback. In the sequel, we introduce the complete estimation framework where we estimate all the parameters jointly.

Case 2. We can define a superset of parameters

$$\boldsymbol{\theta}_t \triangleq \left[\mathbf{G}_t\left(:\right); \mathbf{F}_t\left(:\right); \mathbf{c}_t\right] \tag{41}$$

and formulate an EKF framework for this augmented parameter vector with

$$\boldsymbol{\theta}_{t+1} = \boldsymbol{\theta}_t + \boldsymbol{\varepsilon}_t, \tag{42}$$

which yields

$$\mathbf{x}_t = f_4\left(\boldsymbol{\theta}_t, \mathbf{p}_t\right) + \mathbf{n}_t,$$

$$\begin{pmatrix} \mathbf{p}_{t+1} \\ \boldsymbol{\theta}_{t+1} \end{pmatrix} = \begin{pmatrix} f_5\left(\boldsymbol{\theta}_t, \mathbf{p}_t\right) \\ \boldsymbol{\theta}_t \end{pmatrix} + \begin{pmatrix} \mathbf{v}_t \\ \boldsymbol{\varepsilon}_t \end{pmatrix} + \begin{pmatrix} \mathbf{c}_t \mathbf{w}_t^T \\ 0 \end{pmatrix} \mathbf{n}_t, \tag{43}$$

where

$$f_4\left(\boldsymbol{\theta}_t, \mathbf{p}_t\right) \triangleq \mathbf{F}_t \mathbf{p}_t,$$

$$f_5\left(\boldsymbol{\theta}_t, \mathbf{p}_t\right) \triangleq \left(\mathbf{G}_t - \mathbf{c}_t \mathbf{w}^T \mathbf{F}_t\right) \tag{44}$$

are the corresponding nonlinear equations so that we require EKF.

After some algebra, we get the complete EKF equations as

$$\begin{pmatrix} \mathbf{p}_{t|t} \\ \boldsymbol{\theta}_{t|t} \end{pmatrix} = \begin{pmatrix} \mathbf{p}_{t|t-1} \\ \boldsymbol{\theta}_{t|t-1} \end{pmatrix} + \mathbf{L}_t\left(\mathbf{x}_t - f_4\left(\boldsymbol{\theta}_{t|t-1}, \mathbf{p}_{t|t-1}\right)\right),$$

$$\mathbf{p}_{t+1|t} = f_5\left(\boldsymbol{\theta}_{t|t}, \mathbf{p}_{t|t}\right)$$
$$\qquad\qquad + \mathbf{S}_t \boldsymbol{\Omega}_t^{-1}\left(\mathbf{x}_t - f_4\left(\boldsymbol{\theta}_{t|t-1}, \mathbf{p}_{t|t-1}\right)\right),$$

$$\boldsymbol{\theta}_{t+1|t} = \boldsymbol{\theta}_{t|t},$$

$$\mathbf{L}_t = \mathbf{P}_{t|t-1} \mathbf{H}_t \boldsymbol{\Omega}_t^{-1}, \tag{45}$$

$$\mathbf{S}_t = \begin{pmatrix} 0 & 0 & \mathbf{I} \end{pmatrix} \boldsymbol{\theta}_{t|t-1} \mathbf{w}_t^T \mathbf{R},$$

$$\boldsymbol{\Omega}_t = \mathbf{H}_t^T \mathbf{P}_{t|t-1} \mathbf{H}_t + \mathbf{R},$$

$$\mathbf{P}_{t|t} = \mathbf{P}_{t|t-1} - \mathbf{L}_t \mathbf{H}_t^T \mathbf{P}_{t|t-1},$$

$$\mathbf{P}_{t+1|t} = \mathbf{D}_t \mathbf{P}_{t|t-1} \mathbf{D}_t^T - \mathbf{B}_t \boldsymbol{\Omega}_t^{-1} \mathbf{B}_t^T + \widehat{\mathbf{Q}}_t,$$

$$\mathbf{B}_t = \mathbf{D}_t \mathbf{P}_{t|t-1} \mathbf{H}_t + \begin{pmatrix} \mathbf{S}_t \\ 0 \end{pmatrix},$$

where

$$\mathbf{H}_t = \begin{pmatrix} \left(\nabla_{\mathbf{p}_t} f_4\left(\boldsymbol{\theta}_{t|t-1}, \mathbf{p}_{t|t-1}\right)\right)^T \\ \left(\nabla_{\boldsymbol{\theta}_t} f_4\left(\boldsymbol{\theta}_{t|t-1}, \mathbf{p}_{t|t-1}\right)\right)^T \end{pmatrix},$$

$$\mathbf{D}_t = \begin{pmatrix} \nabla_{\mathbf{p}_t} f_5\left(\boldsymbol{\theta}_{t|t}, \mathbf{p}_{t|t}\right) & \nabla_{\boldsymbol{\theta}_t} f_5\left(\boldsymbol{\theta}_{t|t}, \mathbf{p}_{t|t}\right) \\ 0 & \mathbf{I} \end{pmatrix}. \tag{46}$$

To obtain an expression for $\widehat{\mathbf{Q}}_t$ in terms of $\mathbf{w}_t$, we define the composite error vector $\mathbf{b}_t$ for the state update equation so that

$$\widehat{\mathbf{Q}}_t = E\left[\mathbf{b}_t \mathbf{b}_t^T \mid \mathbf{x}_{t-1}, \mathbf{x}_{t-2}, \ldots\right] \tag{47}$$

with

$$\mathbf{b}_t \triangleq \begin{pmatrix} \mathbf{v}_t \\ \boldsymbol{\varepsilon}_t \end{pmatrix} + \begin{pmatrix} \mathbf{c}_t \mathbf{w}_t^T \\ 0 \end{pmatrix} \mathbf{n}_t. \tag{48}$$

After straightforward algebra, we get

$$\widehat{\mathbf{Q}}_t = \begin{pmatrix} \mathbf{Q} + \mathbf{w}_t^T \mathbf{R} \mathbf{w}_t \boldsymbol{\Gamma}_t & \mathbf{0} \\ \mathbf{0} & \mathbf{U}_t \end{pmatrix}, \tag{49}$$

where

$$\mathbf{Q} = E\left[\boldsymbol{\nu}_t \boldsymbol{\nu}_t^T\right],$$

$$\mathbf{U} = E\left[\boldsymbol{\varepsilon}_t \boldsymbol{\varepsilon}_t^T\right],$$

$$\mathbf{R} = E\left[\mathbf{n}_t \mathbf{n}_t^T\right],$$

$$\boldsymbol{\Gamma}_t \triangleq (\mathbf{0} \ \ \mathbf{I}) \, \mathbf{p}_{t|t-1} \begin{pmatrix} \mathbf{0} \\ \mathbf{I} \end{pmatrix} \tag{50}$$

$$+ (\mathbf{0} \ \ \mathbf{I}) \, \boldsymbol{\theta}_{t|t-1} \begin{pmatrix} \mathbf{0} & \mathbf{0} \\ \mathbf{0} & \mathbf{I} \end{pmatrix} \boldsymbol{\theta}_{t|t-1}^T \begin{pmatrix} \mathbf{0} \\ \mathbf{I} \end{pmatrix}.$$

Given that the system parameters are estimated through the EKF formulation, we next introduce learning algorithms on $\mathbf{w}_t$ in order to change the behavior of the users in a desired manner.

4. Designing a Causal Inference System to Tune User Preferences

After the parameters are estimated through methods described in the previous sections, the complete system framework is given by

$$\mathbf{x}_t = \mathbf{F}_t \mathbf{p}_t + \mathbf{n}_t,$$

$$\mathbf{p}_{t+1} = \left(\mathbf{G}_t + \mathbf{c}_t \mathbf{w}_t^T \mathbf{F}_t\right) \mathbf{p}_t + \mathbf{v}_t + \mathbf{c}_t \mathbf{w}_t^T \mathbf{n}_t, \tag{51}$$

with the estimated

$$\left\{ \mathbf{F}_t = \widetilde{\mathbf{F}}_t, \mathbf{G}_t = \widetilde{\mathbf{G}}_t, \widetilde{\mathbf{c}}_t = \mathbf{c}_t \right\}. \tag{52}$$

Our goal in this section is to design $\mathbf{w}_t$ such that the sequence of preferences $\mathbf{p}_t$ are tuned towards a desired sequence of preferences $\mathbf{q}_t$; for example, one can desire to sway the preferences of a user to a certain product.

In order to tune the user preferences, we design $\mathbf{w}_t$ so that the difference between the preferences $\mathbf{p}_t$ and the desired $\mathbf{q}_t$ is minimized. We define this difference as the loss between the preferences and desired vectors as

$$\sum_{k=1}^{t} l\left(\mathbf{p}_k, \mathbf{q}_k\right), \tag{53}$$

where $l(\cdot)$ is any differentiable loss function. As an example, for the square error loss, this yields

$$\sum_{k=1}^{t} \left\|\mathbf{p}_k - \mathbf{q}_k\right\|^2. \tag{54}$$

To minimize the difference between these two sequences, we introduce a stochastic gradient approach where $\mathbf{w}_t$ is learned in a sequential manner. In the stochastic gradient approach, we have

$$\mathbf{w}_{t+1} = \mathbf{w}_t - \mu \nabla_{\mathbf{w}} l\left(\mathbf{p}_k, \mathbf{q}_k\right), \tag{55}$$

where $\mu > 0$ is an appropriate learning rate coefficient. The learning rate coefficient is usually selected as time varying with two conditions:

$$\mu_t \longrightarrow 0 \quad \text{as } t \longrightarrow \infty,$$

$$\sum_{k=1}^{t} \mu_k \longrightarrow \infty \quad \text{as } t \longrightarrow \infty; \tag{56}$$

for example, $\mu_t = 1/t$.

If these two conditions are met, then the estimated parameters $\mathbf{w}_t$ through the gradient approach will converge to the optimal $\mathbf{w}$ (provided that such an optimal point exists) [21]. To facilitate the analysis, we set

$$l\left(\mathbf{p}_k, \mathbf{q}_k\right) = \left\|\mathbf{p}_k - \mathbf{q}_k\right\|^2 \tag{57}$$

and get

$$\mathbf{w}_{t+1} = \mathbf{w}_t - \mu \nabla_{\mathbf{w}_t} \left\|\mathbf{p}_k - \mathbf{q}_k\right\|^2$$

$$= \mathbf{w}_t - 2\mu \left(\nabla_{\mathbf{w}_t} \mathbf{p}_t\right) \left(\mathbf{p}_t - \mathbf{q}_t\right). \tag{58}$$

In (58), since $\mathbf{p}_t$ is unknown, we use $\mathbf{p}_{t|t-1}$ from the causal loop case, that is, with feedback, and get

$$\mathbf{w}_{t+1} = \mathbf{w}_t - 2\mu \left(\nabla_{\mathbf{w}_t} \mathbf{p}_{t|t-1}\right) \left(\mathbf{p}_{t|t-1} - \mathbf{q}_t\right). \tag{59}$$

To get

$$\nabla_{\mathbf{w}_t} \mathbf{p}_{t|t-1}, \tag{60}$$

we use the EKF recursion as

$$\mathbf{p}_{t|t-1} = \left(\mathbf{G}_t + \mathbf{c}_t \mathbf{w}_t^T \mathbf{F}_t\right)$$

$$\cdot \left(\mathbf{p}_{t-1|t-2} + \mathbf{L}_{t-1} \left[\mathbf{x}_{t-1} - \mathbf{H}_{t-1} \mathbf{p}_{t-1|t-2}\right]\right), \tag{61}$$

$$\mathbf{p}_{t|t-1} = \mathbf{K}_t \mathbf{p}_{t|t-1} + \mathbf{M}_t,$$

where

$$\mathbf{K}_t = \left(\mathbf{G}_t + \mathbf{c}_t \mathbf{w}_t^T \mathbf{F}_t\right) \left(\mathbf{I} - \mathbf{L}_{t-1} \mathbf{H}_{t-1}\right),$$

$$\mathbf{M}_t = \left(\mathbf{G}_t + \mathbf{c}_t \mathbf{w}_t^T \mathbf{F}_t\right) \mathbf{L}_t x_{t-1}. \tag{62}$$

Using (61), we get a recursive update on the gradient as

$$\nabla_{\mathbf{w}_t} \mathbf{p}_{t|t-1} = \nabla_{\mathbf{w}_t} \mathbf{K}_t \mathbf{p}_{t|t-1} + \mathbf{K}_t \nabla_{\mathbf{w}_t} \mathbf{p}_{t|t-1} \nabla_{\mathbf{w}_t} \mathbf{M}_t, \tag{63}$$

From (59), (61), and (63), we get the complete recursive update as

$$\boxed{\begin{aligned} \mathbf{w}_{t+1} &= \mathbf{w}_t - 2\mu \left(\nabla_{\mathbf{w}_t} \mathbf{p}_{t|t-1}\right) \left(\mathbf{p}_{t|t-1} - \mathbf{q}_t\right) \\ \mathbf{p}_{t|t-1} &= \mathbf{K}_t \mathbf{p}_{t|t-1} + \mathbf{M}_t \\ \nabla_{\mathbf{w}_t} \mathbf{p}_{t|t-1} &= \nabla_{\mathbf{w}_t} \mathbf{K}_t \mathbf{p}_{t|t-1} + \mathbf{K}_t \nabla_{\mathbf{w}_t} \mathbf{p}_{t|t-1} \nabla_{\mathbf{w}_t} \mathbf{M}_t \end{aligned}} \tag{64}$$

This completes the derivation of the stochastic gradient update for online learning of the tuning regression vector.

5. Experiments

In this section, we share our simulation results to show that estimated parameters of the system converge to the real values, proving that a system can be designed with the right parameters which allows a sequence of actions or interventions to tune the preferences of a user in a desired manner. Since our goal is mainly to establish a pathway to the possibility of designing a system that can steer user preferences in a desired manner, we consider our basic simulation set to be sufficient based on the mathematical proof we provided in the form of EKF formulations. The true parameters of the system are known to us since we are running our experiments in the form of simulations. Specifically, the preferences of the user, which are not directly observable in real life, are known in case of simulations. We run simulations for the EKF formulations we derived in the previous sections to show that our estimation of the preferences converges to the real preference values. We illustrate the convergence of our algorithms under different scenarios.

In the first scenario, we have the case where the corresponding system has no feedback. As the true system, we choose a second-order linear state-space model, where $\mathbf{G} = 0.95\mathbf{I}$ and $\mathbf{F} = \mathbf{I}$ with $\mathbf{Q} = 3 \times 10^{-3}\mathbf{I}$ and $\mathbf{R} = 3 \times 10^{-3}\mathbf{I}$. For the EKF formulation, we choose two different variances for ε_t, for example, 10^{-3} and 10^{-4}, to demonstrate the effect of this design parameter on the system. We emphasize that neither $\mathbf{F}$ or $\mathbf{G}$ are known; hence, as long as the system is observable, particular choices of $\mathbf{F}$ and $\mathbf{G}$ only change the convergence speed and the final MSE. However, we choose $\mathbf{F}$ to make the system stable.

In Figure 4, we plot the square error difference between the estimated preferences and the real preferences

$$\operatorname{tr} E\left[\left\|\mathbf{p}_t - \mathbf{p}_{t|t-1}\right\|^2\right] \quad (65)$$

with respect to the number of iterations, where we produce the MSE curves after averaging over 100 independent trials. We also plot the cumulative MSE normalized with respect to time, that is,

$$\frac{\sum_{k=1}^{t} \operatorname{tr} E\left[\left\|\mathbf{p}_t - \mathbf{p}_{t|t-1}\right\|^2\right]}{t}, \quad (66)$$

to show that as the iteration count increases, the averaged MSE steadily converges. The plot includes both the average MSE and the cumulative MSE normalized in time for estimation of $\mathbf{F}$ and $\mathbf{G}$. We observe that the estimation of $\mathbf{F}$ and $\mathbf{G}$ is more prone to errors due to the multiplicative uncertainty, single observation, and state update equations. However, both the estimated preferences vectors as well as the system parameters converge.

In the second set of experiments, we have feedback present; that is, $\mathbf{w} \neq \mathbf{0}$. For this case, we now have similar parameters as in the first set of experiments, except $\mathbf{G} = 0.9\mathbf{I}$ to give more decay due to presence of feedback. For this case, we choose two different scenarios, where $\mathbf{w}_t$ and $\mathbf{c}_t$ are fixed or randomly chosen provided that the overall system stays stable after the feedback; that is, $(\mathbf{G} + \mathbf{c}\,\mathbf{w}^T\,\mathbf{F})$ corresponds to a stable

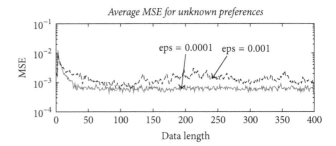

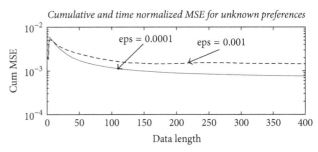

FIGURE 4: Estimation of the underlying preferences vector when there is no feedback. The results are averaged over 100 independent trials. Here, we have no feedback and parameters of both the state equation and the observation equation are unknown. The results are shown for two different noise variances for the EKF formulation.

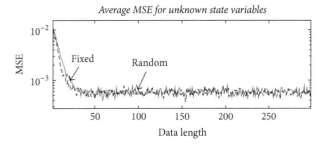

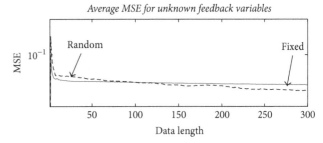

FIGURE 5: Estimation of the underlying vector of preferences and the feedback parameters when there is feedback. The results are averaged over 100 independent trials. Two different configurations are simulated for the feedback as well as for the linear control parameters, for example, the fixed and random initial cases. For both scenarios, our estimation process converges to the true underlying processes.

system. Note that this can be always forced by choosing an appropriate $\mathbf{w}$. However, we choose randomly initialized $\mathbf{w}$ to avoid any bias in our experiments. Here, although $\mathbf{w}$ is known to us, the feedback amount $\mathbf{c}$ and the hidden preferences are unknown. In Figure 5, we plot the MSE between the estimated preference vectors and the true ones. We observe from these simulations that although the feedback produces a multiplicative uncertainty in the state equation and greatly enhances the nonlinearity in the update equation, we are able to recover the true values through the EKF formulation. We observe that although due to feedback we have more colored noise in the state equation, we recover true values due to the whitening effects of the EKF. The MSE errors between the estimated feedback and the true one are plotted, where the MSE curves are produced after 100 independent realizations.

6. Conclusions

In this paper, we model the effects of the machine learning algorithms such as recommendation engines on users through a causal feedback loop. To this end, we introduce a complete state-space formulation modeling: (1) evolution of preference vectors, (2) observations generated by users, and (3) the causal feedback effects of the actions of machine learning algorithms on the system. All these parameters are jointly optimized through an Extended Kalman Filtering framework. We introduce algorithms to estimate the unknown system parameters with and without feedback. In both cases, all the parameters are estimated jointly. We emphasize that we provide a complete set of equations covering all the possible scenarios. To tune the preferences of users towards a desired sequence, we also introduce a linear feedback and introduce an optimization framework using stochastic gradient descent algorithm. Unlike previous works that only use the observations to predict certain desired quantities, we specifically design outputs to "update" the internal state of the system in a desired manner. Through a set of experiments, we demonstrate the convergence behavior of our proposed algorithms in different scenarios.

We consider our work as a significant theoretical first step in designing a system with the right parameters which allows a sequence of actions or interventions to tune the preferences of a user in a desired manner. We emphasize that the main goal of our study is to establish a pathway to designing such a system. We achieve this by first providing mathematical proof and then through a basic set of simulations.

A next step in future studies can be to make the system more stable and also to make the design process easy and practical for system designers. Further analysis on the convergence of the system and more simulations, experiments, and numerical analyses are needed to take our results to the next level. A direct comparison to previous studies is not possible for this first step of our study since, to the best of our knowledge, this is the first time a task of this nature is being undertaken. Our main success criterion is the fact that estimated parameters converge to the real parameter values. However, as our framework evolves, we will be able to track its relative performance.

Another area of focus for future studies is the optimal selection of action sequences. This can be particularly challenging since user preferences can change over time due to the abundance of new products and services. Algorithms to optimally select actions may require online learning and decision making in real time to accommodate these changes.

Conflicts of Interest

The authors declare that there are no conflicts of interest regarding the publication of this article.

Acknowledgments

The authors would like to thank Koc University Graduate School of Social Sciences and Humanities for their support. This work was also supported by the BAGEP Award of the Science Academy.

References

[1] V. Gupta, D. Varshney, H. Jhamtani, D. Kedia, and S. Karwa, "Identifying purchase intent from social posts," in *Proceedings of the 8th International Conference on Weblogs and Social Media (ICWSM '14)*, June 2014.

[2] D. Ruta, "Automated trading with machine learning on big data," in *Proceedings of the 3rd IEEE International Congress on Big Data (BigData Congress '14)*, pp. 824–830, July 2014.

[3] Y. Wang and P. M. Djurić, "Social learning with heterogeneous agents and sequential decision making," *Digital Signal Processing*, vol. 47, pp. 17–24, 2015.

[4] L. Bottou and Y. Le Cun, "On-line learning for very large data sets," *Applied Stochastic Models in Business and Industry*, vol. 21, no. 2, pp. 137–151, 2005.

[5] L. Bottou and O. Bousquet, "The tradeoffs of large scale learning," *In Advances in Neural Information Processing (NISP)*, pp. 1–8, 2007.

[6] J. Yan, N. Liu, G. Wang, W. Zhang, Y. Jiang, and Z. Chen, "How much can behavioral targeting help online advertising?" in *Proceedings of the 18th International World Wide Web Conference (WWW '09)*, pp. 261–270, April 2009.

[7] H. Peng, D. Liang, and C. Choi, "Evaluating parallel logistic regression models," in *Proceedings of the 2013 IEEE International Conference on Big Data (Big Data '13)*, pp. 119–126, October 2013.

[8] L. Bottou, J. Peters, J. Quiñonero-Candela et al., "Counterfactual reasoning and learning systems: the example of computational advertising," *Journal of Machine Learning Research*, vol. 14, pp. 3207–3260, 2013.

[9] Y. C. Sübakan, B. Kurt, A. T. Cemgil, and B. Sankur, "Probabilistic sequence clustering with spectral learning," *Digital Signal Processing: a Review Journal*, vol. 29, no. 1, pp. 1–19, 2014.

[10] Y. Achbany, I. J. Jureta, S. Faulkner, and F. Fouss, "Continually learning optimal allocations of services to tasks," *IEEE Transactions on Services Computing*, vol. 1, no. 3, pp. 141–154, 2008.

[11] M. Jahrer, A. Töscher, and R. Legenstein, "Combining predictions for accurate recommender systems," in *Proceedings of the 16th ACM SIGKDD International Conference on Knowledge Discovery and Data Mining (KDD '10)*, pp. 693–701, July 2010.

[12] A. Töscher, M. Jahrer, and R. Legenstein, "Improved neighborhood-based algorithms for large-scale recommender systems," in *Proceedings of the 2nd KDD Workshop on Large-Scale Recommender Systems and the Netflix Prize Competition (NETFLIX '08)*, August 2008.

[13] D. Chan, R. Ge, O. Gershony, T. Hesterberg, and D. Lambert, "Evaluating online ad campaigns in a pipeline: causal models at scale," in *Proceedings of the 16th ACM SIGKDD International Conference on Knowledge Discovery and Data Mining (KDD '10)*, pp. 7–15, July 2010.

[14] R. Epstein and R. E. Robertson, "The search engine manipulation effect (SEME) and its possible impact on the outcomes of elections," *Proceedings of the National Academy of Sciences of the United States of America*, vol. 112, no. 33, pp. E4512–E4521, 2015.

[15] A. A. Salah, B. Lepri, F. Pianesi, and A. S. Pentland, "Human behavior understanding for inducing behavioral change: application perspectives," in *Proceedings of the 2nd International Workshop on Human Behavior Understanding*, vol. 7065, pp. 1–15, 2011.

[16] T. Z. Zarsky, *Thinking outside The Box: considering Transparency, Anonymity, and Pseudonymity as Overall Solutions to the Problems of Information Privacy in the Internet Society*, vol. 58, University of Miami Law Review, 2004.

[17] P. Wang, D. Yin, M. Meytlis, J. Yang, and Y. Chang, "Rethink targeting: detect 'smart cheating' in online advertising through causal inference," in *Proceedings of the 24th International Conference on World Wide Web (WWW '15)*, pp. 133-134, May 2015.

[18] P. Wang, W. Sun, D. Yin, J. Yang, and Y. Chang, "Robust tree-based causal inference for complex ad effectiveness analysis," in *Proceedings of the 8th ACM International Conference on Web Search and Data Mining (WSDM '15)*, pp. 67–76, February 2015.

[19] K. H. Brodersen, F. Gallusser, J. Koehler, N. Remy, and S. L. Scott, "Inferring causal impact using bayesian structural time-series models," *Annals of Applied Statistics*, vol. 9, no. 1, pp. 247–274, 2015.

[20] W. Sun, P. Wang, D. Yin, J. Yang, and Y. Chang, "Causal inference via sparse additive models with application to online advertising," in *Proceedings of the 29th AAAI Conference on Artificial Intelligence (AAAI '15)*, 2015.

[21] C. M. Bishop, *Pattern Recognition and Machine Learning*, Springer, New York, NY, USA, 2006.

[22] B. D. O. Anderson and J. B. Moore, *Optimal Filtering*, Prentice-Hall, New Jersey, NJ, USA, 1979.

[23] S. S. Kozat, A. C. Singer, and G. C. Zeitler, "Universal piecewise linear prediction via context trees," *IEEE Transactions on Signal Processing*, vol. 55, no. 7, pp. 3730–3745, 2007.

[24] N. D. Vanli and S. S. Kozat, "A comprehensive approach to universal piecewise nonlinear regression based on trees," *IEEE Transactions on Signal Processing*, vol. 62, no. 20, pp. 5471–5486, 2014.

[25] A. C. Singer, S. S. Kozat, and M. Feder, "Universal linear least squares prediction: upper and lower bounds," *IEEE Transactions on Information Theory*, vol. 48, no. 8, pp. 2354–2362, 2002.

4

Uniform Local Binary Pattern for Fingerprint Liveness Detection in the Gaussian Pyramid

Yujia Jiang[ID] **and Xin Liu**

College of Architecture and Artistic Design, Hunan Institute of Technology, Hengyang 421001, China

Correspondence should be addressed to Yujia Jiang; jiangyujiacaad@163.com

Academic Editor: William Sandham

Fingerprint recognition schemas are widely used in our daily life, such as Door Security, Identification, and Phone Verification. However, the existing problem is that fingerprint recognition systems are easily tricked by fake fingerprints for collaboration. Therefore, designing a fingerprint liveness detection module in fingerprint recognition systems is necessary. To solve the above problem and discriminate true fingerprint from fake ones, a novel software-based liveness detection approach using uniform local binary pattern (ULBP) in spatial pyramid is applied to recognize fingerprint liveness in this paper. Firstly, preprocessing operation for each fingerprint is necessary. Then, to solve image rotation and scale invariance, three-layer spatial pyramids of fingerprints are introduced in this paper. Next, texture information for three layers spatial pyramids is described by using uniform local binary pattern to extract features of given fingerprints. The accuracy of our proposed method has been compared with several state-of-the-art methods in fingerprint liveness detection. Experiments based on standard databases, taken from Liveness Detection Competition 2013 composed of four different fingerprint sensors, have been carried out. Finally, classifier model based on extracted features is trained using SVM classifier. Experimental results present that our proposed method can achieve high recognition accuracy compared with other methods.

1. Introduction

With the widespread use of smart applications and phones, it brings convenience to our life. However, the security of identity authentication is an issue that needs to be addressed urgently. Traditional identity authentication method can deal with the security issue, but current problem is that tokens or passwords are easy to be forgotten for a long time and bank cards or identity cards, and so on, are easily stolen or lost. Therefore, recognition systems based on biometric traits gradually replace traditional authentication methods nowadays. For example, smart phone fingerprint recognition device: the personal fingerprint information is stored on the phone, so only the user can access and turn on the smart phone. Biometrics system refers to the identification of human beings based on their physiological and behavioral characteristics. The ease of use and low error rates which promote their widespread use are superior to others methods.

Of course, biometric systems have their own weakness. For example, biometric systems contain vulnerabilities and are also susceptible to various kinds of sophisticated forms of spoofing. Among these, the fingerprint recognition, the ease of use, and high recognition rate are the main factors that contribute to their widespread use, accounting for the vast majority part [1]. Indeed, early identification systems can be easily spoofed by fake fingerprints, which can be reproduced from common materials. Popular fake fingertip materials such as silicon, wood glue and latex [2, 3] consist of large organic molecules which tend to agglomerate during processing. For example, threats to fingerprint systems are spoof finger attack at the sensor, attack on software modules, and so on [4].

Fingerprint liveness detection refers to whether the fingerprints presented are really from a live fingertip or spoofed ones. In order to solve the spoofing, various methods are proposed [5–8] in recent years. The goal of current fingerprint liveness detection research is concerned about how to design a method to discriminate real and fake fingerprints. Because the features of image can be described using textures information, many features based on texture extraction methods spring out according to human vision. In this paper, a novel fingerprint liveness detection method based on uniform local binary pattern in Gaussian pyramid has been proposed. Multiscale analysis using two layers Gaussian pyramid filter has been proved to be more efficient for solving image scale invariance. On the whole, fingerprint liveness detection is regarded as a binary classification problem, in which the given fingerprint image is either a real fingerprint or a spoof one. Feature extraction is a key step for solving the above problem. In our method, Gaussian pyramid filter is introduced to deal with the problem of scale invariance, and feature vectors are constructed using uniform local binary pattern to reduce the number of dimensionality of features. After these, feature vectors of each layer of spatial pyramid image are extracted through using uniform local binary pattern (ULBP). Once the feature vector is generated, the samples classifier model is learnt by using support vector machine. Experimental results based on the LivDet 2013 show that our method exhibits a strong edge.

The paper is organized as follows. In Section 2, a summary of the related work to the present research is given. Our proposed method about the feature vector extraction is introduced in Section 3. The result and comparison are given in Section 4. Conclusions are drawn in Section 5.

2. Related Work

Fingerprint authentication systems are easily cheated by these fake fingerprints, which fake fingerprints that mimic real users' fingerprints. Therefore, fingerprint liveness detection methods are proposed to prevent fingerprint authentication systems from being fake fingerprints. Because of the alternation of the ridges and valleys on them, fingertips surfaces are intrinsically coarse at certain scale. Furthermore, considering the advantage of software-based detection compared with the hardware-based method, software-based fingerprint liveness detection method is proposed in this paper. Because of moisture of sweat glands, the real fingerprint taken using fingerprint sensor devices will change slightly in a short time span. However, it will not happen in spoof ones. Therefore, researchers detect the fingerprint vitality through the analysis perspiration of fingerprint in different time, and the perspiration pattern changes at different time interval were observed (2 seconds in [6] and 5 seconds in [7]). In [7], they can find that the intervals are longer and the wavy nature is more complex based on the spreading of moisture for the real fingerprint. In order to improve the accuracy of Derakhshani's proposed method, Schuckers et al. [8, 9] proposed a novel liveness detection method by using wavelet analysis. In their method, multiresolution analyses are used to extract the low frequency content and wavelet packet analyses are used to extract the high frequency content. Other features related to spectral energy distribution have been used by using different transformation. Thin-plate model has been used by analysing fingertip distortion in [10]. In their method, the tester press his fingertip on the surface of fingerprint

sensor and rotate their fingers in four directions (0 degree, 90 degree, 180 degree and 270 degree) to capture a sequence of frames. Then, relevant features based on the skin deformation based on capturing finger distortion images are constructed. In [11], a liveness detection method using one-way analysis of variance ANOVA and Multiple-Comparison Method to do the statistical tests on the dataset of real fingers and spoof ones was proposed. Because fake fingerprint image quality is not as good as the real fingerprint image, it is difficult to forge a real fingerprint image with the same or better quality fingerprint images. Based on this consideration, [12] uses the coarseness of the fingerprint to discriminate features. Nikam and Agarwal detected the fingerprint liveness based on ridgelet transform to extract texture features using only single fingerprint image [13]. The same method is researched in [14], where 25 quality parameters are used as the measure of performance detection. These methods are such as in [15, 16], in which the features used in the classifier are based on the specific fingerprint measurements, such as ridge strength, continuity, and clarity. Ghiani et al. [16] proposed a fingerprint liveness detection method based on wavelet analysis. In 2013, Ghiani et al. [17] detected the vitality of fingerprint images based on residual Gaussian and the noise of the fingerprint images to estimate the coarseness of fingerprint image. There are many small pores of circular structures in real fingertips, and the attackers observed that we cannot accurately imitate sweat pores in spoofed ones. Reference [18] proposed a new detection method by comparing pore quantity between recorded fingerprints and the query ones. After that, Gragnaniello et al. [19] proposed a novel detection method based on the optimum threshold from correlations peaks to detect which peaks are active pores. Many methods based on texture features have been proposed for liveness detection, such as statistical, signal processing approaches and model based and structural ones [20]. Rao and Jain [21] proposed a fingerprint liveness detection method based on minimizing the energy associated with phase and orientation maps. Multiresolution texture feature analysis in their method and cross ridge frequency analysis techniques are used. Ratha et al. [22] texture features based on the spatial gray level dependence method are extracted by using spatial gray level dependence method (SGLDM) for personal verification and discrimination. In latest literatures, much attention has been also focused on the wavelet transform domain. Jain et al. proposed many fingerprint liveness detection methods, such as the curvelet transform [23, 24], the Gabor filters [12], and the gray level cooccurrence matrices which are combined with the wavelet transform [7, 14, 25].

3. Feature Extraction

The problem of fingerprint liveness detection is seen as two-class classification problem where a given fingerprint image is either real or fake, so the feature extraction is the key step. A general diagram showing different phases of our method is shown in Figure 1, which mainly includes two phases: image training process and image testing process. Next we will give a detailed description on feature extraction of a given image.

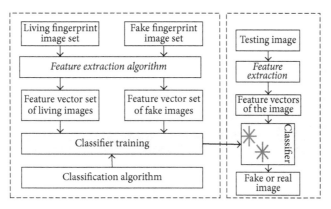

FIGURE 1: The flowchart of the proposed method [9].

3.1. Gaussian Pyramid Filter (GPF). Image pyramid is the major description of image multiscale, and it is an effective but simple structure that interprets image in multiple resolutions. An image pyramid is image set, which comes from the same original image and the resolutions of the image gradually decreases in the form of pyramid. It is sampled by a cascade downsampling until a certain termination condition is researched. We compare a layer of images to a pyramid; the higher the hierarchy, the smaller the image and the lower the resolution. An image pyramid is a series of images sets that are progressively reduced in the shape of a pyramid. At the bottom of the pyramid is the high-resolution, and the top pyramid is low resolution approximation. When moving to the top of the pyramid, the resolutions of images decrease gradually. Because of the size of the base J is $2^J \times 2^J$ or $N \times N$, where $J = \log 2N$; Thus, the size of intermediate j is $2^j \times 2^j$, and the range of j is $0 \leq j \leq J$. The complete pyramid is composed of $J + 1$ resolutions, so the range of size of different resolutions is $2^J \times 2^J$ to $2^0 \times 2^0$. However, most pyramids only have $P + 1$ layers, where $1 \leq P \leq J$. In this paper, Gaussian pyramid is introduced to deal with scale invariance. Two steps are included: (a) the convolution of original Image G_i and Gaussian kernel K are conducted; (b) removing the even rows and columns using downsampling operation. Then the images shrunk to a quarter of the original image. Finally, We can obtain the entire pyramid by iterating over the steps above. The Gaussian kernel K is as follows:

$$K = \frac{1}{16} * \begin{bmatrix} 1 & 4 & 6 & 4 & 1 \\ 4 & 16 & 24 & 16 & 4 \\ 6 & 24 & 36 & 24 & 6 \\ 4 & 16 & 24 & 16 & 4 \\ 1 & 4 & 6 & 4 & 1 \end{bmatrix}. \tag{1}$$

After downsampling operation, the image is scaled to half of the original image. Figure 2(a) shows the original fingerprint image, and Figure 2(b) is an image after one-layer Gaussian kernel operation, and Figure 2(c) is an image after two-layer Gaussian kernel operation.

3.2. Uniform Local Binary Pattern. Local Binary Pattern (LBP), which has scale invariance and gray invariance, is used to describe the image local texture information, and the process of texture features extraction of given image is as follows. Firstly, the pixel values of eight neighbors in 3×3 window are compared with the center pixel of the 3×3 window, respectively, and binary relations are computed by using (2). In (2), z denotes the comparative results between the center pixel and eight adjacent pixels, respectively. Then, the LBP code is weighted by using binary relationship of power of two and summed to obtain the LBP code of the current selected center pixel. Eq. (3) can calculate the LBP code. In (3), I (x_c, y_c) represents the center pixel values of the 3×3 window, and the eight adjacent pixels are $g_0, \ldots, g_7$:

$$s(z) = \begin{cases} 1, & z \geq 0 \\ 0, & z < 0, \end{cases} \tag{2}$$

$$\text{LBP}(x_c, y_c) = \sum_{i=0}^{7} s(g_i, g_c) 2^i. \tag{3}$$

An example of LBP operation is shown in Figure 3. Firstly, Figure 3(a) is the part of image, whose size is 3×3. In the 3×3 window, the pixel value of center pixel is 45. Then, binary relationships are constructed using (2), in which eight adjacent pixel values are compared with the center pixel, respectively. The so-threshold binary values in Figure 3(b) responding to Figure 3(a) using (2) are obtained. Figure 3(c) is a binary relationship of power of two. Next we can calculate, converting the binary number into a decimal number in a clockwise direction by (3), the pixel value of center pixel using LBP. Finally, the local texture feature of image can be shown by counting the histogram of pixel value after LBP operation. Figure 3(c), LBP code of the center pixel: $1 \times 2^0 + 0 \times 2^1 + 0 \times 2^2 + 1 \times 2^3 + 0 \times 2^4 + 1 \times 2^5 + 1 \times 2^6 + 0 \times 2^7 = 1 + 8 + 32 + 64 = 105$.

Therefore, features of image can be described by counting histogram which is formed by 256 LBP codes. However, the current problem is that the binary models after LBP operation are too many. Thus, to solve the problem and improve statistics, uniform local binary pattern is proposed.

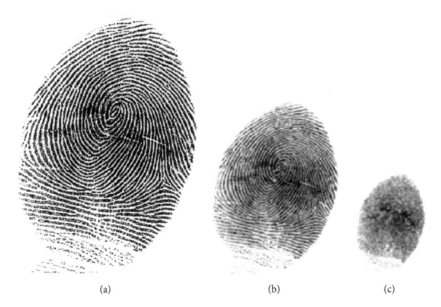

FIGURE 2: The different scale image based downsampling operation.

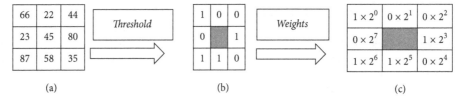

FIGURE 3: An example of the LBP operation.

It finds that the majority transformation of LBP modes only contains two jumps from one to zero or from zero to one, for example, 00000000 (zero jump), 00000111 (only one jump from zero to one), and 10001111 (two jumps are included, one is from one to zero, and another is from zero to one). The above three examples are all uniform local binary pattern. Besides these, others are called mixed model. Based on this finding, uniform local binary pattern is proposed. And for eight adjacent pixel sampling point in the 3×3 window, the number of original binary model is reduced from $2^8 = 256$ to $8 \times (8 - 1) + 2 = 58$ after introducing uniform local binary pattern operation. On one hand, uniform local binary pattern can reduce the dimensionality of feature vectors, on the other hand, it can solve the effects of high frequency noise.

3.3. Support Vector Machine (SVM). Support Vector Machines (SVM) is a general two-class classifier, which is widely used in the research field of computer vision, pattern recognition, and deep learning. The goal of SVM is to find the hyperplane of the classification requirement, which can divide two classification samples correctly; at the same time, the classification interval is the largest. Figure 4 shows the optimal line of classification in linear separable cases. H denotes the optimal line, which can be achieved by maximizing the distance $\max_{\text{margin}=w/2}$ between H_1 and H_2. LIBSVM software package [7, 25, 26] is a most commonly used classification tool. Two key issues need to be considered when using SVM.

One problem is how to select an appropriate kernel function of SVM. The goal of kernel function is that the two classification samples are linearly separable by an appropriate transformation in high-dimensional space; however, the two classification samples are linearly nonseparable in low dimensional space. According to the problem of linear separable and linear inseparable, different kernel functions are chosen. It is noted that the classification labels and features are all nonlinear. In our method, RBF kernel function is selected, which can make nonlinearly mapping to a high-dimensional space.

Another problem is how to select parameters. Two parameters are included in the RBF kernel function: C and Υ. To train a better classifier, parameter optimization operation is used. In LIBSVM, gnuplot.exe is an executable tool, which is used to find the optimal parameters pairs C and Υ, while the goal of the parameter optimization operation is to classify the unknown data. Finally, we can search the results of the optimal parameters by using the "Grid-search and Cross-validation".

4. Experiment

The performance of our method is evaluated by using one official dataset: LivDet 2013 [27], which are the publicly

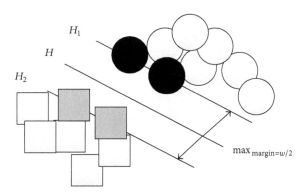

FIGURE 4: The optimal line of classification in linear separable cases.

available datasets provided in the 2013 Fingerprint Liveness Detection Competition. Firstly, a brief introduction about the official databases is given in this section. Secondly, feature vectors are constructed by using our method. Then, the validation criterion is defined which is used to evaluate the performance of our method. Finally, experiments results based on the official dataset LivDet 2013 are obtained, which shows that our proposed method is superior to others' methods.

4.1. Databases Introduction. The Department of Electrical and Computer Engineering of Clarkson University (USA) and the Department of Electronic Engineering of the University of Cagliari (Italy) held the first LivDet competition [5, 27] to help researchers study fingerprints liveness and compare the performance of the proposed state-of-the-art detection methods in 2009. Currently, four publicly official fingerprints datasets are published. And the LivDet 2013 Fingerprint dataset was divided into two parts: one is training part, which is used to learn a trained model classifier, and another set is testing samples, which are used to estimate the performance of the proposed method.

LivDet 2013 fingerprints are obtained through using four different optical fingerprint sensors (such as (a) Italdata ET10 (500 dpi), (b) CrossMatch Verifier 300LC (500 dpi), (c) Biometrika FX2000 (569 dpi), and (d) Swipe (96 dpi)). In this fingerprint set, 8874 real fingerprints and 7979 spoof fingerprints are included, and five different materials, such as Gelatin, Ecoflex, Latex, Modasil, and wood glue, are made fake fingerprints. A part of the fingerprints is used to train the SVM classifiers with the RBF kernel and the rest are used to evaluate the performance of classifier.

The dataset of each fingerprint sensor is divided into two parts: (1) a testing set and (2) a training set. As shown in Table 1, the fingerprint testing set is used to assess the performance of proposed method and the latter is used to learn a classifier model. More detailed parameters about LivDet 2013 are listed in Table 1. In Addition, some fingerprint images of real and spoof are presented in Figure 5. The material used is specified for the generation of the fake fingers, such as Playdoh, Latex, BodyDouble, and Ecoflex. It is hard for our eyes to distinguish the real fingerprints from

the spoof ones. Therefore, our task is designing a method to distinguish the fingerprint liveness.

4.2. Gaussian Multiscale Transformation and Feature Extraction. In this experiment, to solve scale invariance of fingerprint image, Gaussian pyramid structure is used in the fingerprint liveness detection. After Gaussian pyramid operation, features based on uniform local binary pattern are extracted. For example, in Figure 2, the size of the original image Figure 2(a) is 256 × 256. First of all, preprocessing operation is necessary for the given fingerprint images, such as image gray processing. Then, two-layer Gaussian pyramid transformation has been done to solve the image scale invariance by calculating the convolution operation of original fingerprint image and Gaussian filter. After every one-layer Gaussian pyramid transformation, the size of the current image is a quarter of the previous level. Figure 2(b) and Figure 2(c) show the images after Gaussian filter operation. The two images are represented by the symbol GP_1 and GP_2, respectively, whose sizes are 128 × 128 and 64 × 64. To make scale invariance of the extracted texture feature, characteristics of rotation invariance are used based on uniform local binary pattern. Next, features are constructed in original fingerprint image and two-layer pyramids. Since the LBP code can describe local micromode information of the original image, the local features of the fingerprint image can be represented by counting the histogram of pixel values after LBP operation. However, uniform local binary pattern only considers the eight-bit binary of pixel values, which contain two jumps from one to zero or from zero to one in the eight-bit binary. Due to fingerprint images being transformed to two-layer pyramid, feature vectors are extracted based on ULBP in original fingerprint image and two-pyramid image. After constructing the feature vector with uniform local binary pattern, normalization is necessary to unify the data scales. Finally, features are extracted. These features of training sets are trained a classifier model by using SVM, and features of testing sets evaluated the performance of classifier.

4.3. Performance Metrics and Classification Results. The LivDet 2013 Datasets derive from 2013 Fingerprint Liveness Detection Competition, and these fingerprints are downloaded from the website. The performance of method is validated by using the Average Classification Error (ACE), which is considered as standard metric for evaluation of the fingerprint liveness. It is defined as

$$ACE = \frac{(FAR + FRR)}{2}, \qquad (4)$$

where, in (4),

$$FAR$$
$$= \frac{\text{Total Number Imposter Fingerprints Accepted as Genuine}}{\text{Total Number of Forgery Tests Performed}},$$

$$FRR \qquad (5)$$
$$= \frac{\text{Total Number Genuine Fingerprints Accepted as Imposter}}{\text{Total Number of Genuine Matching Tests Performed}}.$$

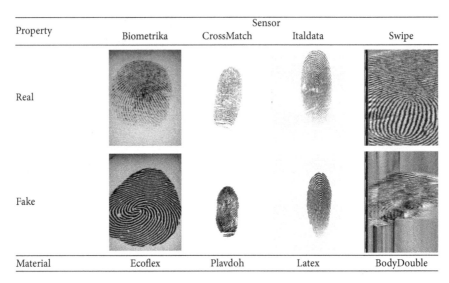

Property	Sensor			
	Biometrika	CrossMatch	Italdata	Swipe
Real				
Fake				
Material	Ecoflex	Plavdoh	Latex	BodyDouble

FIGURE 5: Typical sample images of real and spoof fingerprints those can be found in the LivDet 2013.

TABLE 1: Table of the detailed information of LivDet 2013.

Database ID	Sensor	Model number	Res. (dpi)	Image size	Number of image in training set		Number of images in testing set	
					Real	Fake	Real	Fake
Liv2013-1	Biometrika	FX200	569	352×384	1000	1000	1000	1000
Liv2013-2	CrossMatch	V300LC	500	800×750	1250	1000	1250	1000
Liv2013-3	Italdata	ET10	500	480×640	1000	1000	1000	1000
Liv2013-4	Swipe	—	96	1500×208	1221	979	1153	1000

In (4), FAR (False Accept Rate) accounts for the percentage of fake fingerprints being misclassified as real one, and FRR (False Reject Rate) shows the percentage of real fingerprints being assigned to the spoofed ones. As shown in Figure 1, two successive processes are included: training process and testing processes.

Process 1 (training process). In this process, feature extraction is the key step to achieve fingerprint liveness detection. To solve the scale invariance and reduce the dimensionality of features, Gaussian pyramid in introduced to solve the problem of scale invariance and the uniform local binary pattern is used to reduce the dimensionality of feature. About the construction of feature vectors under different scale image having been talked in Section 4.2. Next, feature vector of original image and each pyramid image is extracted by using our proposed method. Finally, classifier is built by using executable file svm-train.exe to train the obtained feature vectors in SVM. In order to obtain optimal classifier, parameters optimization operation is necessary in this process. During the process, parameter pair (C, Υ) is learnt. Figure 6 shows optimal parameters pair values (C, Υ) for the four different fingerprint sensors. For example, the same color denotes the same value at the same (C, Υ). In Figure 6(a), the green line denotes the optimal parameters pairs when the value

of parameter pair (C, Υ) is $(32768, 8)$. And the classification accuracy is 95.5% in the current parameter pair (C, Υ). That is to say, we can obtain the best classifier model when parameter pair value is set as $(32768, 8)$ in testing process. Similarly, the optimal parameter pairs corresponding Figures 5(b), 5(c), and 5(d) can be found. If not operation, various of different parameter pairs (C, Υ) are needed to try to gain a better classifier model. Finally, the classifier has been trained.

Process 2 (testing process). To distinguish real fingerprint from the spoof ones, fingerprint liveness detection based on uniform local binary pattern in Gaussian pyramid is proposed in this paper. Before constructing feature vectors, image preprocessing operation is necessary. To address the scale invariance of images and reduce the dimensionality of features vectors, Gaussian pyramid filter operation is introduced. Both the Testing process and training processes are conducted based on MATLAB R2014a platform. As mentioned before, the executable file svm-train.exe tool are used to obtain the optimal parameter pair (C, Υ) in this paper. In our experiment, the ACE detection accuracy and its comparison with the current methods for detecting fingerprint vitality are listed in Table 2. The accuracy of best designed methods from LivDet 2013 and the others' results are shown in Table 2. It shows that our method achieves detection

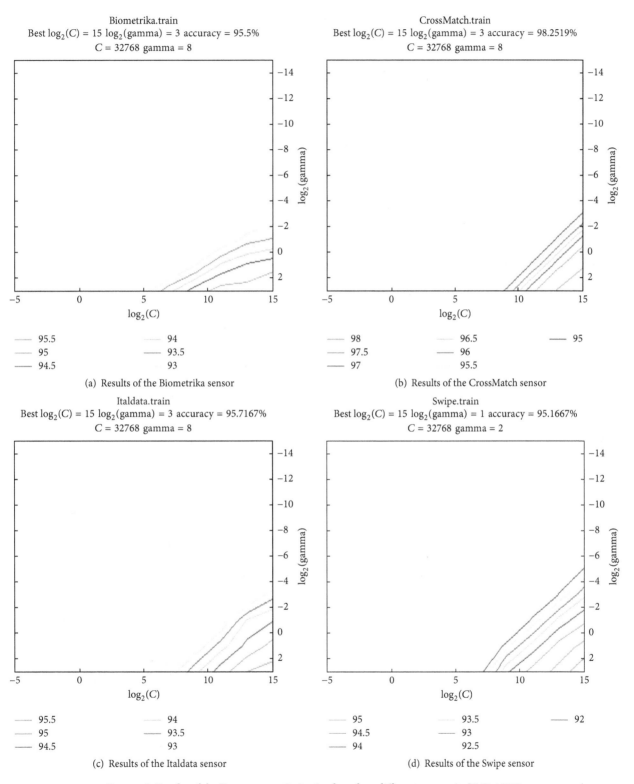

FIGURE 6: Results of the Parameter optimization based on different sensors in LivDet 2013.

TABLE 2: The results of the best different algorithms of LivDet 2013 in terms of average accuracy are cited from [27].

Methods	The average classification error ACE in (%)				
	Bimometrika	Cmatch	Italata	Swipe	Average
Our method	10.68	**46.09**	13.7	14.35	**21.205**
Frassetto2 [28]	25.65	49.87	55.45	**4.02**	33.75
ATVS [27]	**5.05**	54.8	50	46.45	39.08
UniNap2 [27]	6.55	52.13	**9.45**	26.85	23.75
HZ-JLW [27]	32.95	55.56	13.15	15.19	29.21

accuracy superior to other methods proposed in the LivDet 2013. In order to facilitate the comparison of the results, the best obtained results in Table 2 are highlighted in bold. We can clearly notice that the ACE (Average Classification Rate) of our method achieved is obviously superior to other ones in LivDet 2013.

5. Conclusions and Future Work

To solve fingerprint liveness and improve the security of authentication systems, a novel fingerprint liveness detection method based on uniform local binary pattern is proposed in this paper. The advantages of ULBP are that the dimensionality of feature vectors reduced compared with LBP. For the model of 3×3 window, the models of original eight bits binary reduce from 256 to 58. The constructed feature vectors have been evaluated on publicly available databases LivDet 2013, which is a database released in the 2013 LivDet competition [27]. After the obtained features are trained by the SVM classifier, we can get a classifier model. With the help of the trained model, we can predict the classifier accuracy of testing dataset. Furthermore, the our method is part of the software-based solutions and it distinguishes real fingerprint images from the spoof ones; only one fingerprint without extra special hardware devices is added to the sensor. Liveness detection methods such as the one presented in this paper are of great importance in the biometric recognition field as they help to prevent direct attacks from the fake fingerprints (those carried out with synthetic traits and very difficult to detect).

The classifier performance of fingerprints datasets is extremely affected by the noise during the training process and testing process. When noise of fingerprint image is considered, the predicting results are unsatisfactory. Yet, we can get rid of the influence of noise by introducing noise filters with idea from Jin et al. [29]. Besides, more layers Gaussian pyramids are generated to further solve the scale invariance. These will be done in our future works.

Conflicts of Interest

The authors declare that they have no conflicts of interest.

Acknowledgments

This work was supported by the 12th Five-Year Programming of Scientific Research in Education of Hunan Province (Research on Paperless Test System of Art Design Course, no. XJK011CTM015) and Design and Study of Constructing Flipped Class Model Teaching Based On the Instructed Learning Plan + Microlecture (no. XJK015BGD018).

References

[1] D. Maltoni, D. Maio, A. Jain K, and S. Prabhakar, *Handbook of Fingerprint Recognition*, Springer Science Business Media, 2009.

[2] Z. Xia, R. Lv, Y. Zhu, P. Ji, H. Sun, and Y.-Q. Shi, "Fingerprint liveness detection using gradient-based texture features," *Signal, Image and Video Processing*, vol. 11, no. 2, pp. 381–388, 2017.

[3] J. Galbally, R. Cappelli, A. Lumini et al., "An evaluation of direct attacks using fake fingers generated from ISO templates," *Pattern Recognition Letters*, vol. 31, no. 8, pp. 725–732, 2010.

[4] N. K. Ratha, J. H. Connell, and R. M. Bolle, "Enhancing security and privacy in biometrics-based authentication systems," *IBM Systems Journal*, vol. 40, no. 3, pp. 614–634, 2001.

[5] D. Yambay, L. Ghiani, P. Denti, G. L. Marcialis, F. Roli, and S. Schuckers, "LivDet 2011 - Fingerprint liveness detection competition 2011," in *Proceedings of the 2012 5th IAPR International Conference on Biometrics, ICB 2012*, pp. 208–215, India, April 2012.

[6] S. T. V. Parthasaradhi, R. Derakhshani, L. A. Hornak, and S. A. C. Schuckers, "Time-series detection of perspiration as a liveness test in fingerprint devices," *IEEE Transactions on Systems, Man, and Cybernetics, Part C: Applications and Reviews*, vol. 35, no. 3, pp. 335–343, 2005.

[7] R. Derakhshani, S. A. C. Schuckers, L. A. Hornak, and L. O'Gorman, "Determination of vitality from a non-invasive biomedical measurement for use in fingerprint scanners," *Pattern Recognition*, vol. 36, no. 2, pp. 383–396, 2003.

[8] S. Schuckers and A. Abhyankar, "Detecting Liveness in Fingerprint Scanners Using Wavelets: Results of the Test Dataset," in *Biometric Authentication*, vol. 3087 of *Lecture Notes in Computer Science*, pp. 100–110, Springer, Berlin, Germany, 2004.

[9] Z. Xia, C. Yuan, X. Sun, R. Lv, D. Sun, and G. Gao, "Fingerprint liveness detection using difference co-occurrence matrix based texture features," *International Journal of Multimedia and Ubiquitous Engineering*, vol. 11, no. 11, pp. 1–16, 2016.

[10] P. Reddy V, A. Kumar, and S. Rahman, "A new anti-spoofing approach for biometric devices," *IEEE Transactions on Biomedical Circuits Systems*, vol. 2, no. 4, pp. 328–337, 2008.

[11] C. Sousedik and C. Busch, "Presentation attack detection methods for fingerprint recognition systems: a survey," *IET Biometrics*, vol. 3, no. 4, pp. 219–233, 2014.

[12] Y. S. Moon, J. S. Chen, K. C. Chan, K. So, and K. C. Woo, "Wavelet based fingerprint liveness detection," *IEEE Electronics Letters*, vol. 41, no. 20, pp. 1112-1113, 2005.

[13] S. B. Nikam and S. Agarwal, "Ridgelet-based fake fingerprint detection," *Neurocomputing*, vol. 72, no. 10-12, pp. 2491–2506, 2009.

[14] Z. Xia, Y. Zhu, X. Sun, Z. Qin, and K. Ren, "Towards privacy-preserving content-based image retrieval in cloud computing," *IEEE Transactions on Information Forensics and Security*, vol. PP, no. 99, 1 page, 2015.

[15] J. Galbally, F. Alonso-Fernandez, J. Fierrez, and J. Ortega-Garcia, "A high performance fingerprint liveness detection method based on quality related features," *Future Generation Computer Systems*, vol. 28, no. 1, pp. 311–321, 2012.

[16] L. Ghiani, G. L. Marcialis, and F. Roli, "Fingerprint liveness detection by local phase quantization," in *Proceedings of the 21st International Conference on Pattern Recognition, ICPR 2012*, pp. 537–540, November 2012.

[17] L. Ghiani, A. Hadid, G. L. Marcialis, and F. Roli, "Fingerprint Liveness Detection using Binarized Statistical Image Features," in *Proceedings of the 6th IEEE International Conference on Biometrics: Theory, Applications and Systems, BTAS 2013*, pp. 1–6, USA, October 2013.

[18] X. Jia, X. Yang, K. Cao et al., "Multi-scale local binary pattern with filters for spoof fingerprint detection," *Information Sciences*, vol. 268, pp. 91–102, 2014.

[19] D. Gragnaniello, G. Poggi, C. Sansone, and L. Verdoliva, "Fingerprint liveness detection based on Weber Local image Descriptor," in *Proceedings of the 2013 4th IEEE Workshop on Biometric Measurements and Systems for Security and Medical Applications, BioMS 2013*, Italy, September 2013.

[20] Y. Mei, H. Sun, and D. Xia, "A gradient-based combined method for the computation of fingerprints' orientation field," *Image and Vision Computing*, vol. 27, no. 8, pp. 1169–1177, 2009.

[21] A. R. Rao and R. C. Jain, "Computerized flow field analysis: oriented texture fields," *IEEE Transactions on Pattern Analysis Machine Intelligence*, vol. 14, no. 7, pp. 693–709, 1992.

[22] N. K. Ratha, S. Chen, and A. K. Jain, "Adaptive flow orientation-based feature extraction in fingerprint images," *Pattern Recognition*, vol. 28, no. 11, pp. 1657–1672, 1995.

[23] A. K. Jain, L. Hong, S. Pankanti, and R. Bolle, "An identity-authentication system using fingerprints," *Proceedings of the IEEE*, vol. 85, no. 9, pp. 1365–1388, 1997.

[24] H. H. Ahmed, H. M. Kelash, M. Tolba, and M. Badwy, "Fingerprint image enhancement based on threshold fast discrete curvelet transform (FDCT) and gabor filters," *International Journal of Computer Applications*, 2015.

[25] S. B. Nikam and S. Agarwal, "Fingerprint liveness detection using curvet energy and co-occurrence signatures," in *Proceedings of the 5th International Conference on Computer Graphics, Imaging and Visualisation, Modern Techniques and Applications, CGIV*, pp. 217–222, Malaysia, August 2008.

[26] Z. Xia, N. N. Xiong, A. V. Vasilakos, and X. Sun, "EPCBIR: An efficient and privacy-preserving content-based image retrieval scheme in cloud computing," *Information Sciences*, vol. 387, pp. 195–204, 2017.

[27] L. Ghiani, D. Yambay, V. Mura et al., "LivDet 2013 fingerprint liveness detection competition 2013," in *Proceedings of the 6th IAPR International Conference on Biometrics, ICB 2013*, Madrid, Spain, June 2013.

[28] R. Frassetto Nogueira, R. De Alencar Lotufo, and R. Campos Machado, "Evaluating software-based fingerprint liveness detection using Convolutional Networks and Local Binary Patterns," in *Proceedings of the 2014 5th IEEE Workshop on Biometric Measurements and Systems for Security and Medical Applications, BIOMS 2014*, pp. 22–29, Italy, 2014.

[29] Q. Jin, I. Grama, and Q. Liu, "Optimal Weights Mixed Filter for removing mixture of Gaussian and impulse noises," *PLOS ONE*, vol. 12, no. 7, p. e0179051, 2017.

5

Leveraging Fog Computing for Scalable IoT Datacenter using Spine-Leaf Network Topology

K. C. Okafor,[1] **Ifeyinwa E. Achumba,**[2] **Gloria A. Chukwudebe,**[2] **and Gordon C. Ononiwu**[1]

[1]*Department of Mechatronics Engineering, Federal University of Technology Owerri, Ihiagwa, Nigeria*
[2]*Department of Electrical and Electronic Engineering, Federal University of Technology Owerri, Ihiagwa, Nigeria*

Correspondence should be addressed to K. C. Okafor; kennedy.okafor@futo.edu.ng

Academic Editor: Raj Senani

With the Internet of Everything (IoE) paradigm that gathers almost every object online, huge traffic workload, bandwidth, security, and latency issues remain a concern for IoT users in today's world. Besides, the scalability requirements found in the current IoT data processing (in the cloud) can hardly be used for applications such as assisted living systems, Big Data analytic solutions, and smart embedded applications. This paper proposes an extended cloud IoT model that optimizes bandwidth while allowing edge devices (Internet-connected objects/devices) to smartly process data without relying on a cloud network. Its integration with a massively scaled spine-leaf (SL) network topology is highlighted. This is contrasted with a legacy multitier layered architecture housing network services and routing policies. The perspective offered in this paper explains how low-latency and bandwidth intensive applications can transfer data to the cloud (and then back to the edge application) without impacting QoS performance. Consequently, a spine-leaf Fog computing network (SL-FCN) is presented for reducing latency and network congestion issues in a highly distributed and multilayer virtualized IoT datacenter environment. This approach is cost-effective as it maximizes bandwidth while maintaining redundancy and resiliency against failures in mission critical applications.

1. Introduction

Scalability is a desirable feature of a disruptive technology such as the Internet of Things (IoT) and IoE. Ideally, the cloud computing foundations for today's IoT/IoE paradigm have opened up technology perspectives and applications for growing enterprises and their services. IoT is simply defined as the network of physical objects or "things" embedded with sensor electronics and IPv6 connectivity to enable valuable and service oriented exchange of data with a vendor platform, or even other connected devices. This can be achieved through advanced protocols requiring absence of human control.

With today's IoT, it is possible to bring consumer electronic devices including home appliances such as medical devices, fridges, cameras, and sensors into the Internet environment [1]. Machine-to-machine communication which enables "everything" connectivity to the Internet network is not only a reality but also an integral part of day-to-day living and interactions. With IoT, disruptive applications such as smart cities/vibrant ecosystems, smart grid, governance/knowledge-driven platforms, and agricultural and health systems can be repositioned to offer reliable Quality of Service (QoS). For instance, using IoT, intelligent transport system (ITS) applications can monitor city traffic 24/7 using a wireless sensor video surveillance system and then send the gathered information to the users on their smart mobile devices via a global positioning system (GPS) transceiver. This could alert users to avoid traffic jams and prevent accidents.

Interestingly, IoT essentially supports layered integration, real-time data transfer, and analytics of data generated by smart embedded devices (data streams). These will improve the quality of life, enhance urbanization, facilitate efficient health care delivery, and handle natural disasters among other things. In the layered integration, the data plane of the Fog layer enables computing services to be housed at the edge of the network as opposed to servers in a legacy datacenter. For application purposes, the integration framework in context emphasizes proximity to end users. It creates even distribution of local resources, reduces latency for QoS, and facilitates edge stream processing. The overall benefits are availability, consolidated user experience, resilience, and redundancy. This makes the application of IoE paradigm widely accepted and used on a real-time basis. With the layered integration concept discussed in Section 3.2, smart devices, wearable health monitoring devices, connected vehicles, and augmented reality can optimally fit into ISO/IEC 20248 standards which deal with general data aggregation in IoT.

However, Fog IoT model is fundamentally built into cloud datacenters [2–4]. These cloud datacenter structures are classified into two major categories. The first is the switch-centric datacenter, which organizes switches into structures other than trees and puts the interconnection intelligence on switches. Some notable examples are Fat-Tree [5], VL2 [6], PortLand [7], Dragonfly [8], and PERCS [9]. The second category is server-centric datacenter, which leverages the rapid growth scale of the server hardware including its multiple Network Interface Card (NIC) ports to put the interconnection and routing intelligence on the servers principally. Examples are DCell [10], FiConn [11], BCube [12], and BCN [13]. The other types are the containerized datacenters [14–17].

For these datacenters, their environment is mainly used to process, store, and analyze large volumes of data on demand. Also, with the cloud datacenters, hosting of IoT applications, storage of a large volume of data, and execution of live data analytics require a robust architecture. Similarly, within a typical cloud datacenter, a large number of servers are found interconnected by network devices using a specific networking structure. These networks have high performance switches which serve as an interface connecting and sharing the data in a distributed fashion. But, in a typical IoT transaction, network bandwidth congestion can arise when large volumes of data are moved to edge node or cluster in the cloud datacenter environment. This will normally violate service level agreement (SLA). Obviously, most cloud datacenters offer scalability via redundancy and resilience. However, as virtualization, cloud computing, and distributed cloud computing become increasingly popular in the IoT datacenters, there is an urgent need to evolve well balanced network support for IoT services.

It is obvious that the traditional datacenter network having the core, aggregation, and access model performs well for north-south traffic, that is, traffic that travels in and out of the datacenter. However, HTTP/S web service, exchange, FTP, and e-mail services require a lot of remote client/server communication. In this case, their network architecture is normally designed for core redundancy and resiliency against outages or failure. More so, in a production scenario, about 50% of the critical network link path is blocked by the spanning-tree protocol (STP). This is in order to prevent event based network loops. As such, these paths constitute redundant backup wasting about 50% maximum bandwidth.

In this paper, with the possibility of latency issues (data offloading), wastage of bandwidth, and network outage as a result of saturated STP in these traditional networks, a better alternative is considered. In this case, a Fog computing network (FCN) for scalable IoT datacenter is proposed. This is based on a spine-leaf network topology. The use of this type of computing would relieve enormous real-time workloads, reduce latency issues, and make for smarter responses as more people use IoT applications and services. This is because the Fog DC is the most useful in facilitating Big Data and real-time analytics, while delivering and moving data closer to the user. With Fog DC, location awareness and global aggregation for the edge devices are made possible for IoE. The major components in its integration layer are the Fog data plane having its typical instances:

(i) Real-time pooling of end user idle computing (e.g., storage/bandwidth resources)

(ii) Content caching at the edge and bandwidth management services

(iii) Client-driven distributed broadcast

(iv) Client-to-client direct communications (e.g., WiMAX, LTE 3/4G, and Wi-Fi)

(v) Cloudlets with mini datacenters

The second component is the control plane which has the following instances:

(i) Smart Over-the-Top (SOTT) content management procedure

(ii) Fog-driven radio access network, for example, Radio Network Controllers (RNC)

(iii) Client-based protocol controls from the edge

(iv) Client-controlled cloud storage from the edge

(v) Session management at the edge

(vi) Ubiquitous crowd sensing of network states at the edge

(vii) Edge analytics and real-time stream processing (data mining) from the edge

Furthermore, the isolated benefits of Fog DC include the following:

(i) Real-time processing and cyberphysical system control especially in tactile Internet and edge data analytics, as well as interfacing between humans and objects

(ii) Intelligence and cognition awareness for end-to-end communication via edge/client devices

(iii) Network efficiency via pooling of local resources by objects at the edge

(iv) Scalability and agility which make for faster and cheaper computation at the client and edge devices

(v) Security via encrypted and multipath traffic in the end-to-end network system

With the above background, this paper is now organized as follows. In Section 2, a review of classical works in scalable computing, applications, and services is presented. Also, scalable IoT networks are studied while highlighting their limitations. In Section 3, a framework for building a cost-effective, fault-tolerant, and symmetrical Fog spine-leaf network structure for IoT datacenter is presented. In this regard, a Fog computing system architecture, including its architectural framework, and the IoT requirements are discussed. In Section 4, the design of the proposed scalable IoT network using spine-leaf topology is presented. In addition, the merits and limitations of the network are presented. Section 5 discusses the design implementation, integration techniques, and SL-FCN interfaces. Section 6 presents the performance evaluation while focusing on simulation case studies for scalable IoT networks. Conclusion and future works are discussed in Section 7.

2. Related Works

To facilitate scalability in IoT based datacenter networks, various schemes have been proposed in the literature. This section will look at scalable IoT networks and the overall research gaps of the traditional computing DCNs.

2.1. Scalable Strategies to IoT Networks. Meng et al. [18] proposed a Software Defined (SD) approach to network virtualization in cloud datacenters. By optimizing the placement of VMs on host machines, traffic patterns among VMs can be better aligned with the communication distance between them. The work used traffic traces collected from production datacenters to evaluate their proposed VM placement algorithm while showing performance improvement compared to existing generic methods that do not take advantage of traffic patterns and datacenter network characteristics. Wells et al. [19] proposed a Mixed-Mode Multicore (MMM) system to support such changing requirements in a virtual cloud network. In this network, certain applications (or portions of applications) run in high performance mode using a single core, while other applications (including the system software) run in a highly reliable mode using Dual-Modular Redundancy (DMR) [20]. These are considered as fault-tolerant schemes. Wang et al. [21] proposed a joint optimization strategy for achieving energy efficiency of datacenter networks. This was done by proposing a unified optimization framework. In their framework, the work considered taking advantage of the application characteristics and topology features to integrate virtual machine assignment and traffic engineering. Under this framework, two algorithms were proposed for assigning virtual machines and routing traffic flows, respectively. However, emphasis was excluded from Fog computing.

Wang and Ng [22] highlighted that most cloud service providers use machine virtualization strategies to provide flexible and cost-effective resource sharing among users. Such scalability as found in Amazon EC2 [23] and GoGrid [24] uses Xen virtualization [25] to support multiple virtual machine instances on a single physical server. The virtual machine instances share physical processors and I/O interfaces with other instances achieving some form of scalability. Virtualization was obviously identified as a scalable strategy

that impacts the computation and communication performance of IoT cloud services. For instance, Xen [25] represents an open-source x86 virtual machine monitor which can create multiple virtual machines on a physical machine running enterprise cloud service. In this regard, each virtual machine runs an operating system instance while using a scheduler which runs in the Xen hypervisor to schedule virtual machines on the processors.

Besides, Huang and Peng [26] proposed a novel model NetCloud of data placement and query for cloud computing in DCN based on the DCell datacenter design model. The work analyzed an efficient, fault-tolerant, self-organizing data placement and query model NetCloud based on DCell datacenter design architecture. Other works on fault-tolerant and scalable datacenter networks were carried out in [27–32]. Interestingly, most of the works on scalable computing networks provide full real-time visibility of both physical and virtual infrastructure.

2.2. Research Gaps. It was observed that some cloud scalable networks lack key capabilities such as multihypervisor support, integrated security, end-to-end mapping for IoT application placement, and ease of maintenance.

(i) Again, the software network virtualization strategy treats physical and virtual infrastructure as separate entities and denies end users the ability to manage computer resources as well as allowing for QoS monitoring and management.

(ii) Traditional datacenter tree-like structures previously enumerated have a variety of challenges, such as limited server-to-server connectivity, vulnerability to single point of failure, lack of agility, insufficient scalability, and smart resource fragmentation. To achieve a scalable IoT network with low-latency (response time) performance and fault recovery under variable data streams, there is a need to support adaptive, scalable load balancing and elastic runtime scaling of cloud reducers. This has the capacity of taking care of workload variation on the datacenter system.

(iii) Also, there is a need to develop a low-latency and fault-tolerant mechanism that has minimal overhead during regular operations. Hence, real-time parallel fault recovery is vital. This paper has a perspective that all these limitations of traditional cloud computing will adversely affect scalable IoT design.

3. Fog Computing System Architecture

3.1. Architectural Framework. Fog computing is a distributed computing paradigm that extends the services provided by the cloud to the edge of the network [1]. With Fog grid, this enables seamless fusion of cloud and edge resources for efficient data offloading in a short time. It offers efficient resource provisioning, management, and programming of computing, networking, and storage services between datacenters and edge end devices. Essentially, this type of computing essentially involves wireless data transfer to distributed devices

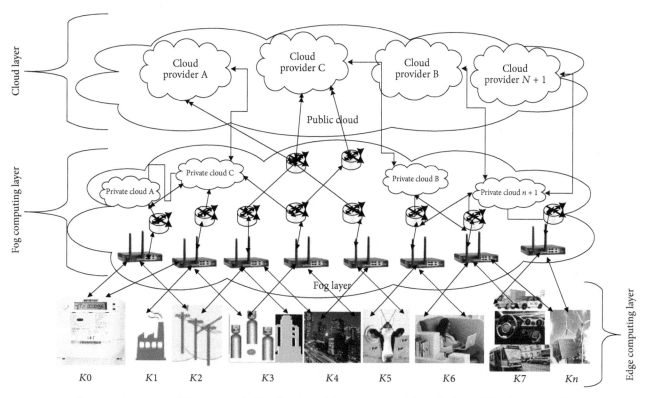

FIGURE 1: A conceptual framework for Fog distributed data processing (the author's model with Visio 2013).

in the Internet of Things (IoT) network cloud. Unlike with cloud computing where there is an on-demand network use of a shared pool of configurable computing resources (such as networks, servers, storage, applications, and services) that is usually provisioned with minimal vendor management efforts, Fog computing has its application services and components running on both cloud and end devices via its smart gateways and routers.

Figure 1 illustrates distributed data processing in a Fog computing environment. With the Fog layer, edge computing devices can seamlessly connect to the federated cloud to facilitate data offloading from the cloud. In this case, computing is dynamically distributed across the cloud sites. The network elements for scalability and QoS can be determined. With Fog computing, there is no need for storage renting infrastructure or even renting of computing services and applications. Rather, the Fog layer is optimized to support Internet of things (IoT) and Internet of Everything (IoE) smarter mobility, seamless resource and interface heterogeneity, handshake with the cloud, and distributed data analytics. This is to address requirements of IoT/IoE applications that require low latency with a wide and dense geographical distribution [1]. In context, this computing concept leverages both edge and cloud computing. In other words, it uses edge devices for close proximity to the endpoints (edge) and also leverages the on-demand scalability of cloud resources.

With the established framework, novel network integration for the emerging Internet of Everything (IoE) applications (K_1-K_n) is expedient. This is because these applications have serious demand for real-time and predictable latency

(e.g., industrial automation, agriculture, renewable energy, transportation, and networks of sensors and actuators). The network depends on the wide geographical distribution Fog system model for real-time Big Data and real-time analytics. Invariably, this will support remote and densely distributed data collection points, thereby enhancing critical Big Data dimensions, that is, volume, variety, and velocity, as the fourth axis. In this paper, the conceptual framework has support for application enabled platforms, management and automation, Fog data stream computing, physical and cybersecurity components, data analytics, and cloud network connectivity. A layered architecture is presented in Section 3.2.

3.2. IoT Requirements in Fog Computing Architecture. In deploying a new IoT device or network, new and more vigorous demands will be placed on the networks. Applications and services such as high-speed wireless networks, high-definition IP video services, and real-time measuring systems require high-bandwidth connectivity. In addition, extremely low-latency applications, such as high-speed motion controls, demand high-speed connections to be indispensable. Figure 2 shows the architecture of Fog computing environment for the proposed spine-leaf datacenter integration.

The architecture shows the hierarchical arrangement of Fog edge devices throughout the network between sensors and the cloud core shown in Figure 1. In the architecture, IoT sensors are located at layer 1 of the Fog architecture stack. In reality, this is distributed in multitenanted geographical locations. In essence, the sensing environment propagates the generated data stream values to the Fog middleware using

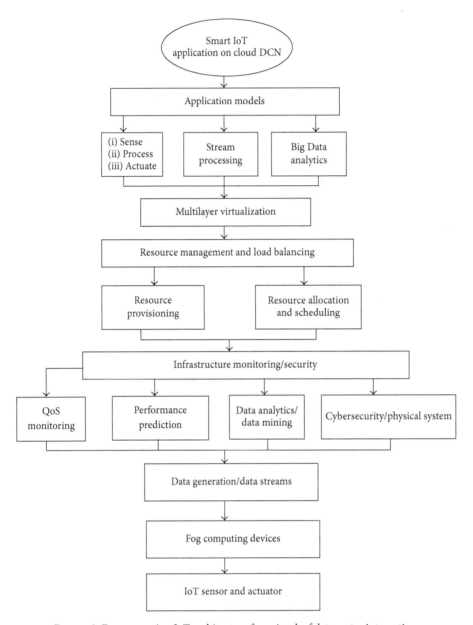

FIGURE 2: Fog computing IoT architecture for spine-leaf datacenter integration.

intelligent gateways. This is used for extended distributed processing and filtering.

In layer 1, IoT actuators serve as a control system designed to communicate real-time deviations or changes in environments when the sensors detect any event. In this regard, the IoT data streams from sensors form the datasets for analytics. The Fog devices in Figure 2 basically host the application modules that are connected to sensors. An integrated service gateway links these sensors to the Internet. Besides, cloud resources provisioned on demand from geographically distributed datacenters are encapsulated in Figure 2.

The multilayer virtualization gives support for resource management and load balancing on the cloud. In this case,

scheduling and resource provisioning are included for Fog and IoT environments.

At the infrastructure monitoring (components) layer, the QoS monitoring checks and ensures stable resource utilization, throughput, and availability of sensors and actuators. Also, it ensures that Fog devices and network elements are at an optimal level. Performance monitoring of the applications and services on the infrastructure is addressed by these components. Without resource management, the QoS expectations will be truncated while allowing for resource wastage. By providing active load balancing and scheduling, the available resources for workloads will be uniformly shared. Other profiles monitored are power and application program interfaces (APIs) for the IoT system. Finally, the architectural models supported for IoT applications are as follows:

(i) *Smart Sensing, Processing, and Actuation (SSPA).* In this case, the information gathered by sensors is emitted as data streams, which are acted upon by applications running on Fog devices. Hence, the resultant control signals are sent to actuators.

(ii) *Smart Stream Processing (SSP).* With the SP model, this uses its network of application modules running on Fog devices to continuously process data streams emitted from sensors. The generated information mined from the incoming streams is stored in datacenters for large-scale and long-term Big Data analytics.

The above considerations engendered the need for a flexible and scalable network infrastructure. This type of network can easily deploy applications from the cloud down to the Fog edge while serving myriads of devices joining the network. Furthermore, the IoT network infrastructure must be secured and scalable. Hence, resilience at scale, integrated security, and converged networking are the key IoT requirements for conceptual Fog conceptual framework in Figure 1. The benefits include scalable network for real-time analytics, support for cloud to Fog and edge data processing, and reliable QoS provisioning.

Considering the Fog architecture, some useful IoT network technologies that can be considered in the implementation stage from Cisco systems [33] include embedded service routers (Cisco 59xx series), switches Cisco 2020, Industrial Ethernet 4000 Series Switches, Cisco ASR 900 (i.e., Aggregation Services Router), and Cisco 1000 Series Connected Grid Router. These devices meet the IoT needs of the various market segments such as energy, manufacturing, oil and gas, utilities, transportation, mining, and public sector.

4. Spine-Leaf Network Topology

4.1. System Description. So far, the importance of allowing intrinsic data processing locally in a scalable network has been discussed. This is very important in supporting applications like smart traffic systems, energy grids, smart cars, health care systems, and so forth, as shown in Figure 1. With localized data processing/data offloading, it is possible to create an efficient network model that is relatively cost-effective. The main task of Fog offloading is to position information near the user at the network edge as shown in Figure 1. Figure 3 shows the proposed scalable SL-FCN. With such system, important alerts and other details would still be sent to the cloud.

Also, the use of spine-leaf Fog computing would relieve larger workloads, reduce latency issues, and make for smoother responses as more people engage the IoT layers. However, SL-FCN is proposed for scalability considering the Fog IoT era. This type of datacenter network is well positioned for data analytics and distributed data collection points. End services like setup boxes and access points can be easily

hosted using SL-FCN. This improves QoS metrics generally. Moreover, since there is an increased focus on real-time massive data transfers as well as instantaneous data trajectory in the network, the legacy three-tier design within a datacenter can be replaced by the Fog leaf-spine design. This model is obviously adaptable to the continuously changing needs of services and applications in the Big Data domain, hence bringing about enterprise scalability of instantaneous stream workloads. The advantages are enumerated in Section 4.2.

4.2. Advantages of Spine-Leaf FCN. With Smart Sensing, Processing, and Actuation (SSPA) and Smart Stream Processing (SSP) in Figure 2, the highlighted advantages of the massively scaled Fog computing network are enumerated as follows:

(i) Massive scalability arising from multihypervisor virtualized systems with bandwidth optimized paths

(ii) Reduction in data movement across the network resulting in reduced congestion, cost, and latency

(iii) Elimination of disturbances resulting from centralized computing systems

(iv) Improved security of encrypted data from edge devices as the edge layer stays closer to the end user, reducing exposure to unfavourable elements

(v) Eliminating the core computing environment, thereby reducing centralized computing and point of failure instances

(vi) Enhance edge security, as data are encoded when moving towards the network edge

(vii) Integrated support for edge computing while providing low-latency response to end users

(viii) Using dynamic layer 3 routing for interconnecting various layers

(ix) Providing high levels of reliability and fault tolerance

(x) Consequent lower bandwidth consumption generally

(xi) Removal of STP between the legacy access and aggregation layers using dynamic layer 3 routing results in a much more stable environment

4.3. Spine-Leaf FCN Limitations. There are few issues regarding the proposed system. The only limitations of the proposed network are as follows:

(i) It literally introduces issues on the selection of cabling technology platforms for link paths.

(ii) The other major disadvantage arises from the use of layer 3 routing. This has obviously eliminated the spanning of VLANs (virtual LAN) across a network. In context, the VLANs in a spine-leaf FCN are localized to each individual leaf switch; as such, any VLAN microsegments left on a leaf switch will be inaccessible by the other leaf instances. Problems can arise from this type of scenario, for instance, when guest virtual machine mobility is introduced within a datacenter.

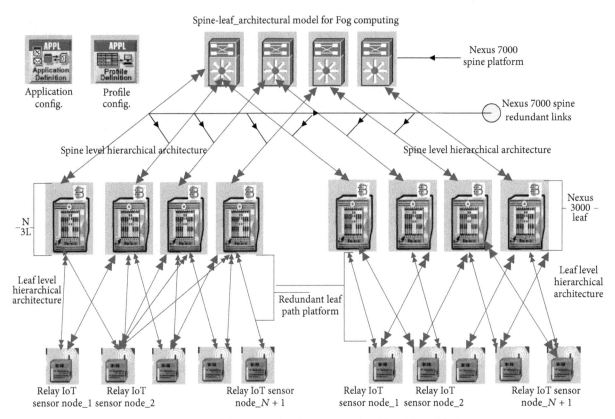

FIGURE 3: Design of Fog computing datacenter using Cisco Nexus Platforms.

5. Design Implementation

The implementation of SL-FCN is constituted by the simulated Fog cloud entities and services. First, a description on how the elements of architecture are modelled is presented. In this paper, SL-FCN was developed using the event simulation functionalities found in CloudSim [34] and Riverbed Modeller Version 15.6.11 [35].

In this regard, entities in object palette CloudSim, like Nexus datacenter multilayer switches, communicate between each other by message passing operations (sending events) via the link paths as demonstrated in Figure 3. With the design setup, the super spine core layer is responsible for handling events between Fog computing components in CloudSim C++ class of Riverbed Modeller. The main classes of network topology as introduced in Figure 3 include Fog device sensors, physical topology, actuators, object placement mapping, application edge, controllers for Fog devices, and configuration application engine (Table 1).

5.1. Integration Techniques. Using the C++ library of the modeller simulator, the network application module placement strategies include the traditional cloud placement and Fog placement in the spine-leaf scenarios. The cloud placement strategy is based on the traditional cloud implementation where all modules of an application run in legacy three-tier datacenter. With the proper sensor placement, the sense-process-actuate applications are implemented by having the

IoT sensors transmit sensed data to the cloud for real-time processing. After the processing, any other legitimate action can be enforced by the actuator.

Also, in the Fog layer placement scenario, application deployment is made close to the network edge as depicted in Figure 3. This is because the Fog devices such as smart gateways and access points placed close to the edge of the network lack robust computational stability to host bandwidth intensive applications.

Essentially, the redundant Nexus platform at the Fog layer is cascaded as much as possible to support Fog application modules placed between the network edge and the cloud. This is necessary to stabilize the QoS.

5.2. Spine-Leaf-FCN Graphical Interface. The SP-FCN network topology illustrated in Figure 3 has its graphic user interface built over the C++ library of the modeller simulator application logic. The interface allows for representing the actual physical elements such as Fog Nexus devices, sensors, actuators, and connecting links. The defining attributes of these entities are captured into the topology using the GUI application engine templates. After developing the design, this was saved and reloaded for testing from its trace file (JSON) format. With rich JAVA APIs, it is also possible to develop the same physical topologies. The SP-FCN has layer 1 sensors, smart gateways, and cloud virtual machines, as well as the link path connection depicted in Figure 3. For testing the scalable Fog IoT design, the basic steps for the simulation

TABLE 1: Description of the physical topology for IoT FCN.

Fog Nexus Router (spine node)	Cisco 7000
Fog Nexus Router (leaf node)	Cisco 3000
Total ISR/switch in topology	4 spine + 8 leaf (small); 4 spine + 16 leaf (medium); 8 spine + 16 leaf (small)
Fog devices	11
Wi-Fi access points	8
Fog C++ library	Enabled
Path link	40 GB
Multilayer virtualization	Type 1
Routing type	Dynamic layer-3
Redundancy	Active ($N + 1$)

are discussed below. The design was then analyzed to show the performance of the system.

(1) Using the imported C++ libraries, the physical entities were created while outlining their capabilities and specification configurations. The actual entities used include IoT RF sensors, Nexus gateways (ISR), cloud virtual machines, and link paths (40 GB links). These are connected layer by layer.

(2) The workload of the system was carefully realized by setting transmit rates of layer 1 sensor using transmit distribution attribute in SensorClass (sensor MAC).

(3) The definition of placement and scheduling policies that map application modules to Fog devices is made. In all cases, these policies in context only considered end-to-end processing latency, network availability, and network resource usage constraints. The traces file Module Placement and Controller (MPC) classes were used in implementing the required placement logic.

(4) The identification of QoS profile for workload is made so as to ascertain the network latency, availability, and network resource usage at incremental loading.

(5) The result analysis was carried out for the QoS metrics in an Excel worksheet after the design completion.

6. Performance Evaluation

This work will now present the two simulation case studies for scalable IoT network. In this regard, the simulation study was carried out for a period of 1000 seconds. The study focused on introducing a latency-sensitive application on the SL-FCN. The latency-critical application involves augmented event based sensing and data-offload interaction. In the design, the real-time processing in context requires that the application be hosted very close to the source of data for possible evaluations. This was done to show the impact of scalable SL-FCN for the event based application case study. In this regard, the efficiencies of two placement strategies (i.e., legacy cloud and Fog layer) were evaluated in terms of latency, network usage, and resource availability.

6.1. Evaluation of Case Study 1: Latency Profile for Scalable Spine-Leaf-FCN Placement. In analyzing latency metric, the simulation experiment for this case study was carried out for a period of 2 hours in extended Riverbed DES while taking cognizance of the report metrics collected. The results of the simulation experiment demonstrate how the different input workloads and placement strategies impact the overall end-to-end latency. In essence, each IoT edge device establishes a communication link while gaining access to the Internet through Wi-Fi gateways. This is then connected to the smart ISP gateway. For the purpose of testing SL-FCN performance, the topology sizes and the number of Wi-Fi gateways were varied while keeping the edge devices connected to each Wi-Fi gateway and ISR constant. The two configurations of physical topology simulated are the Fog placement and cloud placement in configuration model, namely, Scenario 1 and Scenario 2. Initially, each case had 8 Wi-Fi gateways and 10 Nexus ISR in Figure 1. For testing/validation in Figure 3, four identical Nexus 7000 devices were used as the spine platform for hosting the cloud placement, while eight Nexus 3000 Fog devices were used for the leaf platform which connects all the Fog and edge devices/applications. In this case, each gateway is connected to edge devices/applications for event based services. The performance of an application on the Fog depends on latencies of the links connecting the Fog devices. Hence, 40 GB Ethernet link was introduced in the simulation topology. A real-time communication between the edge devices and cloud domain hosting its services with efficient processing is very expedient in the event based communication/sensing. Any lag in real-time reporting will severely affect user experience at large. Figure 4 illustrates the average delay/latency in execution of data-offloading sequence. It was observed that latency execution dramatically increases for cloud application (about 87.5) and services placement. However, it decreases for edge-ward placement strategy (about 12.5%) where Fog devices are utilized for processing. This reduction is more significant when Fog topology size increases.

6.2. Evaluation of Case Study 2: Network Usage Profile for Scalable Spine-Leaf-FCN Placement. Figure 5 shows the network usage of the spine-leaf FCN. An increase in the number of devices connected to the application significantly increases the load on the network where both cloud and Fog

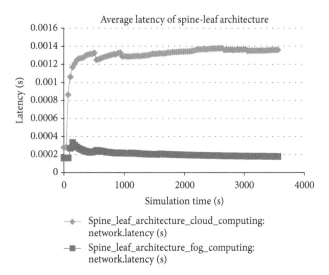

FIGURE 4: Average latency profile of SLFCN.

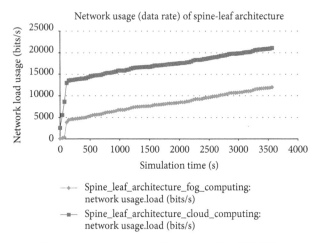

FIGURE 5: Average network usage profile of SLFCN.

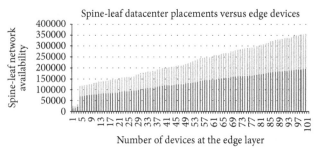

FIGURE 6: Spine-leaf DCN placement for services availability.

resources are used. As shown in Figure 5, when Fog devices are considered, the network usage considerably decreased. This is not the case for cloud layer placement or usage incidence. The network density seems to be very high relative to Fog computing. For network usage, SP-FCN offers self-learning, self-organization, and self-healing for massively scaled IoE scenario. This makes congestion and latency issues less significant while providing the necessary platform managing heterogeneous and distributed real-time services with minimal impact on QoS.

6.3. Evaluation of Case Study 3: Network Availability Profile for Scalable Spine-Leaf-FCN Placement. As shown in Figure 6, it was observed that as the number of devices connected to the network increases, the load on the network increases significantly in the case of cloud deployment. This is in contrast to Fog layer deployment. However, with the application placement strategies, the implication is that, with spine-leaf FCN, there will be high guarantee of network

availability. Scalable network environments must not necessarily have high throughput; rather, stability remains a desirable consideration. Consequently, with spine-leaf FCN, scalability guarantee as well as optimal bandwidth utilization will obviously improve the network performance. This will invariably make multitenanting an interesting dimension in the IoT/IoE computing era.

7. Conclusion and Future Works

This paper has dealt with Fog computing in the context of scalable IoT datacenter network perform. This network is shown to complement cloud computing functionalities in meeting the demands of the emerging IoT stream processing paradigms. The spine-leaf FCN is a scalable model developed which works side by side with cloud computing datacenter networks. This can be used for data offloading and for high-end batch processing workloads in today's IoT era. Existing cloud networks have issues with policy framework for QoS management. Also, for the traditional datacenter tree-like structures, issues such as limited server-to-server connectivity, vulnerability to single point of failure, lack of agility, insufficient scalability, and smart resource fragmentation are still affecting the cloud domain. Hence, a conceptual IoT framework is developed. This was based on comprehensive architectural decomposition such as application models, multilayer virtualization, resource management/load balancing, infrastructure monitoring, data streams, and IoT edge sensors/actuators. To further validate the work, network usage, latency, and availability metrics were considered for both Fog and cloud spine-leaf architectures. The results show that scalable FCN can offer reliable QoS while remaining fault-tolerant for traffic workloads. It can be concluded that Fog computing and cloud computing will complement each other regardless of their merits and limitations. Even if Fog computing grows exponentially in the emerging network contexts, scalability and low-latency processing are key issues that must be taken into consideration for satisfying high-end computing demands. This will invariably reduce cost.

Future work will focus on using a production spine-leaf network environment for validating the IoT data stream processing. Other areas of future research include priority-aware resource management strategies for multitenant environments, modelling and analysis of failure modes in Fog and edge devices considering scheduling, and recovery policies for a wide range of applications. Also, work on the validation Fog cloud virtualization techniques (Full, Para, and OS virtualization) in IoT environments is necessary.

Conflicts of Interest

The authors declare that there are no conflicts of interest regarding the publication of this article.

Acknowledgments

This research was carried out as an extended work on Distributed Cloud Computing Network for SGEMS/EETACP project commissioned by the Department of Electronic Engineering, University of Nigeria Nsukka.

References

[1] H. Gupta, A. V. Dastjerdi, S. K. Ghoshy, and R. Buyya, "iFogSim: a toolkit for modeling and simulation of resource management techniques in internet of things," *Edge and Fog Computing Environments*, pp. 1–22, 2016.

[2] S. Kuppusamya, V. Kaniappanb, D. Thirupathic, and T. Ramasubramanian, "Switch Bandwidth Congestion Prediction in Cloud Environment," pp. 235–243, 2015, Proceedings of the 2nd International Symposium on Big Data and Cloud Computing (ISBCC '15), Published by Elsevier B.V. 2015.

[3] Y. Zhang and N. Ansari, "On architecture design, congestion notification, TCP incast and power consumption in data centers," *IEEE Communications Surveys and Tutorials*, vol. 15, no. 1, pp. 39–64, 2013.

[4] K. C. Okafor, *development of a model for smart green energy management system using distributed cloud computing network [Ph.D. thesis]*, Department of Electronic Engineering, University of Nigeria Nsukka, 2015.

[5] M. A. Fares, A. Loukissas, and A. Vahdat, "A scalable, commodity data center network architecture," in *Proceedings of the SIGCOMM*, Seattle, Wash, USA, 2008.

[6] A. Greenberg, N. Jain, S. Kandula et al., "Vl2: a scalable and flexible data center network," in *Proceedings of the SIGCOMM*, vol. 12, Barcelona, Spain, 2009.

[7] R. Mysore, A. Pamboris, and N. Farrington, "Portland: a scalable fault-tolerant layer 2 data center network fabric," in *Proceedings of the SIGCOMM*, Barcelona, Spain, 2009.

[8] J. Kim, W. J. Dally, S. Scott, and D. Abts, "Technology-driven, highly-scalable dragonfly topology," in *Proceedings of the 35th International Symposium on Computer Architecture (ISCA '08)*, pp. 77–88, Beijing, China, June 2008.

[9] B. Arimilli, R. Arimilli, V. Chung et al., "The PERCS high-performance interconnect," in *Proceedings of the 18th IEEE Symposium on High Performance Interconnects (HOTI '10)*, pp. 75–82, Mountain View, Calif, USA, August 2010.

[10] C. Guo, H. Wu, K. Tan, L. Shi, Y. Zhang, and S. Lu, "Dcell: a scalable and fault-tolerant network structure for data centers," in *Proceedings of the SIGCOMM*, Seattle, Wash, USA, 2008.

[11] D. Li, C. Guo, H. Wu, K. Tan, Y. Zhang, and S. Lu, "FiConn: using backup port for server interconnection in data centers," in *Proceedings of the 28th Conference on Computer Communications (IEEE INFOCOM '09)*, pp. 2276–2285, Rio de Janeiro, Brazil, April 2009.

[12] C. Guo, G. Lu, D. Li et al., "Bcube: a high performance, server-centric network architecture for modular data centers," in *Proceedings of the SIGCOMM*, Barcelona, Spain, 2009.

[13] D. Guo, T. Chen, D. Li, Y. Liu, X. Liu, and G. Chen, "BCN: expansible network structures for data centers using hierarchical compound graphs," in *Proceedings of the 30th IEEE International Conference on Computer Communications (INFOCOM '11)*, pp. 61–65, Shanghai, China, April 2011.

[14] J. Hamilton, "An architecture for modular data centers," in *Proceedings of the 3rd CIDR Conference*, pp. 306–313, Pacific Grove, Calif, USA.

[15] M. M. Waldrop, "Data center in a box," *Scientific American*, vol. 297, no. 2, pp. 90–93, 2007.

[16] D. Li, M. Xu, H. Zhao, and X. Fu, "Building mega data center from heterogeneous containers," in *Proceedings of the 19th IEEE International Conference on Network Protocols (ICNP '11)*, pp. 256–265, Vancouver, Canada, October 2011.

[17] H. Wu, G. Lu, D. Li, C. Guo, and Y. Zhang, "MDCube: a high performance network structure for modular data center interconnection," in *Proceedings of the ACM Conference on Emerging Networking Experiments and Technologies (CoNEXT '09)*, pp. 25–36, Rome, Italy, December 2009.

[18] X. Meng, V. Pappas, and L. Zhang, "Improving the scalability of data center networks with traffic-aware virtual machine placement," in *Proceedings of the IEEE INFOCOM*, San Diego, Calif, USA, March 2010.

[19] P. M. Wells, K. Chakraborty, and G. S. Sohi, "Dynamic heterogeneity and the need for multicore virtualization," *ACM SIGOPS Operating Systems Review*, vol. 43, no. 2, pp. 5–14, 2009.

[20] P. M. Wells, K. Chakraborty, and G. S. Sohi, "Mixed-mode multicore reliability," in *Proceedings of the 14th International Conference on Architectural Support for Programming Languages and Operating Systems (ASPLOS '09)*, pp. 169–180, March 2009.

[21] Lin Wang, Fa Zhang, Athanasios V. Vasilakos, and C. H. Z. Liu, *Joint Virtual Machine Assignment and Traffic Engineering for Green Data Center Networks*, Greenmetrics, Pittsburgh, Pa, USA, 2013.

[22] G. Wang and T. S. E. Ng, "The impact of virtualization on network performance of Amazon EC2 Data Center," in *Proceedings of the IEEE INFOCOM*, March 2010.

[23] Amazon ec2, http://aws.amazon.com/ec2/.

[24] Gogrid, http://www.gogrid.com/.

[25] P. Barham, B. Dragovic, K. Fraser et al., "Xen and the art of virtualization," in *Proceedings of the 19th ACM Symposium on Operating Systems Principles (SOSP '03)*, October 2003.

[26] X. Huang and Y. Peng, "A Novel Method of Fault-Tolerant Decentralized Lookup Service for the Cloud Computing," vol. 29, pp. 3234–3239, 2012, Proceedings of the International Workshop on Information and Electronics Engineering (IWIEE '12).

[27] M. Isard, M. Budiu, Y. Yu, A. Birrell, and D. Fetterly, "Dryad: distributed data-parallel programs from sequential building blocks," *ACM SIGOPS Operating Systems Review*, vol. 41, no. 3, 2007.

[28] M. Zaharia, M. Chowdhury, M. J. Franklin, S. Shenker, and I. Stoica, "Spark: cluster computing with working sets," *HotCloud*, 2010.

[29] S. Bykov, A. Geller, G. Kliot, J. R. Larus, R. Pandya, and J. Thelin, "Orleans: cloud computing for everyone," in *Proceedings of the 2nd ACM Symposium on Cloud Computing (SOCC '11)*, p. 16, ACM, October 2011.

[30] J. Ekanayake, H. Li, B. Zhang et al., "Twister: a runtime for iterative MapReduce," in *Proceedings of the 19th ACM International Symposium on High Performance Distributed Computing (HPDC '10)*, pp. 810–818, June 2010.

[31] P. Bhatotia, A. Wieder, R. Rodrigues, U. A. Acar, and R. Pasquini, "Incoop: MapReduce for incremental computations," in *Proceedings of the 2nd ACM Symposium on Cloud Computing (SOCC '11)*, ACM, October 2011.

[32] A. Shaout and S. Sreedharan, "fault-tolerant storage system for cloud datacenters," in *Proceedings of the 13th International Arab Conference on IT (ACIT '12)*, pp. 241–248, December 2012.

[33] Cisco IoT System, http://www.cisco.com/go/iotsystem, 2015.

[34] R. N. Calheiros, R. Ranjan, A. Beloglazov, C. A. F. De Rose, and R. Buyya, "CloudSim: a toolkit for modeling and simulation of cloud computing environments and evaluation of resource provisioning algorithms," *Software—Practice and Experience*, vol. 41, no. 1, pp. 23–50, 2011.

[35] Riverbed Modeler Academic Edition 17.5 PL6: Available Online: https://splash.riverbed.com/community/product-lines/steelcentral/university-support-center/blog/2014/06/11/riverbed-modeler-academic-edition-release.

6

Cloud Platform based on Mobile Internet Service Opportunistic Drive and Application Aware Data Mining

Ge Zhou

School of Information Engineering, Chongqing Youth Vocational & Technical College, Chongqing 400712, China

Correspondence should be addressed to Ge Zhou; gezhou_cy@163.com

Academic Editor: James Nightingale

Because the static cloud platform cannot satisfy the diversity of mobile Internet service and inefficient data mining problems, we presented a reliable and efficient data mining cloud platform construction scheme based on the mobile Internet service opportunistic driving and application perception. In this scheme, first of all data selection mechanism was established based on mobile Internet service opportunistic drive. Secondly, through the cloud platform different cloud and channel aware, nonlinear mapping from the service to a data set of proposed perceptual model is applied. Finally, on the basis of the driving characteristics and extraction of perceptual features, the cloud platform would be constructed through the service opportunities of mobile Internet applications, which could provide robust and efficient data mining services. The experimental results show that the proposed mechanism, compared to the cloud platform based on distributed data mining, has obvious advantages in system running time, memory usage, and data clustering required time, as well as average clustering quality.

1. Introduction

The cloud platform has high performance of data management and efficient data mining [1], which has been widely applied in various fields, such as knowledge discovery and Leaf Spot dynamics [2], and ERP applications [3]. So, the cloud platform [4, 5] has played an important role for quality of service guarantee and data mining of mobile Internet.

In data mining, Rakocevic et al. [6] embedded a distributed data mining algorithm into a sensor network, which used local predictors on each sensor node to make a local prediction and offers several original voting schemes. The architecture of the huge amount 3D video data was proposed by [7], which designed a model of Key Encryption Model for protecting the privacy video data. Ronowicz et al. [8] researched the cause-effect relationships between pellet formulation characteristics, as well as the selected quality attribute.

About the service driver, Ghosh et al. [9] developed the cost analysis and optimization framework by using stochastic availability and performance models of an IaaS cloud. The economic model as a Bayesian network was proposed by Ye et al. [10] for selecting and composing cloud services. The importance and challenges in designing event-driven mobile services were discussed [11], which could detect conditions of interest to users and notify them accordingly.

In addition, the fast scalable video coding- (SVC-) based channel-recommendation system for IPTV on a cloud and peer-to-peer (P2P) hybrid platform was studied in [12]. The mechanisms for orchestrating cloud-enabled hardware and software resources were proposed by Petcu et al. [13], which should be supported by a recently developed open-source platform as a service. The novel monitoring architecture was proposed by Alcaraz Calero and Aguado [14], which should be addressed to the cloud provider and the cloud consumers.

However, these research results ignored the relationship between data set of cloud platform and service requirements of mobile Internet and lack the in-depth study of influence of Internet application on cloud platform. Hence, we proposed the cloud platform with mobile Internet service opportunistic drive and application aware data mining.

The rest of the paper is organized as follows. Section 2 describes the mobile Internet services driven data selection mechanism. In Section 3, we design the application perception model. In Section 4, we proposed the efficient

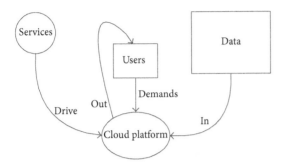

FIGURE 1: Services architecture in mobile Internet.

data mining cloud platform. Simulation results are given in Section 5. Finally, we conclude the paper in Section 6.

2. Data Selection Mechanism Driven by Mobile Internet Services

In mobile Internet, we assume a service data set function, which was used to optimize data selection for satisfying the service demands and provided the optimal data set for service. This is the role scheme which was used to solve the combination issue of mobile Internet and cloud computing. In general, the mobile Internet service architecture model is shown in Figure 1. Data input was driven by service set and stored in the cloud platform. When the service request was received successfully, the cloud platform would select the data and sent output feedback to the user according to the request.

There are some problems that should be considered in the progress of data selection, which are as follows:

(1) whether the data is corresponding to the service and whether it can meet the service needs,

(2) lack of user information feedback mechanism which is used to judge whether the user is satisfied with the data,

(3) how to coordinate multiple user needs,

(4) how to coordinate the input and output of data without increasing the load of the cloud platform.

The mapping relationship of user set and data set is shown in Figure 2. Here, the relationship was constructed by the services, which include the following cases:

(1) single user to intersection of multiple data sets,

(2) single data set to multiple users,

(3) single user to the union of data sets.

According to the above problems, we give the following service driven definition:

(1) $\mathrm{SE}_{\mathrm{set}}(n)$: service set and its length which is n,

(2) $\mathrm{DA}_{\mathrm{set}}(m)$: data set and its length which is m,

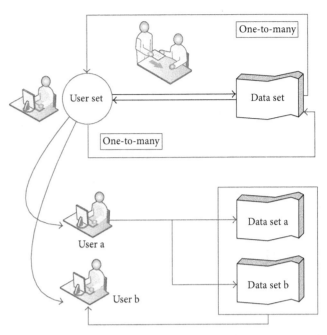

FIGURE 2: Mapping relationship and correlation between users and data set.

(3) $\mathrm{US}_{\mathrm{set}}(p)$: user set and its length which is p,

(4) $\mathrm{QE}(i)$: service satisfaction of the i data,

(5) $L_{\mathrm{CP}}(j)$: the number of data services in the i unit time,

(6) $T(i)$: the time consumed by the k data service,

(7) $L_{\mathrm{CP}}(a,b)$: the number of service sessions between a and b.

According to the above stations, there is the relationship shown as formula (1) in mobile Internet application:

$$N = L_{\mathrm{CP}}\left(\mathrm{US}_{\mathrm{set}}(1), \mathrm{DA}_{\mathrm{set}}(u) \mid 1 < u \le m\right)$$
$$+ L_{\mathrm{CP}}\left(\mathrm{US}_{\mathrm{set}}(v) \mid 1 < v \le n, \mathrm{DA}_{\mathrm{set}}(1)\right),$$
$$T = \sum_{i=1}^{N} \mathrm{QE}(i)\,T(i), \qquad (1)$$
$$T_h = \sum_{i=1}^{N} \mathrm{SE}_{\mathrm{set}}(i)\,L_p L_{\mathrm{CP}}(i).$$

Here, let N denote the number of sessions. Let L_p denote the length of data packet. Let T denote the time of completing the N services. Let T_h denote the throughput.

So, formula (2) gives the data selection model based on service opportunistic driven. Here, service request launched the service opportunistic driven in accordance with the probability. The data sets to meet the service request through the cloud platform. For the request of hybrid multiple data sets of service, the data set could be computed with XOR operation

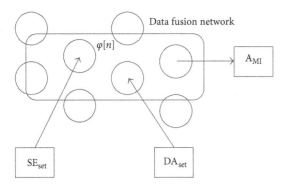

FIGURE 3: Nonlinear mapping relationship.

to form a single data set, for selecting the data without interference and avoiding the performance degradation:

$$DA_{set}(SE)$$

$$= \begin{cases} T_h, & dataType = 0, \\ \sum_{type=1}^{T_y} DA_{type}(T_h) \oplus DA_{type+1}(T_h), & dataType = 1, \end{cases}$$

$$SE_{set} = [SE_1, SE_2, \ldots, SE_n],$$

$$(2)$$

$$D_{rv} = SE_{set} \begin{bmatrix} a_1 \\ \vdots \\ a_n \end{bmatrix}.$$

Here, let D_{rv} denote the service opportunistic request driven factor. Vector $[a_1, \ldots, a_n]$ denotes the service opportunistic weight. The value of dataType could be set according to the ability of satisfying the service requests. If dataType is 0, the current data set can be independent of the service request. If dataType is 1, more than 2 data sets could satisfy the current service request. Let T_y denote the number of data sets. $DA_{set}(SE)$ denote the data set which gives feedback to users.

3. Application Perception Model

In the processing progress of mobile Internet applications, cloud platforms can be achieved through nonlinear mapping between different clouds and channel from the service to the data set, which could meet the needs of different data sets from different cloud data fusion. Here, it is important to coordinate transmission and fusion of multicloud applications, as shown in Figure 3. Here, the cycle symbol of Figure 3 denotes the cloud of platform.

Based on the same service request and being located in the same area, data transmission coordination network composed of multicloud needs to be aware of the application and keep the time synchronization. When the application requests are met in different regions, in order to guarantee the space synchronization, the time must keep asynchronous, as shown in formula (3). Based on the above time and space of synchronous request and asynchronous operation, formula

(4) illustrated the application of perception matrix and data output matrix and relationship:

$$T(i) = T(j),$$

$$S_{pace}(DA_{set}(i)) = S_{pace}(DA_{set}(j)),$$

$$T(i) \neq T(j),$$

$$S_{pace}(DA_{set}(i)) \neq S_{pace}(DA_{set}(j)).$$

$$(3)$$

Here, i and j represent the different application request. Let function $S_{pace}(DA_{set}(i))$ denote the data set location of the application mapping:

$$A_{MI}[n] = T \otimes (\nabla A_{MI}[n-i] \oplus N(i)),$$

$$i = 1, 2, \ldots, \sqrt{n},$$

$$\varphi[n] = \ln\left(\frac{\nabla A_{MI}[n-i]}{\sqrt{n}}\right),$$

$$(4)$$

$$O_{MI} = e^{A_{MI}[n]} DA_{set}(SE)^{\varphi[n]}.$$

Here, let $A_{MI}[n]$ denote application perception matrix. Let $\varphi[n]$ denote the multicloud coordination flux. Let O_{MI} denote the output matrix of data set.

Hence, the data output flow of mobile Internet application perception is as follows:

(1) initializing the vector and parameters according to the principles and models,

(2) computing the matrix A_{MI} according to formula (4),

(3) O_{MI} is set to 1, which means service request is active and waiting for data output,

(4) data selection and integration after the activation of cloud devices,

(5) the consistency and time of the region are judged according to formula (3),

(6) if the space is consistent, the time synchronization is obtained by formula (4),

(7) If the space is not the same, the time is asynchronous. The cloud platform is in a stable state. In an asynchronous cycle, the multiple cloud segmentation data are activated. The end of the independent data set is obtained after data integration.

4. Efficient Data Mining Cloud Platform

According to the service opportunities driving characteristics and extraction of perceptual features, how to build cloud platform for mobile Internet applications to provide robust and efficient data mining service has become a key issue of QoS guarantee in mobile Internet. In cloud platform, the customer service satisfaction $QE(DA_{set})$ could be computed by adding each data service satisfaction as shown in formula (5):

$$QE(DA_{set}) = \sum_{i=1}^{n} QE(i).$$

$$(5)$$

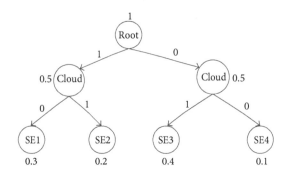

FIGURE 4: Service driven tree.

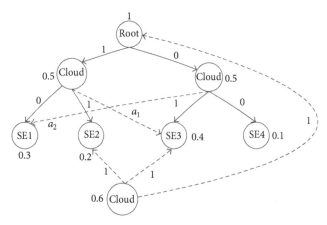

FIGURE 5: Service opportunistic driven tree.

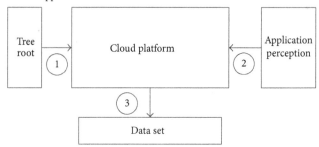

FIGURE 6: Cloud platform architecture for efficient data mining.

TABLE 1: Service driven.

Service ID	Weight	Service vector	Data mining complexity
SE1	0.3	10	High
SE2	0.2	11	Low
SE3	0.4	01	High
SE4	0.1	00	Low

TABLE 2: Service opportunistic driven.

Service ID	Weight	Service vector	Cloud weight	Data mining complexity
SE1	$a_2/0.3$	10/00	0.5/0.6	High/low
SE2	0.2	11	0.5	Low
SE3	$a_1/0.4$	01/11	0.5/0.6	High/low
SE4	0.1	00	0.5	Low

If customer service demand satisfaction of data sets is larger than the user specified minimum value, the data sets are robust. Otherwise, the data sets should be reconstructed through data mining.

In order to facilitate the service opportunity to play the driving characteristics, we defined the service drive tree. The tree consists of K leaf nodes. Each leaf node represents a service identifier and the opportunity probability. The intermediate node indicates the subtree ability which is denoted by the summary of service opportunities driven weight of leaf nodes. The service driven tree is shown in Figure 4. If the current node and the child nodes are time synchronization, the link will be recorded as 1; otherwise, it is denoted by 0. From the root node to any leaf node, a set of binary bit strings could be obtained. Each leaf node can access the service based on adaptive driving vector, which could reduce data mining complexity. The service opportunities driven tree is shown in Figure 5.

Here, we set 4 leaf nodes and service initiation probability of each leaf node is given. The sum of 4 leaf nodes probability is equal to 1. The service opportunity driven weight of root node is equal to 1. The intermediate nodes are composed of 2 clouds, which are shown as in Table 1.

As shown in Table 1, although the SE4 opportunity weight is low, the service driven path vector is all asynchronous, the data mining complexity is low, and the data clustering service can be obtained with higher real-time. Although the SE3 has the best chance, but the service driven path is heterogeneous,

the data mining is complex, so the data clustering is poor, and the real-time performance is poor. In addition, the value of SE1, SE2, SE3, and SE4 could be computed based on the service requests and service driven tree as shown in Figure 4.

As shown in Table 2, with opportunistic driven scheme, the data mining complexity of 4 leaf nodes has been reduced. For SE2 and SE3, we can establish the path of multiple data transmission through the opportunity weighting, so as to ensure the real-time and accuracy of data clustering. In addition, the cloud platform could be constructed by choosing the same area of the current leaf nodes and service opportunities driven. Based on the above service opportunity driving features and application of data clustering mining, the architecture of the cloud platform is as shown in Figure 6. Here, ① expresses the analysis of service opportunistic drive characteristics; ② denotes the feature extraction of application perception; ③ denotes the clustering data mining. The construction algorithm is described as follows.

Algorithm 1. Construction of cloud platform is as follows.

Input. It includes $SE_{set}(n)$, $DA_{set}(m)$, $US_{set}(p)$, $QE(i)$, and data mining complexity threshold DM_{th}.

Output. It includes data set $DA_{set}(C\_P)$ and cloud platform C_P_{DM}.

Begin

    While (1)

    Initial parameters: $L_{CP}(j)$, $L_{CP}(a, b)$;

    Obtain the value of N

    While $i \geqslant N$

    If QE(i) = 1 or QE(i) = 3

    Count time;

    i++;

    End while

    Computing the value of T and T_h based on QE(i) and $T(i)$;

    Obtain the service opportunity request drive factor D_{rv};

    Constructing the service opportunity driven tree;

    Analyzing the data mining complexity DM;

    If DM is larger than DM$_{th}$

    Updating the tree;

    Else

    If $S_{pace}(DA_{set}(i)) = S_{pace}(DA_{set}(j))$

    Time synchronization

    Else

    Time asynchronous

    End if

    End if

    Computing multicloud coordination flux $\varphi[n]$

    Select the optimal clouds to construct the cloud platform C_P$_{DM}$

    Activate the multicloud segmentation data and obtain the final independent data set DA$_{set}$(C_P) after the fusion data

    End while

End

5. Performance Evaluation

In order to verify the cloud platform performance and data mining performance of the proposed cloud platform based on opportunities in the service of mobile Internet driver and data mining of application perception (CP-SAD), we designed the experiment with 1 GB storage space and 100 data sets randomly distributed in 10 pieces of cloud equipment and evaluated with the transaction data base server. Verification metrics include the system running time and memory occupancy rate, the time required for data clustering, and the average clustering quality, which compared with the cloud computing mechanism with distributed data mining (CP-DDM); the results are as shown in Figure 7.

From Figure 7(a), we found that CP-DDM mechanism system running time increases linearly with increasing data set, while the operating time of the proposed CP-SAD mechanism remained stable, because the use of service opportunities driven model and real-time analysis of the characteristics of the driver can accurately grasp the service request, optimize the system initialization and service driven and application aspects of perception in the delay, not only shorten the operation time but also smooth the delay jitter.

Figure 7(b) proved that the proposed mechanism could optimize the memory capacity, because of the application of perceptual features extraction mechanism, which can not only be aware of the applications required data scale and distribution, but also optimize the composition of the cloud platform, by combining with the opportunity to serve driver tree. The proposed mechanism can increase the utilization ratio of memory, avoiding the cloud platform system performance degradation caused by memory overflow.

From Figure 7(c), we can see that the required time of data mining clustering increases first and then decreases with the increase of cloud scale activation. This is because the large computation result is more time consuming in initialization phase. However, the proposed CP-SAD mechanism can complete cloud equipment initialization and reduce data mining time faster and earlier. The CP-SAD mechanism can complete initialization after the first cloud device activation, and CP-DDM mechanism complete initialization when three-cloud device is activated, which wasted a lot of time for data mining clustering stage. This is because the distributed data mining is composed of a cloud platform data distributed storage and application features and service requests are not built for nonlinear mapping, resulting in data mining delay being large.

Clustering quality average is shown in Figure 7(d) with the increase of the size of the cloud. In the activation of the cloud number from 0 to 4, the average clustering quality of two mechanisms changes in the same law, and the gap is about 10 percentage points. With a further increase in the cloud, the average clustering quality of CP-DDM mechanism began to decline, until 10 clouds are activated to rise to 60%. However, the average clustering quality of CP-SAD mechanism has stalled when there are four clouds and then increases linearly. This is because the CP-SAD mechanism can effectively grasp the opportunity to drive characteristics and extraction of perceptual features and construct, for mobile Internet applications to provide robust and efficient data mining service cloud platform, mobile Internet applications for improving the efficient and reliable quality of service.

The iteration number analysis results of time complexity of CP-DDM and CP-SAD were shown in Figure 7(e). The proposed mechanism could compute the data efficiently and mine the data accurately with less iteration number than one of CP-DDM, which has the very low time complexity.

6. Conclusions

In order to improve the cloud platform of the mobile Internet services with quality assurance and data mining efficiency, we researched the opportunities in the service of mobile Internet driver, as well as the reliable and efficient application aware

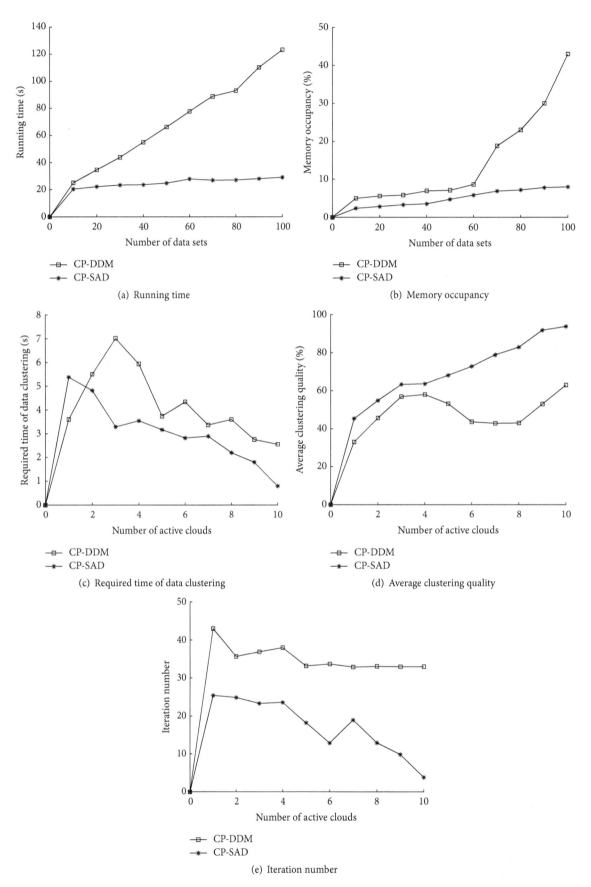

(a) Running time

(b) Memory occupancy

(c) Required time of data clustering

(d) Average clustering quality

(e) Iteration number

FIGURE 7: Performance evaluation.

data mining. Firstly, a data selection mechanism is designed based on the analysis of the characteristics of the mobile Internet service opportunity driving. Second, based on the relationship between the Internet service and data set, the nonlinear mapping between cloud and the Internet channel was established, and it established an Internet application perception model. Third, based on the characteristics of service opportunity driven and application perception, a cloud platform is proposed to provide efficient and robust data mining services for mobile Internet applications. The experimental results show that the proposed mechanism in the runtime and memory occupancy rate, data clustering, and the time required for the average clustering quality are better than the cloud platform based on distributed data mining.

Conflict of Interests

The author declares that there is no conflict of interests regarding the publication of this paper.

References

[1] A. Cuzzocrea, "Models and algorithms for high-performance data management and mining on computational grids and clouds," *Journal of Grid Computing*, vol. 12, no. 3, pp. 443–445, 2014.

[2] A. K. Tripathy, J. Adinarayana, K. Vijayalakshmi et al., "Knowledge discovery and Leaf Spot dynamics of groundnut crop through wireless sensor network and data mining techniques," *Computers and Electronics in Agriculture*, vol. 107, pp. 104–114, 2014.

[3] C.-S. Chen, W.-Y. Liang, and H.-Y. Hsu, "A cloud computing platform for ERP applications," *Applied Soft Computing*, vol. 27, pp. 127–136, 2015.

[4] J. Carretero and J. G. Blas, "Introduction to cloud computing: platforms and solutions," *Cluster Computing*, vol. 17, no. 4, pp. 1225–1229, 2014.

[5] H. Qi, M. Shiraz, J.-Y. Liu, A. Gani, Z. Abdul Rahman, and T. A. Altameem, "Data center network architecture in cloud computing: review, taxonomy, and open research issues," *Journal of Zhejiang University SCIENCE C*, vol. 15, no. 9, pp. 776–793, 2014.

[6] G. Rakocevic, Z. Tafa, and V. Milutinovic, "A novel approach to data mining in wireless sensor networks," *Ad-Hoc & Sensor Wireless Networks*, vol. 22, no. 1-2, pp. 21–40, 2014.

[7] T. Xu, W. Xiang, Q. Guo, and L. Mo, "Mining cloud 3D video data for interactive video services," *Mobile Networks and Applications*, vol. 20, no. 3, pp. 320–327, 2015.

[8] J. Ronowicz, M. Thommes, P. Kleinebudde, and J. Krysiński, "A data mining approach to optimize pellets manufacturing process based on a decision tree algorithm," *European Journal of Pharmaceutical Sciences*, vol. 73, pp. 44–48, 2015.

[9] R. Ghosh, F. Longo, R. Xia, V. K. Naik, and K. S. Trivedi, "Stochastic model driven capacity planning for an infrastructure-as-a-service cloud," *IEEE Transactions on Services Computing*, vol. 7, no. 4, pp. 667–680, 2014.

[10] Z. Ye, A. Bouguettaya, and X. Zhou, "Economic model-driven cloud service composition," *ACM Transactions on Internet Technology*, vol. 14, no. 2-3, Article ID 2651420, pp. 255–273, 2014.

[11] A. Boukerche, A. A. F. Loureiro, E. F. Nakamura, H. A. B. F. Oliveira, H. S. Ramos, and L. A. Villas, "Cloud-assisted computing for event-driven mobile services," *Mobile Networks & Applications*, vol. 19, no. 2, pp. 161–170, 2014.

[12] H.-Y. Chang, C.-C. Lai, and Y.-W. Lin, "A fast SVC-based channel-recommendation system for an IPTV on a cloud and P2P hybrid platform," *Computer Journal*, vol. 57, no. 12, pp. 1776–1789, 2013.

[13] D. Petcu, S. Panica, C. Crăciun, M. Neagul, and C. Şandru, "Cloud resource orchestration within an open-source component-based platform as a service," *Concurrency and Computation: Practice and Experience*, vol. 27, no. 9, pp. 2443–2469, 2015.

[14] J. M. Alcaraz Calero and J. G. Aguado, "MonPaaS: an adaptive monitoring platformas a service for cloud computing infrastructures and services," *IEEE Transactions on Services Computing*, vol. 8, no. 1, pp. 65–78, 2015.

7

Disordered and Multiple Destinations Path Planning Methods for Mobile Robot in Dynamic Environment

Yong-feng Dong,[1] **Hong-mei Xia,**[2] **and Yan-cong Zhou**[3]

[1]*School of Computer Science and Engineering, Big Data Computing Key Laboratory of Hebei Province, Hebei University of Technology, No. 5340 Xiping Road, Shuangkou, Beichen District, Tianjin 300401, China*
[2]*School of Computer Science and Engineering, Hebei University of Technology, No. 5340 Xiping Road, Shuangkou, Beichen District, Tianjin 300401, China*
[3]*School of Information Engineering, Tianjin University of Commerce, Tianjin, China*

Correspondence should be addressed to Hong-mei Xia; 727001435@qq.com

Academic Editor: Sook Yoon

In the smart home environment, aiming at the disordered and multiple destinations path planning, the sequencing rule is proposed to determine the order of destinations. Within each branching process, the initial feasible path set is generated according to the law of attractive destination. A sinusoidal adaptive genetic algorithm is adopted. It can calculate the crossover probability and mutation probability adaptively changing with environment at any time. According to the cultural-genetic algorithm, it introduces the concept of reducing turns by parallelogram and reducing length by triangle in the belief space, which can improve the quality of population. And the fallback strategy can help to jump out of the "U" trap effectively. The algorithm analyses the virtual collision in dynamic environment with obstacles. According to the different collision types, different strategies are executed to avoid obstacles. The experimental results show that cultural-genetic algorithm can overcome the problems of premature and convergence of original algorithm effectively. It can avoid getting into the local optimum. And it is more effective for mobile robot path planning. Even in complex environment with static and dynamic obstacles, it can avoid collision safely and plan an optimal path rapidly at the same time.

1. Introduction

The development of science and technology makes smart home concept realizable, where mobile robots play a very important role. There is a heavy need in daily life for a robot to work continuously in an environment which contains disordered and multiple destinations. Path planning for a mobile robot working in such an environment is a challenging task and has attracted more and more attention of scholars worldwide. This paper presents disordered and multiple destinations path planning methods for mobile robot in an environment with dynamic obstacles. Path planning problem can be understood as an optimization problem with constraints. It refers to how a robot searches one optimal or approximates optimal route with specific performance (such as the shortest distance, less time, or the minimum energy consumption) from starting point to target point in the environment with obstacles.

There are many studies in the literature about path planning. Depending on the methods and principles used in the path planning, the robot path planning methods are divided into two types: traditional path planning methods and intelligent path planning methods. Traditional path planning methods include visibility graph method, grid decoupling method, graph searching method, and artificial potential method [1]. Intelligent path planning methods include fuzzy logic [2], ant colony algorithm [3], neural networks [4], and genetic algorithm [5]. In order to solve the shortcomings of these algorithms, scholars have conducted a lot of researches. In some particular work environments, the ants will fall into traps. Yu and Shiyong [6] proposed the ant rollback strategy to solve this problem, which could reduce the operating efficiency of the algorithm. By analysing the shortcomings of the artificial potential field method, Tang et al. [7] proposed an obstacle avoidance method based on gravity chain. For solving the "dead cycle" problem in U-shaped obstacles, a systemic neural-fuzzy control algorithm was proposed by Bao et al. [8]. An Obstacle Avoidance Algorithm (OAA) and Distinguish Algorithm (DA) were proposed to generate the initial population by Yun et al. [9] in order to improve the efficiency by selecting only the feasible paths during the evolution of genetic algorithm. But it inhibits the diversity of the population. To overcome the premature convergence in the traditional genetic algorithm, Hu and Feng [10] proposed a new way to generate the genetic operator, by means of modifying insert a space before (SAGA). In order to avoid infeasible path and improve the convergence speed, Tuncer and Yildirim [11] proposed a new mutation operation, which selected the mutated node with the best fitness value after being replaced with the original node (BMFGA). In dynamic uncertain environments, Wei et al. [12] proposed the incremental replanning which reused the information of previous. At the same time, it could also reduce the possibility of finding the optimal path. Zhu [13] used the virtual ants to predict the potential collision with the moving obstacles. The local motions planning for avoiding collisions were scheduled under the ACO, which can plan optimal path rapidly in cluttered environment. These algorithms solve only the problem with certain aspects, but they are not very comprehensive consideration. Some algorithms do not consider the operating efficiency, or the probability of finding the optimal path is too low, or the ability of real-time processing is poor. This paper presents a simple and effective dynamic obstacle avoidance strategy.

2. The Mobile Robot Path Planning Based on the Evolutionary Genetic Algorithm

2.1. Encoding Scheme. In this paper, we set the sequence number for each grid. The basic sequence is from left to right, top to bottom. The upper border is x-axis, and the left border is y-axis. We use grid method to model the working environment as the paper [14]. Minkowski and the principle of expanding obstacles [15] are adopted to divide the work space into a number of grids. In the grid domain, a black grid denotes an obstacle and a white grid denotes free space. Robot path is indicated by the index numbers, which can save memory and express more succinctly compared with the method of coordinate. What is more important is that the genetic operations (such as the selection operator, crossover operator, and mutation operator) are simpler.

2.2. Sequencing. There are disordered destinations in the task of robot in practical work. For example, the robot goes to the kitchen to get a cup and pour water, goes to the living room to take drug, and finally goes to the bedroom. In the workflow, the sequence of robot taking drug and taking the cup is arbitrary. But the sequence of taking cup and pouring is determined. Therefore, the robot must determine the order of each destination according to the work environment firstly.

We propose the sequencing rule to determine the order of each destination. The sequencing rule can be denoted by

$$C_i = O_{num} * w_{num} + L_{pre} * w_{pre} + L_{next} * w_{next}. \quad (1)$$

C_i is the fitness value of the disordered destination D_i. O_{num} is the number of barrier grids in the rectangle which diagonal is the line segment from the former destination (or starting point) to the destination D_i. L_{pre} is the length from the destination D_i to the former destination (or starting point). L_{next} is the length from the destination D_i to the next destination (or goal point). w_{num}, w_{pre}, and w_{next} are the weight coefficients, and $w_{num}+w_{pre}+w_{next} = 1$. In considering the population diversity and the efficiency of finding the optimal path, through repeated testing, the best combination of weight coefficients is obtained ($w_{num} = 0.6$, $w_{pre} = 0.2$, and $w_{next} = 0.2$). If the value of C_i is smaller, D_i has the higher priority. Robot determines the destination sequence based on this standard. Within each branching process, execute genetic operation, find the optimal path, and then get the optimal path in the static environment.

2.3. Initialization of Population. A good initial population in the feasible region is very effective to enhance the speed of evolution. We present the law of attractive destination. According to the relative position of the starting point and destination in each branching process, we adopt different strategy to generate the set of feasible paths. We categorize the relative positions of the starting point and its associated destination into four types as shown in Figure 1. Figure 1(a) represents that the destination is in the first quadrant of the starting point. Figure 1(b) represents that the destination is in the second quadrant of the starting point. Figure 1(c) represents that the destination is in the third quadrant of starting point. Figure 1(d) represents that the destination is in the fourth quadrant of the starting point. R represents the robot and D represents the direction of destination. When the robot chooses the next grid to move, we give priority to the grid marked with "1," which is closer to the destination in the region whose diagonal is a line segment from the starting point to the destination. If the grids marked with "1" are not in the feasible region of robot, we consider the grids marked with "2." If the grids marked with "2" are also not in the feasible region of robot, we consider the grids marked with "3." At the same time, the fallback phenomenon appears. We will set the current grid as the barrier grid to enhance the speed of population initialization and avoid the circuitous path effectively. When the starting point and destination are in the same horizontal or vertical line, we use the method in Figure 1(a). Looking for the next grid, the same horizontal (or vertical) coordinate is expanded 3 units from the left and right, respectively, and forms the search rectangle.

If the robot selects the next grid all in accordance with the law of attractive destination in the process of initial population, it is easy to fall into the local optimal. Therefore, when the number of walking steps is an integer multiple of 3, the robot selects the next walking grid randomly in the feasible region, which can increase the diversity of population.

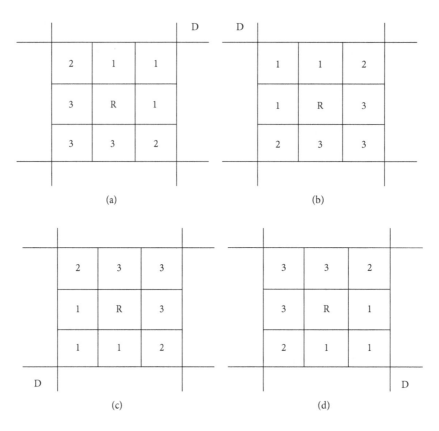

FIGURE 1: Schematic diagram of direction selection priority.

After the initialization, we simplify the individuals. We will delete the path between the repeated grids, which can improve the quality of initial population. For example, the original individual is (0, 1, 11, 13, 22, 32, 34, 23, 24, 34, 45, 56, 66, 77, 87, 88, 99); the individual is (0, 1, 11, 13, 22, 32, 34, 45, 56, 66, 77, 87, 88, 99) after being simplified.

2.4. Fitness Function. In the process of walking, the path length and energy consumption are the two important considered factors. The energy consumption is mainly correlated with the number of turns [16]. According to the above analysis, we adopt the fitness function as follows:

$$F = \frac{100}{\left(1 + 1/\sqrt{1+n}\right) \times D \times w_d + \text{curve} \times w_c},\quad (2)$$

where n is the number of all grids in the path, $1/\sqrt{1+n}$ is a correction item, D is the length of path, and curve is the total number of turns. w_d and w_c are the weights, and $w_d + w_c = 1$. According to the requirement about these three standards, the weight coefficient is customized. This paper sets $w_d = 0.8$, $w_c = 0.2$. We define the path length by Euclidean distance, so the length of an edge with the points $p_i(x_i, y_i)$ and $p_{i+1}(x_{i+1}, y_{i+1})$ is given as follows: $d = \sqrt{(x_{i+1} - x_i)^2 + (y_{i+1} - y_i)^2}$. So the total length is $D = \sum_{i=1}^{n-1} \sqrt{(x_{i+1} - x_i)^2 + (y_{i+1} - y_i)^2}$.

2.5. Design of Genetic Operator

2.5.1. Selection Method. The main principle of the selection method is that the best genes on the chromosome should be survived and transferred to next generation. So we use the roulette wheel method to choose the next generation population, which is good at protecting the better individuals. The better path has the higher probability to be selected as the next generation.

2.5.2. Crossover Operator and Mutation Operator. In this paper, we adopt a new improved adaptive genetic algorithm, which changes the crossover probability and mutation probability adaptively, according to the population and the distribution of fitness values. Change curves of the crossover probability and mutation probability are from the oscillation to stability gradually. In the early evolution, it can generate the larger cross probability and mutation probability, which can enhance the search ability. In the later evolution, we take a relatively low crossover probability and mutation probability to make the best individual preserved, which can weaken the bad influences caused by the too larger crossover probability and mutation probability that are generated because of the fitness close to the average fitness values or maximum fitness values. At the same time it also overcomes the evolutionary stagnate and the problem of the local optimum. SAGA is expressed as follows:

$$p_c$$

$$= \begin{cases} \dfrac{p_{c1} + p_{c2}}{2} + \dfrac{p_{c1} - p_{c2}}{2} * \sin\left(\dfrac{f' - f_{\text{avg}}}{f_{\text{max}} - f_{\text{avg}}} * \dfrac{\pi}{2}\right) & f' \geq f_{\text{max}} \\ p_{c1} & f' < f_{\text{avg}} \end{cases}$$

$$p_m$$

$$= \begin{cases} \dfrac{p_{m1} + p_{m2}}{2} + \dfrac{p_{m1} - p_{m2}}{2} * \sin\left(\dfrac{f' - f_{\text{avg}}}{f_{\text{max}} - f_{\text{avg}}} \dfrac{\pi}{2}\right) & f' \geq f_{\text{max}} \\ p_{m1} & f' > f_{\text{avg}}, \end{cases}$$

$$(3)$$

where p_c and p_m represent the mutation probability value and mutation probability value, respectively, f_{max} represents the maximum fitness value in the population, f_{avg} represents the average fitness value in the population, f' represents the larger values between the two crossed individuals, p_{c1} and p_{c2} are the maximum and minimum crossover probability values, respectively, and p_{m1} and p_{m2} are the maximum and minimum mutation probability values, respectively. The single-point crossover is adopted in the adjacent chromosomes. The point which can make the path owing the maximum fitness value is the mutation point in the mutation points set.

2.6. The Cultural Algorithm. The main idea of the cultural algorithm is that individuals in the population space have individual experience during the evolutionary process, and the individual experience will influence the belief space through Accept( ) function. In belief space, after the formation of the group experience, the behavior of individuals in the population space will be modified by Influence( ) function, in order to enable individuals to achieve higher evolutionary efficiency [17]. The basic framework of cultural algorithm is as shown in Figure 2.

In the population space, the algorithm mainly completes the selection, crossover, and mutation operations. The concepts of reducing turns by parallelogram and reducing length by triangle are adopted by the belief space.

Through reducing turns by parallelogram [18], we can reduce energy consumption in the robot walking and enhance the path fitness value, as shown in Figures 3 and 4. We select three consecutive break points. If line 1 from the first break point to the node which is in front of the first break point is parallel to line 2 from the second break point to the third break point, we make the three break points as the three points of a parallelogram. Then we add an extra edge to draw a complete parallelogram based on the three points. If the extra edge does not contain any barrier grid, we remove the original path of the parallelogram, join the extra edge, and form a new path. That will reduce the three break points to two or one.

As we all know, the hypotenuse is the shortest in the right angled triangle. We propose a right angled triangle optimization strategy using this theorem. The length of the path after optimization is shorter than the original. The central idea of the strategy is to find a right angle and two angled sides. Intuitively, this is to draw the hypotenuse as long as possible while it is feasible. The effect drawings are

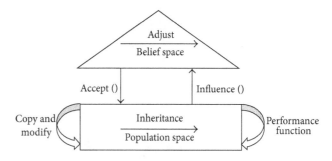

FIGURE 2: Basic framework of cultural algorithm.

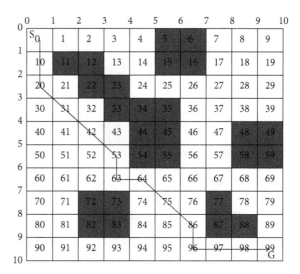

FIGURE 3: Original path diagram.

as shown in Figures 5 and 6. The whole flow chart is as shown in Figure 7.

In order to improve the convergence speed, we adopt the population replacement strategy from literature [17]. Replacement rate is p $(0 < p < 1)$. The offspring may destroy the excellent parent individuals, after the selection, crossover, mutation operation, and optimization in the belief space. Therefore, keeping the excellent parent individuals can accelerate the convergence speed of the algorithm. Offspring individuals with poorer fitness are replaced by the parent individuals with better fitness. In order to improve convergence speed and the global searching capability of the algorithm, we set p from 0.3 to 0.6, as in the literature.

3. Routing Optimization Based on the Evolutionary Genetic Algorithm in the Static Environment

To deal with the multiple destinations after the orders being determined, we take the following activities within each branching process. (1) Generate the high quality initial population, in the feasible region. (2) Put forward the appropriate

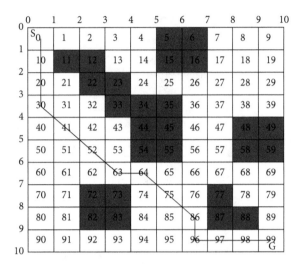

FIGURE 4: Path diagram after reducing the break points.

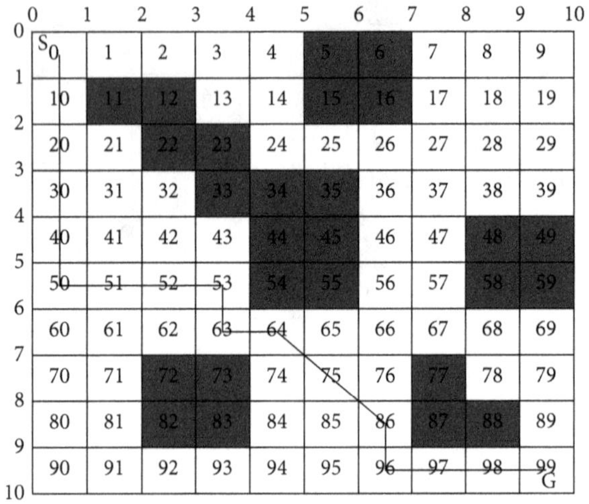

FIGURE 5: Original path diagram.

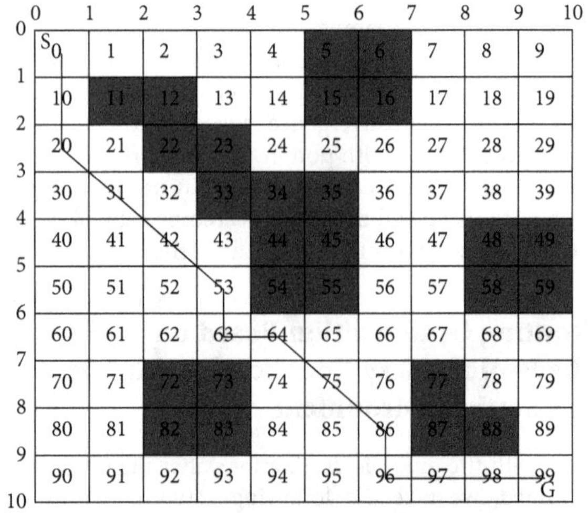

FIGURE 6: Path diagram after optimization.

fitness function. (3) Adopt adaptive genetic algorithm and get different crossover probability and mutation probability for different population. (4) Enhance the quality of path by reducing turns by parallelogram and reducing length by triangle in the belief space. The whole algorithm flow chart is as shown in Figure 8.

The general steps for solving the routing optimization problem by cultural-genetic algorithm are as follows.

The steps in the population space are as follows.

(1) Grid method is used to model the working environment. The sequencing rule is used to determine the order of each destination. Set the number of destinations goal_num = 1.

(2) Initialize the algorithm. Generate the feasible path of robot path which is the initial population in shunt process by the law of attractive destination. Set the current experiment iterations $t = 1$.

(3) According to the fitness function, calculate fitness of each individual in the population; then the roulette wheel selection is used to produce the new population.

(4) To get new chromosomes, we use the single-point crossover in the adjacent chromosomes.

(5) To produces new individuals, mutation operation is performed on the part of the individuals.

(6) According to the Accept( ) function, the new population is passed to the belief space.

(7) According to the function of Influence( ) in the belief space, we get the parent population for new generation.

(8) If the termination condition is satisfied, output the best individual of shunt process and go to step (10). Otherwise, continue to optimize the operation.

(9) Set iteration $t = t + 1$ and go to step (3).

(10) If it arrives at the final destination, the robot's final optimal individual is spliced by the best individual of shunt process. Otherwise, set iteration goal_num = goal_num + 1 and go to step (2).

The steps in the belief space are as follows.

In the belief space, we use the concept of reducing turns by parallelogram and reducing length by triangle to improve the quality of population. The strategy of population replacement is used to get the new parent population. Then, we pass the new parent populations to the population space.

4. Dynamic Path Planning

In a dynamic environment, the position of dynamic obstacle changes with time. In order to simplify complexity, we make the following assumptions.

(1) Simulate the size of a dynamic obstacle as a grid. Dynamic obstacle walks integral multiple of grids in a unit time.

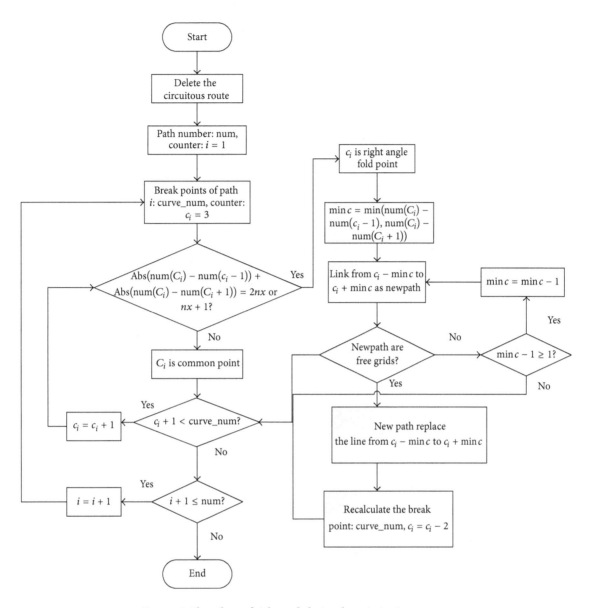

FIGURE 7: Flow chart of right angled triangle optimization strategy.

(2) The movement of the dynamic obstacles is in uniform linear motion and speed is not known.

(3) The robot can detect the movements of obstacles in the domain while walking.

The robot walks along the optimal path of static environment, which has been discussed in last section. The speed and the direction of the robot are R_{dir} and R_v. Visual domain radius is r unit grid. Through the simulation of virtual collision, we can predict the collision point and the speed of dynamic obstacle (D_v) and the direction of dynamic obstacle (D_{dir}). Therefore, we can choose different obstacle avoidance rules for obstacle avoidance.

We divide the collision into three types: (1) side collision: when the robot and dynamic obstacle have collision, their direction of motion is not in a straight line, (2) collision after turning: When the robot and dynamic obstacle have collision, their direction of motion is in a straight line, but the moving direction of robot last step and the moving direction of dynamic obstacle are not in a straight line, and (3) other collisions.

Different strategies have been applied for different collision types under specific conditions as shown in Table 1.

5. Simulation

5.1. Simulation Environment and Parameter Settings. All parameters are shown in Table 2.

5.2. Simulation Results in Static Environment. In order to study the efficiency of the algorithm, we set one destination in the work environment firstly, as shown in Figure 3.

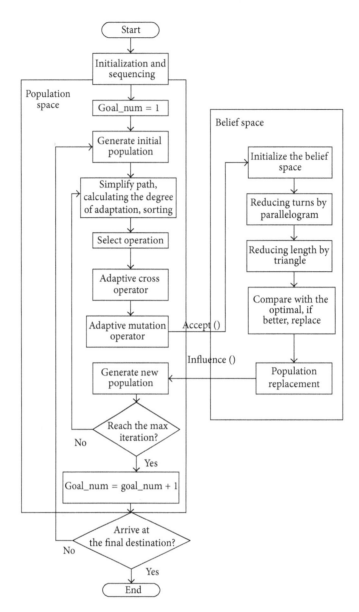

FIGURE 8: Flow chart of improved genetic algorithm.

The 0 and 99 are the starting point and the destination point, respectively.

We make the comparison with three algorithms: the evolutionary genetic algorithm (EGA), the BMFGA, and the SAGA. The three algorithms are all run 50 times, where the success probability and average fitness of the three algorithms are compared. The results are shown in Figure 9 and Table 3.

Randomly select one result from the 50 running times; the optimal fitness convergence results are shown in Figure 10. From the figures, we can conclude that the EGA has better convergence than others.

What can we see from the experimental results is that EGA has the biggest probability of searching the optimal path, with fastest convergence speed. From the above results, EGA has higher success rate, and the convergence speed is also fast in the static environment, which has only one destination.

The working environment with disordered and multiple destinations is shown Figure 11, where S and G are the starting point and final destination, respectively, $D1$ and $D2$ are disordered destinations, and $D3$, $D4$, and $D5$ are destinations of determined sequence. According to (1), we can determine the running order, which is (S, $D1$, $D2$, $D3$, $D4$, $D5$, and G). By using this algorithm, we get the optimal path as shown in Figure 11.

5.3. Simulation Results in Dynamic Environment. Robot avoids dynamic obstacles in the dynamic environment as shown in Figure 12. The robot walks along the optimal path,

TABLE 1: Collision avoidance strategy.

Type of collision	Collision avoidance strategy
Side collision	Waiting strategy: the robot waits for unit time in the current position, which can avoid the collision with dynamic obstacles.
Collision after turning	Rollback strategy: because the motion direction of the robot on the last step is not on the same line with the dynamic obstacle, the robot just needs back up one step, which can avoid collision.
Other collisions	Hiding in the nearby: the robot finds a point as the collision avoidance point in the vicinity of the current location. After avoiding dynamic obstacles successfully, it goes back to the current position.

TABLE 2: Parameters.

Population size	Number of iterations	P_{c1}	P_{c2}	P_{m1}	P_{m2}	p
150	150	0.75	0.25	0.2	0.01	0.3

which is shown in Figure 11. When the robot walks to the grid 60, it detects a dynamic obstacle in the grid 60. Through virtual collision, we get that the collision point is grid 81, and the type is side collision. According to Table 1, we choose the waiting strategy. The robot avoids collision successfully for the first time. The robot continues moving along the original path. When the robot walks to the grid 207, it detects a dynamic in the grid 201. Through virtual collision, we get that the collision point is grid 81, and the type is collision after turning. According to Table 1, we choose the rollback strategy first and then choose the waiting strategy. The robot avoids collision successfully for the second time. When moving to the grid 257, the robot detects a dynamic obstacle in the grid 297. Through virtual collision, we get that the collision point is grid 277, and the type is other collisions. According to Table 1, we choose the strategy of hiding in the nearby. The robot avoids collision successfully for the third time. The robot arrives at the final destination, as shown in Figure 12. We can see from the experimental results that the collision avoidance strategy is simple and effective.

6. Conclusion

Aiming at the working environment with disordered and multiple destinations in the smart home, we determine the order of destinations by the sequencing rule. Then the initial feasible path set is generated according to the law of attractive destination. We use adaptive genetic algorithm to optimize the population. The work above focuses on exploring the population space of cultural-genetic algorithm. We introduce the concept of reducing turns by parallelogram and reducing length by triangle in the belief space, which can improve the quality of population and accelerate the convergence speed. Static simulation results show that the EGA can search the optimal path quickly and accurately; it can solve the problems of local optimal and early maturing. Obstacle avoidance method in this paper is simple, efficient, and safe.

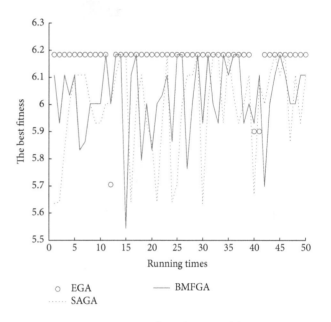

FIGURE 9: Convergence curves about the optimal fitness running 50 times.

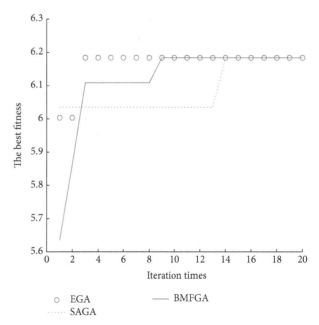

FIGURE 10: Convergence curves about the optimal fitness.

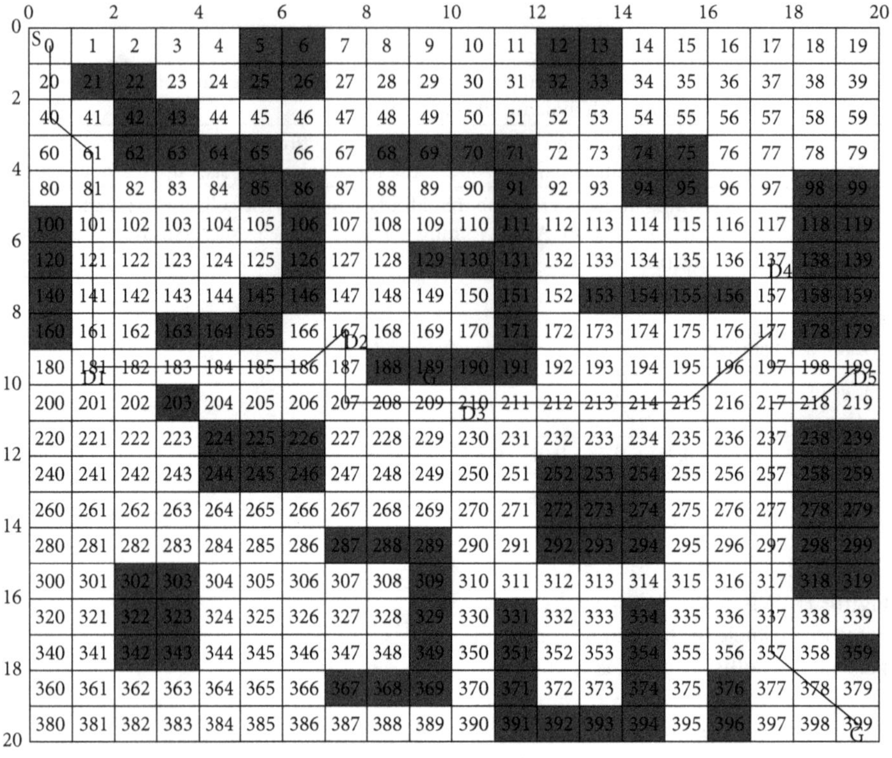

FIGURE 11: Ptimal path in the disordered and multiple destinations.

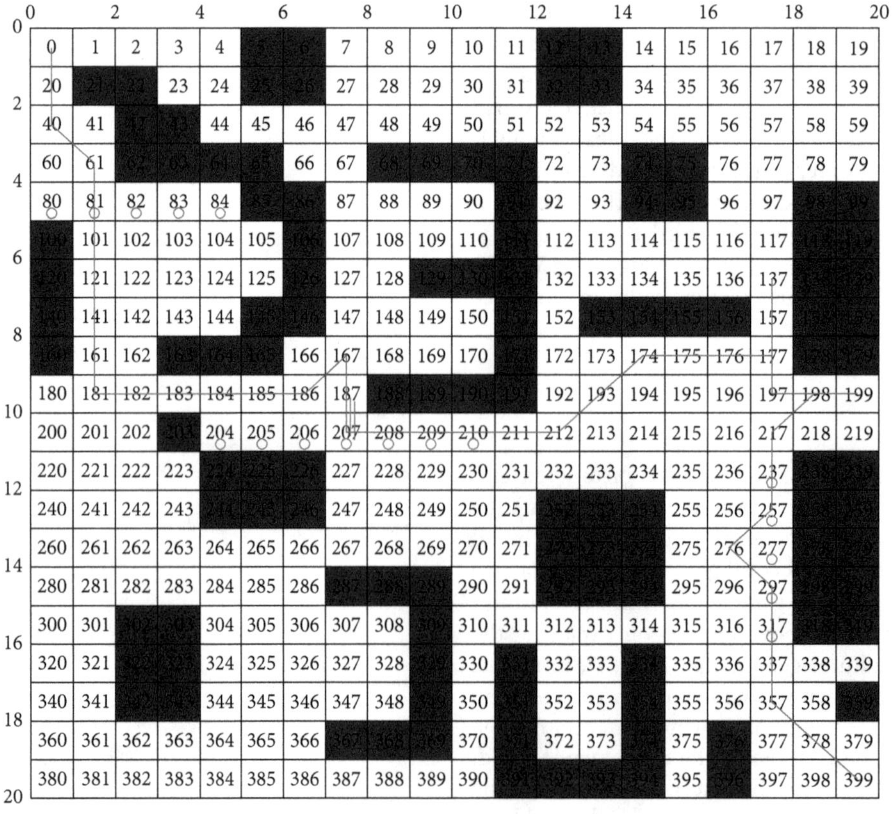

FIGURE 12: Arrival at the final destination.

TABLE 3: Performance comparison.

Planning algorithm	Average fitness	Optimal fitness	The percentage of the optimal path
EGA	6.1634	6.1843	95%
BMFGA	5.9974	6.1843	12%
SAGA	5.9880	6.1843	18%

Competing Interests

The authors declare that they have no competing interests.

References

[1] D.-F. Zhang and F. Liu, "Research and development trend of path planning based on artificial potential field method," *Computer Engineering & Science*, vol. 35, no. 6, pp. 88–95, 2013.

[2] V. Ganapathy, C. Y. Soh, and J. Ng, "Fuzzy and neural controllers for acute obstacle avoidance in mobile robot navigation," in *Proceedings of the IEEE/ASME International Conference on Advanced Intelligent Mechatronics (AIM '09)*, pp. 1236–1241, July 2009.

[3] M. Brand, M. Masuda, N. Wehner, and X.-H. Yu, "Ant colony optimization algorithm for robot path planning," in *Proceedings of the International Conference on Computer Design and Applications (ICCDA '10)*, pp. V3-436–V3-440, IEEE, Qinhuangdao, China, June 2010.

[4] W. Wang, S. M. Wei, Y. Q. Yang, Y. F. Jiang, and L. I. DuanLing, "Path planning for a mobile robot using neural networks," *Journal of Beijing University of Technology*, vol. 45, no. 10, pp. 221–225, 2009.

[5] I. Al-Taharwa, A. Sheta, and M. Al-Weshah, "A mobile robot path planning using genetic algorithm in static environment," *Journal of Computer Science*, vol. 4, no. 4, pp. 341–344, 2008.

[6] G. Yu and L. Shiyong, "Path planning for robot based on improved ant colony algorithm," *Computer Measurement & Control*, vol. 17, no. 1, pp. 187–189, 2009.

[7] L. Tang, S. Dian, G. Gu, K. Zhou, S. Wang, and X. Feng, "A novel potential field method for obstacle avoidance and path planning of mobile robot," in *Proceedings of the 3rd IEEE International Conference on Computer Science and Information Technology (ICCSIT '10)*, vol. 9, pp. 633–637, July 2010.

[8] F. Bao, Y.-H. Pan, and W.-B. Xu, "Dynamic path plan of mobile robot based on neural-fuzzy control system," *Computer Engineering and Applications*, vol. 45, no. 10, pp. 221–225, 2009.

[9] S. C. Yun, V. Ganapathy, and L. O. Chong, "Improved genetic algorithms based optimum path planning for mobile robot," in *Proceedings of the 11th International Conference on Control, Automation, Robotics and Vision (ICARCV '10)*, pp. 1565–1570, Singapore, December 2010.

[10] C.-B. Hu and W.-Y. Feng, "Optimization problem of mobile robot route with improved adaptive genetic algorithm," *Journal of Lanzhou University of Technology*, vol. 37, no. 5, pp. 11–15, 2011.

[11] A. Tuncer and M. Yildirim, "Dynamic path planning of mobile robots with improved genetic algorithm," *Computers and Electrical Engineering*, vol. 38, no. 6, pp. 1564–1572, 2012.

[12] W. Wei, D.-T. Ouyang, S. Lu, and Y.-X. Feng, "Multi objective path planning under dynamic uncertain environment," *Chinese Journal of Computers*, vol. 34, no. 5, pp. 836–838, 2011.

[13] Q.-B. Zhu, "Ants predictive algorithm for path planning of robot in a complex dynamic environment," *Chinese Journal of Computers*, vol. 28, no. 11, pp. 1898–1892, 2005.

[14] J. Ma, Z.-P. Fan, and L.-H. Huang, "A subjective and objective integrated approach to determine attribute weights," *European Journal of Operational Research*, vol. 112, no. 2, pp. 397–404, 1999.

[15] S. Sun and Y. Qu, "Robot motion planning using genetic algorithm," *Journal of Northwestern Polytechnical University*, vol. 16, no. 1, pp. 79–83, 1998.

[16] Z.-Y. Deng and C.-K. Chen, "Mobile robot path planning based on improved genetic algorithm," *Machinery Design & Manufacture*, vol. 7, pp. 147–149, 2010.

[17] J. Cao and C. Sun, "Path planning based on multi-objective genetic algorithm for AUV on VCF electronic chart," *Geomatics and Information Science of Wuhan University*, vol. 35, no. 4, pp. 441–445, 2010.

[18] Y.-C. Zhou, Y.-F. Dong, H.-M. Xia, and J.-H. Gu, "Routing optimization of intelligent vehicle in automated warehouse," *Discrete Dynamics in Nature and Society*, vol. 2014, Article ID 789754, 14 pages, 2014.

8

Security Enrichment in Intrusion Detection System using Classifier Ensemble

Uma R. Salunkhe[1] and Suresh N. Mali[2]

[1]*Smt. Kashibai Navale College of Engineering, Savitribai Phule Pune University, Pune, India*
[2]*Sinhgad Institute of Technology and Science, Savitribai Phule Pune University, Narhe, Pune, India*

Correspondence should be addressed to Uma R. Salunkhe; umasalunkhe@yahoo.com

Academic Editor: Arun K. Sangaiah

In the era of Internet and with increasing number of people as its end users, a large number of attack categories are introduced daily. Hence, effective detection of various attacks with the help of Intrusion Detection Systems is an emerging trend in research these days. Existing studies show effectiveness of machine learning approaches in handling Intrusion Detection Systems. In this work, we aim to enhance detection rate of Intrusion Detection System by using machine learning technique. We propose a novel classifier ensemble based IDS that is constructed using hybrid approach which combines data level and feature level approach. Classifier ensembles combine the opinions of different experts and improve the intrusion detection rate. Experimental results show the improved detection rates of our system compared to reference technique.

1. Introduction

With the wide usage of Internet, Information Security is an important domain for research. Intrusion Detection System (IDS) is a major concern of security. IDS is designed to monitor the network traffic and identify the suspicious patterns representing network intrusion that may compromise the system. That is, it continuously inspects network traffic for potential vulnerabilities [1]. Whenever IDS finds security breach or any kind of compromise to the system, it generates an alert to indicate the existence of intrusion. IDS play a crucial role in enhancing security of networking environment. Based on the approaches that are used to detect the intrusions, IDS can be categorized into following groups [2].

(1) Signature Based IDS. IDS monitor the network and compare actual behavior with known suspicious patterns that are maintained in a database of attack signatures. Matching behavior indicates the existence of attack and generates an alert. The database does not cover any unknown or newly introduced threat whose signature is not available. If any unknown attack occurs, IDS cannot detect it as its signature does not match with those in the database. This indicates that

success of intrusion detection is limited by the availability of the recent attack signatures in the database. These systems have proved efficient for known attacks.

(2) Anomaly Based IDS. Signature based IDS effectively detect known attacks but are ineffective for unknown attacks. In order to overcome this limitation, anomaly based IDS compare actual behavior with the baseline that defines the normal state of the system, that is, parameters such as protocols, traffic load, and typical packet size [3]. Deviation from the baseline indicates the anomalous behavior and generates an alert. Sometimes normal behavior can be misclassified as attack due to incomplete description of normal behavior.

(3) Hybrid IDS. Hybrid IDS makes combined use of signature based and anomaly based ones in order to gain advantages of both [4]. That is, they try to increase detection rates of known attacks and decrease false positive rates of novel attacks.

The rest of this paper is organized as follows. Section 2 presents a review of related work. Section 3 describes the proposed Intrusion Detection System and its algorithm is discussed in Section 4. Section 5 presents the experimental setup used. Section 6 focuses on obtained results and discussions. Finally, conclusions are given in Section 7.

2. Related Work

Buczak and Guven [4] reviewed machine learning methods for intrusion detection with respect to parameters like complexity of algorithm, challenges in security enhancement, and so forth. Authors suggested different criteria such as accuracy, algorithm complexity, and time complexity to select the effective technique for intrusion detection.

Khor et al. [5] proposed a cascaded classifier approach for IDS that enhances the detection rates of the attacks which belong to the rare category. The proposed technique first separates out the rare intrusions from nonrare intrusion category so that each expert can focus on fewer categories. The method helps to diminish the effects of dominant intrusion category which has shown increased detection rates for rare intrusions. Also double filtering of network traffic improves detection rates and computational cost of the approach is less.

Aburomman and Ibne Reaz [6] presented a novel classifier ensemble approach for Intrusion Detection System in order to improve the accuracy. Authors have constructed an ensemble by using proposed PSO generated weights scheme and compared the results with that of the Weighted Majority Algorithm (WMA) approach. LUS metaoptimization of the set of generated weights has resulted in the performance improvements of IDS.

Qassim et al. [7] reviewed the set of features that is more suitable for detecting wide range of anomalies from the network traffic. Authors introduced A-IDS, an alarm classifier that can automatically analyze and categorize the anomalies monitored by a packet header based anomaly detection system. Proposed method monitors the network traffic flow, selects appropriate features, and compares traffic flows representing attack to existing data.

Govindarajan [8] introduced a new hybrid Intrusion Detection System by combining radial basis function and support vector machine. Experimentation carried out on various data sets of intrusion detection proves effectiveness of heterogeneous models compared with homogeneous models. Liu et al. [9] presented a hybrid approach SmoteAdaNL that applies resampling in order to increase number of flows in minority class and then diversified ensemble technique to improve the generalization of classifier. Weight assignment to the misclassified flows helps to improve the classification performance.

Al-Jarrah et al. [1] introduced a traffic based IDS (T-IDS) for botnet, which includes number of compromised machines known as bots, remotely controlled by a machine known as botmaster. The proposed approach makes use of a novel randomized data partitioned learning method (RDPLM) and analyzes packet header rather than packet payload to identify intrusion. Authors developed a novel feature selection technique to create a subset of features which will be helpful for correct detection of intrusions. Approach has proved to improve detection accuracy with lower computational cost and is scalable to large networks.

Hu et al. [10] proposed a distributed intrusion detection framework in which each node constructs a global detection model that combines local parametric models created using a small set of samples. Hence a node can detect attack signatures present in other nodes, though it does not have representative samples of that attack. Li et al. [11] proposed nonnegative matrix factorization (NMF) based method for classification of networked text. Proposed algorithm puNet initially identifies clusters with the help of NMF method and then learning algorithm is trained with available labeled data.

Hu et al. [12] proposed a novel intrusion detection algorithm that has low computational complexity and high detection rate. If any false detection of attack is made, next iteration of AdaBoost focuses on it and improves the detection rate. The proposed approach also handles overfitting issue where detection of attack is not very specific and new attacks will be also detected effectively.

Yu et al. [13] presented an automatically tuning IDS (ATIDS) that can automatically tune the detection model based on the feedback about the false predictions. Whenever deployed detection model encounters novel data, it adapts to that data so that model performance is improved. Experimental results on KDDCup'99 dataset have shown 35% improvements in detecting the anomalous behavior.

Alrajeh et al. [14] discussed few existing IDS and research issues relevant to Wireless Network Security (WSN). Authors briefed different categories of IDS and choosing appropriate type of IDS for specified WSN. They suggested use of anomaly based IDS for small sized WSN due to their lightweight nature. Relatively larger WSN should prefer signature based IDS while very large WSN should choose hybrid type of IDS. Authors suggest not to prefer cross layer IDS for WSN with limited resources.

Machine learning techniques have helped in correctly identifying the intrusions in IDS which in turn helps to improve the security of IDS. Although there is much work on IDS, still some issues in this area need further attention of researchers. Skewed nature of training datasets of IDS is such an important issue that may have significant impact on performance of IDS. The number of instances belonging to positive class is very low compared to that of negative class. The classifier that is trained on skewed data may be biased towards negative class in decision making. This has motivated us to address the imbalance between the classes in order to avoid this issue. The first concern in the proposed system is to reduce the imbalance between the classes by resampling the dataset and then apply classifier ensemble technique to improve the classification performance.

3. Proposed System

Basically, Intrusion Detection System involves analysis of network traffic collected and comparison with the baseline defined for the system that indicates the normal behavior of the system. If a mismatch is found, it indicates that someone has intruded the system.

Intrusion Detection System comprises the following elements.

(1) Monitoring of Network Traffic. This involves monitoring the user and system activity in order to collect network traffic data.

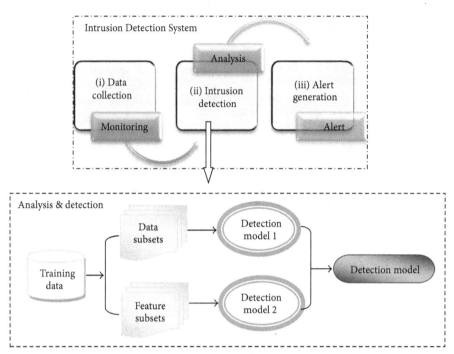

FIGURE 1: Proposed system.

(2) Analysis and Detection. Figure 1 represents the analysis and detection process of the proposed system.

This element incorporates generation of a prediction model for intrusion detection that can correctly detect the intrusion.

In this paper, we propose a classification-based framework for the analysis and detection of intrusions. First concern of this work is to focus on intrusions of rare category. Such category has few representative instances and hence detection model trained on such data may not be efficient in detecting the intrusions of that category. In order to avoid this, initially resampling of minority category is done. Synthetic data is introduced to such attack category. Also samples of category having relatively high number of instances are reduced. Such preprocessed data is provided as input for learning of detection models. Preprocessing also involves identification of noisy data or data with missing values.

Existing studies have shown improved rates of detection with the usage of classifier ensemble approach. Hence proposed system creates a novel classifier ensemble that combines opinions of individual experts. Two level ensembles are constructed by using two different approaches of creating the ensemble. That is, data level and feature level method is used to generate two detection models.

Detection Model 1. Data subsets $D_1, D_2, \ldots, D_n$ are created by extracting subset of original training data and are provided as input to the individual base classifier. Results of those classifiers are combined to get predicted output of ensemble named Detection Model 1.

Detection Model 2. Feature subsets $S_1, S_2, \ldots, S_n$ are created by extracting subsets of features from the original training

dataset and individual classifiers are trained with those subsets. Their results are combined to get Detection Model 2.

Outputs of Detection Model 1 and Detection Model 2 are combined to get the final prediction of whether intrusion exists or not.

(3) Alert Generation. If any malicious activity is detected, an alert will be generated to inform the administrator about the existence of intrusion.

The detailed algorithm is explained in Section 4.

4. Algorithm

Algorithm 1 (GenerateClassifier)

T: Original Training data set

T_1, T_2, T_3: Training Subsets by using different datasets

S_1, S_2, S_3: Training Subsets by using different feature sets

T': Modified data set after Pre-processing

F: Final classifier Ensemble model

CE: Classifier Ensemble

Steps

(1) Apply pre-processing to original training data set T

$$S' = \text{Over\_sample } (T)$$
$$B' = \text{under\_sample } (T)$$

(2) For $i = 1$ to K do //create k models

(3) Create a new training dataset T_i by extracting different data subsets $T_i = S' \cup B'$

(4) Train and learn a base classifier using T_i

$$B_i = \text{BuildClassifier } (T_i)$$

(5) Create a new training dataset S_i by extracting different feature subsets

$$S_i = \text{Feature subset } (T')$$

(6) Train and learn a base classifier J48 using S_i

$$M_i = \text{BuildClassifier } (S_i)$$

(7) Construct first level classifier ensembles

$$E_1 = \text{CE } (B_1, B_2, B_3)$$

(8) Construct first level classifier ensembles

$$E_2 = \text{CE } (M_1, M_2, M_3)$$

(9) Final classifier is

$$F = \text{CE } (E_1, E_2)$$

5. Experimental Investigation

For experimentation, we have chosen KDDCup'99 dataset that is publicly available in UCI repository [13]. Many existing works in the area of IDS have been evaluated by using KDD-Cup'99 data as standard dataset. Dataset includes various intrusions simulated in a military network environment for several weeks. The dataset consists of a training dataset with 494,021 records and a test dataset with 311,029 records [6] described with 41 attributes.

Attacks in the KDDCup'99 dataset can be categorized into four main categories [4]: Remote to Local (R2L), User to Root (U2R), Probing, and Denial of Service (DOS). R2L is a type of attack in which attacker tries to gain access to network or machine [6]. In U2R attack, attacker has access to victim machine but aims to get superuser privileges. Probing is an attack in which attacker executes scanning in order to identify possible vulnerabilities in the victim system. Identified weaknesses can be used to harm the system. DOS is a kind of attack that aims to make the resources unavailable to authorized users. Usually this is achieved by flooding systems or networks with excess traffic, disrupting the connection or services. This will result in delayed or inefficient services.

In this work, we have selected subset of attacks from KDDCup'99 dataset including attacks such as the following.

(a) Teardrop. It involves sending fragmented IP packets that are overlapping with each other to the target machine. After receiving, target machine tries to reassemble them but cannot succeed. Windows 95 and Windows NT contain one bug related to overlapping due to which system cannot handle

TABLE 1: Datasets used in the experiment.

Attack name	Number of records
Normal	3987
Phf	3
Teardrop	50
Loadmodule	7
Smurf	43
Total	4090

overlapping packets in an effective way. As a result, system may crash or reboot.

(b) Smurf. It is a kind of Distributed DOS attack in which attacker spoofs the target system and broadcasts Internet Control Message Protocol (ICMP) packets with target system's IP. Most of the networked devices reply to the source IP which generates a huge traffic and floods the target system. Hence its services will not be available to authorized users.

For our experimentation, we have chosen subset of the KDDCup'99 dataset. The details of the dataset used in our experimentation are shown in Table 1.

Evaluation of the system performance is done by using detection rate as an evaluation measure. Accuracy is a measure that represents fraction of intrusions that are correctly identified.

6. Results and Discussion

Performance of proposed system is compared with existing multiclass classifier ensemble. Experimentation is carried out for different individual classifiers, namely, Logistic Regression, J48, and Naive Bayes. Table 2 summarizes the detection rates of proposed and other reference techniques.

Figure 2 depicts performance evaluation of proposed method in terms of detection rate. Though the performance improvement seems smaller, correct identification of intrusion is extremely important and proves beneficial.

Analysis of the graphs presented in Figure 2 clearly shows improved accuracy of detecting intrusions with the use of proposed method. The major aim of the experimentation was to investigate the effect on detection rates of the proposed IDS by selecting different individual classifiers as base classifiers of ensemble. This has helped to derive some conclusions about the suitable classifiers for IDS. Analysis of the results leads to some findings that can help in choosing the appropriate base classifier to be used for ensemble designed for Intrusion Detection System. Three classifiers, namely, J48, Logistic Regression, and Naive Bayes, were tested as base classifiers of proposed ensemble technique. Logistic Regression has proved more beneficial as a base classifier in detecting the intrusions. Usage of preprocessing helps to detect the attacks of rare category correctly and improves the performance of classifier. But it has overhead as it requires more time for the learning phase of model. Overall, the proposed method improves performance of IDS by using a simpler design and easier approach.

TABLE 2: Performance evaluation using detection rate (%).

Base classifier	Logistic Regression		J48		Naive Bayes	
Attack	Model 1	Proposed method	Model 1	Proposed method	Model 1	Proposed method
Phf	98.73	100	57	81.3	66.7	71
Teardrop	99.11	100	100	100	100	100
Normal	100	99.9	99.9	99.9	98.6	99
Smurf	97.7	97.7	100	100	100	100
Loadmodule	57.1	71.4	67.4	74.2	85.7	85.7

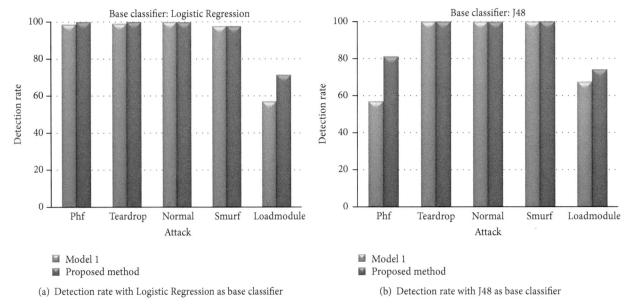

(a) Detection rate with Logistic Regression as base classifier

(b) Detection rate with J48 as base classifier

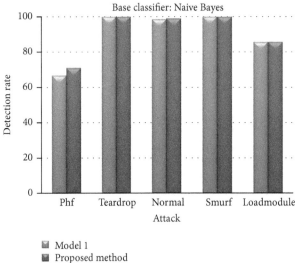

(c) Detection rate with Naive Bayes as base classifier

FIGURE 2: Performance evaluation.

7. Conclusion

In this work, we proposed a novel classifier ensemble method for intrusion detection that is diversified by using two different approaches. That is, it uses different feature sets and training sets both. The methodology also makes use of resampling technique that emphasizes the attack of rare category. The comparison of proposed approach with reference techniques shows significant improvement in detecting the intrusions correctly. The procedure can be further extended to adjust the ensemble size dynamically according to the size of dataset. That is, decision of number of base classifiers to be used for constructing ensemble should be done dynamically. If the size is decided statistically, it may not prove effective for different dataset sizes with varying imbalance ratios. Hence adaptively changing the size by analyzing these factors will help to improve performance with relatively less overhead. Also performance of the approach can be tested for more number of attack categories.

Conflicts of Interest

The authors declare that they have no conflicts of interest.

References

[1] O. Y. Al-Jarrah, O. Alhussein, P. D. Yoo, S. Muhaidat, K. Taha, and K. Kim, "Data randomization and cluster-based partitioning for botnet intrusion detection," *IEEE Transactions on Cybernetics*, vol. 46, no. 8, pp. 1796–1806, 2016.

[2] K. Kumar and S. Singh, "Intrusion Detection Using Soft Computing Techniques," 2016.

[3] S. Rajasegarar, C. Leckie, J. C. Bezdek, and M. Palaniswami, "Centered hyperspherical and hyperellipsoidal one-class support vector machines for anomaly detection in sensor networks," *IEEE Transactions on Information Forensics and Security*, vol. 5, no. 3, pp. 518–533, 2010.

[4] A. L. Buczak and E. Guven, "A survey of data mining and machine learning methods for cyber security intrusion detection," *IEEE Communications Surveys and Tutorials*, vol. 18, no. 2, pp. 1153–1176, 2016.

[5] K.-C. Khor, C.-Y. Ting, and S. Phon-Amnuaisuk, "A cascaded classifier approach for improving detection rates on rare attack categories in network intrusion detection," *Applied Intelligence*, vol. 36, no. 2, pp. 320–329, 2012.

[6] A. A. Aburomman and M. B. Ibne Reaz, "A novel SVM-kNN-PSO ensemble method for intrusion detection system," *Applied Soft Computing Journal*, vol. 38, pp. 360–372, 2016.

[7] Q. S. Qassim, A. M. Zin, and M. J. Ab Aziz, "Anomalies classification approach for network—based intrusion detection system," *International Journal of Network Security*, pp. 1159–1171, 2016.

[8] M. Govindarajan, "Evaluation of ensemble classifiers for intrusion detection," *World Academy of Science, Engineering and Technology, International Journal of Computer, Electrical, Automation, Control and Information Engineering*, vol. 10, no. 6, pp. 876–884, 2016.

[9] Z. Liu, R. Wang, and M. Tao, "SmoteAdaNL: a learning method for network traffic classification," *Journal of Ambient Intelligence and Humanized Computing*, vol. 7, no. 1, pp. 121–130, 2016.

[10] W. Hu, J. Gao, Y. Wang, O. Wu, and S. Maybank, "Online adaboost-based parameterized methods for dynamic distributed network intrusion detection," *IEEE Transactions on Cybernetics*, vol. 44, no. 1, pp. 66–82, 2014.

[11] M. Li, S. Pan, Y. Zhang, and X. Cai, "Classifying networked text data with positive and unlabeled examples," *Pattern Recognition Letters*, vol. 77, pp. 1–7, 2016.

[12] W. Hu, W. Hu, and S. Maybank, "AdaBoost-based algorithm for network intrusion detection," *IEEE Transactions on Systems, Man, and Cybernetics, Part B: Cybernetics*, vol. 38, no. 2, pp. 577–583, 2008.

[13] Z. Yu, J. J. P. Tsai, and T. Weigert, "An automatically tuning intrusion detection system," *IEEE Transactions on Systems, Man, and Cybernetics, Part B: Cybernetics*, vol. 37, no. 2, pp. 373–384, 2007.

[14] N. A. Alrajeh, S. Khan, and B. Shams, "Intrusion detection systems in wireless sensor networks: a review," *International Journal of Distributed Sensor Networks*, vol. 9, no. 5, Article ID 167575, 2013.

9

A Retrieval Optimized Surveillance Video Storage System for Campus Application Scenarios

Shengcheng Ma ⓘ,[1] **Xin Chen ⓘ,**[1] **Zhuo Li ⓘ,**[2] **and Yingjie Yang**[1]

[1]*School of Computer Science, Beijing Information Science and Technology University, Beijing, China*
[2]*Beijing Key Laboratory of Internet Culture and Digital Dissemination Research, School of Computer Science, Beijing Information Science and Technology University, Beijing, China*

Correspondence should be addressed to Xin Chen; chenxin@bistu.edu.cn

Academic Editor: Attila Kertesz

This paper investigates and analyzes the characteristics of video data and puts forward a campus surveillance video storage system with the university campus as the specific application environment. Aiming at the challenge that the content-based video retrieval response time is too long, the key-frame index subsystem is designed. The key frame of the video can reflect the main content of the video. Extracted from the video, key frames are associated with the metadata information to establish the storage index. The key-frame index is used in lookup operations while querying. This method can greatly reduce the amount of video data reading and effectively improves the query's efficiency. From the above, we model the storage system by a stochastic Petri net (SPN) and verify the promotion of query performance by quantitative analysis.

1. Introduction

With the promotion of the smart city, the smart campus, and other projects, the demands of the video surveillance system deployment have become more fine-grained and multipoint. The development tendency of the video surveillance system is moving towards "digital, networked, high-definition, and intelligent" [1]. The number of monitoring devices is increasing, the quality of video is continually improving, and the duration time of the video retention is extending. All these changes increase the amount of data produced by the video surveillance system rapidly. How to effectively organize these mass monitoring video data and how to quickly locate the relevant video in the postverification are the important requirements of surveillance video storage system.

With the development of distributed file systems and cloud storage [2], a large number of surveillance video storage systems are based on the IP-SAN technologies [3]. These technologies ensure system scalability, load balancing, high availability, data backup, and recovery, but these common storage technologies only design storage systems focusing on the writing efficiency of storage. Previous designs concern the ability to write multiple video data concurrently as fast as possible, but the optimal design of video content query is lacking. Some effective video organization methods [4] are proposed, but there is little consideration about the storage of large amounts of video data. However, the campus environment surveillance video data has its unique application characteristics. The surveillance video data is a write-based data. There is no spike or trough in the generation of data. The writing of the monitored video data is sequential. Video data is streaming media data with large file size; compared to the random writing of small size file, the speed of video data writing is fast, because there is not too much OPEN/CLOSE operation. As a kind of evidential data, there is little need for modification after writing. The content of data changes regularly with the school schedule. Query operation is relatively little, but the workload is quite large when it happens. It needs to read and match the mass data which have been stored. Sometimes it needs to intervene in manual operation and the time consumption is huge.

In view of the above summary of campus surveillance video data read and write characteristics, as well as organizational storage problems, we propose a surveillance video storage system CSVS (campus surveillance video storage) for campus applications.

The main contributions of this paper can be summarized as follows:

(1) We use a mature distributed file system to address the video data writing problem, the space scalable problems, data backup, and recovery issues.

(2) We put forward a video key-frame extracted function according to the school schedule time on the impact of video data. Design an index subsystem that combines video metadata with video key frames. This index system can greatly reduce the amount of data read when retrieving. And it can improve the retrieval efficiency and reduce the workload of manual intervention.

(3) We implement the prototype of the CSVS system. The system is modeled by stochastic Petri net that can help us to analyze the efficiency of the real environment in long-time running. According to performance analysis and evaluation, it proves that the number of queries fulfilled by key-frame index is 5 times that of the manual search in the same period.

The rest of this paper is organized as follows. Section 2 summarizes related works of video data storage system. We present a campus surveillance video storage system in Section 3. In particular, we illustrate the architecture of this system and explain how we solve the problem regarding scalability and security, and the organization of data and key frame extraction method are presented in this part. In Section 4, we introduce the experimental environment and conduct the performance evaluation. We conclude this paper in Section 5.

2. Related Work

Because of the development of security system, the surveillance video storage technology has been developed more maturely. According to the characteristics of surveillance video data and SAN storage technology, researchers have proposed a video surveillance storage system based on IP-SAN [5]. Each video frame is stored in a fixed-size data area. And the memory caching technology for video metadata improves search efficiency. But this cache technology is only suitable for data sets with relatively small amount of data. In addition, the memory is a volatile storage device, so it is difficult to guarantee the data recovery after the failure. In article [6], a video data cache VDB (video data buffer) is designed based on the image group GOP, but this design is optimized only for writing. When the cache data area is full, the data will be written to disk and no longer live in the cache, so it is not helpful to the video content retrieval. To speed up writing, a cache write storage system with IO polling mechanism is proposed [7]. Each video stream corresponds to a thread written to disk. When the buffer is full, the thread triggers the write mechanism and flushes all the cache data into the disk. It converts random writing to sequential writing, thereby improving data writing efficiency. However, in the support of data retrieval, only based on the time to optimize the search, it does not support the search based on video content.

A high-performance disk array called ripple-raid for continuous data storage is proposed by [8]. Surveillance video data is a kind of continuous data, so the design features of the program can improve the video data writing efficiency. Their updating strategy and incremental generation of checksum data function not only improve the performance of data writing but also improve the energy efficiency of the system. A surveillance video storage system called THNVR based on SAN is proposed in [9]; this system uses the SQLite database to store metadata information of video. It saves nonstructured surveillance video data with fixed length files. Metadata and video data are indexed separately to improve storage and indexing performance. Fixed-length file can avoid the generation of disk fragmentation, but SQLite only supports relational data and has no high availability considerations. It is not suitable for large data storage.

Le et al. [10] propose a scheme for using SMR (shingled magnetic recording) disks in RAID arrays to accelerate the speed of storage system. Compared to traditional disk write, SMR technology can enlarge the density of data and is suited for saving the log-structure data which is like the surveillance video. A new block I/O scheduling scheme called BID (bulk I/O dispatch) is designed in [11]. By organizing the order of block I/O requests to be served, the BID scheme changes random I/Os into sequential I/Os. This operation can save CPU wait time, so the performance is promoted. Because this scheduler is especially suited for the MapReduce kind of applications and the surveillance videos are almost sequential I/Os, it is not very suitable for video storage system.

In [12], the authors propose a distributed video recording system based on IaaS; the Hadoop HDFS is used as the storage file system, and MapReduce is proposed to analyze the video data. However, with the increasing amount of video data, there is a problem of bottleneck in the metadata center when high concurrent retrieval happened. To solve the problem of high concurrent retrieving, mass storage, and so on, Cao's team proposes a high-performance distributed storage system DVSS [1]; it uses multiple storage nodes to support system linear expansion and to solve the problem of large capacity. It uses the Redis database as metadata index to improve the efficiency of high concurrent retrieval. But its GOP-based video frame operation mode is only optimized for writing. It is not considering the function based on video content retrieval.

3. Design and Implementation of CSVS

The development of video surveillance system, with the digital and network trend, has transformed from the original analog signal transmission, through the digital signal transmission, to the network digital transmission in the present. The DVR (disk video recorder) as the representative of the digital surveillance system is gradually replaced by NVR (network video recorder). DVR combines video control with video storage to make the system more integrated and more applicable, but it can only store data on the disk of the local computer, which limits the size of the system data. NVR has the function of receiving IPC (IP camera) data, video codec, storage, real-time display, and so on. It can also forward the stored video data to other storage systems through the network [13] (Figure 1 shows an example).

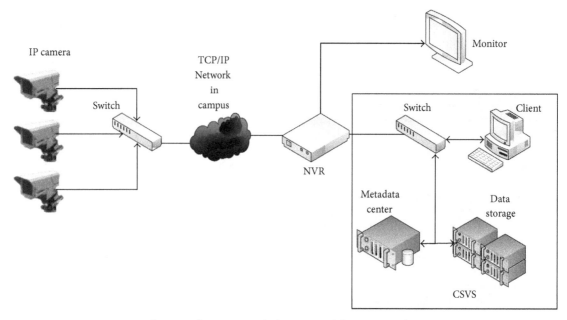

FIGURE 1: Video surveillance system deployment and the position of CSVS system.

The CSVS (campus surveillance video storage) system proposed in this paper is located at the back end of NVR. It provides massive video storage for monitoring system, and it also provides fast and accurate content-based video retrieval.

The implementation goals of CSVS system are as follows: scalability, where the system needs to support massive data storage and storage space scalability, security, where it is required to support data backup, storage, and lost data recovery, Fast query, where metadata information and video data are separately stored in the system, and the index of video frames is generated asynchronously. The query function based on video content is supported.

3.1. CSVS System Architecture.
The CSVS system consists of three parts: the client, the metadata cluster, and the data storage cluster. The metadata cluster includes the video key-frame index center. System structure is shown in Figure 2.

The client of the system is responsible for the initiation of the tasks and the collection of operational results. The client provides internal and external APIs and video data import and export functions based on metadata and video content querys and other operations. All of these operations are launched by the client.

The metadata cluster is responsible for storing metadata information that describes the video sent by the client. The picture data generated by the key-frame extraction task are associated with the metadata information. It also provides search query function to the client. The cluster achieves load balance in order to make all the servers in the cluster undertake the tasks together.

The data storage cluster is responsible for reading and writing of video data. In the form of storage volumes, data replications are stored on different server nodes to ensure backup and achieve automatic recovery when data is abnormal. The entire cluster consists of multiple storage

volumes, and the storage volume is composed of multiple storage service nodes. When a service node fails, the others still guarantee service. Linear extensions of space can be achieved by increasing the storage volumes.

3.2. System Scalability and Data Security.
The metadata cluster is implemented based on MongoDB database, and the metadata information of the video is organized into Bson format for storage [14]. Because metadata information is mainly text, it occupies very little storage space compared to video data, so the main expansion of pressure is in the data storage cluster.

The data storage cluster is implemented based on the GlusterFS distributed file system [15]. According to this application scenario of surveillance video, we select specific features to serve our system. We use the replica function to automatically backup the data and the strip ribbon function to improve the writing performance. The strip ribbon function, which is like the RAID0 technique, makes different disks write different parts at the same time, so it accelerates the speed of writing.

3.3. Organization Form of Data.
In order to provide a fast and accurate retrieval function, we save the metadata and video data in separated way. We save metadata to the Mongodb database cluster in key-value form.

The metadata field includes the video ID, the video name, the shooting position, the start time, the end time, the video duration, the video file size, the video storage path, the key-frame flag, and the key-frame storage path, as shown in Figure 3.

The ID field is the unique identifier of the metadata in the database. Video_name is the file name of the video data. Position is the position information where the video data is recorded; Start_time is the recording start time of the video

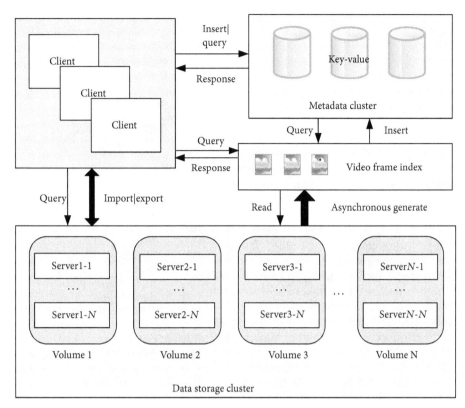

FIGURE 2: Architecture of CSVS.

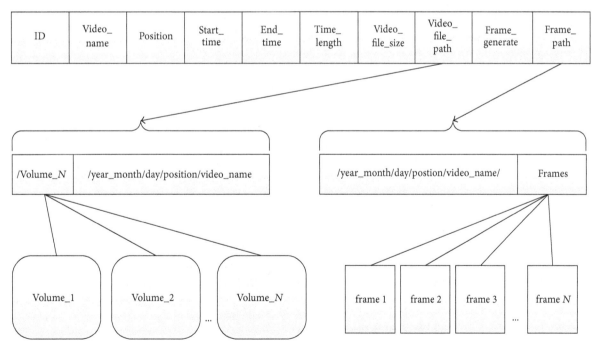

FIGURE 3: Metadata fields.

data. End_time is the shooting end time of the video data. Time_length is the duration of the video data which is equal to the shooting end time minus the shooting start time. Video_file_size is the file size of the video data. Video_file_path field saves the video file storage path. It has two parts: the first part is directory of storage path which represents the number of the storage volumes in the data cluster, and the second part is the directory of the video file to be stored in.

The Frame_generate field is used to identify whether a key-frame group has been generated. The Frame_path field holds the storage path of the key-frame group of the video. This path stores the picture files generated by the asynchronous key frame extraction task, and it provides the index for video based on content retrieval.

3.4. Key-Frame Extraction of Surveillance Video. Surveillance video is different from other videos. The video shooting angle is stabilized. So the video background does not change too much. According to this feature, the difference between the frames in the video is compared with the way of calculating the histogram distance, and the video key frame is extracted [16]. Because the campus has fixed life schedule, the video data content is also regular.

Before class time and at school canteen dinner time, video content is the most abundant, but during the class and night hours, there is no change in the content of the video. If we retrieve video content through the human eye, it will inevitably increase unnecessary workload. If we do match content in each frame of the video by the machines, there is also a huge amount of computation. To solve this problem, combined with the above characteristics, we calculate the histogram difference as the rule to extract the video key frame [17] and build the content index of video.

In the operation of key-frame extraction, the formula for calculating histogram distance [18] has four methods: CORREL, Chi-Square, Bhattacharyya, and INTERSECT.

The CORREL method is defined as

$$d_{\text{correl}}(H_1, H_2) = \frac{\sum_i H_1'(i) \cdot H_2'(i)}{\sqrt{\sum_i H_1'(i) \cdot H_2'(i)}}, \quad (1)$$

where H_1 and H_2 represent two histograms and $H_1'(i)$ is defined as follows:

$$H_k'(i) = H_k(i) - \left(\frac{1}{n}\right)\left(\sum_j H_k(j)\right), \quad (2)$$

where n is the number of the bins.

The Chi-Square formula is as follows:

$$d_{\text{chi-square}}(H_1, H_2) = \sum_i \frac{(H_1(i) - H_2(i))^2}{H_1(i) + H_2(i)}. \quad (3)$$

Bhattacharyya is defined as

$$d_{\text{Bhattacharyya}}(H_1, H_2) = \sqrt{1 - \sum_i \frac{\sqrt{H_1(i) \cdot H_2(i)}}{\sum_i H_1(i) \cdot H_2(i)}}. \quad (4)$$

At last, the INTERSECT method has the following formula:

$$d_{\text{intersect}}(H_1, H_2) = \sum_i \min(H_1(i), H_2(i)). \quad (5)$$

Our strategy for extracting key frames is to use as few frames as possible to summarize the complete video content. In order to improve the computational efficiency, we use the INTERSECT method, which is the minimum and fastest histogram distance calculation method.

```
INPUT: VideoPath, OutputPath, Threshold;
OUTPUT: Frames;
(1)     ret = access(VideoPath);
(2)     if ret == False then
(3)        exiterror_code;
(4)     end if
(5)     ret = access(OutputPath);
(6)     if ret == False then
(7)        mkdir(OutputPath);
(8)     end if
(9)     cap = captureFromFile(VideoPath);
(10)    frame = QueryFrame(cap);
(11)    baseHistogram = CalcHist(Frames);
(12)    while frame = QueryFrame(cap)! = NULL do
(13)       curHistogram = CalcHist(Frames);
(14)       HistogramError = CompareHist
(15)       (baseHistogram, curHistogram,
(16)       COMP_INTERSECT);
(17)       curHistogram = CalcHist(Frames);
(18)       if instogramError < Threshold then
(19)          SaveImage(Frames);
(20)          CopyHist(baseHistogram, curHistogram);
(21)       end if
(22)       ReleaseHist(baseHistogram);
(23)       ReleaseHist(curHistogram);
(24)       ReleaseCap(cap);
(25)    end while
```

ALGORITHM 1: Key-frame extraction.

For implementation of key-frame extraction algorithm description, see Algorithm 1.

The threshold is a floating point variable between 0 and 1. The closer the threshold is to 1, the more key-frames are written. Key-frame naming is a long integer + extension format. The long integer is the sequence number of the frames in the video. A frame sequence number can be used to locate the time point in which the frame appears in the video.

$$\text{Time} = \frac{\text{num}}{\text{frame\_rate}} + 1. \quad (6)$$

For example, if the duration of a video is 1000 seconds and 25 frames per second (frame_rate), the video is composed of 25000 frames. If the key-frame to be queried is the 1024th frame (num), the frame can be matched in the 41 seconds of the video according to (6).

3.5. Writing and Retrieving Data

3.5.1. Data Writing. The writing of the video data is initiated by the client. The client acquires the video data from the NVR. It generates the metadata information based on the video data and starts the writing operation.

The writing procedure is as follows:

(i) Get video data from NVR.

(ii) Read the video data file, parse out the video file, the video camera position, video start time, and end time, calculate the duration of the video, parse out the video file size, generate a video file path, set the flag as 0 which means key-frames extraction is needed, and generate a key-frame storage path.

(iii) Insert data into the metadatabase.

(iv) Write the video data according to the storage path and continue processing the next video data.

(v) Start the asynchronous key-frame extraction task and check which key-frame flag is 0.

(vi) Extract the key frames and write them into storage path and set the flag to 1; writing operation is finished.

3.5.2. Retrieval of Video Data. The retrieval of video data is divided into ordinary retrieval and video content retrieval. Ordinary retrieval only needs to operate on the metadata database. The retrieval of video content is based on the key-frame index.

Ordinary Retrieval Process

(i) According to the search conditions, such as start time, end time, duration, shooting point, or the combination of these conditions, a query can be initiated to the metadatabase by a lookup operation.

(ii) The metadatabase returns all the data entries that match the conditions.

(iii) Parse the video storage path from all of the data entries.

(iv) Read video file directly based on the video storage path.

Video Content Retrieval Process

(i) Search in database based on metadata conditions (the same process as the ordinary retrieval process).

(ii) The metadatabase returns all the data entries that match the conditions.

(iii) Parse the key frame storage paths from the returned items one by one.

(iv) Compare the video content to key-frame group saved in storage path.

(v) Return the closest key frame, parse the video storage path of the frame, and calculate the time appearing in the video.

(vi) Locate the video based on the storage path and the time when it appears.

4. Experiment and Performance Evaluation

4.1. Experimental Environment. CSVS system relies on campus video surveillance system. We use 11 Hikvision DS-2CD5026XYD HD cameras and 1 Hikvision DS-8632N-I8 network video recorder in our system. We use 5 virtual machines to build the cluster of metadata and storage center. Each machine has Intel Xeon 2.5 GHz Core*4, CPU, 12 GB memory, and 100 GB hard disk.

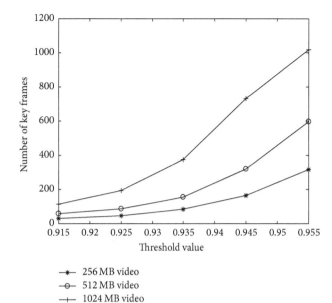

FIGURE 4: Threshold and number of key frames.

4.2. Threshold and Key Frames. According to our key-frame extracting algorithm, the threshold parameter decides the quantity of key frames generated from video. The content of each frame in video changes slowly with time. For calculating the extent of difference between each of the frames, we use histogram distance to measure them. The threshold is the criterion to identify which histogram distance is large enough to represent the frame that needs to be saved. The bigger threshold is, the more frames will be saved.

In Figure 4, we use three different size videos to verify the relationship between threshold and number of key frames. The test video sizes are 256 MB, 512 MB, and 1024 MB. We choose five numerical values of threshold from 0.915 to 0.955 to generate the key frames. The result shows that number of key frames will increase when threshold value gets bigger. Shown as 1024 MB video file, the number of key frames increases from 113 to 1018. A large number of key frames make the index more accurate but take up more storage space. So it is very useful to tune the threshold value to weigh the storage space and the index efficiency.

4.3. Efficiency of Content Retrieval. We have done some exercises to check the working efficiency of key-frame index function. The retrieval time is a criterion to compare our method with the GOP index method without key-frame index. We have obtained the result shown in Figure 5.

We save a group of video files in our CSVS storage system and DVSS system. These files' size is from 64 MB to 2048 MB. We choose a frame of video as target to retrieve in these two systems. The difference value of time cost between two methods will become bigger and bigger when the video files' size is increasing. The retrieval time of common method will rise sharply. By contrast, the key-frame index method will lift the time cost line gently.

TABLE 1: System comparison.

Exist/our work	Storage model	Fault tolerance	Scalability	Retrieval speed	Content retrieval
THNVR	SQLite + FS	Poor	Poor	Low	No
DSFS	CSM	SPOF	Poor	Low	No
DVSS	Redis + logical volume	Strong	Strong	High	No
CSVS	Key-frame + GlusterFS	Strong	Strong	High	Yes

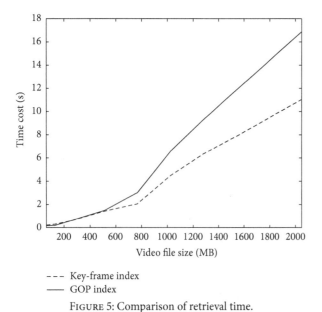

--- Key-frame index
— GOP index

FIGURE 5: Comparison of retrieval time.

TABLE 2: Meaning of transition.

Transition	Meaning
T0	Search from metadata center
T1	Parse result to get path
T2	Retrieve data by path
T3	Match key frames
T4	Retrieve data by key frames
T5	Return video by storage path
T6	Return video and time point by key frames

4.4. Comparison with Relative Work. Considering the function of content retrieval, our storage system has advantages compared with other existing systems. The statistical function results are shown in Table 1.

4.5. Performance Evaluation. Our surveillance video storage system is built in campus and operated by our team. It runs well but the workload is low. How to evaluate the performance in long-time runs if the workload is increasing?

To do the performance evaluation, a transient stochastic state classes method is proposed [19]. The authors provide an approach to continuous time transient analysis. Transitive closure of transitions identifies a transient stochastic graph. It is convenient to map a transient stochastic tree to do the classes analysis. The approach is applicable for any Generalized Semi-Markov Process. It is also suitable for performance evaluation in real-time systems. While this method is complex, Balsamo and his colleagues provide a powerful, general, and rigorous route to product forms in large stochastic models [20]. They present a building block concept composed by a group of logically related places and transitions. The state probability of building block equals the sum of the places' state probability in the group. This technique can effectively avoid the problem of the state space explosion. If the model is complex and difficult to solve, we can adopt this method to address the state space explosion problem. Our purpose is to obtain the stationary

state probability. Therefore we adopt ordinary stochastic Petri nets (SPNs) to model and evaluate the performance.

Stochastic Petri nets is a powerful tool for system performance evaluation [21–23]. In this paper, the basic theory of stochastic Petri nets is applied to model and evaluate performance of storage systems. According to [24], we assume that the firing rates of transitions are independent random variables with (negative) exponential distributions and represent the frequency of the data process for each function in our system. The isomorphic relationship between the stochastic Petri net and the Markov chain is used to calculate the stationary state probability, and the performance evaluation of query efficiency in storage system is provided.

According to the retrieval process in CSVS system, the stochastic Petri nets model is established by using PIPE (Platform Independent Petri Net Editor) tool [25]. As shown in Figure 6, it consists of 8 places, $P0$, $P1$, $P2$, $P3$, $P4$, $P5$, $P6$, and $P7$, and 7 transitions, $T0$, $T1$, $T2$, $T3$, $T4$, $T5$, and $T6$.

$P0$ represents query conditions based on metadata, $P1$ represents the query result based on the video content, $P2$ represents the query result returned by the metadata, $P3$ represents the video storage path, $P5$ represents the key-frame storage path, $P4$ represents the time of the key-frame in the video, $P6$ represents the ordinary retrieval and getting the results, and $P7$ represents the video content retrieval by matching key frame group and finding the results.

Table 2 shows the meaning of each transition in the CSVS system.

The reciprocal of firing rate is service time. We set $\tau = \{\tau_0, \tau_1, \tau_2, \tau_3, \tau_4, \tau_5, \tau_6\}$ as service time. We compare every cost time of data processing functions in CSVS which represent the service time of transitions. Then we get the ratio of them, $T0$, $T1$, $T4$, $T5$ and $T6$ cost one unit of time to process the same amount of data. Retrieving data by path (i.e., $T2$) will cost ten units of time. Matching key frames (i.e., $T3$) will cost two units of time. Above all, $\tau = \{1, 1, 10, 2, 1, 1, 1\}$. All the

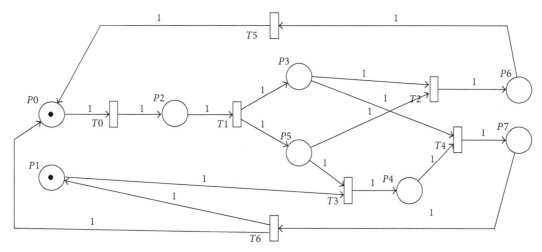

FIGURE 6: Retrieval process in CSVS system modeling by PIPE tool.

data of unit time cost are obtained from our prototype system. Then $\lambda = 1/\tau$; firing rate is $\lambda = \{10, 10, 1, 5, 10, 10, 10\}$.

According to the running time of the function, which corresponds to the transition in our retrieval subsystem, we set the firing rate $\lambda = \{10, 10, 1, 5, 10, 10, 10\}$ for the transitions $T0$, $T1$, $T2$, $T3$, $T4$, $T5$, and $T6$ as the time stochastic parameters subject to exponential distribution. Assuming an initial marking of one token in place $P0$ and $P1$ and no tokens in the rest of places, we can obtain a state matrix:

$$\begin{pmatrix} & P0 & P1 & P2 & P3 & P4 & P5 & P6 & P7 \\ M0 & 1 & 1 & 0 & 0 & 0 & 0 & 0 & 0 \\ M1 & 0 & 1 & 1 & 0 & 0 & 0 & 0 & 0 \\ M2 & 0 & 1 & 0 & 1 & 0 & 1 & 0 & 0 \\ M3 & 0 & 0 & 0 & 1 & 1 & 0 & 0 & 0 \\ M4 & 0 & 1 & 0 & 0 & 0 & 0 & 1 & 0 \\ M5 & 0 & 0 & 0 & 0 & 0 & 0 & 0 & 1 \end{pmatrix}. \quad (7)$$

Let Q be the transition probability matrix, and $X = (x_0, x_1, x_2, x_3, x_4, x_5)$ is the stationary state probability of the above $M0$, $M1$, $M2$, $M3$, $M4$, and $M5$. According to the Markov processes, there are linear equations as follows:

$$XQ = 0$$
$$\sum_i x_i = 1, \quad 0 \leqslant i \leqslant 5. \quad (8)$$

Solve the equations to obtain the stationary state marking probability [26]:

$P[M0] = 0.18182, \; P[M1] = 0.18182.$

$P[M2] = 0.30303, \; P[M3] = 0.15152.$

$P[M4] = 0.0303, \; P[M5] = 0.15152.$

At the same time, we can deduce the stationary state probability of each place:

$P[M(P0) = 1] = P[M0] = 0.18182.$

$P[M(P1) = 1] = P[M0] + P[M1] + P[M2] + P[M4] = 0.69697.$

$P[M(P2) = 1] = P[M1] = 0.18182.$

$P[M(P3) = 1] = P[M2] + P[M3] = 0.45455.$

$P[M(P4) = 1] = P[M3] = 0.15152.$

$P[M(P5) = 1] = P[M2] = 0.30303.$

$P[M(P6) = 1] = P[M4] = 0.0303.$

$P[M(P7) = 1] = P[M5] = 0.15152.$

We focus on $P[M(P6) = 1]$ and $P[M(P7) = 1]$; $P6$ represents ordinary retrieval, and $P7$ represents video content retrieval, and $P[M(P7) = 1]$ is almost equal to $5 * P[M(P6) = 1]$. From the analysis, the retrieval hit count of video content is five times that of ordinary retrieval during the same length of time.

Through the simulation and performance evaluation of the stochastic Petri net, it can be concluded that the CSVS system based on the key-frame index function can effectively improve the efficiency of video retrieval.

5. Conclusions

We propose a video storage system (CSVS) to cope with the problem of the low efficiency of video content retrieval in video storage system; a surveillance video storage system (CSVS) for campus applications is proposed in this paper. While achieving storage space scalability and high data availability, the key-frame extraction technology is applied to the storage index function of CSVS system. In the content-based retrieval operation, we find the video through the key frame and locate the time in seconds when the frame appeared in the video. The CSVS system is modeled and evaluated by stochastic Petri nets. According to the characteristics of stochastic Petri nets and Markov process isomorphism, the stationary probability of the marking is obtained. The probability provides the evidence for analyzing the efficiency of system running. In the light of quantitative analysis above, we can find that the CSVS system with key-frame index can improve the efficiency of query based on video content.

In the follow-up works of CSVS system, the method of key-frame extraction will be studied continually. We will improve the algorithm based on histogram distance calculation and find a more accurate key-frame extraction technique. We also plan to optimize the algorithm for the matching process of the key-frame querying. And we need to further improve the efficiency of retrieval based on video content.

Conflicts of Interest

The authors declare that they have no conflicts of interest.

Acknowledgments

This work was supported by the following: the National Natural Science Foundation of China (nos. 61370065 and 61502040), National Key Technology Research and Development Program of the Ministry of Science and Technology of China (no. 2015BAK12B03-03), and Beijing Municipal Program for Excellent Teacher Promotion (no. PXM2017_014224.000028).

References

[1] S. D. Cao, Y. Hua, D. Feng, Y. Y. Sun, and P. F. Zuo, "High-Performance distributed storage system for large-scale high-definition video data," *Ruan Jian Xue Bao/Journal of Software*, vol. 28, no. 8, 2017, in Chinese.

[2] Z. Zhao, X. Cui, and H. Zhang, "Cloud storage technology in video surveillance," *Advanced Materials Research*, vol. 532-533, pp. 1334–1338, 2012.

[3] W. Zheng and X. J. Zhang, "Research and Application of IP-SAN," *Journal of Electrical and Computer Engineering*, 2003.

[4] J. Calic and E. Izquierdo, "Efficient key-frame extraction and video analysis," in *Proceedings of the International Conference on Information Technology: Coding and Computing, ITCC 2002*, pp. 28–33, USA, April 2002.

[5] J. He, *Study on key technique in video surveillance storage system based on IP-SAN*, Shanghai, Shanghai Jiaotong University, 2011, in Chinese.

[6] JX. Tang, *The software design of storage subsystem for network video surveillance system*, Zhejiang University, Zhejiang, 2013, in Chinese.

[7] M. Jiang, Z. Y. Niu, and S. P. Zhang, "Design and implementation of video surveillance storage system," *Computer Engineering and Design*, vol. 35, no. 12, pp. 4195–4201, 2014 (Chinese).

[8] Z. Z. Sun, Q. X. Zhang, Y. A. Tan, and Y. Z. Li, "Ripple-RAID: A high-performance and energy-efficient RAID for continuous data storage," *Ruan Jian Xue Bao/Journal of Software*, vol. 26, no. 7, pp. 1824–1839, 2015 (Chinese).

[9] J. Y. Wu, Y. Gu, D. P. Ju, and D. S. Wang, "THNVR: Distributed large-scale surveillance video storage system," *Computer Engineering and Applications*, vol. 45, no. 31, pp. 56–59, 2009 (Chinese).

[10] Q. M. Le, A. Amer, and J. Holliday, "SMR Disks for Mass Storage Systems," in *Proceedings of the IEEE 23rd International Symposium on Modeling, Analysis, and Simulation of Computer and Telecommunication Systems, MASCOTS 2015*, pp. 228–231, USA, October 2015.

[11] P. Mishra, M. Mishra, and A. K. Somani, "Bulk I/O storage management for big data applications," in *Proceedings of the 24th IEEE International Symposium on Modeling, Analysis and Simulation of Computer and Telecommunication Systems, MASCOTS 2016*, pp. 412–417, UK, September 2016.

[12] C.-F. Lin, M.-C. Leu, S.-M. Yuan, and C.-T. Tsai, "A framework for scalable cloud video recorder system in surveillance environment," in *Proceedings of the 2012 9th International Conference on Ubiquitous Intelligence & Computing and 9th International Conference on Autonomic & Trusted Computing (UIC/ATC)*, pp. 655–660, IEEE, Fukuoka, September 2012.

[13] H. E. Xiao-Feng, *Analysis and Application of Network Video Recorder (NVR) Storage Technology*, China Science & Technology Information, 2011.

[14] Y. Gu, X. Wang, S. Shen et al., "Analysis of data storage mechanism in NoSQL database MongoDB," in *Proceedings of the 2nd IEEE International Conference on Consumer Electronics - Taiwan, ICCE-TW 2015*, pp. 70-71, June 2015.

[15] P. Zhou, F. Dong, Z. Xu, J. Zhang, R. Xiong, and J. Luo, "ECStor: A Flexible Enterprise-Oriented Cloud Storage System Based on GlusterFS," in *Proceedings of the 4th International Conference on Advanced Cloud and Big Data, CBD 2016*, pp. 13–18, China, August 2016.

[16] G. Liu and J. Zhao, "Key frame extraction from MPEG video stream," in *Proceedings of the 3rd International Symposium on Information Processing, ISIP 2010*, pp. 423–427, China, November 2010.

[17] Y. Yang, F. Dadgostar, C. Sanderson, and B. C. Lovell, "Summarisation of surveillance videos by key-frame selection," in *Proceedings of the 2011 5th ACM/IEEE International Conference on Distributed Smart Cameras, ICDSC 2011*, Belgium, August 2011.

[18] R. Bradski G and A. Kaehler, *Learning OpenCV*, OReilly Media, 2014.

[19] A. Horváth, M. Paolieri, L. Ridi, and E. Vicario, "Transient analysis of non-Markovian models using stochastic state classes," *Performance Evaluation*, vol. 69, no. 7-8, pp. 315–335, 2012.

[20] S. Balsamo, P. G. Harrison, and A. Marin, "Methodological construction of product-form stochastic Petri nets for performance evaluation," *The Journal of Systems and Software*, vol. 85, no. 7, pp. 1520–1539, 2012.

[21] M. K. Molloy, "Performance Analysis Using Stochastic Petri Nets," *IEEE Transactions on Computers*, vol. C-31, no. 9, pp. 913–917, 1982.

[22] A. Marin, S. Balsamo, and P. G. Harrison, "Analysis of stochastic Petri nets with signals," *Performance Evaluation*, vol. 69, no. 11, pp. 551–572, 2012.

[23] S. Distefano, F. Longo, and M. Scarpa, "Marking dependency in non-Markovian stochastic Petri nets," *Performance Evaluation*, vol. 110, pp. 22–47, 2017.

[24] W. M. Zuberek, "Performance evaluation using unbounded timed Petri nets," in *Proceedings of the Third International Workshop on Petri Nets and Performance Models (PNPM89)*, pp. 180–186, 1989.

10

Hybrid Intrusion Detection System for DDoS Attacks

Özge Cepheli,[1] Saliha Büyükçorak,[1,2] and Güneş Karabulut Kurt[1]

[1]*Department of Electronics and Communication Engineering, Istanbul Technical University, 34469 Istanbul, Turkey*
[2]*Gebze Technical University, 41400 Kocaeli, Turkey*

Correspondence should be addressed to Özge Cepheli; irmakoz@itu.edu.tr

Academic Editor: Andrea Ceccarelli

Distributed denial-of-service (DDoS) attacks are one of the major threats and possibly the hardest security problem for today's Internet. In this paper we propose a hybrid detection system, referred to as hybrid intrusion detection system (H-IDS), for detection of DDoS attacks. Our proposed detection system makes use of both anomaly-based and signature-based detection methods separately but in an integrated fashion and combines the outcomes of both detectors to enhance the overall detection accuracy. We apply two distinct datasets to our proposed system in order to test the detection performance of H-IDS and conclude that the proposed hybrid system gives better results than the systems based on nonhybrid detection.

1. Introduction

Distributed denial-of-service (DDoS) attacks stand as a crucial threat to Internet services. A DDoS attack is launched by producing an extremely large amount of traffic to exhaust resources of target systems. As shown in Figure 1, the attack is generally initiated by a single attacker, exploiting and taking control of several devices referred to as zombies. Frequently zombie devices are not aware of the fact that they are being used to perform an attack. The attacker usually makes a sweep operation to determine the devices that are eligible for being used as a zombie, for example, a device with an open port. After this stage, the attack is initiated by the attacker using zombie devices. As the number of zombies can be around hundreds or thousands (and theoretically it is possible to have even more) the detection of the attacker becomes a very hard task.

A number of methods have been proposed to prevent DDoS attacks in the literature, though there is still lack of a methodology addressing all requirements. Therefore, DDoS attacks are still a huge threat to network security. In this paper we propose a novel framework named as hybrid intrusion detection system (H-IDS) to detect DDoS attacks. In this system, in order to achieve more accurate detection we use both anomaly-based and signature-based detection techniques. Anomaly-based detector part of the

proposed H-IDS is designed by using multidimensional Gaussian mixture models (GMMs) from a training dataset, while signature-based detector is formed by using SNORT [1]. In addition to this, we design a node referred to as hybrid detection engine (HDE) in order to control and evaluate outputs of these detectors. The proposed H-IDS enhanced the overall performance of DDoS attack detection and shortened the detection delay through using two detectors separately but in an integrated fashion. The proposed H-IDS can be implemented as a module in any IDS solution, as well as being used as a separate DDoS detection system. For the detection performance evaluation of the proposed hybrid detector, we utilize the widely used DARPA 2000 dataset and a dataset provided by a commercial bank in Turkey during a penetration test. With the H-IDS, true positive rate (TPR) is obtained as 92.1% for DARPA and 99.9% for the commercial bank dataset. The TPR is increased by 27.4% with the proposed H-IDS when compared to the signature-based detector for the dataset DARPA.

The remainder of this paper is organized as follows. In Section 2, a detailed overview of the related literature is given. In Section 3, the proposed H-IDS and its components are detailed along with working principles of this hybrid detector. In Section 4, we evaluate experiments by using two distinct datasets to validate our detection model. We conclude this paper in Section 5.

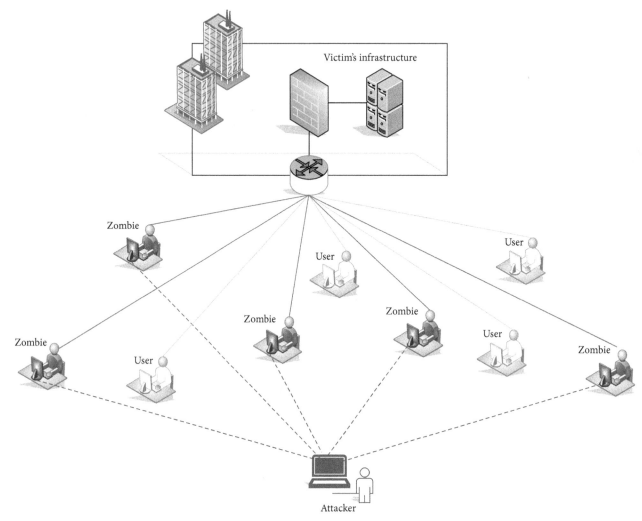

FIGURE 1: DDoS attack model.

2. Literature Overview

The entropy based DDoS countermeasure methods are independent of the specific attack features. In [2], Tao and Yu proposed a flow entropy based DDoS attack detector. The effectiveness of this method is shown thorough various experiments and simulations. The authors offered a mechanism for IP traceback against DDoS attacks based on entropy variations between normal and attack traffic. This is fundamentally different from commonly used packet marking [3, 4]. Xiang et al. proposed a novel low-rate DDoS attacks detector ground on new information metrics (i.e., the generalized entropy metric and the information distance metric). It is demonstrated that these metrics can expressly reduce the false positive rate by using actual DDoS datasets [5, 6].

DDoS attacks can be detected by examining of the network traffic changes. There are many proposed countermeasure methods based on self-similarity of the network. In [7], the authors introduced a real-time DDoS attack detector based on network self-similarity. It is shown that the attacks can be detected effectively and precisely using

the rescaled range algorithm. In the study performed by Chonka et al. [8], by using the property of network self-similarity, a chaotic model is developed to find out DDoS flooding attack traffic. Chen et al. [9] proposed a DDoS intrusion detection algorithm ground on preprocessing network traffic and chaos theory that can detect an anomaly caused either by bursty legitimate traffic or by DDoS flooding attacks. The proposed algorithm's performance is improved by utilizing an exponential smoothing model as forecasting model [10].

Probabilistic methods are also frequently used to detect DDoS attacks. Joshi et al. [11] tested the efficiency of the cloud traceback (CTB) by using a back propagation neural network, named cloud protector, and came to the conclusion that the proposed CTB helps to find out the real sources of attacking packets. Thing et al. [12] proposed a new and high speed nonintrusive traceback technique based on the rationale that packets relating to a particular source-destination flow follow a relatively static path through routers. In [13], the authors introduced a novel anomaly detector ground on hidden semi-Markov model to detect the application layer based DDoS attacks. The effectiveness of this method is demonstrated

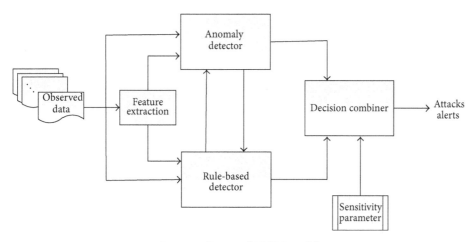

FIGURE 2: Proposed H-IDS model.

by conducting experiments using real web traffic data. The authors reached the conclusion that identifier/location separation can help to prevent DDoS attacks by investigating numerical results based on the real data [14].

In the study performed by Barati et al. [15], by using a machine learning technique composed of genetic algorithm and artificial neural network, it is shown that the accuracy of DDoS attack detection is improved. Yu et al. [16] guaranteed the quality of service for legitimate users by using a dynamic resource allocation strategy to confront DDoS attacks that target individual cloud customers. Thapngam et al. [17] investigated a detector based on the pattern behavior of traffic sources by observing packet arrivals. It is shown through experiments with several datasets that the proposed detector can discriminate DDoS attack traffic from flash crowd with a quick response.

There are also many hybrid detection algorithms proposed for DDoS attack detection. Hwang et al. [18] proposed a hybrid system that combines a signature-based IDS with an anomaly detection system in a cascade structure, achieving twice the detection accuracy of IDS only system. Gómez et al. [19] extended SNORT by adding an anomaly detection preprocessor. Afterwards, various hybrid systems are proposed following the same aim, to have the strengths of both signature- and anomaly-based detection.

In this paper, we propose a novel hybrid intrusion detection system (H-IDS) to accurately detect DDoS attacks. Our developed system makes use of both anomaly-based and signature-based detection methods in parallel. The decision combiner, which is the core processing unit of the system, combines outputs of the detectors and then generates an attack alarm with a tunable sensitivity parameter. Note that our proposed H-IDS differs from the existing studies in the literature, with its parallel detection methodology, due to its flexible nature with decision combiner and having tunable parameters.

3. Hybrid Intrusion Detection System (H-IDS)

The H-IDS designed within this paper is based on an original approach, where the outputs of an anomaly-based detector

and a signature-based detector are collected. The parameters of the detectors are controlled by a centralized node. This node is referred to as hybrid detection engine (HDE). The design goal of this intrusion detection system is to enhance the overall performance of DDoS attack detection, by shortening the detection delay, while increasing the detection accuracy. The block diagram of the proposed H-IDS is shown in Figure 2. As can be seen from this figure, the observed data containing normal traffic and DDoS attacks is processed to extract some features; then processed data is linked to signature-based and anomaly-based detector blocks to detect attacks. Outputs of these detectors are examined by a decision combiner and an alarm gets produced according to sensitivity parameter. The components of the hybrid IDS are explained in detail in the following subsections.

3.1. Feature Extraction and Activity Model Calculation. The first step of the proposed detection process is to analyze the network traffic and to extract some features to build an activity model. In order to give an a priori idea of the detection problem, time analysis of DARPA 2000 dataset is given in Figure 3. From this figure, one can conclude that it is not an easy task to even distinguish between normal and attack periods by solely observing traffic density.

The model of normal network traffic can be achieved by using training data. The training data period can be as short as hours or as long as weeks, similar to the case in DARPA dataset. As the length of the training period affects the model accuracy greatly (but results in a delay), the time required for the training should be optimized in implementation.

In our study, the following features widely used in DDoS studies are selected: packet interarrival times, packet sizes, and protocol frequencies. Note that there are several features that can be used in order to achieve maximum performance.

3.2. Anomaly Detector. In this work, by using multidimensional Gaussian mixture models (GMMs), an anomaly-based detector is designed to distinguish normal and abnormal traffic in the data obtained from the feature extraction step. Expectation maximization (EM) algorithm is used

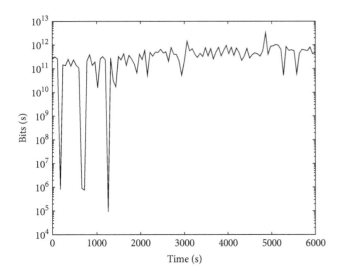

FIGURE 3: Time domain analysis of DARPA data showing traffic density in bits per second (bps) in logarithmic scale.

to estimate the parameters of the GMMs. Afterwards, the distance between the parameters is investigated and detection is made based upon comparison of this distance with defined thresholds, which constitutes the sensitivity parameter in H-IDS. The output of the anomaly detector is defined as isAlarm$_a$.

3.2.1. Expectation Maximization Algorithm. EM algorithm is commonly used for simplifying difficult maximum likelihood estimate (MLE) problems that are frequently encountered in mixture models and cannot be analytically solved [18, 20]. This algorithm is a practical parameter estimation technique and named as parametric methods, where the number of mixture components needs to be known a priori.

Let $X = \{\mathbf{x}_1, \mathbf{x}_2, \ldots, \mathbf{x}_N\}$ be a given dataset, where $\mathbf{x}_i$ is an M-dimensional vector measurement. In a mixture model, the probability density function (pdf), $p(\mathbf{x})$, can be defined as in the following with a finite K component [20–22]:

$$p(\mathbf{x} \mid \Theta) = \sum_k \omega_k p_k(\mathbf{x} \mid \theta_k), \tag{1}$$

where $p_k(\mathbf{x} \mid \theta_k)$ is defined with parameters θ_k over $p(\mathbf{x})$ and refers to each component of the mixture. $k = 1, 2, \ldots, K$ is the number of mixture components and ω_k is the proportion of kth mixing component in the mixture (which are positive and sum to one). $\Theta = (\omega_1, \omega_2, \ldots, \omega_K, \theta_1, \theta_2, \ldots, \theta_K)$ is the complete set of parameters in a mixture model with K components. The component density $p_k(\cdot)$ is a multidimensional Gaussian distribution defined as

$$p_k(\mathbf{x} \mid \theta_k)$$
$$= \frac{1}{(2\pi)^{M/2} \det(\Sigma)^{1/2}} \exp\left[-\frac{1}{2}(\mathbf{x} - \boldsymbol{\mu}_k) \Sigma_k^{-1} (\mathbf{x} - \boldsymbol{\mu}_k)\right], \tag{2}$$

where $\theta_k = (\boldsymbol{\mu}_k, \Sigma_k)$ represents parameters of each component in the mixture. $\boldsymbol{\mu}_k$ is the mean vector of length M and Σ_k is the covariance matrix of size $M \times M$. As defined in (1) and

(2), Gaussian mixture models assume that all the data points are originated from a mixture of a finite number of Gaussian distributions with unknown parameters.

The EM algorithm begins with some initial estimated Θ values and proceeds by iteratively updating Θ until convergence. Each iteration consists of two steps: the expectation step (E-step) and the maximization step (M-step) [22, 23].

In the E-step, the membership coefficients of data point $\mathbf{x}_i$ in component k are calculated by using the current parameter values Θ as [22]

$$\gamma_{ik} = \frac{\omega_k p_k(\mathbf{x}_i \mid \theta_k)}{\sum_{k=1}^{K} \omega_k p_k(\mathbf{x}_i \mid \theta_k)}, \quad 1 \le k \le K, \ 1 \le i \le N, \tag{3}$$

where $\mathbf{x}_i$ refers to the data in the kth mixture and $\sum_{k=1}^{K} \gamma_{ik} = 1$.

In the M-step, parameter values are updated as mean, covariance, and mixing proportion belonging to each component in the mixture model, by using the membership coefficients obtained in the E-step and the dataset. The new mixture weights are calculated as

$$\widehat{\omega}_k = \frac{1}{N} \sum_{i=1}^{N} \gamma_{ik}, \quad 1 \le k \le K. \tag{4}$$

The updated mean values are obtained as

$$\widehat{\boldsymbol{\mu}}_k = \frac{\sum_{i=1}^{N} \gamma_{ik} \mathbf{x}_i}{\sum_{i=1}^{N} \gamma_{ik}}, \quad 1 \le k \le K. \tag{5}$$

Note that this is a vector equation since $\widehat{\boldsymbol{\mu}}_k$ and $\mathbf{x}_i$ are both M-dimensional vectors. Lastly, the covariance matrices of each component are calculated as

$$\widehat{\Sigma}_k = \frac{\sum_{i=1}^{N} \gamma_{ik} (\mathbf{x}_i - \widehat{\boldsymbol{\mu}}_k)(\mathbf{x}_i - \widehat{\boldsymbol{\mu}}_k)^T}{\sum_{i=1}^{N} \gamma_{ik}}, \quad 1 \le k \le K. \tag{6}$$

The M-step is defined by calculating new whole parameters and then membership weights are recalculated by going back to the E-step. The algorithm iteratively calculates estimation values with maximum likelihood for parameters by applying the E- and M-steps, iteratively.

3.2.2. Information Distance Metrics. The information distance metrics can be described as methods to measure the norm of the similarity between two pdfs. In this work, these metrics are used to quantify the distance between the pdfs of normal and abnormal traffic, and the distance $\mathcal{D}$ is chosen as the output of the anomaly detector.

Let $\mathcal{P} = (p_1, p_2, \ldots, p_{\mathcal{T}})$ and $\mathcal{Q} = (q_1, q_2, \ldots, q_{\mathcal{T}})$ represent two discrete probability distributions. The Kullback-Leibler ($\mathcal{KL}$) distance can be described as [2]

$$\mathcal{D}_{\mathcal{KL}}(\mathcal{P}, \mathcal{Q}) = \sum_t p_t \log_2 \frac{p_t}{q_t}. \tag{7}$$

Here, we note that $\mathcal{KL}$ distance cannot be a perfect metric due to the asymmetry properties, which will result in potential problems. There are a few metrics (i.e., Jeffrey distance,

Sibson distance, and Hellinger distance) that can handle the asymmetric problem of the $\mathscr{KL}$ distance [2, 17].

The Sibson distance can be calculated based on the $\mathscr{KL}$ distance as

$$\mathscr{D}_{\mathscr{S}}(\mathscr{P}, \mathscr{Q}) = \frac{1}{2}\left[\mathscr{D}_{\mathscr{KL}}\left(\mathscr{P}, \frac{1}{2}(\mathscr{P} + \mathscr{Q})\right)\right. \tag{8}$$
$$\left. + \mathscr{D}_{\mathscr{KL}}\left(\mathscr{Q}, \frac{1}{2}(\mathscr{P} + \mathscr{Q})\right)\right].$$

In the literature, it is indicated that the Sibson distance is a suitable candidate for DDoS detection in terms of data sensitivity and statistical features [2, 17]. Accordingly, in our numerical experiments, we choose Sibson distance and get a constant value as threshold (α) from HDE and calculated isAlarm$_a$ as

$$\text{isAlarm}_a = \begin{cases} 0, & \mathscr{D}_{\mathscr{S}}(\mathscr{P}, \mathscr{Q}) < \alpha \\ 1, & \mathscr{D}_{\mathscr{S}}(\mathscr{P}, \mathscr{Q}) \geq \alpha. \end{cases} \tag{9}$$

3.3. Signature-Based Detector. Signature-based detector is a type of attack detectors that uses predefined signature sets in order to detect an alarm. The main principle is to extract some features from the traffic data and compare the values of these features with the predefined rules. This process usually does not depend on the application specific cases; however it is usually easier to implement and manage.

The first approach to detect network attacks is to use rule sets. This is the basis of all current IDS or intrusion prevention systems (IPSs) that are used in practice. Hence, there are many tools available, developed by various groups/companies. In addition to the proprietary solutions as the IPS feature of Palo Alto Next Generation Firewall and Juniper IDP, there are also open source signature-based solutions as SNORT [1] and Suricata [24]. In the scope of this study, we used SNORT as our signature-based detector. We specifically choose the rules that are commonly applied in the literature.

SNORT is a free and open source intrusion detection and prevention system (IDPS), created by Martin Roesch in 1998. After the acquisition by Cisco Systems on October 7, 2013, it continues to be developed as an open source solution. It is a widely used solution for network intrusion detection both for practical and for research implementation.

SNORT can be configured to run in three modes:

(i) Sniffer mode, which simply reads the packets off the network and displays them in a continuous stream on the console (screen).

(ii) Packet logger mode, which logs the packets to disk.

(iii) Network IDS mode, which performs detection and analysis on network traffic; this is the most complex and configurable mode.

The rule set of SNORT can be modified for special requirements. Note that different rule sets should be chosen for different performance results. However, in general, extensive optimization of all the rules in the rule set is not aimed

at during the implementation of a signature-based solution. Instead one can use the periodically updated rule sets and further create additional rules for special requirements [24]. Granularity of the rule set can be changed on the run to control the security level of the detector. Hence, the amount of work that is necessary to configure the rule-based approach is less than that of the anomaly-based one. In our system, the granularity of the rule set is set by the HDE. The output of SNORT is denoted by isAlarm$_r$ and calculated based on the value $\mathscr{A}(k)$, where k is the time frame index and $\mathscr{A}(k)$ is chosen as the number of generated alerts within the kth time frame. Using $\mathscr{A}(k)$, isAlarm$_r$ is calculated as

$$\text{isAlarm}_r = \begin{cases} 0, & \mathscr{A}(k) = 0 \\ 1, & \mathscr{A}(k) \geq 0. \end{cases} \tag{10}$$

3.4. Hybrid Detection Engine. In this paper, we make use of anomaly- and signature-based detectors and combine their output in order to enhance the overall performance. Also, the hybrid detection engine controls the sensitivity levels of the anomaly- and signature-based detectors according to the calculated suspicion value. The functionalities of HDE can be listed as follows:

(i) Collecting the outputs of anomaly-based detector and signature-based detector.

(ii) Calculating the attack probability.

(iii) Controlling the security levels of the detectors.

(iv) Updating anomaly detector's normal network model.

(v) Updating the signature-based detectors rule set.

These functionalities are detailed below.

3.4.1. Collecting the Outputs of Detectors. The collection of outputs can be conducted in two different approaches: hard detection and soft detection. In hard detection, the outputs of the detectors are the isAlarm value, which is a binary number indicating if there is an attack or not. In soft detection, the outputs of the detectors are collected as a value referring to probability of an attack. As stated previously, hard detection is used within this study, for the results given in the next section. However, we propose the framework of HDE enabling the use of soft detection.

3.4.2. Calculation of the Attack Probability. The HDE calculates the final decision on the probability of an attack by using the collected outputs of the anomaly- and signature-based detectors. The calculation is performed according to a weighted correlation of the two detector inputs. For a hard decision we can define the process as a function as shown in Figure 4. The overall performance is highly related to the threshold selection (th$_1$ and th$_2$) of this function.

When using more than one detector, there is always a possibility that one of the detectors detects an intrusion while the other does not. In case of such an output (the blue fields in Figure 4), one option is to use "OR" relation, which means to decide on presence of an attack even if only one of the

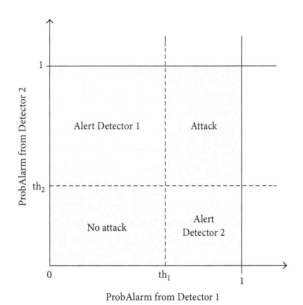

FIGURE 4: Detection function of HDE.

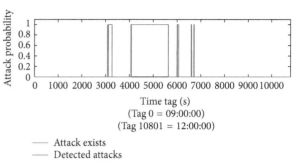

FIGURE 5: Hard detection results of DARPA dataset.

detectors detects an attack. The other option is to use "AND" relation, where the final decision is presence of the attack if and only if both of the detectors report an intrusion.

For the soft decision, one should provide a probability value for every point in the 2D plane in Figure 4.

3.4.3. Controlling the Security Levels of the Detectors. The security levels of the detectors are controlled by HDE, according to the suspicion level (attack probability). In lower security levels, H-IDS is on a light-working mode; the detector works with a less granular traffic model which has a lower processing power requirement. Hence, it is suitable for systems with high volume of data and lower processing abilities. The security levels can be configured in an adaptive manner according to the production requirements.

The security level of anomaly detector controls the detail level of the traffic modeling. The anomaly detector works with the most detailed model (more Gaussian mixture components) in the highest security level, while it uses a simple network activity model (one or two Gaussian mixture components) for other cases.

The security level of the signature-based detector controls the richness of the applied rule set. For lower security levels, a simple rule set is used while in higher security levels the content of the rule set is extended.

3.4.4. Updating Anomaly Detector's Normal Network Model. One of the most important properties of H-IDS is the feedback feature. If there is an attack that one of the detectors detects and the other does not, it usually means that one of the detectors has missed an attack or the other one gave a false alarm. If the signature-based method detects an alarm with a high probability and the anomaly detector has not detected any anomaly, then we should update the normal network activity model accordingly. This way, we can ensure that the normal network model does not involve an attack situation.

3.4.5. Updating the Signature-Based Detectors Rule Set. Similar to the update process of the anomaly-based detector's model, HDE also updates the rule set of the signature-based detectors, if it determines that the rule set has missed an attack. The updates of rule parameters are made directly, while rule additions may require a decision support system.

4. Numerical Results

In order to test the performance of our proposed system, the H-IDS is applied to DARPA 2000 dataset and a dataset acquired from a commercial bank in Turkey. The performance indicators are chosen as true positive rate (TPR) and false positive rate (FPR), which are calculated by

$$
\begin{aligned}
\text{TPR} &= \frac{N_{\text{TD}}}{N_A}, \\
\text{FPR} &= \frac{N_{\text{FD}}}{N_{\text{NA}}},
\end{aligned}
\tag{11}
$$

where N_{TD} and N_{FD} are the numbers of true detection instances and false detection instances, respectively. N_A represents the number of attack packets, whereas N_{NA} is the number of normal (nonattack) packets.

For the first step in our experiments, a low security level H-IDS using the OR rule is implemented with hard decision and the following results are achieved.

4.1. DARPA 2000 Dataset. We used the dataset DARPA 2000 Lincoln Laboratory Scenario (DDoS) 1.0 which is provided by MIT [25]. This dataset has been used in many studies to test performance of DDoS attack detection.

The attack scenario is carried out over multiple network and audit sessions. These sessions have been grouped into 5 attack phases over the course of which the attacker probes, breaks in, installs Trojan mstream DDoS software, and launches a DDoS attack against an off-site server.

The DARPA dataset is analyzed by using the H-IDS with a hard decision system and by using the OR rule. The obtained results for the first and second weeks of the available data are given in Figure 5. Here, we can see that we have detected the attack with 98.7% TPR and 0.73% FPR by utilizing the proposed H-IDS. Using the AND rule instead of the OR rule, we would have 61.6% TPR and 0.01% FPR.

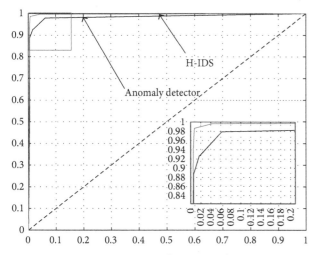

FIGURE 6: ROC curve for DARPA dataset.

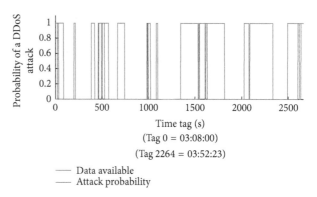

FIGURE 7: Hard detection results of a commercial bank penetration test dataset.

We also analyzed the sole detection rates of anomaly detector and signature-based detector. With anomaly detector we get a 92.1% TPR and 1.8% FPR, and with signature-based detector we get 64.7% TPR and 13.2% FPR. We can easily see that the attack detection with the H-IDS with OR rule outperforms both systems. This result is similar to the results of [18], as the H-IDS outperforms the single detector systems. Please note that as the authors in [18] have used a different dataset, combining the real-life traffic with the MIT/LL attack dataset, it is not possible to make an exact comparison. However, they reported a 47% detection rate for their system at 1% false alarms and 60% detection rate if the false alarms can be tolerated up to 30%. SNORT has almost a constant 30% detection rate with less than 0.1% false alarm rate.

In Figure 6, the receiver operating characteristic (ROC) curves for both anomaly detector and H-IDS are given for various thresholds (α). The curves show the trade-off between the detection rate and false positive rate under various attacks. Our detection scheme achieves closer to ideal detection performance than the sole use of anomaly detector. This result proves the effectiveness of our H-IDS detection mechanism.

4.2. Dataset of a Commercial Bank from a Penetration Test. The dataset provided by a commercial bank includes banking network data in production and a DDoS attack which is deliberately performed by 400 nodes (zombies) from Amazon.com servers to one web server in the bank's network. There were several ICMP echo attacks within a 45-minute period, each active for 3–7 minutes. The dataset contains 17239 unique IP addresses as destination IP where only one of them is the attack target. The dataset is analyzed and a hard decision system is made on available data. The results are given in Figure 7. Here, our system has a 99.9% TPR and 0.01% FPR, which is very successful. However please note that this particular DDoS attack was easy to detect scenario that is deployed in a penetration test, with very little background traffic and a traceable behavior. The detection

performance would probably be lower if more stealthy attacks were performed, especially when attackers try to evade traces that are detectable by the signature-based detector. However even in this case the anomaly detector may detect changes in the network model.

5. Conclusion

In this paper we propose a novel hybrid detection system referred to as H-IDS, which is composed of anomaly-based and signature-based detection techniques for more accurate DDoS attack detection. The proposed detection system can be adopted to networks with varying traffic patterns due to the flexibility provided through the used decision combiner and the associated sensitivity parameter. We test the proposed H-IDS's performance against systems based on nonhybrid detection by using two distinct datasets (i.e., DARPA and a commercial bank penetration test). The results are satisfactory, which shows that the proposed hybrid system can be an efficient solution in the DDoS detection process. We also state that more sophisticated DDoS attacks may evade the signature-based detector rules, which are commonly known, and the system performance may decrease as the detection success solely depends on the anomaly detector. Also the training need of anomaly detector stands as a limitation on the overall system performance. The training data may not reflect the real network model in a practical system or even may be unavailable, which may result in decreased performance. Improvements to the present system, including the enhancement of aforementioned limitations, are left as future work.

Competing Interests

The authors declare that they have no competing interests.

Acknowledgments

This work was supported in part by the ITEA2 Project ADAX and the TUBITAK under Grant no. 9130016.

References

[1] Snort, http://www.snort.org/.

[2] Y. Tao and S. Yu, "DDoS attack detection at local area networks using information theoretical metrics," in *Proceedings of the 12th IEEE International Conference on Trust, Security and Privacy in Computing and Comm*, pp. 233–240, Melbourne, Australia, July 2013.

[3] S. Yu, W. Zhou, R. Doss, and W. Jia, "Traceback of DDoS attacks using entropy variations," *IEEE Transactions on Parallel and Distributed Systems*, vol. 23, no. 3, pp. 412–425, 2012.

[4] S. Yu, W. Zhou, and R. Doss, "Information theory based detection against network behavior mimicking DDoS attacks," *IEEE Communications Letters*, vol. 12, no. 4, pp. 318–321, 2008.

[5] Y. Xiang, K. Li, and W. Zhou, "Low-rate DDoS attacks detection and traceback by using new information metrics," *IEEE Transactions on Information Forensics and Security*, vol. 6, no. 2, pp. 426–437, 2011.

[6] M. H. Bhuyan, D. K. Bhattacharyya, and J. K. Kalita, "Information metrics for low-rate DDoS attack detection: a comparative evaluation," in *Proceedings of the 7th International Conference on Contemporary Computing (IC3 '14)*, pp. 80–84, IEEE, Noida, India, August 2014.

[7] Y. Xiang, Y. Lin, W. L. Lei, and S. J. Huang, "Detecting DDOS attack based on network self-similarity," *IEE Proceedings: Communications*, vol. 151, no. 3, pp. 292–295, 2004.

[8] A. Chonka, J. Singh, and W. Zhou, "Chaos theory based detection against network mimicking DDoS attacks," *IEEE Communications Letters*, vol. 13, no. 9, pp. 717–719, 2009.

[9] Y. Chen, X. Ma, and X. Wu, "DDoS detection algorithm based on preprocessing network traffic predicted method and chaos theory," *IEEE Communications Letters*, vol. 17, no. 5, pp. 1052–1054, 2013.

[10] X. Wu and Y. Chen, "Validation of chaos hypothesis in NADA and improved DDoS detection algorithm," *IEEE Communications Letters*, vol. 17, no. 12, pp. 2396–2399, 2013.

[11] B. Joshi, A. S. Vijayan, and B. K. Joshi, "Securing cloud computing environment against DDoS attacks," in *Proceedings of the International Conference on Computer Communication and Informatics (ICCCI '12)*, pp. 1–5, IEEE, Coimbatore, India, January 2012.

[12] V. L. Thing, M. Sloman, and N. Dulay, "Locating network domain entry and exit point/path for DDoS attack traffic," *IEEE Transactions on Network and Service Management*, vol. 6, no. 3, pp. 163–174, 2009.

[13] Y. Xie and S.-Z. Yu, "Monitoring the application-layer DDoS stacks for popular websites," *IEEE/ACM Transactions on Networking*, vol. 17, no. 1, pp. 15–25, 2009.

[14] H. Luo, Y. Lin, H. Zhang, and M. Zukerman, "Preventing DDoS attacks by identifier/locator separation," *IEEE Network*, vol. 27, no. 6, pp. 60–65, 2013.

[15] M. Barati, A. Abdullah, N. I. Udzir, R. Mahmod, and N. Mustapha, "Distributed Denial of Service detection using hybrid machine learning technique," in *Proceedings of the 4th International Symposium on Biometrics and Security Technologies (ISBAST '14)*, pp. 268–273, Kuala Lumpur, Malaysia, August 2014.

[16] S. Yu, Y. Tian, S. Guo, and D. O. Wu, "Can we beat DDoS attacks in clouds?" *IEEE Transactions on Parallel and Distributed Systems*, vol. 25, no. 9, pp. 2245–2254, 2014.

[17] T. Thapngam, S. Yu, W. Zhou, and G. Beliakov, "Discriminating DDoS attack traffic from flash crowd through packet arrival patterns," in *Proceedings of the IEEE Conference on Computer Communications Workshops (INFOCOM WKSHPS '11)*, pp. 952–957, Shanghai, China, April 2011.

[18] K. Hwang, M. Cai, Y. Chen, and M. Qin, "Hybrid intrusion detection with weighted signature generation over anomalous internet episodes," *IEEE Transactions on Dependable and Secure Computing*, vol. 4, no. 1, pp. 41–55, 2007.

[19] J. Gómez, C. Gil, N. Padilla, R. Baños, and C. Jiménez, "Design of a snort-based hybrid intrusion detection system," in *Distributed Computing, Artificial Intelligence, Bioinformatics, Soft Computing, and Ambient Assisted Living*, pp. 515–522, Springer, Berlin, Germany, 2009.

[20] R. A. Redner and H. F. Walker, "Mixture densities, maximum likelihood and the EM algorithm," *SIAM Review*, vol. 26, no. 2, pp. 195–239, 1984.

[21] G. J. McLachlan and T. Krishnanl, *The EM Algorithm and Extensions*, Wiley Series in Probability and Statistics, 2nd edition, 2008.

[22] J. Bilmes, "A gentle tutorial of the EM algorithm and its application to parameter estimation for Gaussian mixture and hidden Markov models," Tech. Rep. TR-97-021, International Computer Science Institute (ICSI), 1997.

[23] J. Rennie, "A short tutorial on using expectation-maximization with mixture models," 2004, http://people.csail.mit.edu/jrennie/writing/mixtureEM.pdf.

[24] E. Albin and N. C. Rowe, "A realistic experimental comparison of the Suricata and Snort intrusion-detection systems," in *Proceedings of the 26th IEEE International Conference on Advanced Information Networking and Applications Workshops (WAINA '12)*, pp. 122–127, Fukuoka, Japan, March 2012.

[25] MIT Lincoln Laboratory, Information Systems Technology, 2015, http://www.ll.mit.edu/ideval/data/2000data.html.

11

User Utility Oriented Queuing Model for Resource Allocation in Cloud Environment

Zhe Zhang and Ying Li

Institute of Software, Nanyang Normal University, Nanyang, Henan 473061, China

Correspondence should be addressed to Ying Li; lying1024@163.com

Academic Editor: James Nightingale

Resource allocation is one of the most important research topics in servers. In the cloud environment, there are massive hardware resources of different kinds, and many kinds of services are usually run on virtual machines of the cloud server. In addition, cloud environment is commercialized, and economical factor should also be considered. In order to deal with commercialization and virtualization of cloud environment, we proposed a user utility oriented queuing model for task scheduling. Firstly, we modeled task scheduling in cloud environment as an $M/M/1$ queuing system. Secondly, we classified the utility into time utility and cost utility and built a linear programming model to maximize total utility for both of them. Finally, we proposed a utility oriented algorithm to maximize the total utility. Massive experiments validate the effectiveness of our proposed model.

1. Introduction

Providers of cloud services usually provide different computing resources with different performances and different prices, and the requirements of users for performance and cost of resources differ greatly too. So how to allocate available resources for users to maximize the total system utilization is one of the most important objectives for allocating resources and scheduling tasks [1] and is also a research focus in cloud computing.

Traditional resource allocation models mainly focus on the response or running time, saving energy of the whole system, and fairness of task scheduling and do not take user utility into consideration [2]. However, the utility of a user in cloud environment is the usage value of services or resources, and it describes how the user is satisfied with the proposed services or resources while occupying and using them [3, 4]. In order to maximize the total utility of all users in cloud environment, it is necessary to analyze and model user utility first and then optimize it to get a maximum [5]. The modeling of user utility is very complex, as it needs a formal description considering many factors, such as the processing time that tasks have passed by [6], the ratio of finished tasks [7], the costs of finished and unfinished tasks [8], and the parallel speedup [9].

In a cloud server, requests of users, called tasks, come randomly, and a good description of these tasks is the Poisson distribution assumption. At the same time, under the commercialization constraint of the cloud environment, the utility of cloud server becomes much more important. In this paper, we formalized and quantified the problem of task scheduling based on queuing theory, divided the utility into time utility and cost utility, and proposed a linear programming method to maximize the total utility. The contributions of the paper are as follows:

(i) We modeled task scheduling as $M/M/1$ queuing model and analyzed related features in this queuing model.

(ii) We classified utility into time utility and cost utility and built a linear programming method to maximize total utility for each of them.

(iii) We proposed a utility oriented and cost based scheduling algorithm to get the maximum utility.

(iv) We validated the effectiveness of the proposed model with massive experiments.

The rest of the paper is organized as follows. In Section 2, we review related works about resource allocation and task scheduling in cloud computing. In Section 3, we formalize the tasks in cloud environment based on the queuing theory, define a random task model for random tasks, describe our proposed user utility model, and design a utility oriented time-cost scheduling algorithm. Experiments and conclusion are given in Sections 4 and 5, respectively.

2. Related Works

In cluster systems that provide cloud services, there is a common agreement in researchers that the moments, when tasks come into the system, conform to the Poisson distribution, and both the intervals between two coming tasks and the serviced time of tasks are exponentially distributed. In this situation, heuristic task scheduling algorithms, such as genetic algorithm and ant colony algorithm, have better adaptability than traditional scheduling algorithms. However, the deficit of heuristic algorithms is that they have complex problem-solving process, so they can only be applied in small cluster systems. The monstrous infrastructure of cloud systems usually has many types of tasks, a huge amount of tasks, and many kinds of hardware resources, which makes heuristic algorithms unsuitable.

There are a lot of researches about resource allocation or task scheduling in cloud environment, especially for the MapReduce programming schema [10]. Cheng et al. [11] proposed an approximate algorithm to estimate the remaining time (time to end) of tasks in MapReduce environment and the algorithm scheduled tasks with their remaining time. Chen et al. [12] proposed a self-adaptive task scheduling algorithm, and this algorithm computed the running progress (ratio of time from beginning to total running time) of the current task on a node based on its historical data. The advantage of [12] is that it can compute remaining time of tasks dynamically and is more suitable to heterogeneous cloud environment than [11]. In addition, Moise et al. [13] designed a middleware data storage system to improve the performance and ability of fault tolerance.

Traditional task scheduling algorithms mainly focus on efficiency of the whole system. However, some researchers introduce economic models into task scheduling, and the basic idea is optimizing resource allocation by adjusting users' requirements and allocating resources upon price mechanism [14]. Xu et al. [15] proposed a Berger model based task scheduling algorithm. Considering actual commercialization and virtualization of cloud computing, the algorithm is based on the Berger social allocation model and adds additional cost constraints in optimization objective. According to experiments on the CloudSim platform, their algorithm is efficient and fair when running tasks of different users. In addition, with respect to the diversity of resources in cloud environment, more researchers believe that the diversity will increase as time goes on with update of hardware resources. In order to alleviate this phenomenon and ensure quality of services, Yeo and Lee [16] found that while the resources were independently identically distributed, dropping resources

that needed three times the number of minimal response time could make the whole system use less total response time and thus less energy.

The study of random scheduling began in 1966, and Rothkopf [17] proposed a greedy optimal algorithm based on the weights of tasks and expected ratios of finished time to total time. If all tasks had the same weights, then this algorithm became the shortest expected processing time algorithm. Möhring et al. [18] proved the optimal approximation for scheduling tasks with random finished time. They began with the relaxation of linear programming, studied the problem of integer linear programming for systems with homogeneous tasks, and got an approximate solution with the lower limit of the linear programming. Based on the above research, Megow et al. [19] proposed a better optimal solution with better approximation. In addition, Scharbrodt et al. [20] studied how to schedule independent tasks randomly. They analyzed the problem of scheduling n tasks on m machines randomly and gave the worst performance of random scheduling under homogeneous environment theoretically, and their result was the best among related works.

All of the above algorithms focus on the response or running time of users' requirements, saving energy of the whole system and fairness of tasks, and do not take user utility into consideration. However, utility of users is very important in cloud service systems. In order to maximize the total utility of all users in cloud environment, we analyze and model user utility first and then optimize it to get a maximal solution.

In addition, Nan et al. [21] studied how to optimize resource allocation for multimedia cloud based on queuing model, and their aim is to minimize the response time and the resource cost. However, in this paper, we deal with commercialization and virtualization of cloud environment, and our aim is maximizing utility. Xiao et al. [22] presented a system that used virtualization technology to allocate data center resources dynamically. Their aim is to minimize the number of servers in use considering the application demands and utility, whereas in this paper we aim to maximize the system's total utility under a certain cloud environment.

3. Proposed Model

3.1. Queuing Model of Tasks. In this paper, we describe randomness of tasks with the $M/M/1$ model of queuing theory, and the model is illustrated in Figure 1. The model consists of one server, several schedulers, and several computing resources. When user tasks are submitted, the server analyzes and schedules them to different schedulers and adds them to local task queue of the corresponding scheduler. Finally, each scheduler schedules its local tasks to available computing resources. In Figure 1, $t(d)$ is the waiting time of a task in the queue and $t(e)$ is the running time.

3.2. Modeling Random Tasks. In the following, we will analyze the waiting time, running time, and queue length of the proposed $M/M/1$ model.

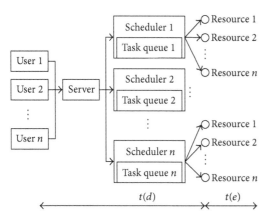

FIGURE 1: Scheduling model of user tasks in cloud environment.

Definition 1. If the average arrival rate of tasks in a scheduler is λ, the average service rate of tasks in a scheduler is μ, and then the service intensity ρ is

$$\rho = \frac{\lambda}{\mu}. \qquad (1)$$

The service intensity describes the busyness of the scheduler. When ρ approaches zero, the waiting time of tasks is short, and the scheduler has much idle time; when ρ approaches one, the scheduler has less idle time, and thus tasks would have long waiting time. Generally speaking, the average arrival rate should be equal to or smaller than the average service rate, otherwise there will be more and more waiting tasks in the scheduler.

Definition 2. If we denote the expected length of tasks in a scheduler as L, the expected length of tasks in queuing as L_q, the expected total time (including both waiting time and running time) of a task as W, and the expected waiting time of a task in queuing as W_q, then we have the following equations according to queuing theory [17]:

$$
\begin{aligned}
L &= \frac{\lambda}{(\mu - \lambda)} = \rho(1 - \rho) \\
L_q &= \frac{\lambda^2}{\mu(\mu - \lambda)} = \rho^2(1 - \rho) = L \cdot \rho \\
W &= \frac{1}{(\mu - \lambda)} \\
W_q &= \frac{\lambda}{\mu(\mu - \lambda)} = W \cdot \rho.
\end{aligned}
\qquad (2)
$$

In addition, let $P_n = P\{N = n\}$ be the possibility of number of tasks in a scheduler at any moment; then, we have the following equation:

$$P_n = \rho(1 - \rho). \qquad (3)$$

If $n = 0$, then P_0 is the possibility that all virtual machines are idle.

3.3. Model of User Utility

3.3.1. Time Utility of Tasks. As we can see from Figure 1, the total time that a user takes from submitting a request to getting the result includes both waiting time $t(d)$ and running time $t(e)$. Here, the computing resources are virtual resources managed by virtual machines. Let T be total time; then, we have

$$T = t(d) + t(e). \qquad (4)$$

In (4), the running time $t(e)$ is the sum of used time $t(f)$ and remaining time $t(u)$; that is,

$$t(e) = t(f) + t(u). \qquad (5)$$

In order to calculate the time requirement of a task, the system needs to calculate the remaining time $t(u)$ and schedules $t(u)$ for different tasks to different virtual machines.

For analyzing the remaining time, we classified tasks into set $P = \{p_i \mid 1 \leq i \leq m\}$ and nodes into set $V = \{p_j \mid 1 \leq j \leq n\}$. According to statistical computing, we can get the average executing rate of task p_i on node v_j; that is, $R = \{r_{i,j} \mid 1 \leq i \leq m, \ 1 \leq j \leq n\}$, and then the remaining time of p_i on v_j is

$$t(u)_{i,j} = \frac{(w - w_u)}{r_{i,j}}, \qquad (6)$$

where w is the number of total tasks and w_u is the number of finished tasks. For computing intensive tasks, w is the total input data and w_u is the already processed input data. Schedulers schedule tasks on virtual machine resources according to their remaining time and assure all tasks are finished on time.

A task can be executed either on one virtual machine or on n virtual machines in parallel, while being divided into m subtasks. We denoted the subtask set as $D = \{d_k \mid 1 \leq k \leq m\}$. While these subtasks are executed on different virtual machines, especially different physical nodes, the communication cost increases, and we use speedup to measure the parallel performance

$$s = \frac{T_1}{T_p}, \qquad (7)$$

where T_1 is the time of a task in one node and T_p is the time of a task in p nodes. In order to make sure $s \leq S_0$, all subtasks run in parallel, and total time of the task is

$$T = t(d) + \max\{t(e)_{k,j}\}, \qquad (8)$$

where $t(e)_{k,j}$ is the time of subtask d_k on v_j and $\max\{t(e)_{k,j}\}$ is the maximal time of all subtasks.

3.3.2. Cost Utility of Tasks. In this paper, we assume that the cost rate of nodes is proportional to CPU and I/O speed, and tasks of different types consume different energy, different bandwidth, and different resource usage. So different tasks will have different cost rates.

Definition 3. Let $C = (c_{i,j} \mid 1 \leq i \leq m, \; 1 \leq j \leq n)$ be the cost matrix of task p_i on node c_j, and then total cost of a task is the product of node cost and running time; that is,

$$M = C \times T = \sum_{i=1}^{m} \sum_{j=1}^{n} \left(c_{i,j} \times t(e)_{i,k,j} \right), \qquad (9)$$

where $c_{i,j}$ is the unit cost of task p_i on node v_j and $t(e)_{i,k,j}$ is the time of subtask d_k on node v_j.

3.3.3. Formalization and Optimization of User Utility

Definition 4. Let the time utility function be U_t and let the cost utility function be U_c; then, the total utility is

$$U = a \times U_t + b \times U_c, \qquad (10)$$

where $a + b = 1, 0 \leq a \leq 1$ and $0 \leq b \leq 1$.

In (10), both time utility and cost utility are between 0 and 1 and a and b are the weights of time utility and cost utility, respectively.

The aim of utility oriented task scheduling is to maximize the total utility, and the constraints are expected time of tasks, expected cost, finished rate, speedup, and so on. In this paper, we classify user tasks into time sensitive and cost sensitive.

For time sensitive user tasks, change of running time for a task will affect the time utility a lot, and its definition is as follows.

Definition 5. The utility model of time sensitive user tasks is defined by the following equations:

$$U = a \times U_t + b \times U_c,$$

$$U_t = \frac{k}{(\ln(t-a) \times b)}, \qquad (11)$$

$$U_c = a \times c + b.$$

The constrains are

$$F(D) = 1, \qquad (12)$$

$$0 \leq UT < U_t \leq 1, \qquad (13)$$

$$0 \leq UC < U_c \leq 1, \qquad (14)$$

$$t(d) + t(e) < T_0, \qquad (15)$$

$$\frac{L_q}{\lambda} < T_1, \qquad (16)$$

$$\max\left\{ t(e)_{k,j} \right\} < T_2, \qquad (17)$$

$$C \times T < M_0, \qquad (18)$$

$$s > S_0, \qquad (19)$$

where D is the set of subtasks for all tasks, and the aim is to maximize total utility U.

For cost sensitive user tasks, change of running cost for a task will affect the cost utility a lot, and its definition is as follows.

Definition 6. The utility model of cost sensitive user tasks is defined by the following equations:

$$U = a \times U_t + b \times U_c,$$

$$U_c = \frac{k}{(\ln(c-a) \times b)}, \qquad (20)$$

$$U_t = a \times t + b.$$

The constrains are

$$F(D) = 1, \qquad (21)$$

$$0 \leq UT < U_t \leq 1, \qquad (22)$$

$$0 \leq UC < U_c \leq 1, \qquad (23)$$

$$t(d) + t(e) < T_0, \qquad (24)$$

$$\frac{L_q}{\lambda} < T_1, \qquad (25)$$

$$\max\left\{ t(e)_{k,j} \right\} < T_2, \qquad (26)$$

$$C \times T < M_0, \qquad (27)$$

$$s > S_0. \qquad (28)$$

In both Definitions 5 and 6, their aims are maximizing the total utility U, but the differences are the computation of U_c and U_t. Based on the above definitions, we propose a utility oriented and cost based scheduling algorithm. The details of the algorithm are as follows:

(1) Analyze user type for each user and select computing equations for U_c and U_t.

(2) Initialize parameters in constraints for $UT, UC, T_0, T_1, T_2, M_0$, and S_0.

(3) Compute L_q and W_q for each scheduler according to (1) to (3).

(4) With the results of step (3), tag X schedulers with least waiting time.

(5) Input some data into the X schedulers and set the highest priority for these tasks.

(6) Execute the above tasks, and record the running time and cost (see Pseudocode 1).

(7) Predict running time, cost, and corresponding utility of all tasks with time and cost of results from step 6, and tag the scheduler with the maximal utility.

(8) Schedule tasks in the scheduler with maximal utility, and optimize user utility (see Pseudocode 2).

(9) Wait until all tasks finish, and record the running time, cost, and corresponding utility.

```
if (user task is time sensitive) {
    select nodes with quickest speed, execute the above tasks, such that s < S_0;
} else {
    Select nodes with lowest cost, execute the above tasks, such that s < S_0;
}
```

PSEUDOCODE 1

```
initialize upgrade = 1;
while (task is time sensitive and upgrade = 1) {
    let previous user of current be current user;
    unit time cost of current user = unit time cost × (1 + v%);
    unit time cost of previous user = unit time cost × (1 − w%);
    if (both cost of current user and previous user do not decrease) {
        upgrade = 1;
    else {
        upgrade = 0;
        rescore current user bo be current user;
    }
}
```

PSEUDOCODE 2

TABLE 1: Hardware configuration parameters.

Number	CPU	Amount	Memory (GB)
1	4-core, 3.07 GHz	10	4
2	4-core, 2.7 GHz	10	4

4. Experiments

4.1. Experimental Setup. We do experiments on two hardware configurations and the configurations are in Table 1. Both of the two hardware configurations run on CentOS5.8 and Hadoop-1.0.1.

There are total 20 computing nodes in our experimental environment, and each computing node starts up a virtual computing node. We start 10 schedulers, and each scheduler manages 2 virtual nodes (computing nodes). The application that we use in the experiments is WordCount.

According to (1) to (3), we computed the service intensity ρ, the expected number of tasks in a scheduler L, the expected length of queuing L_q, the expected finishing time of tasks W, and the expected waiting time of queuing W_q. Figure 2 describes the expected waiting time $T(w)$ on each scheduler. As we can see from the figure, the waiting time from schedulers 1, 3, 5, and 7 satisfied (14) and (23), and thus we can copy and execute some subtasks (data with size 1 KB) on them. If the user task is time sensitive, then we run the task on node with faster speed; and if the user is cost sensitive, then we run the task on node with lower cost.

4.2. Experiments for Time Sensitive User Utility Model. In order to select the parameters for time utility and cost utility functions, we normalize them first and get the following

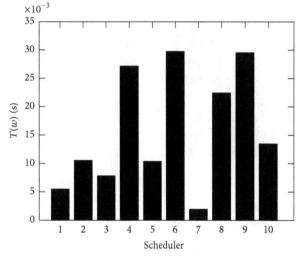

FIGURE 2: Expected waiting time for each scheduler.

equations. Figure 3 describes the curves of the following two equations:

$$U_t = \frac{8}{(\ln(t - 20) \times 5)},$$
$$U_c = -\left(\frac{1}{63}\right) \times c + \frac{61}{63}. \tag{29}$$

Based on running time and rate, total time, cost, and utility from schedulers 1, 3, 5, and 7, we set $a = 0.7$ and $b = 0.3$ in (10). Under constrains from (12) to (19), we compute the total utility. In Figure 4, U_t is the predicted time utility, U_c is the predicted cost utility, U' is the predicted total utility, U is

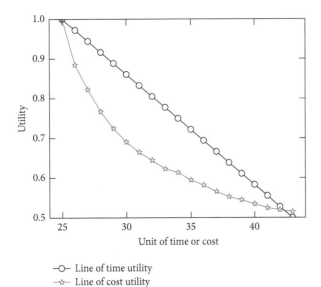

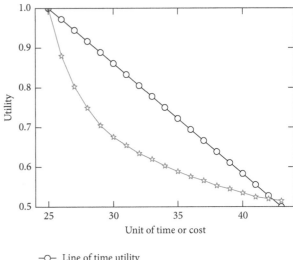

FIGURE 3: Time and cost utility lines for time sensitive user tasks.

FIGURE 5: Time and cost utility lines for cost sensitive user tasks.

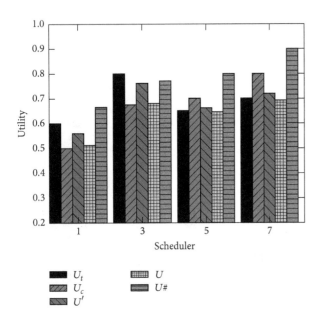

FIGURE 4: Utility distribution of time sensitive user tasks.

4.3. Experiments for Cost Sensitive User Utility Model.

In order to select the parameters of time utility and cost utility functions for cost sensitive user tasks, we also normalize them and get the following two equations. Figure 5 describes the curves of the following two equations:

$$U_t = -\left(\frac{1}{63}\right) \times t + \frac{61}{63},$$

$$U_c = \frac{8}{(\ln(c - 20) \times 5)}. \tag{30}$$

From Figure 6 we can see that the predicted total utility U' in scheduler 5 is the highest, and if we schedule tasks on scheduler 5, we would have the highest actual total utility $U\#$. So if user tasks have different time and cost requirements, we can choose different computing nodes to execute them and make the total utility maximal. In addition, after rescheduling the tasks, all tasks have higher actual total utility $U\#$ than predicted utility U' and actual total utility U, which validates the effectiveness of our proposed algorithm.

4.4. Comparison Experiments.

In this experiment, we selected 10 simulating tasks and compared our algorithm with both Min-Min and Max-Min algorithms. The Min-Min algorithm schedules minimum task to the quickest computing node every time, and the Max-Min algorithm schedules maximum task to the quickest computing node every time. We implemented two algorithms for both time sensitive and cost sensitive user tasks and denoted them as MaxUtility-Time and MaxUtility-Cost. The experimental result is in Figure 7.

In Figure 7, the total utilities of MaxUtility-Time and MaxUtility-Cost algorithms are higher than the other two algorithms and are also stable; both Min-Min and Max-Min algorithms have lower total utilities, and their values fluctuate very much. Both Min-Min and Max-Min algorithms only consider the running time of tasks and ignore requirements of

the actual total utility, and $U\#$ is the total utility that we get by rescheduling tasks on the above 1, 3, 5, and 7 schedulers.

In Figure 4, for scheduler 1, U_t, U_c, U', and U are all the lowest; for scheduler 3, U_t is the highest, U_c is much lower, and U' is the highest too; for schedulers 5 and 7, although their U_c is higher than scheduler, their U' is lower than scheduler 3. According to the rule of maximizing utility, we should choose scheduler 3 as the scheduler. However, in order to further improve the total utility, we applied the proposed algorithm in Section 3.3.3. By rescheduling the tasks in queuing, we get the actual total utility $U\#$ for each scheduler. In schedulers 5 and 7, $U\#$ is much higher than U' of scheduler 3.

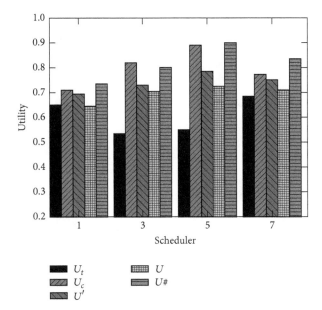

FIGURE 6: Utility distribution of cost sensitive user tasks.

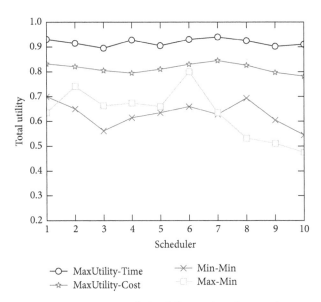

FIGURE 7: Comparison result for different algorithms under simulating tasks.

both time and cost, which makes them get lower total utilities and fluctuate very much. In particular, when running tasks 8, 9, and 10, total utility of the Max-Min algorithm drops quickly. The reason is that it schedules long-running tasks to computing nodes with high performance, which makes the utility very low.

5. Conclusion

In this paper, we introduced utility into the cloud environment, quantified the satisfaction of users to services as utility, and proposed utility oriented queuing model for task scheduling. We classified utility into time and cost utility,

rescheduled tasks according to their remaining time, and minimized the total utility by constraints. With the proposed model, we can reschedule remaining tasks dynamically to get the maximum utility. We validated our proposed model by lots of experiments.

Conflict of Interests

The authors declare that there is no conflict of interests regarding the publication of this paper.

References

[1] A. Beloglazov and R. Buyya, "Energy efficient resource management in virtualized cloud data centers," in *Proceedings of the 10th IEEE/ACM International Symposium on Cluster, Cloud, and Grid Computing*, pp. 826–831, IEEE, Melbourne, Australia, May 2010.

[2] C. S. Yeo and R. Buyya, "Service level agreement based allocation of cluster resources: handling penalty to enhance utility," in *Proceedings of the IEEE International Conference on Cluster Computing (CLUSTER '05)*, pp. 1–10, Burlington, Mass, USA, September 2005.

[3] J. N. Silva, L. Veiga, and P. Ferreira, "Heuristic for resources allocation on utility computing infrastructures," in *Proceedings of the 6th International Workshop on Middleware for Grid Computing (MGC '08)*, pp. 93–100, ACM, Leuven, Belgium, December 2008.

[4] G. Song and Y. Li, "Utility-based resource allocation and scheduling in OFDM-based wireless broadband networks," *IEEE Communications Magazine*, vol. 43, no. 12, pp. 127–134, 2005.

[5] T. T. Huu and J. Montagnat, "Virtual resources allocation for workflow-based applications distribution on a cloud infrastructure," in *Proceedings of the 10th IEEE/ACM International Symposium on Cluster, Cloud, and Grid Computing (CCGrid '10)*, pp. 612–617, IEEE, Melbourne, Australia, May 2010.

[6] Y. Yakov, "Dynamic resource allocation platform and method for time related resources," U.S. Patent Application 10/314,198[P], 2002.

[7] G. Wei, A. V. Vasilakos, Y. Zheng, and N. Xiong, "A game-theoretic method of fair resource allocation for cloud computing services," *The Journal of Supercomputing*, vol. 54, no. 2, pp. 252–269, 2010.

[8] D. López-Pérez, X. Chu, A. V. Vasilakos, and H. Claussen, "Power minimization based resource allocation for interference mitigation in OFDMA femtocell networks," *IEEE Journal on Selected Areas in Communications*, vol. 32, no. 2, pp. 333–344, 2014.

[9] X. Wang and J. F. Martínez, "XChange: a market-based approach to scalable dynamic multi-resource allocation in multicore architectures," in *Proceedings of the 21st IEEE International Symposium on High Performance Computer Architecture (HPCA '15)*, pp. 113–125, IEEE, Burlingame, Calif, USA, February 2015.

[10] L. Thomas and R. Syama, "Survey on MapReduce scheduling algorithms," *International Journal of Computer Applications*, vol. 95, no. 23, pp. 9–13, 2014.

[11] D. Cheng, J. Rao, Y. Guo, and X. Zhou, "Improving MapReduce performance in heterogeneous environments with adaptive task tuning," in *Proceedings of the 15th International Middleware*

Conference (Middleware '14), pp. 97–108, ACM, Bordeaux, France, December 2014.

[12] Q. Chen, D. Zhang, M. Guo, Q. Deng, and S. Guo, "SAMR: a self-adaptive mapreduce scheduling algorithm in heterogeneous environment," in *Proceedings of the 10th IEEE International Conference on Computer and Information Technology (CIT '10)*, pp. 2736–2743, IEEE, Bradford, UK, July 2010.

[13] D. Moise, T.-T.-L. Trieu, L. Bougé, and G. Antoniu, "Optimizing intermediate data management in MapReduce computations," in *Proceedings of the 1st International Workshop on Cloud Computing Platforms (CloudCP '11)*, pp. 37–50, ACM, Salzburg, Austria, April 2011.

[14] R. Buyya, D. Abramson, J. Giddy, and H. Stockinger, "Economic models for resource management and scheduling in grid computing," *Concurrency Computation Practice and Experience*, vol. 14, no. 13–15, pp. 1507–1542, 2002.

[15] B. Xu, C. Zhao, E. Hu, and B. Hu, "Job scheduling algorithm based on Berger model in cloud environment," *Advances in Engineering Software*, vol. 42, no. 7, pp. 419–425, 2011.

[16] S. Yeo and H.-H. S. Lee, "Using mathematical modeling in provisioning a heterogeneous cloud computing environment," *Computer*, vol. 44, no. 8, Article ID 5740825, pp. 55–62, 2011.

[17] M. H. Rothkopf, "Scheduling with random service times," *Management Science*, vol. 12, no. 9, pp. 707–713, 1966.

[18] R. H. Möhring, A. S. Schulz, and M. Uetz, "Approximation in stochastic scheduling: the power of LP—based priority policies," *Journal of the ACM*, vol. 46, no. 6, pp. 924–942, 1999.

[19] N. Megow, M. Uetz, and T. Vredeveld, "Models and algorithms for stochastic online scheduling," *Mathematics of Operations Research*, vol. 31, no. 3, pp. 513–525, 2006.

[20] M. Scharbrodt, T. Schickinger, and A. Steger, "A new average case analysis for completion time scheduling," *Journal of the ACM*, vol. 53, no. 1, pp. 121–146, 2006.

[21] X. Nan, Y. He, and L. Guan, "Optimal resource allocation for multimedia cloud based on queuing model," in *Proceedings of the 3rd IEEE International Workshop on Multimedia Signal Processing (MMSP '11)*, pp. 1–6, Hangzhou, China, November 2011.

[22] Z. Xiao, W. Song, and Q. Chen, "Dynamic resource allocation using virtual machines for cloud computing environment," *IEEE Transactions on Parallel and Distributed Systems*, vol. 24, no. 6, pp. 1107–1117, 2013.

12

An Efficient Stream Data Processing Model for Multiuser Cryptographic Service

Li Li [ID],[1,2] Fenghua Li [ID],[3,4] Guozhen Shi,[5] and Kui Geng[3]

[1]*College of Communication Engineering, Xidian University, Xi'an 710071, China*
[2]*Department of Electronic and Information Engineering, Beijing Electronics Science and Technology Institute, Beijing 100070, China*
[3]*State Key Laboratory of Information Security, Institute of Information Engineering, CAS, Beijing 100093, China*
[4]*School of Cyber Security, University of Chinese Academy of Sciences, Beijing 100049, China*
[5]*Department of Information Security, Beijing Electronic Science and Technology Institute, Beijing 100070, China*

Correspondence should be addressed to Fenghua Li; lfh@iie.ac.cn

Academic Editor: Jar Ferr Yang

In view of the demand for high-concurrency massive data encryption and decryption application services in the security field, this paper proposes a dual-channel pipeline parallel data processing model (DPP) according to the characteristics of cryptographic operations and realized cryptographic operations of cross-data streams with different service requirements in a multiuser environment. By encapsulating cryptographic operation requirements in job packages, the input data flow is divided by the dual-channel mechanism and job packages parallel scheduling, which ensures the synchronization between the processing of the dependent job packages and parallel packages and hides the processing of the independent job package in the processing of the dependent job package. Prototyping experiments prove that this model can realize the correct and rapid processing of multiservice cross-data streams. Increasing the pipeline depth and improving the processing performance in each stage of the pipeline are the key to improving the system performance.

1. Introduction

With the development of computer and network technology, the large number of users and businesses of all kinds of business systems bring huge challenges to data analysis, processing, and storage of business systems. Meanwhile, the urgent need for the security service capabilities of business systems is also put forward. Not only security needs are reflected in financial business, but also the big data analysis for user behavior can easily expose users' personal privacy. The vulnerability of information transmission in the Internet of Things can easily become a security risk in the field of industrial control. The use of cryptographic techniques to ensure the security of business and data and the protection of user privacy are urgent tasks at this stage and even in the future. Therefore, it is necessary to study fast cryptographic operations for mass data. Therefore, considering the security and high-speed processing requirements, it is urgent to design a parallel system that can meet the requirements of different algorithms and different cryptographic working modes.

As the mainstream of computer architecture research and design, multicore has an irreplaceable role in improving computing performance. People have done a lot of research on the high-speed design and implementation of cryptographic algorithm itself, as well as heterogeneous multicore crypto processors. However, there is a lack of research on the high-speed processing of cryptographic services that cross each other in multiuser scenarios. This dissertation takes the design of high-performance cryptographic server as research background. According to the characteristics of cryptographic operations, under the demand of high-concurrency massive data encryption and decryption application service, an efficient stream data processing model for multiuser cryptographic services is proposed to meet the requirements of user-differentiated cryptographic service requirements and achieve high-speed cryptographic service performance.

This paper is organized as follows: Section 2 reviews the existing research. Section 3 introduces the thread separation of the cryptographic operations based on the characteristics of cryptographic operation in different working modes. In Section 4, the dual-channel pipeline parallel data processing model DPP is proposed. Section 5 implements and tests the model.

2. Related Research

As the mainstream of processor architecture development, multicore processors have led to the research upsurge of parallel processing. The speed of data processing is improved by multicore parallel execution. There are two issues involved here: multithread parallelism and multitask parallelism. For multithreaded tasks, concurrent execution of multiple threads by multicore processors can improve the processing performance. For example, one task can be divided into three threads to complete, in the following order: initialization I, operation C, and results output T. Then we can complete it with three cores, as shown in Figure 1. A single-threaded task is usually ported to multiple cores for execution through automatic parallelization techniques. There are many studies on the automatic parallelization of loops. The traditional loop parallel methods include DOALL [1, 2] and DOACROSS [3]. When there is no dependency between iterations of the loop, the DOALL method is used to perform the parallelization sequentially; when there are dependencies between iterations of the loop, the DOACROSS method is used. This automatic parallelization technique cannot achieve good results for general loops containing complex control flow, recursive data structures, and multiple pointer accesses. For this reason, Ottoni proposed an instruction-level automatic task parallel algorithm called Decoupled Software Pipelines (DSWP) [4]. It divides the loop into two parts, the instruction stream and the data stream, and completes parallelism through synchronization between instructions and data. The implementation flow of DSWP and DOACROSS is shown in Figures 2(a) and 2(b), respectively.

DSWP reduce interaction between cores compared to DOACROSS. Whether it is DSWP or DOACROSS, there is a synchronous relationship between threads that are automatically parallelized. For example, the execution time of thread I and thread C needs to be consistent; otherwise, it will result in the waiting consumption of cores. Therefore, synchronization (or coordination) is a key issue that must be considered for parallelization. Concurrency must achieve high performance without significant overhead. Synchronization between threads often leads to the sequentialization of parallel activities, thereby undermining the potential benefits of concurrent execution. Therefore, the effective use of synchronization and coordination is critical to achieving high performance. One way to achieve this goal is speculative execution, which enables concurrent synchronization through thread speculation or branch prediction [5–8]. Successful speculation will reduce the portion of continuous execution, but false speculation will increase revocation and recovery overhead. Simultaneous implementation of the

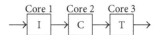

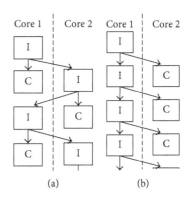

FIGURE 1: The execution of multithreaded task.

FIGURE 2: (a) DOACROSS. (b) DSWP.

speculative mechanism in the traditional control flow architecture requires a large amount of software and hardware overhead.

In multitask parallelism, if each task is a multithreaded task, due to the independence of the tasks and the independence of the threads, the processing method is equivalent to a multithreaded task. If there are single-threaded tasks, after they are parallelized into multiple threads, there will be some associated threads in the process of multitask parallel execution, which must be treated differently.

The cryptographic service involves multiple elements. For example, a block cipher algorithm involves cryptographic algorithms, KEYs, initial vectors, working modes, etc. Different cryptographic services have different operational elements. The rapid implementation of multiuser cryptographic services belongs to the multitask parallel domain. As a device for realizing multiuser and massive data cryptographic services, the high-performance cryptographic server must achieve the following two points: First is the correctness of user services: the processing request of different users cannot be confused, and the second is the rapidity of data processing. There are many researches on the fast implementation of the cryptographic algorithm itself, such as improving the computing performance of block cipher algorithm through pipelining [9–13] and optimizing the key operations of public-key cryptography algorithm to improve the operation speed [14–16]. Some studies also accelerate the performance of cryptographic operations through multicore parallelism. For example, the literature uses GPU to implement parallel processing of part of cryptographic algorithms [17–19]. These research results are usually the performance improvement of a single cryptographic algorithm. The literature adopts a heterogeneous multicore approach to complete the parallel processing of multiple cryptographic algorithms [20–22]. However, there is no proposed data processing method for multiuser cryptographic services in the presence of multiple cryptographic algorithms, multiple KEYs, and multiple data streams.

This paper proposes a dual-channel pipeline parallel data processing model (DPP), which includes parallel scheduling, algorithm preprocessing, algorithmic operation, and result acquisition. The DPP is designed and implemented in a heterogeneous multicore parallel architecture. This parallel system performs a variety of cryptographic algorithms and supports linear expansion of the algorithm operation unit. Each algorithm operation unit adopts dual channels to receive data and realizes parallel operations among multiple tasks.

3. Thread Split

As mentioned above, different cryptographic services have different computing elements, which is expressed as

$$Service = \{ID, crypto, key, IV, mode\}$$

ID is the service number that is set for multiple users.

The cryptographic operations are usually carried out in blocks and user's data can be divided into several blocks. According to different cryptographic algorithms, the size of the block also varies. Here UB is used to represent the size of a single block. The research in this paper is based on the following assumptions:

(1) Parallel processing with UB granularity.

(2) Each cryptographic algorithm core completes the operation of one block. The algorithm core adopts the full pipeline design.

The fast implementation of cryptographic algorithm core is not discussed here. Under the premise of meeting the interface conditions, any kind of full pipeline implementation scheme of the cryptographic algorithm can be applied to the algorithm core in this model. This paper focuses on the parallelism between different blocks of cryptographic service.

3.1. Symmetric Cryptographic Algorithm. The parallelism between blocks of symmetric cryptography algorithms must consider the working mode adopted by the cryptographic algorithm. The commonly used working modes are ECB, CBC, CFB, OFB, CTR [23–27], and so on. Assume that C_i denotes the ith ciphertext block, P_i denotes the ith plaintext block, Enc denotes the encryption algorithm, Dec denotes the decryption algorithm, key denotes the KEY, IV denotes the initial vector, n is the number of plaintext/ciphertext blocks, T_i is the counter value, which increases by 1 with the increment of the block, and u is the length of the last block.

(1) ECB working mode

Encryption: $C_i = Enc(key, P_i), \quad 0 \le i < n,$
Decryption: $P_i = Dec(key, C_i), \quad 0 \le i < n.$

(2) CTR working mode

Encryption:
$$\begin{cases} C_i = P_i \ XOR \ Enc(key, T_i), & i = 0, 1, 2, \ldots, n-2, \\ C_{n-1} = P_{n-1} \ XOR \ MSB_u(Enc(key, T_{n-1})). \end{cases}$$

Decryption:
$$\begin{cases} C_i = P_i \ XOR \ Enc(key, T_i), & i = 0, 1, 2, \ldots, n-2, \\ C_{n-1} = P_{n-1} \ XOR \ MSB_u(Enc(key, T_{n-1})). \end{cases}$$

(3) CBC working mode

Encryption:
$$\begin{cases} C_0 = Enc(key, XOR(IV, P_0)), \\ C_i = Enc(key, XOR(C_{i-1}, P_i)), & 0 < i < n. \end{cases}$$

Decryption:
$$\begin{cases} P_0 = Dec(key, C_0)XORIV, \\ P_i = Dec(key, C_i) \ XOR \ C_{i-1}, & 0 < i < n. \end{cases}$$

(4) CFB working mode

Encryption:
$$\begin{cases} C_0 = Enc(key, IV)XOR \ P_0, \\ C_i = Enc(key, C_{i-1}) \ XOR \ P_i, & 0 < i < n. \end{cases}$$

Decryption:
$$\begin{cases} P_0 = Enc(key, IV) \ XOR \ C_0, \\ P_i = Enc(key, C_{i-1}) \ XOR \ C_i, & 0 < i < n. \end{cases}$$

(5) OFB working mode

Encryption:
$$\begin{cases} C_0 = Enc(key, IV) \ XOR \ P_0, \\ C_i = Enc(key, C_{i-1}) \ XOR \ P_i, & 0 < i < n. \end{cases}$$

Decryption:
$$\begin{cases} S_0 = Enc(key, IV), \\ S_i = Enc(key, S_{i-1}), & 0 < i < n, \\ P_i = S_i XORC_i, & 0 \le i < n. \end{cases}$$

Because there is no dependency between blocks in the ECB and CTR modes, blocks can be processed in parallel. So ECB and CTR are parallel modes and are very suitable for parallel processing. CBC, CFB, and OFB modes have certain dependencies among blocks, so CBC, CFB, and OFB are serial modes. When using multicore parallel operations in multiuser scenarios, attention must be paid to coordination and synchronization among blocks.

By analyzing each working mode, we can divide the encryption and decryption operation into 3 threads. Thread 1 completes the acquisition of the algorithm core input data, thread 2 completes the encryption/decryption operation of a single block, and thread 3 completes the output of the ciphertext/plaintext data. Taking CBC encryption mode and OFB decryption mode as examples, the thread splitting is shown in Table 1.

In this way of splitting, the function of thread 2 is relatively simple, which is the cryptographic algorithm operation of one UB. Since encryption and decryption operations usually require multiple rounds of confusion and iterative operations, the operation time of thread 2 is longer than that of thread 1 and thread 3. Taking the $SM4$ algorithm as an example, each block needs 32 rounds of function operations. In the full pipeline approach, the algorithm architecture is shown in Figure 3, where F0 to F31 represent 32 rounds of

TABLE 1: Thread split.

CBC encryption mode	OFB decryption mode
Thread 1: $result\ 1 = XOR(X, Pi)$ $X = \begin{cases} IV, & i = 0, \\ C_{i-1}, & 0 < i < n. \end{cases}$	Thread 1: $result\ 1 = \begin{cases} IV, & i = 0, \\ result\ 2_{i-1}, & 0 < i < n. \end{cases}$
Thread 2: $result\ 2 = Enc(Key, result\ 1)$	Thread 2: $result\ 2_i = Enc(Key, result\ 1_i)$
Thread 3: $C_i = result\ 2$	Thread 3: $P_i = result\ 2\ XOR\ C_i$ $0 \leq i < n$

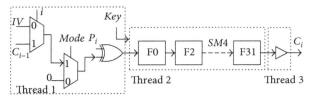

FIGURE 3: $SM4$ 3-thread algorithm operation.

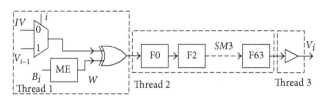

FIGURE 4: $SM3$ 3-thread algorithm operation.

function operations. Different blocks without dependencies can be executed in parallel within it.

For example, $service\ 1 = \{ID1,SM4,key1,IV1,CBC\}$ and $service\ 2 = \{ID2,SM4,key2,none,ECB\}$ correspond to the data streams data 1 and data 2, if data 1 can be split into m UB blocks and data 2 can be split into n UB blocks. That is

$$data\ 1 = \{p_{11}, p_{12}, \ldots, p_{1m}\},$$
$$data\ 2 = \{p_{21}, p_{22}, \ldots, p_{2n}\}, \tag{1}$$

when p_{1i} is operated in module $F_k\ (0 \leq k \leq 31)$, $p_{1(i+1)}$ cannot enter the thread 1 module, but p_{2j} can enter the thread 1 and $F_{k'}\ (k' < k)$ modules. So we can insert the block data of the parallel mode between blocks of the serial working mode and hide the execution time of the parallel mode block data inside that of the serial working mode block data. The thread 2 pipeline depth determines the number of independent blocks that can be inserted between dependent blocks.

3.2. Hash Algorithm.

The Hash function needs to obtain the hash value of the message through multiple iterations of the block data, so the Hash operation has dependencies between the blocks. By analyzing, Hash algorithm can also be divided into 3 threads: message expansion (ME), iterative compression, and hash value output. The message expansion completes the calculation of parameters required for the iterative compression function, and the hash value output is used for the output of the final result. Taking $SM3$ as an example, the algorithm architecture is shown in Figure 4. The parallelism of Hash operations can only occur between blocks of different data streams.

4. DPP Parallel Data Processing Model

The parallel computing models based on PRAM, BSP, and LogP [28, 29] are all computing oriented, lacking pertinence to data processing and are not suitable for practical application of massive data. It can be seen from the above description that the cryptographic operation data in the multiuser environment have the following characteristics:

(1) Different user data streams intersect each other. (2) Independent blocks and dependent blocks exist in mutual intersections. Therefore, the parallel processing model must have the following two mechanisms: (1) distinguish between different user data streams and (2) distinguish between data stream dependencies. For this purpose, we encapsulate the data stream and add certain attribute information to the block data, so as to express its properties, thereby facilitating subsequent parallel processing.

The cryptographic operations of streaming data are data-intensive applications. Its typical feature is that the data value is time-sensitive, so the system requires low latency. When a large amount of multiuser data reaches the system in a continuous, fast, time-varying, and cross way, it must be quickly sent to each cryptographic algorithm operation node. Otherwise, data loss may occur due to limited storage space of the system receiver. Referring to the MapReduce data stream processing strategy, specialized module is used to distribute data streams.

The three threads of cryptographic operations of different working modes are implemented by three modules: preprocessing module, operation module, and result output module. The data reorganization module completes the integration of the data stream packages of each service. Figure 5 shows the dual-channel pipeline parallel data processing model proposed in this paper. The data stream processing is divided into six stages: job package encapsulation (PE), parallel scheduling (PS), job package preprocessing (PP), algorithm operation (AO), result output (RO), and data reorganization (DR). The job package encapsulation and data reorganization are completed by the node P_0, the parallel scheduling is completed by the node P_0, and the job package preprocessing, algorithm operation, and result output are completed by the algorithm operation unit cry_IP. Each algorithm corresponds to a cluster of algorithm operation units. For example, the operation module cry_IP_{i1} is an encryption operation unit of algorithm s_i and cry_IP_{i2} is a decryption operation unit of algorithm s_i. The dual channel is embodied in the two channels of input and output data of algorithm operation unit.

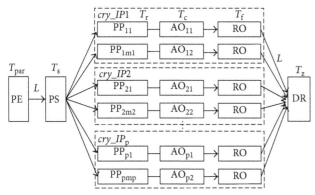

FIGURE 5: Dual-channel pipeline parallel data processing model (DPP).

In the DPP model, data processing is performed in units of job packages. No explicit synchronization process is required between job packages. Synchronization is implicit in the algorithm preprocessing. Each job package is completed by a fixed algorithm operation unit, and there is no data interaction between the algorithm operation units in the job package processing.

4.1. Encapsulation.

The encapsulation is completed by the master node. The format of the encapsulated job package is as follows:

$$P = \{ID, crypto, key, IV, mode, No, flag, l\}$$

ID is the service number set for multiuser and is used to distinguish different data streams; $Crypto$ represents the specific demand for cryptographic algorithms and encryption/decryption operations, key is the KEY, IV is the initial vector, and $mode$ is the working mode, which can be used to distinguish the dependency property of the job package; No. is the job package serial number, which is used to reassemble the data stream after the algorithm operation. $Flag$ is the tail package identifier, which indicates whether the service data flow is end. l is the length of the job package and is consistent with the size of the unit block of the cryptographic algorithm.

The flow data received by the system is described as $Task = \{P_{ij}\}$, where i corresponds to the service number and j corresponds to the sequence number of the service. We refer to job packages in parallel mode as independent job packages and job packages in serial mode as dependent job packages.

4.2. Dual Channel and Parallel Scheduling.

According to the thread splitting, under the same algorithm requirements, the difference of package processing of different working modes is embodied in the preprocessing module and the result output module. The operation module does not consider the correlation among the job packages and only processes the input job packages. For this reason, it is necessary to distinguish the input data of the preprocessing module and the result output module. We adopt dual channels to receive job packages and classify independent job packages and dependent job packages.

4.2.1. Dual Receiving Channel of the Preprocessing Module.

Channel 1 is used for the transfer of independent job packages. Considering that the first job package of a data stream in the serial mode is not associated with job packages of other data streams, the job package transmitted in channel 1 satisfies the condition:

$$(mode = ECB|CTR) \quad or \quad (mode = CBC|CFB|OFB \quad and \quad No. = 1)$$

Channel 2 is used for the transfer of dependent job packages. The job package that is transmitted in channel 2 satisfies the condition:

$$(mode = CBC|CFB|OFB) \ and \ No. = /1$$

Suppose that the working mode of four services that request cry_IP_{ab} operation is as follows: service 1. mode = service 2.mode = CBC, service 3.mode = service 4. mode = ECB, the job packages on channel 1 and channel 2 after parallel scheduling are shown in Figure 6.

The selection of channel is determined by the control signal Si, and the default selection is channel 1, that is, $Si = 0$. cnt is used to record the execution time of the dependent job package in the algorithm operation unit. When module cnt senses that the preprocessing module inputs a dependent job package, the counting starts. It is assumed that the algorithm operation unit needs m clock cycles to complete the operation of the dependent job package. When $cnt = m$, the counter clears, $cnt = 0$, sets $Si = 1$ to select channel 2, and inputs the next dependency job package. In other cases, $Si = 0$ and channel 1 is selected. The state flow diagram is shown in Figure 7.

4.2.2. Dual Receiving Channel of the Result Output Module.

Channel 3 is used for the transfer of independent job packages. The job package that is transmitted in channel 3 satisfies the condition:

$$(mode = ECB|CTR) \quad or \quad (mode = CBC|CFB|OFB \quad and \quad flag = 1)$$

Channel 4 is used for the transfer of dependent job packages. The job package that is transmitted in channel 4 satisfies the condition:

$$(mode = CBC|CFB|OFB) \ and \ flag = /n$$

Channel 4 provides support for storing intermediate states in serial mode. Since the result of the tail package does not need to be used as an intermediate state, the tail package's result in serial mode is also output through channel 3.

The choice of channel is determined by the control signal So, and channel 3 is the default, that is $So = 0$. The channel selection control signal is the same as that of the preprocessing module. When $cnt = m$, So is set to 1 and channel 4 is selected. In other cases, $So = 0$ and channel 3 is selected. When $So = 1$, the job package transmitted by channel 4 has the same ID as the job package received by the preprocessing module, as shown in Figure 8.

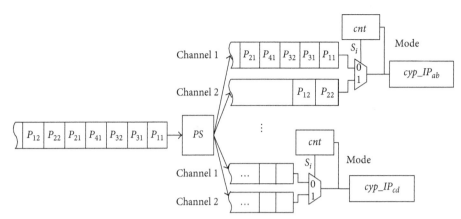

FIGURE 6: Parallel scheduling and dual receiving channel of preprocessing module.

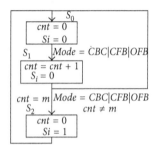

FIGURE 7: Dual-channel selection control of preprocessing module.

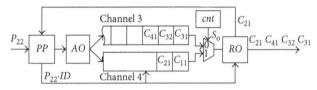

FIGURE 8: Dual-channel control of output module.

4.2.3. Parallel Scheduling. The process of parallel scheduling is as follows:

> *Step 1.* Determine the algorithm operation unit according to *crypto*.
>
> *Step 2.* Select the input channel of the preprocessing module of the algorithm operation unit according to *mode* and *No.*

This scheduling method realizes fast transfer of incoming data streams and continuous processing of job packages. The use of dual channels reduces the interaction between modules and hides the processing time of independent job packages in the processing time of dependent job packages, facilitating the parallel execution of job packages.

4.2.4. Data Processing Steps

> *Step 1.* The algorithm application process splits the data to be processed, adds attribute information, and encapsulates it as job package.

Step 2. The algorithm operation unit is determined according to the *crypto* field in the job package, and the input channel of its preprocessing module is selected according to *mode* and *No.* The job package is sent to the corresponding input channel.

Step 3. The preprocessing module obtains the input data of the algorithm operation module, namely, data, *KEY*, and *IV*, according to the package field of *mode* and *No.*

Step 4. The algorithm operation module performs pipeline processing on the received data and sends the result to the receiving channel of the result output module according to *mode* and *flag.*

Step 5. The result output module outputs the received job package to the result receiving process and determines whether to feed the job package back to the preprocessing module according to *mode* and *flag* of the job package.

Step 6. The result receiving process recombines the received job package based on *ID.*

4.3. Parallel Execution Time. Assume that P_0 is the job package encapsulation and reorganization node, and P_a, P_b, and P_c are algorithm operation nodes. T_{par} is the package encapsulation time, and T_z is the data reorganization time. g is the communication interval, that is, the minimum time interval during which node P_0 continuously transmits and receives job packages. The reciprocal of g corresponds to the communication bandwidth. L is the maximum communication delay, which is the time taken to transmit a job package from node P_0 to the scheduling node. T_s indicates the parallel scheduling time of job packages, T_r indicates the job package preprocessing time, T_c indicates the job package operation time, and T_f indicates the job package output time. g represents the calculated load, which is the set of job packages. m is the algorithm operation module pipeline depth. The message delivery process of the job package on DPP is shown in Figure 9.

The continuous sending and receiving of messages needs to meet the conditions:

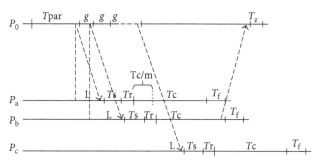

FIGURE 9: Message delivery on the DPP model.

$$L + T_s + T_r + \frac{T_c}{m} \leq g + L + T_s + T_r,$$

(2)

$$g \geq \frac{T_c}{m}.$$

Conclusion 1. The system communication bandwidth can be improved by two ways: increasing the operation speed of the algorithm operation module and increasing the pipeline depth of it.

If g job packages come from α data streams, consider two scenarios:

(1) Each data stream adopts a parallel mode; that is, job packages are all independent. The load processing time is as follows:

$$T = T_{\text{par}} + (n-1)g + T_s + T_r + T_c + T_f + T_z + 2L.$$

(3)

(2) Each data stream adopts a parallel mode, so that job packages of the same service data stream are mutually dependent, and job packages of different service data streams are mutually independent. Assume that the maximum number of service job packages is w', in the extreme case, the first job packet of this data flow appears after other service data flows, and then, the operation time of other service data flows is hidden during that of the longest service data flow. The load processing time is as follows:

$$T = T_{\text{par}} + (w - w' - 1)g + w'(T_s + T_r + T_c + T_f) + T_z + 2L.$$

(4)

For the data stream mixed in the serial/parallel mode, due to the pipeline design of the algorithm operation module, in the process of dependent job packages, the independent job packages can be executed in parallel, so the execution time of independent job packages is hidden in the execution time of the dependent job package. Therefore, the execution time T of the multitask mixed mode data stream is as follows:

$$T = T_{\text{par}} + (n-1)g + T_s + T_r + T_c + T_f + T_z + 2L \leq T \leq T_{\text{par}} + (w - w' - 1)g + w'(T_s + T_r + T_c + T_f) + T_z + 2L.$$

(5)

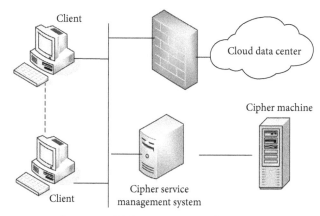

FIGURE 10: Multiuser cryptographic service.

Conclusion 2. The execution time of mixed cross-data streams is limited to the execution time of the data streams with the most job packages. On the premise of constant pipeline depth, improving the processing performance of each module in the pipeline is the key to improve the processing method.

5. Implementation and Testing

5.1. Hardware Implementation. We prototyped the model to verify its validity. The architecture is shown in Figure 10. The cipher server management system completes the reception of multiuser cryptographic service data streams, the encapsulation of job packages, and the data reorganization service of the operation results. The cryptographic algorithm operation is performed by a crypto machine as a coprocessor. The crypto machine is designed using Xilinx XC7K325t FPGA, which includes parallel scheduling module, *SM3* and *SM4* cryptographic algorithm cores.

The hardware implementation block diagram of the cipher machine is shown in Figure 11. The cipher machine adopts the PCIe interface and receives the job package split by the algorithm application process of the cipher server management system in the way of *DMA* and stores them in *DOWN_FIFO* in the downlink data storage area.

Parallel scheduling module *PSCHEDULE*: Determine the algorithm core according to the *crypto* field of the job package, determine the receiving *FIFO* according to the *mode* and *No.* fields, and realize the transfer of the job package. *FIFO1* corresponds to channel 1 in the model, and *FIFO2* corresponds to channel 2 in the model.

Preprocessing module *IP_CTRL*: Acquire algorithm core input data, including *IV*, *KEY*, and the result of the preorder dependent job package, and calculate the input data to cryptographic cores.

Operation modules *SM4* and *SM3*: Cryptographic cores; perform algorithm operations on input data in pipelining way, and send the result of the operation to *uFIFO* or *RAM*. *uFIFO* corresponds to channel 3 in the model, and *RAM* corresponds to the channel 4.

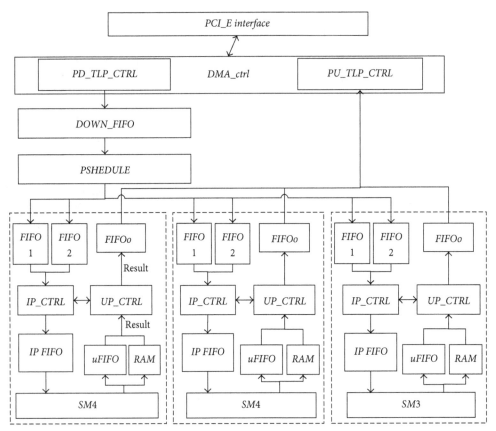

FIGURE 11: Hardware architecture of partem.

Result output module *UP_CTRL*: If *IP_CTRL* gives the *ID* number, the data of the same *ID* number are extracted from *RAM*, and the output result *result'* is calculated, and fed back to *IP_CTRL* and output to the output *FIFOo* at the same time. If *IP_CTRL* has no *ID* number output, the data in *uFIFO* are extracted, and *result'* is calculated and sent to *FIFOo*. The data in *FIFOo* are fed back to the result reception process of the cipher server management system through the interface module in *DMA* mode.

5.2. Test. The test environment is as follows: The main frequency of the heterogeneous multicore parallel processing system implemented by Xilinx XC7K325t FPGA is 160 MHz, and the interface with the upper application is PCIe 2.0 * 8.

Test 1. SM4 CBC encryption for a 4000 MB file. The end of the test operation takes 114.390935 s, so the data stream processing rate is: 4000 * 8/114.390935 = 279.742446 Mbps.

Test 2. Test 2.1 to Test 2.4 use eight 400 MB files, and job packages of the eight files enter the cipher machine in an interleaving manner. These files use different *IVs* and *KEYs* in different working modes. The end time of each file processing is shown in Table 2. For the data set, the maximum end time is the total time it takes. The data flow processing rate is derived from the following formula:

TABLE 2: Cipher operation time under cross files.

	File	File 1	File 2	File 3	File 4
	Mode		SM4 CBC		
	Time (s)	13.5175	13.4912	13.4994	13.4831
Test 2.1	File	File 5	File 6	File 7	File 8
	Mode		SM4 CBC		
	Time (s)	13.4788	13.4872	13.4950	13.5014
	Processing rate: 3200 * 8/13.5175 s = 1.89 Gbps					
	File	File 1	File 2	File 3	File 4
	Mode		SM4 ECB		
	Time (s)	12.5029	12.4946	12.4988	12.4784
Test 2.2	File	File 5	File 6	File 7	File 8
	Mode		SM4 CBC		
	Time (s)	12.4825	12.4906	12.4864	12.5052
	Processing rate: 3200 * 8/12.5052 s = 2.05 Gbps					
	File	File 1	File 2	File 3	File 4
	Mode		SM4 ECB		
	Time (s)	4.3340	4.3166	4.0397	4.1721
Test 2.3	File	File 5	File 6	File 7	File 8
	Mode		SM4 ECB		
	Time (s)	4.3433	4.9895	4.1908	4.3623
	Processing rate: 3200 * 8/4.9895 s = 5.13 Gbps					
	File	File 1	File 2	File 3	File 4
	Mode	SM3		SM4 ECB	
	Time (s)	12.8909	12.4151	13.0394	13.1713
Test 2.4	File	File 5	File 6	File 7	File 8
	Mode	SM4 CBC		SM4 OFB	
	Time (s)	12.7424	12.6119	13.1909	12.4842
	Processing rate: 3200 * 8/13.1909 = 1.94 Gbps					

$$\text{rate (bps)} = \frac{\text{size of data flow (bit)}}{\text{the total time (s)}}. \tag{6}$$

Analysis: Because Test 1 has only one file in the *CBC* mode, the job packages are interrelated and all are executed serial. Although packages of each file are interrelated, the files of Test 2.1 are independent of each other, so the data flow processing rate of Test 2.1 is higher than that of Test 1. In Test 2.2, 4 files are in the *ECB* work mode, and the independent job packages operation time can be hidden within the operation time of the dependency packages, so the data flow processing rate of Test 2.2 is higher than that of the Test 2.1. Similarly, the data processing rate of Test 2.3 is the highest. Test 2.4 has 2 files with independent job packages and 6 files with dependent packages, but they are allocated in two algorithm units, so the operation rate is close to Test 2.1.

Test 3. Processing rate compare of dual channel and single channel. The total amount of job packages is 10000, and they are randomly assigned to j files. If N_i represents the number of job packages in $file_i$, $\sum_{i=1}^{j} N_i = 10000$. If j is 10, 20, 30, 40, the *ECB* or *CBC* encryption mode is adopted. Change the number of files in *CBC* encryption mode and compare the completion time of data flow in single-channel architecture and dual-channel architecture. The average value of data flow processing time is run several times, and the comparison result is shown in Figure 12. Single 0% means that all files use *ECB* mode, and the system adopts single-channel architecture. Dual 50% indicates that 50% of the files in the data stream use *CBC* mode, and the system is dual-channel architecture, and so on.

As can be seen from Figure 12, when the data flow is an independent data flow, the algorithm operation unit adopts the pipeline design, so the processing rate under the dual channel is close to the processing rate under the single channel; with the increase of the associated job packages in the data flow, the advantage of the data processing rate of dual channel is gradually displayed, and with the increase of the number of files in the data stream, the advantage of the data processing rate is more obvious.

6. Conclusion

Based on the characteristics of cryptographic operations, this paper proposes a dual-channel pipeline parallel data processing model DPP to implement cryptographic operations for cross-data streams with different service requirements in a multiuser environment. The model ensures synchronization between dependent job packages and parallel processing between independent job packages and data streams. It hides the processing of independent job packages in the process of dependent job packages to improve the processing speed of cross-data streams. Prototype experiments prove that the system under this model can realize correct and rapid processing of multi-service and personalized cross-data streams. Increasing the depth of the cryptographic algorithm pipeline and

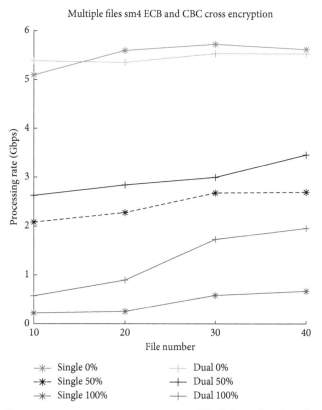

FIGURE 12: Processing rate comparison of dual channel and single channel.

improving the processing performance of each module in the pipeline can improve the overall performance of the system.

Conflicts of Interest

The authors declare that they have no conflicts of interest.

Acknowledgments

This work was supported by the National Key R&D Program of China (no. 2017YFB0802705) and the National Natural Science Foundation of China (no. 61672515).

References

[1] Y. Song and Z. Li, "Applying array contraction to a sequence of DOALL loops," in *Proceedings of the International Conference on Parallel Processing (ICPP'04)*, vol. 1, pp. 46–53, Montreal, Canada, August 2004.

[2] G. Elsesser, V. Ngo, S. Bhattacharya, and W. T. Tsai, "Load balancing of DOALL loops in the Perfect Club," in *Proceedings of the 1993 Proceedings Seventh International Parallel Processing Symposium*, pp. 129–133, Newport, CA, USA, April 1993.

[3] D. K. C. Ding-Kai Chen and P. C. Y. Pen-Chung Yew, "Statement re-ordering for DOACROSS loops," in *Proceedings of the 1994 Internatonal Conference on Parallel Processing*, vol. 2, pp. 24–28, Raleigh, NC, USA, August 1994.

[4] G. Ottoni, R. Rangan, A. Stoler, and D. I. August, "Automatic thread extraction with decoupled software pipelining," in *Proceedings of the 38th Annual IEEE/ACM International Symposium on Microarchitecture (MICRO'05)*, pp. 105–118, Barcelona, Spain, November 2005.

[5] V. Krishnan and J. Torrellas, "A chip-multiprocessor architecture with speculative multithreading," *IEEE Transactions on Computers*, vol. 48, no. 9, pp. 866–880, 1999.

[6] A. S. Rajam, L. E. Campostrini, J. M. M. Caamaño, and P. Clauss, "Speculative runtime parallelization of loop nests: towards greater scope and efficiency," in *Proceedings of the 2015 IEEE International Parallel and Distributed Processing Symposium Workshop (IPDPSW)*, pp. 245–254, Hyderabad, India, May 2015.

[7] S. Aldea, A. Estebanez, D. R. Llanos, and A. Gonzalez-Escribano, "An OpenMP extension that supports thread-level speculation," *IEEE Transactions on Parallel and Distributed Systems*, vol. 27, no. 1, pp. 78–91, 2016.

[8] J. Salamanca, J. N. Amaral, and G. Araujo, "Evaluating and improving thread-level speculation in hardware transactional memories," in *Proceedings of the 2016 IEEE International Parallel and Distributed Processing Symposium (IPDPS)*, pp. 586–595, Chicago, IL, USA, May 2016.

[9] Z. Ying and B. Qinghai, "The scheme for improving the efficiency of block cipher algorithm," in *Proceedings of the 2014 IEEE Workshop on Advanced Research and Technology in Industry Applications (WARTIA)*, pp. 824–826, Ottawa, ON, Canada, September 2014.

[10] P. Kitsos and A. N. Skodras, "An FPGA implementation and performance evaluation of the seed block cipher," in *Proceedings of the 2011 17th International Conference on Digital Signal Processing (DSP)*, pp. 1–5, Corfu, Greece, July 2011.

[11] L. Bossuet, N. Datta, C. Mancillas-López, and M. Nandi, "ELmD: a pipelineable authenticated encryption and its hardware implementation," *IEEE Transactions on Computers*, vol. 65, no. 11, pp. 3318–3331, 2016.

[12] P. U. Deshpande and S. A. Bhosale, "AES encryption engines of many core processor arrays on FPGA by using parallel, pipeline and sequential technique," in *Proceedings of the 2015 International Conference on Energy Systems and Applications*, pp. 75–80, Pune, India, October 2015.

[13] T. Kryjak and M. Gorgon, "Pipeline implementation of the 128-bit block cipher CLEFIA in FPGA," in *Proceedings of the 2009 International Conference on Field Programmable Logic and Applications*, pp. 373–378, Prague, Czech Republic, August 2009.

[14] S. Lin, S. He, X. Guo, and D. Guo, "An efficient algorithm for computing modular division over GF(2m) in elliptic curve cryptography," in *Proceedings of the 2017 11th IEEE International Conference on Anti-counterfeiting, Security, and Identification (ASID)*, pp. 179–182, Xiamen, China, 2017.

[15] K. M. John and S. Sabi, "A novel high performance ECC processor architecture with two staged multiplier," in *Proceedings of the 2017 IEEE International Conference on Electrical, Instrumentation and Communication Engineering (ICEICE)*, pp. 1–5, Karur, India, April 2017.

[16] M. S. Albahri, M. Benaissa, and Z. U. A. Khan, "Parallel implementation of ECC point multiplication on a homogeneous multi-core microcontroller," in *Proceedings of the 2016 12th International Conference on Mobile Ad-Hoc and Sensor Networks (MSN)*, pp. 386–389, Hefei, China, December 2016.

[17] W. K. Lee, B. M. Goi, R. C. W. Phan, and G. S. Poh, "High speed implementation of symmetric block cipher on GPU," in *Proceedings of the 2014 International Symposium on Intelligent Signal Processing and Communication Systems (ISPACS)*, pp. 102–107, Kuching, Malaysia, December 2014.

[18] J. Ma, X. Chen, R. Xu, and J. Shi, "Implementation and evaluation of different parallel designs of AES using CUDA," in *Proceedings of the 2017 IEEE Second International Conference on Data Science in Cyberspace (DSC)*, pp. 606–614, Shenzhen, China, June 2017.

[19] W. Dai, Y. Doröz, and B. Sunar, "Accelerating NTRU based homomorphic encryption using GPUs," in *Proceedings of the 2014 IEEE High Performance Extreme Computing Conference (HPEC)*, pp. 1–6, Waltham, MA, USA, September 2014.

[20] G. Barlas, A. Hassan, and Y. A. Jundi, "An analytical approach to the design of parallel block cipher encryption/decryption: a CPU/GPU case study," in *Proceedings of the 2011 19th International Euromicro Conference on Parallel, Distributed and Network-Based Processing*, pp. 247–251, Ayia Napa, Cyprus, February 2011.

[21] H. Kondo, S. Otani, M. Nakajima et al., "Heterogeneous multicore SoC with SiP for secure multimedia applications," *IEEE Journal of Solid-State Circuits*, vol. 44, no. 8, pp. 2251–2259, 2009.

[22] S. Wang, J. Han, Y. Li, Y. Bo, and X. Zeng, "A 920 MHz quad-core cryptography processor accelerating parallel task processing of public-key algorithms," in *Proceedings of the IEEE 2013 Custom Integrated Circuits Conference*, pp. 1–4, San Jose, CA, USA, September 2013.

[23] M. Alfadel, E. S. M. El-Alfy, and K. M. A. Kamal, "Evaluating time and throughput at different modes of operation in AES algorithm," in *Proceedings of the 2017 8th International Conference on Information Technology (ICIT)*, pp. 795–801, Amman, Jordan, May 2017.

[24] A. Abidi, S. Tawbi, C. Guyeux, B. Bouallègue, and M. Machhout, "Summary of topological study of chaotic cbc mode of operation," in *Proceedings of the 2016 IEEE Intl Conference on Computational Science and Engineering (CSE) and IEEE Intl Conference on Embedded and Ubiquitous Computing (EUC) and 15th Intl Symposium on Distributed Computing and Applications for Business Engineering (DCABES)*, pp. 436–443, Paris, France, August 2016.

[25] S. Najjar-Ghabel, S. Yousefi, and M. Z. Lighvan, "A high speed implementation counter mode cryptography using hardware parallelism," in *Proceedings of the 2016 Eighth International Conference on Information and Knowledge Technology (IKT)*, pp. 55–60, Hamedan, Iran, September 2016.

[26] H. M. Heys, "Analysis of the statistical cipher feedback mode of block ciphers," *IEEE Transactions on Computers*, vol. 52, no. 1, pp. 77–92, 2003.

[27] M. A. Alomari, K. Samsudin, and A. R. Ramli, "A study on encryption algorithms and modes for disk encryption," in *Proceedings of the 2009 International Conference on Signal Processing Systems*, pp. 793–797, Singapore, 2009.

[28] L. Wang, H. M. Cui, L. Chen, and X. B. Feng, "Research on task parallel programming model," *Journal of Software*, vol. 24, no. 1, pp. 77–90, 2013.

[29] K. Huang, G. C. Fox, and J. J. Dongarra, *Distributed and Cloud Computing: From Parallel Processing to the Internet of Things*, Morgan Kaufmann, Burlington, MA, USA, 2011.

13

A Fast and Robust Key Frame Extraction Method for Video Copyright Protection

Yunyu Shi,[1] Haisheng Yang,[2] Ming Gong,[2] Xiang Liu,[1] and Yongxiang Xia[1]

[1]*School of Electronic and Electrical Engineering, Shanghai University of Engineering Science, Shanghai, China*
[2]*Shanghai Media Group, Shanghai, China*

Correspondence should be addressed to Xiang Liu; morningcall@sues.edu.cn

Academic Editor: Hui Cheng

The paper proposes a key frame extraction method for video copyright protection. The fast and robust method is based on frame difference with low level features, including color feature and structure feature. A two-stage method is used to extract accurate key frames to cover the content for the whole video sequence. Firstly, an alternative sequence is got based on color characteristic difference between adjacent frames from original sequence. Secondly, by analyzing structural characteristic difference between adjacent frames from the alternative sequence, the final key frame sequence is obtained. And then, an optimization step is added based on the number of final key frames in order to ensure the effectiveness of key frame extraction. Compared with the previous methods, the proposed method has advantage in computation complexity and robustness on several video formats, video resolution, and so on.

1. Introduction

Video data has been increased rapidly due to rapid development of digital video capture and editing technology. Therefore, video copyright protection is an emerging research field and has attracted more and more attention. Digital video watermark is a traditional method for video copyright protection. However there are some faults about the above method and it is not suitable for huge video data on the Internet.

Key frame extraction is a powerful tool that implements video content by selecting a set of summary key frames to represent video sequences. Most of the existing key frames extraction methods are not suitable for video copyright protection, as they do not meet specific requirements.

Generally, key frame extraction techniques can be roughly categorized into four types [1], based on shot boundary, visual information, movement analysis, and cluster method. And then sometimes it could be completed in compressed domain [2]. Nowadays, cluster-based methods are mostly applied in video content analysis research. In these methods, key frame extraction is usually modeled as a typical clustering

process that divides one video shot into several clusters and then one or several frames are extracted based on low or high level features [3–6]. The methods in compressed domain usually are not suitable for diverse formats of videos from the Internet. Transcoding may increase time complexity and inaccuracy.

How to achieve a meaningful key frame is an important problem in various communities. The focus of the work is to represent the video content adequately and fast [7, 8]. In this paper, an active detection method is proposed. First, the key frame is defined for video copyright protection. And then, a key frame extraction algorithm based on two-step method with low level features is proposed.

The distinct features of our algorithm are as follows. (1) The definition of key frame is specific for video copyright protection. (2) The method is with lower computation complexity. (3) The method is robust for online videos regardless of video formats, video resolution, and so on.

The rest of the paper is organized as follows. The proposed key frame extraction method is presented in Section 2, while experimental results are listed in Section 3. Finally the conclusions are drawn in Section 4.

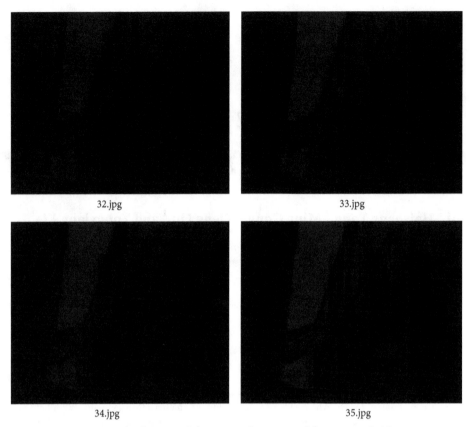

32.jpg

33.jpg

34.jpg

35.jpg

FIGURE 1: Four frames with low gray value extracted from a tested video.

2. The Proposed Key Frame Extraction Method

2.1. Definition of Key Frame for Video Copyright Protection. There are some distinct features about the key frame for video copyright protection. So, the key frame for video copyright protection is defined firstly before video preprocessing and key frame extracting.

The key frames should meet the following three conditions.

(1) The gray value of a key frame is within a certain range to allow viewers to have subjective perception about the video content. Four images with low gray value in Figure 1 are extracted from a single video, which is difficult for almost viewers to recognise the content.

(2) The final key frame sequence must be arranged in chronological order consistent with original video sequence, in order to satisfy temporal features and to be different from the short promotion trailer.

(3) Appropriate redundancy of some key frames is allowed to ensure the periods or intervals along the processing of video content. Figure 2 indicates the condition by selecting four images from a tested video, which are with similar content, that is to say, one judge in the show every once in a while.

In general, radio and television programs need to convey certain visual content; that is, video images that are too dark

or too bright do not meet these subjective feelings. Four images in Figure 1 are extracted form a tested video, which are always too dark for viewers to perceive the video content. The phenomenon is sometimes with gradual transitions of shots. In order to distinguish and program trailers and other programs, the intervals between extracted key frames must be consistent with the frames from the original video. As online video piracy is often divided into smaller video files for playback, thus mastering the key frame extraction should allow appropriate redundancy to ensure a period of time. Taking the talent show as an example, the moderator reviewing screen may arise for every player in a game situation, as shown in Figure 2; then the time of video frames' critical information is reserved for the key frame extraction processing.

2.2. Two-Stage Method for Key Frame Extraction. Figure 3 is the key frame extraction overall flowchart for digital video copyright protection. First, a digital video is decomposed into video frames. The downloaded video from the network includes several video formats, such as f4v, flv, and mp4. In order to improve the universality of video key extraction algorithm, the present method does not consider the specific format and video stream structure, and the video is decoded before the processed video frame decomposition. It is seen from Figure 3 that the program to extract key frame is divided into two steps. Firstly, alternative key frame sequence based on the color characteristics of the original difference

25.jpg 669.jpg

1061.jpg 1778.jpg

FIGURE 2: Four frames with similar content extracted from a tested video.

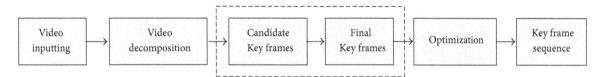

FIGURE 3: Flowchart of the proposed key frame extraction method.

between video frames is obtained; then key frame sequence is got according to the structure characteristic differences between alternative key frames sequence, and finally it is determined by the number of key frames in order to ensure the effectiveness of key frames.

Based on the above considerations, the frame difference method is used to extract key frames by analyzing the presence of spatial redundancy and temporal redundancy. In order to improve operational efficiency, it is worth mentioning that this method is different from the traditional shot segmentation method [9], for that the traditional approach is to conduct a video shot segmentation, then to extract key frames from each shot, and finally to compose key frame sequence of the video. In this method, the segmentation is not considered and then to extract key frames directly from the video.

2.2.1. Alternative Key Frame Sequence Based on Color Features. Color is one of the important properties of the image and is often used to characterize the statistics of the image [10, 11], and even for some specified domain video, color information can be expressed directly semantics, such as soccer video, usually on behalf of green grass. In addition, different color space of the sensory perception of visual effects is inconsistent. In order to achieve an effective balance between the key frame extraction efficiency and the speed,

the RGB color space is used and the color histogram for each frame is calculated. Then the color histogram difference between adjacent frames is adopted in the present method, as shown in Figure 4.

Based on the number of key frames, color feature extraction method for video sequence obvious video content conversion has a good ability to judge, but to little effect, or change the gradient color; light detection effect is not ideal, because the color histogram for pretty gradients and lighting effects such as gradients are very sensitive to the frame between a few dozen frames of video content; despite little change between adjacent frames, the significant changes between color histogram features are occurring. As previously stressed, in order to quickly and effectively perform key frame extraction, the video shot segmentation will not be adopted directly. Although motion estimation, optical flow analysis, and motion modeling method are effective in the previous method, the time complexity is also too high; these problems have a serious impact on the practical application of copyright in video monitoring.

2.2.2. Final Key Frame Sequence Based on Structure Features. Figure 5 is a key frame sequence optimization based on structural features. The program uses the first frame extraction based on color features alternate key and then extracted key frames to optimize based on structural features; that is, the

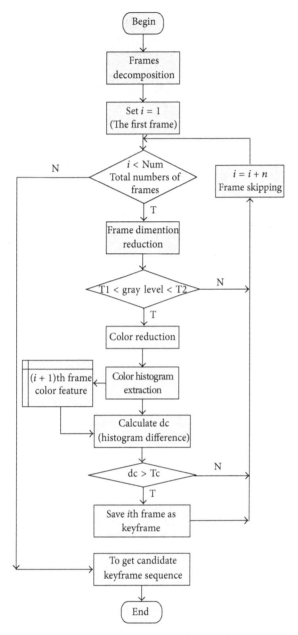

FIGURE 4: Flowchart of generating candidate key frame sequence.

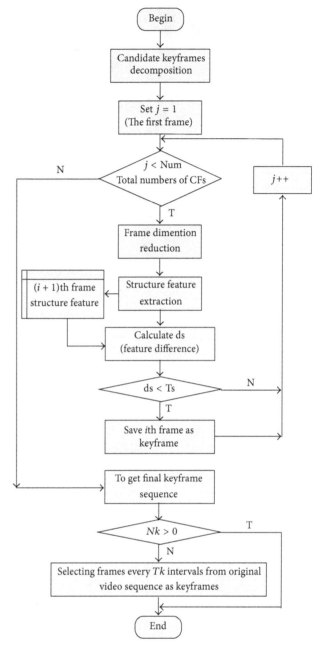

FIGURE 5: Flowchart of generating final key frame sequence and optimization based on key frames number.

alternative key frame structure similarity between adjacent frames is determined to further reduce key frames.

The method is derived from the structural similarity evaluation method for image quality evaluation [12] and is a measure of the similarity of the two images; the value closer to 1 indicates that the two images' quality is more similar. Structural similarity theory states that natural image signal is highly structured and that there is a strong correlation between pixels, especially airspace closest pixels; this correlation contains important information visual objects in the scene structure. Human visual system (HVS) main function is to extract structured information from view; it can be used as a measure of structural information perceived image quality of approximation. In this scenario, the structure is similar to

the concept introduced to the key frame optimization process; thereby removing the extraction of the frame structure information is not sensitive to this problem based on color feature key.

The program uses only similarity index structure similar to the structure of the components. From the perspective of an image composition, structural information is defined as an independent component from brightness and contrast in the theory of structural similarity index. And it could reflect the properties of objects in the scene. The covariance is selected as a structural similarity metric. The main calculation is as follows.

FIGURE 6: Examples of alternative key frames.

Covariance as a structural similarity measure for the image block x, y of the correlation coefficient, namely, the covariance of x and y, is calculated as

$$\sigma_{xy} = \frac{1}{N-1} \sum_{i-1}^{N} \left(x_i - \mu_i \right) \left(y_i - \mu_i \right), \tag{1}$$

where N is the number of the patches and μ_i is the average value.

In the alternative key frame sequence, the front frame could be as the original image, and the adjacent frame is set as the test image. According to the two corresponding image blocks at the same position x (in the original image) and y (in the test image), the structure similarity component between the two image blocks is calculated as (x, y):

$$s\left(x, y \right) = \frac{\sigma_{xy} + C}{\sigma_x \sigma_y + C}, \tag{2}$$

where $C = ((KL)^2/2)$, $K \ll 1$, $L \in (0, 255]$ and σ_x, σ_y are x and y variance, respectively.

If the component values of $s(x, y)$ are small, then the distinction between the contents of the information is not; at the same time they do not have to be retained as a key frame, which can be extracted only as a key frame is optimized.

2.3. Optimization Based on the Number of Key Frames. After extracting alternative key frames based on color features and key frames based on structural features, the number of key frames will be determined to meet the demand. If no key frame is extracted from a video, then it will extract the appropriate number of key frames from the original video, in accordance with isochronous interval. Usually this occurs in the lens without the division, such as newscasts broadcast of a piece with only anchor shot. There are no significant changes in color and structural features between video frames.

3. Experiments and Analysis

The method is applied to a lot of online videos downloaded from several video websites and the digital linear tapes are from Shanghai Media Group. The algorithm was implemented in C++ and OpenCV 2.0, and then the experiments were conducted on a Windows 7 system with an Intel i7 processor and 16 GB RAM.

Firstly, we took television show "SUPER DIVA" to verify the effectiveness and robustness of the proposed method. More than 20 versions of the copies or near-duplicates were downloaded, which may be different in video formats (.mp4, .rm, .wmv, .flv, etc.), spatial resolutions (1920 ∗ 1080, 1080 ∗ 720, 720 ∗ 576, etc.), video lengths (such as short clips cut from a full video), and so on. The results which are got from the downloaded video with mp4 format are partly shown in Figures 6 and 7.

From Figure 6, we could see that most key frames are covering the video content exactly. There are also some frames similar with content, such as the three frames in the 2nd and 3rd row. The difference among these frames is color background, especially the bubble lights. So the final key frames are extracted based on the structural difference from the alternative key frames, as shown in Figure 7. In general, these final key frames meet the three conditions mentioned in Section 2. The frame content could be viewed definitely and their order consisted with the original video, and there

FIGURE 7: Examples of final key frames extracted from Figure 6.

FIGURE 8: Three sets of key frames from different versions of the tested video.

is appropriate redundancy, such as the third frame in the 1st row and the last frame in the 3rd row.

Secondly, three different versions of SUPER DIVA were tested to get the final key frames. They are different in formats or resolutions and are noted in V1 (.mp4, 640 * 352), V2 (.flv, 608 * 448), and V3 (.avi, 512 * 288). The results are partly shown in Figure 8. It should be noted that the frames listed in Figure 8 are cropped to the same size for the appearance. Generally, each set of key frames are consistent with others, especially with almost the same video content and the same time line. The reason for the different key frames may be because of the same feature difference thresholds, Tc and Ts.

Thirdly, the optimization step based on the number of key frames was tested and the results are listed in Figure 9. The original video is a short promotion trailer about a famous movie. There's almost no feature difference among these original frames, only the mouth movements and few hand movements of the introducer. So no key frames are extracted based on the color and structure information. Therefore, the optimization based on the a fixed time interval is needed in order to satisfy the key frame demand and ensure the following processes for video copyright detection.

4. Conclusions

A key frame extraction method based on frame difference with low level features is proposed for video copyright protection. Exactly, a two-stage method is used to extract accurate key frames to cover the content for the whole video sequence. Firstly, an alternative sequence is obtained

FIGURE 9: Optimized key frames based on the frame number.

based on color characteristic difference between adjacent frames from original sequence. Secondly, the final key frame sequence is obtained by analyzing structural characteristic difference between adjacent frames from the alternative sequence. And thirdly, an optimization step based on the number of final key frames is added in order to ensure the effectiveness for video copyright protection processes. Tested with several television videos with different content, formats, and resolutions, it is shown that the proposed method has advantages in computation complexity and robustness on several video formats, video resolution, and so on. In the future the adaptive threshold is the primary research point.

Conflicts of Interest

The authors declare that they have no conflicts of interest.

Acknowledgments

Shanghai College Young Teachers Training Program (no. ZZGCD15002) and Local Colleges and Universities' Capacity Construction Project of Shanghai Science and Technology Commission (no. 15590501300) are gratefully acknowledged.

References

[1] J. M. Zhang, H. Y. Liu, and S. M. Sun, "Keyframe extraction based on improved ant algorithm and agglom erative," *Computer Engineering and Applications*, vol. 49, no. 3, pp. 222–225, 2013.

[2] X. Guo and F. Shi, "Quick extracting keyframes from compressed video," in *Proceedings of the 2nd International Conference on Computer Engineering and Technology (ICCET '10)*, pp. V4163–V4165, Chengdu, China, April 2010.

[3] S. Angadi and V. Naik, "Entropy based fuzzy C means clustering and key frame extraction for sports video summarization," in *Proceedings of the 5th International Conference on Signal and Image Processing (ICSIP '14)*, pp. 271–279, January 2014.

[4] Q. Guo, C. Zhang, Y. Zhang, and H. Liu, "An efficient SVD-based method for image denoising," *IEEE Transactions on Circuits & Systems for Video Technology*, vol. 26, no. 5, pp. 868–880, 2016.

[5] J. Peng and Q. Xiao-Lin, "Keyframe-based video summary using visual attention clues," *IEEE Multimedia*, vol. 17, no. 2, pp. 64–73, 2010.

[6] L. Liu and G. Fan, "Combined key-frame extraction and object-based video segmentation," *IEEE Transactions on Circuits & Systems for Video Technology*, vol. 15, no. 7, pp. 869–884, 2005.

[7] M. Chatzigiorgaki and A. N. Skodras, "Real-time Keyframe extraction towards video content identification," in *Proceedings of the 16th International Conference on Digital Signal Processing (DSP '09)*, pp. 68–73, grc, July 2009.

[8] S. Lei, G. Xie, and G. Yan, "A novel key-frame extraction approach for both video summary and video index," *The Scientific World Journal*, vol. 2014, Article ID 695168, 9 pages, 2014.

[9] J. Li, Y. Ding, Y. Shi, and Q. Zeng, "DWT-based shot boundary detection using Support Vector Machine," in *Proceedings of the 5th International Conference on Information Assurance and Security (IAS '09)*, pp. 435–438, September 2009.

[10] Z. Sun, K. Jia, and H. Chen, "Video key frame extraction based on spatial-temporal color distribution," in *Proceedings of the 4th International Conference on Intelligent Information Hiding and Multiedia Signal (IIH-MSP '08)*, pp. 196–199, August 2008.

[11] J. Zhang, X. Jiang, G. Li, and L. Jiang, "Key frame extraction based on particle swarm optimization," *Journal of Computer Applications*, vol. 31, no. 2, pp. 358–361, 2011.

[12] Y. Shi, Y. Ding, R. Zhang, and J. Li, "Structure and hue similarity for color image quality Assessment," in *Proceedings of the International Conference on Electronic Computer Technology (ICECT '09)*, pp. 329–333, February 2009.

14

QoE Guarantee Scheme based on Cooperative Cognitive Cloud and Opportunistic Weight Particle Swarm

Weihang Shi

College of Software Technology, Zhengzhou University, Zhengzhou, Henan 450002, China

Correspondence should be addressed to Weihang Shi; shiwh@zzu.edu.cn

Academic Editor: James Nightingale

It is well known that the Internet application of cloud services may be affected by the inefficiency of cloud computing and inaccurate evaluation of quality of experience (QoE) seriously. In our paper, based on construction algorithms of cooperative cognitive cloud platform and optimization algorithm of opportunities weight particle swarm clustering, the QoE guarantee mechanism was proposed. The mechanism, through the sending users of requests and the cognitive neighbor users' cooperation, combined the cooperation of subcloud platforms and constructed the optimal cloud platform with the different service. At the same time, the particle swarm optimization algorithm could be enhanced dynamically according to all kinds of opportunity request weight, which could optimize the cooperative cognitive cloud platform. Finally, the QoE guarantee scheme was proposed with the opportunity weight particle swarm optimization algorithm and collaborative cognitive cloud platform. The experimental results show that the proposed mechanism compared is superior to the QoE guarantee scheme based on cooperative cloud and QoE guarantee scheme based on particle swarm optimization, compared with optimization fitness and high cloud computing service execution efficiency and high throughput performance advantages.

1. Introduction

With the rapid development of cloud computing technology and diversification of user requirements of mobile Internet, how to provide the scalable service and how to optimize the hardware and software platforms have been the hot research issue [1]. Particularly, according to the computing service of the cloud platform [2], we have to obtain the comprehensive understanding of user experience requirements and quality evaluation, which could not only create the maximum interests of services providers but also satisfy the requirements of users. The cloud platform could be adjusted with the real-time dynamic state information adaptively, to further enhance the cloud computing service support capabilities. A series of research results have been obtained, such as Seamless QoE Support [3], Context-Aware QoE [4], and Policy-Based and QoE-Aware Content Delivery [5].

About cooperative cognition technology and cloud computing algorithm, Kaewpuang et al. [6] provided the guarantee of mobile applications by studying and sharing the radio and computing with mobile cloud computing environment. Lei et al. [7] proposed a novel cognitive cooperative vehicular ad hoc network for solving the contradiction between the increasing demand of diverse vehicular wireless applications and the shortage of spectrum resource. Feteiha and Hassanein [8] addressed the area of heterogeneous wireless relaying vehicular clouds and devised an advanced vehicular relaying technique for enhanced connectivity in densely populated urban areas. The spectrum leasing strategy based on cooperative relaying for cognitive radio networks was proposed in [9]. The implementation of the CCRN framework applied to IEEE 802.11 WLANs was proposed by [10].

On the other hand, the fast cloud-based web service composition approach was proposed according to the characteristics of notion of Skyline [11]. The task-based system load balancing method using particle swarm optimization (TBSLB-PSO) was proposed for achieving system load balancing by only transferring extra tasks from an overloaded VM instead of migrating the entire overloaded VM [12].

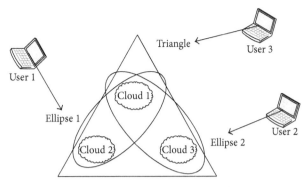

FIGURE 1: Architecture of cloud platform.

This paper puts forward a cloud theory-based particle swarm optimization (CTPSO) algorithm proposed by Ma and Xu [13], which is used to solve a variant of the vehicle routing problem. Multiple Strategies Based Orthogonal Design PSO was presented by Qin et al. [14], which is used with a small probability to construct a new exemplar in each iteration. The hybrid methods for fuzzy clustering were proposed in [15].

In view of the deficiency of the above research results, we studied the cloud platform construction method based on cooperative cognition of data processing units. Then we researched the optimization algorithm with opportunistic weight particle swarm. Finally, we proposed a reliable and efficient QoE guarantee scheme.

The rest of the paper is organized as follows. Section 2 describes the cooperative cognitive cloud. In Section 3, we design the opportunistic weight particle swarm. The QoE guarantee scheme is proposed in Section 4. Experiment results are given in Section 5. Finally, we conclude the paper in Section 6.

2. Cooperative Cognitive Cloud Platform

The cloud platform can store the large scale data. For achieving load balance and dynamic adjustment, the cloud platform would provide different services for different Internet users. The cloud platform can avoid the system performance degradation, which may be caused by user service competition. The cloud platform can also satisfy the service quality reliability simultaneously. The cloud platform architecture is shown in Figure 1.

In Figure 1, there are three clouds in the cloud platform. Every cloud is made up of the computer. According to the needs of different users, the sub platform is different. The service of User 1 is provided by elliptical 1 cloud platform consisting of cloud 1 and cloud 2. The service of User 2 is provided by elliptical 2 cloud platform consisting of cloud 1 and cloud 3. The service of User 3 is provided by triangle cloud platform consisting of cloud 1, cloud 2, and cloud 3.

Cloud platform is defined as the state vector $S_{cp} = \{C_N, \text{RAM}_{\text{MAX}}, \text{RAM}_{\text{AVE}}, \text{DIS}_{\text{MAX}}, \text{DIS}_{\text{AVE}}, \text{CH}_{\text{MAX}}, \text{CH}_{\text{AVE}}, \text{CPU}_{\text{MAX}}, \text{CPU}_{\text{AVE}}\}$.

Here, C_N denotes the number of computers in subcloud platform, RAM_{MAX} denotes the total member size of subcloud platform, RAM_{AVE} denotes the average member size, DIS_{MAX} denotes the total disk size, DIS_{AVE} denotes the average disk size, CH_{MAX} denotes the maximum channel bandwidth, CH_{AVE} denotes the average channel bandwidth, CPU_{MAX} denotes the maximum CPU operating frequency, and CPU_{AVE} denotes the average CPU operating frequency.

The user cloud computing service request is set to 1. The request includes 4 metrics, which are E_{RAM}, E_{DIS}, E_{CH}, and E_{CPU}. Here, $E_{\text{RAM}} + E_{\text{DIS}} + E_{\text{CH}} + E_{\text{CPU}} = 1$.

The matching vector F between cloud platform and user demand is defined as $\{C_N, E_{\text{RAM}} * \text{RAM}_{\text{MAX}}, (E_{\text{RAM}}/C_N) * \text{RAM}_{\text{AVE}}, E_{\text{DIS}} * \text{DIS}_{\text{MAX}}, (E_{\text{DIS}}/C_N) * \text{DIS}_{\text{AVE}}, E_{\text{CH}} * \text{CH}_{\text{MAX}}, (E_{\text{CH}}/C_N)\text{CH}_{\text{AVE}}, E_{\text{CPU}} * \text{CPU}_{\text{MAX}}, (E_{\text{CPU}}/C_N)\text{CPU}_{\text{AVE}}\}$.

Hence, cloud platform and user request evaluation results are as shown in the following formula:

$$a = E_{\text{RAM}}\text{RAM}_{\text{MAX}} + E_{\text{DIS}}\text{DIS}_{\text{MAX}},$$
$$b = E_{\text{CH}}\text{CH}_{\text{MAX}} + E_{\text{CPU}}\text{CPU}_{\text{MAX}}, \tag{1}$$
$$E_{(S_{\text{CP}}, \text{User})} = \frac{a + b}{C_N}.$$

In order to satisfy the request of users, the cloud platform load is shown in the following:

$$\text{RAM}_T = \sum_{t=1}^{T} \sum_{i=1}^{C_N} E^t{}_{\text{RAM}}\text{RAM}^t_{\text{AVE}},$$

$$\text{DIS}_T = \sum_{t=1}^{T} \sum_{i=1}^{C_N} E^t{}_{\text{DIS}}\text{DIS}^t_{\text{AVE}},$$

$$\text{CH}_T = \sum_{t=1}^{T} \sum_{i=1}^{C_N} E^t{}_{\text{CH}}\text{RAM}^t_{\text{CH}}, \tag{2}$$

$$\text{CPU}_T = \sum_{t=1}^{T} \sum_{i=1}^{C_N} E^t{}_{\text{CPU}}\text{RAM}^t_{\text{CPU}}.$$

Whether the cloud platform is able to satisfy the user request or not could be judged by the following formula:

$$Y \ (\mathrm{RAM}_T + \mathrm{DIS}_T + \mathrm{CH}_T + \mathrm{CPU}_T) \leq E_{(S_{\mathrm{CP}}, \mathrm{User})},$$
$$N \ (\mathrm{RAM}_T + \mathrm{DIS}_T + \mathrm{CH}_T + \mathrm{CPU}_T) > E_{(S_{\mathrm{CP}}, \mathrm{User})}. \qquad (3)$$

Here, Y denotes that the could platform can satisfy the requirements and N denotes that it cannot do this.

After the subcloud platform satisfies the requirements, the user should broadcast the signal to clouds. The neighbor users could listen to the channel and receive the signal. The collection of service requests for multiple neighbor users is shown in the following formula:

$$U_R^{N_U} = \bigcup_{i=1}^{N_U} \sum_{i=1}^{4} E_i U_R^i. \qquad (4)$$

Here, $U_R^{N_U}$ denotes the collection of user cognitive service requests, N_U denote the user number of joining the cognitive networks, E denote the 4 aspects of comprehensive evaluation of user's cloud computing service request, and U_R denote the evaluation value of a neighbor's service request.

The channel bandwidth is shown in formula (5) between the sending request user and the cognitive users:

$$S_T = \sum_{i=1}^{C_N} \mathrm{CH}^i{}_T,$$
$$S_{\mathrm{AVE}} = \frac{a+b}{C_N},$$
$$a = E_{\mathrm{RAM}} \mathrm{RAM}_{\mathrm{AVE}} + E_{\mathrm{DIS}} \mathrm{DIS}_{\mathrm{AVE}}, \qquad (5)$$
$$b = E_{\mathrm{CH}} \mathrm{CH}_{\mathrm{AVE}} + E_{\mathrm{CPU}} \mathrm{CPU}_{\mathrm{AVE}},$$
$$B_W = \sum_{i=1}^{N_U} \sum_{j=1}^{C_N} \ln \left(S^i{}_T S^j{}_{\mathrm{AVE}} \right).$$

Here, S_T is used to analyze the resource of subcloud platform and S_{AVE} is used to analyze the average data processing ability of subcloud platform. The channel bandwidth could be obtained by the combination of neighbor users and subcloud platform resources. So, the cloud platform could be constructed based on the cooperative cognition of sending request user, cognitive users, and computers of subcloud platform. The architecture is shown in Figure 2.

To sum up, the optimization of cloud resource management platform could be provided by the cooperative control of cloud platform data processing units and cooperative transmission of the sending request user and the cognition neighbor users, which is shown in the following formula:

$$\text{minimize:} \quad \sum_{i=1}^{SCP_N} S^i{}_{\mathrm{CP}}$$

$$\text{subject to:} \quad
\begin{cases}
\displaystyle \sum_{i=1}^{N_U} \sum_{j=1}^{C_N} \ln \left(E^i{}_{\mathrm{RAM}} \mathrm{RAM}^j{}_{\mathrm{MAX}} \right) \geq E \left[\sum_{j=1}^{C_N} \mathrm{RAM}^j{}_{\mathrm{AVE}} \right] \\[6pt]
\displaystyle \sum_{i=1}^{N_U} \sum_{j=1}^{C_N} \ln \left(E^i{}_{\mathrm{DIS}} \mathrm{DIS}^j{}_{\mathrm{MAX}} \right) \geq E \left[\sum_{j=1}^{C_N} \mathrm{DIS}^j{}_{\mathrm{AVE}} \right] \\[6pt]
\displaystyle \sum_{i=1}^{N_U} \sum_{j=1}^{C_N} \ln \left(E^i{}_{\mathrm{CH}} \mathrm{CH}^j{}_{\mathrm{MAX}} \right) \geq E \left[\sum_{j=1}^{C_N} \mathrm{CH}^j{}_{\mathrm{AVE}} \right] \\[6pt]
\displaystyle \sum_{i=1}^{N_U} \sum_{j=1}^{C_N} \ln \left(E^i{}_{\mathrm{CPU}} \mathrm{CPU}^j{}_{\mathrm{MAX}} \right) \geq E \left[\sum_{j=1}^{C_N} \mathrm{CPU}^j{}_{\mathrm{AVE}} \right].
\end{cases} \qquad (6)$$

Here, the function E is used to compute the mean of all data processing unit of the relevant resources in cloud platform.

3. Opportunistic Weight Particle Swarm

Through considering the various types of user requests and the opportunistic weight, we used and improved the particle swarm optimization algorithm to realize the optimization objectives of cooperative cognitive cloud platform and guarantee quality of the user experience.

Assume that the cognitive cooperative cloud platform is a particle swarm and composed of m particles, which is denoted as $\mathrm{CC} = \{\mathrm{CC}_1, \mathrm{CC}_2, \ldots, \mathrm{CC}_m\}$.

The j particle expresses the data service progress of the data packet, which is denoted by vector $KP = \{KP_1, KP_2, \ldots, KP_K\}$. Here, K denotes the user experience quality of the data packet, which includes the real-time performance, reliability, size, number of hops, and distance.

The sending power of the j particle Pj is $\{P_{j1}, P_{j2}, \ldots, P_{jK}\}$. The extremal optimization cloud platform

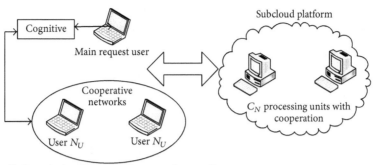

(i) Constructing the cooperative networks according to the resources and status of mobile users

(ii) Selecting the users from cooperative networks based on the value of E_{RAM}, E_{DIS}, E_{CH}, and E_{CPU}

FIGURE 2: Cooperative cognitive cloud platform.

LO is $\{\mathrm{LO}_1, \mathrm{LO}_2, \ldots, \mathrm{LO}_K\}$. Extremal optimization cloud platform FO is $\{\mathrm{FO}_1, \mathrm{FO}_2, \ldots, \mathrm{FO}_K\}$.

Transmission power opportunity renewal model is shown in the following formula:

$$P_{j+1} = P_j + \sum_{i=1}^{K} \lambda_i KP_i + \sqrt{\left| P_j^2 - P_{j-1}^2 \right|}. \tag{7}$$

Here, the optimization of j particle is realized based on j and $j - 1$ particle. The sending power could be updated with the opportunistic dynamical scheme.

Resource opportunity renewal model is shown in the following formula:

$$\mathrm{RAM}_{j+1} = \sum_{i=1}^{C_N} E^j_{i,\mathrm{RAM}} \sum_{l=1}^{K} KP_l \mathrm{RAM}^j_{i,\mathrm{AVE}},$$

$$\mathrm{DIS}_{j+1} = \sum_{i=1}^{C_N} E^j_{i,\mathrm{DIS}} \sum_{l=1}^{K} KP_l \mathrm{DIS}^j_{i,\mathrm{AVE}},$$

$$\mathrm{CH}_{j+1} = \sum_{i=1}^{C_N} E^j_{i,\mathrm{CHS}} \sum_{l=1}^{K} KP_l \mathrm{CH}^j_{i,\mathrm{AVE}}, \tag{8}$$

$$\mathrm{CPU}_{j+1} = \sum_{i=1}^{C_N} E^j_{i,\mathrm{CPU}} \sum_{l=1}^{K} KP_l \mathrm{CPU}^j_{i,\mathrm{AVE}}.$$

Request weight updating model is shown in the following formula:

$$E^{j+1}_{(S_{\mathrm{CP}},\mathrm{User})} = \frac{\sum_{i=1}^{K} KP_i \left(E^j_{(S_{\mathrm{CP}},\mathrm{User})} + E^{j-1}_{(S_{\mathrm{CP}},\mathrm{User})} \right)}{\sqrt{N_U C_N \left| E^j_{(S_{\mathrm{CP}},\mathrm{User})} - E^{j-1}_{(S_{\mathrm{CP}},\mathrm{User})} \right|}}. \tag{9}$$

In order to guarantee and sustain dynamic characteristic and diversity of cloud platform in the particle swarm dynamic evolution process, based on subcloud platform optimization

extreme and cloud platform extremal optimization, the real-time evaluation function is established and shown in the following formula:

$$\mathrm{RH}|_{j \to j+l} = \frac{\sqrt{j+l}}{l} \sum_{i=1}^{K} KP_i \mathrm{RH}_{j+i},$$

$$\mathrm{RH}_j = \log_2 \left(\sum_{i=1}^{K} KP_i \right)^j \sum_{i=1}^{K} \frac{\mathrm{LO}^j_i}{\mathrm{FO}_i}. \tag{10}$$

Flow of the cooperative cognitive cloud platform with opportunity weight particle swarm optimization algorithm is shown in Figure 3; the optimal fitness is shown in Figure 4. From the results of Figure 4, based on the best adaptation degree and the average fitness, this opportunity weight particle group optimization algorithm can satisfy the demand for data optimization cooperative cognitive cloud platform well. With the growing particle size, the best fitness increases gradually and the data clustering effect remains good, which not only enhance the local search ability but also achieve good global optimization effect.

4. QoE Guarantee Scheme

In view of the cooperative cognitive cloud platform, with the opportunity weight particle swarm optimization algorithm, the QoE guarantee mechanism is established from the perspective of the user. The QoE guarantee problem can be transformed into a multiobjective optimization problem, as shown in the following formula:

$$\begin{aligned} \mathrm{Min} \quad & \mathrm{FO}\,(kp) \\ \mathrm{s.t.} \quad & kp \in KP. \end{aligned} \tag{11}$$

Here, based on the global optimization, the user experience quality guarantee scheme is established based on multiobjective optimization.

Based on the user experience quality optimization model, we defined the user data service expectations of the target function UE and the expected execution efficiency of EE.

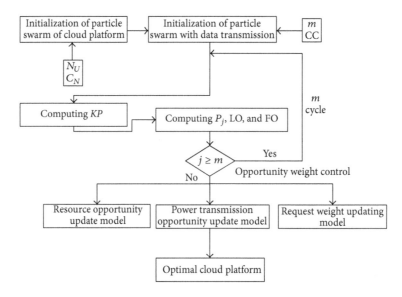

FIGURE 3: Flow of the weight particle swarm optimization algorithm.

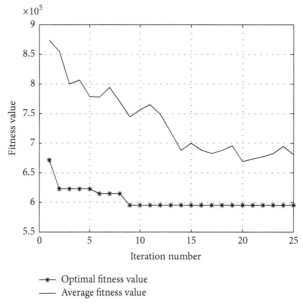

FIGURE 4: Particle swarm optimization.

After sending the service request to cognitive cooperative cloud platform by users, the expectation objective function UE of user data service is used to realize the optimization goal based on the cloud platform during initialization, particle swarm optimization, updating a series of operations, and so forth. This function is shown in formula (12).

The desired execution efficiency of EE: this means the execution time of the data service tasks and the ratio of the required cloud platform resources, which are shown in formula (13):

$$\text{UE} = \ln\left(\frac{\max\left\{\text{RAM}^j{}_{\text{MAX}}, \text{DIS}^j{}_{\text{MAX}}, \text{CH}^j{}_{\text{MAX}}, \text{CPU}^j{}_{\text{MAX}}\right\} - S_{\text{AVE}}}{1 + \max\left\{\text{RAM}^j{}_{\text{AVE}}, \text{DIS}^j{}_{\text{AVE}}, \text{CH}^j{}_{\text{AVE}}, \text{CPU}^j{}_{\text{AVE}}\right\}}\right), \tag{12}$$

$$\text{EE} = \ln\left(\frac{\text{UE} - \sum_{i=1}^{K} KP_i\left(E^j{}_{(S_{\text{CP}},\text{User})} + E^{j-1}{}_{(S_{\text{CP}},\text{User})}\right)}{1 + \left|E^j{}_{(S_{\text{CP}},\text{User})} - E^{j-1}{}_{(S_{\text{CP}},\text{User})}\right|}\right). \tag{13}$$

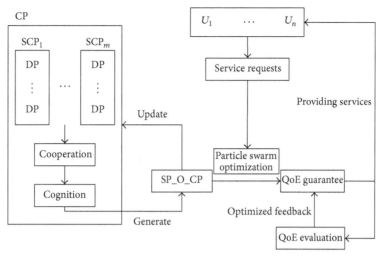

CP: cloud platform
DP: data processing unit
SCP: subcloud platform

U: user
SP_O_CP: service provider of optimal
cloud platform

FIGURE 5: QoE guarantee mechanism architecture.

Above all, based on formulas (11), (12), and (13), the objectives of QoE guarantee mechanism are shown in formula (14), which could minimize the parameters of UE, P, and FO and maximize EE:

$$\text{Min UE} = \ln \sum_{i=1}^{K} KP_i \left(\frac{\max\left\{\text{RAM}^j_{\text{MAX}}, \text{DIS}^j_{\text{MAX}}, \text{CH}^j_{\text{MAX}}, \text{CPU}^j_{\text{MAX}}\right\} - S_{\text{AVE}}}{1 + \max\left\{\text{RAM}^j_{\text{AVE}}, \text{DIS}^j_{\text{AVE}}, \text{CH}^j_{\text{AVE}}, \text{CPU}^j_{\text{AVE}}\right\}} \right),$$

$$\text{Max EE} = \ln \left(\frac{\text{UE} - \left(E^j_{(S_{\text{CP}},\text{User})} + E^{j-1}_{(S_{\text{CP}},\text{User})}\right)}{1 + \left|E^j_{(S_{\text{CP}},\text{User})} - E^{j-1}_{(S_{\text{CP}},\text{User})}\right|} \right)^{1/\sum_{i=1}^{K} KP_i},$$

$$\text{Min } P = \frac{1}{P_N} \sum_{j=1}^{P_N} \lambda_j \sum_{i=1}^{K} KP_i + \sqrt{\left|P_j^2 - P_{j-1}^2\right|} P_j,$$

$$\text{Min FO} = \frac{\alpha\text{UE} + \beta\text{EE} + \gamma P}{\sqrt{\alpha^2 \beta^2 \gamma^2}}.$$

(14)

The architecture is shown in Figure 5. The workflow of the proposed scheme is described as follows.

Step 1. Construct the cooperative cognitive cloud platform according to the cloud platform state and user requests.

Step 2. Divide the subcloud platform by selecting cooperative users and updating the cloud state.

Step 3. Execute the opportunistic weight particle swarm algorithm.

Step 4. Establish the QoE guarantee mechanism from the user's point of view.

5. Performance Evaluation

In order to validate the performance of the QoE guarantee mechanism based on cooperative cognitive clouds and opportunity weight particle swarm (Q-CCC-OWPW), we designed and developed 6 clouds in the rectangular area of 4000 meters * 4500 meters. Each cloud includes several computers. The setting of the experiment is shown in Table 1. The topology of experiment is illustrated as in Figure 6.

The QoE guarantee scheme based on opportunity weight particle swarm (Q-OWPW) and QoE guarantee scheme based on cooperative cognitive clouds (Q-CCC) and Q-CCC-OWPW are compared and analyzed from the aspects of

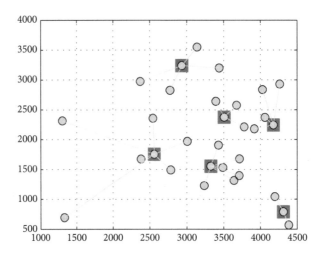

FIGURE 6: Experiment platform.

TABLE 1: Cloud settings.

Cloud	Number of computers	Location	Configuration	Disk usage
1	4	(2500, 2400)	Same	30%
2	5	(3400, 2600)	Same	10%
3	5	(4100, 2400)	Same	20%
4	3	(2400, 1700)	Same	25%
5	6	(3500, 1600)	Same	15%
6	3	(4300, 800)	Same	35%

optimal adaptive degree, throughput rate, and user's demand error and execution efficiency. The results are shown in Figure 7.

With the increase of the number of iterations, the optimal fitness curves of three QoE guarantee mechanisms are shown in Figure 7(a). Among them, Q-CCC-OWPW has the best fitness and gradually tends to be stable. This has benefited from the cooperation of the data processing computer and the opportunity particle swarm optimization, not only the perception of the cloud platform resources and dynamic adjustment according to the channel quality. However, Q-CCC can only sense the channel quality and Q-OWPW can only perceive the cloud platform resources, so the performance is poor.

Figure 7(b) gives the error of the throughput of the three mechanisms of and the throughput of the user's request. It was found that the error of Q-CCC and Q-OWPW is greater than that of the proposed Q-CCC-OWPW. When the active computer number is between 11 and 19, the performance of Q-OWPW is better than the one of Q-CCC. This is because the Q-OWPW cannot obtain the information of cloud resources.

User service request execution efficiency is shown in Figure 7(c). The execution efficiency of the three mechanisms gradually increases as the experimental time increases. This is because the cloud platform initialization, the cloud platform

and user channel competition, and resource allocation stage require a certain period of time; after the completion of the above operations, the execution efficiency of the system increased significantly. However, the efficiency of Q-OWPW prior to 500 s is lower than that of Q-CCC, which is due to the long time required for the optimization of particle swarm optimization. After more than 500 s, the efficiency of Q-CCC is higher than that of Q-OWPW. This is because the particle swarm optimization algorithm obtains the gain of data transmission. For Q-CCC-OWPW, the construction of the opportunity weight particle swarm optimization, to achieve global optimization, has higher efficiency.

6. Conclusions

In order to improve the execution efficiency of cloud and guarantee the quality of experience, we put forward the efficient and reliable QoE guarantee mechanism based on the cooperative cognitive cloud platform construction algorithms and opportunities weight particle swarm clustering optimization algorithm. First, according to the sending requests user and the cognitive neighbor users, the computers of subcloud platform through cooperative cognitive scheme cloud platform would be constructed and updated. Then, in order to realize the optimization objectives of cooperative cognitive cloud platform and improve quality of user experience, particle swarm optimization algorithm was improved for clustering by considering the user end of various types of requests the weight changes in the dynamic of opportunities. Finally, based on the cooperative cognitive cloud platform and the opportunity weight particle swarm optimization algorithm, the QoE guarantee mechanism was proposed from the user's point of view. The experimental results show that the proposed mechanism has obvious advantages in optimizing the degree of adaptation, the efficiency of the implementation of cloud computing services, and the throughput rate.

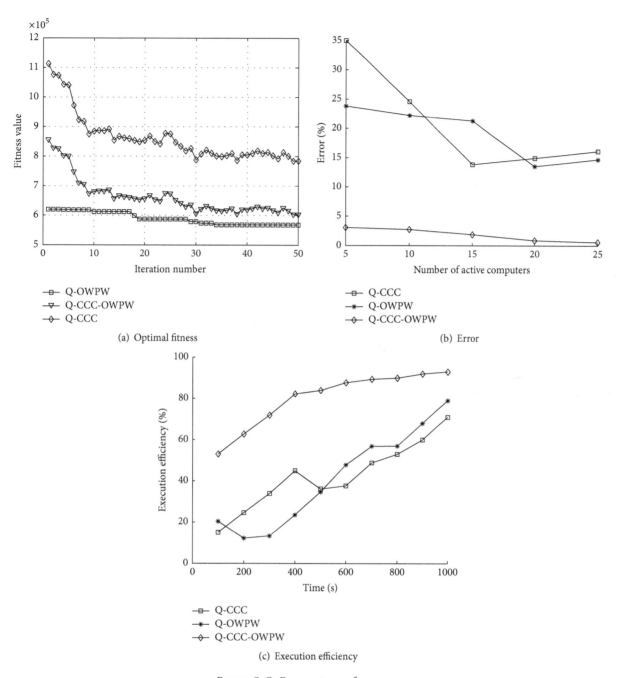

(a) Optimal fitness

(b) Error

(c) Execution efficiency

FIGURE 7: QoE guarantee performance.

Conflict of Interests

The authors declare that there is no conflict of interests regarding the publication of this paper.

References

[1] M. Jarschel, D. Schlosser, S. Scheuring, and T. Hoßfeld, "Gaming in the clouds: QoE and the users' perspective," *Mathematical and Computer Modelling*, vol. 57, no. 11-12, pp. 2883–2894, 2013.

[2] J. He, Y. Wen, J. Huang, and D. Wu, "On the cost-QoE tradeoff for cloud-based video streaming under Amazon EC2's pricing models," *IEEE Transactions on Circuits and Systems for Video Technology*, vol. 24, no. 4, pp. 669–680, 2014.

[3] G. Kim, S. Lee, and S. G. Lee, "Seamless QoE support for mobile cloud services using IEEE802.21 MIH and the GENI future internet framework," *International Journal of Software Engineering and Knowledge Engineering*, vol. 24, no. 7, pp. 1039–1063, 2014.

[4] K. Mitra, A. Zaslavsky, and C. Ahlund, "Context-aware QoE modelling, measurement, and prediction in mobile computing systems," *IEEE Transactions on Mobile Computing*, vol. 14, no. 5, pp. 920–936, 2015.

[5] M. Olli, Y. F. Zarrar, M. Petteri, and J. Lessmann, "Policy-based and QoE-aware content delivery using Q-learning method,"

Wireless Personal Communications, vol. 83, no. 1, pp. 315–342, 2015.

[6] R. Kaewpuang, D. Niyato, P. Wang, and E. Hossain, "A framework for cooperative resource management in mobile cloud computing," *IEEE Journal on Selected Areas in Communications*, vol. 31, no. 12, pp. 2685–2700, 2013.

[7] Z. Lei, L. Tao, L. Wei, Z. Siting, and L. Jianfeng, "Cooperative spectrum allocation with QoS support in cognitive cooperative vehicular ad hoc networks," *China Communications*, vol. 11, no. 10, pp. 49–59, 2014.

[8] M. F. Feteiha and H. S. Hassanein, "Enabling cooperative relaying VANET clouds over LTE-A networks," *IEEE Transactions on Vehicular Technology*, vol. 64, no. 4, pp. 1468–1479, 2015.

[9] K. Ma, J. Yang, G. Hu, and X. Guan, "Cooperative Relay-Aware Spectrum leasing based on Nash bargaining solution in cognitive radio networks," *International Journal of Communication Systems*, vol. 28, no. 7, pp. 1250–1264, 2015.

[10] M. B. Pandian, M. L. Sichitiu, and H. Dai, "Optimal resource allocation in random access cooperative cognitive radio networks," *IEEE Transactions on Mobile Computing*, vol. 14, no. 6, pp. 1245–1258, 2015.

[11] S. Wang, Q. Sun, H. Zou, and F. Yang, "Particle swarm optimization with skyline operator for fast cloud-based web service composition," *Mobile Networks & Applications*, vol. 18, no. 1, pp. 116–121, 2013.

[12] F. Ramezani, J. Lu, and F. K. Hussain, "Task-based system load balancing in cloud computing using particle swarm optimization," *International Journal of Parallel Programming*, vol. 42, no. 5, pp. 739–754, 2014.

[13] Y. Ma and J. Xu, "A cloud theory-based particle swarm optimization for multiple decision maker vehicle routing problems with fuzzy random time windows," *Engineering Optimization*, vol. 47, no. 6, pp. 825–842, 2015.

[14] Q. Qin, S. Cheng, Q. Zhang, Y. Wei, and Y. Shi, "Multiple strategies based orthogonal design particle swarm optimizer for numerical optimization," *Computers & Operations Research*, vol. 60, pp. 91–110, 2015.

[15] T. M. Silva Filho, B. A. Pimentel, R. M. C. R. Souza, and A. L. I. Oliveira, "Hybrid methods for fuzzy clustering based on fuzzy c-means and improved particle swarm optimization," *Expert Systems with Applications*, vol. 42, no. 17-18, pp. 6315–6328, 2015.

15

Inaccuracy-Tolerant Sparse-to-Dense Depth Propagation for Semiautomatic 2D-to-3D Conversion

Hongxing Yuan (ID)

School of Electronics and Information Engineering, Ningbo University of Technology, Ningbo 315211, China

Correspondence should be addressed to Hongxing Yuan; yuanhx@mail.ustc.edu.cn

Academic Editor: Jit S. Mandeep

Current semiautomatic 2D-to-3D methods assume that user input is perfectly accurate. However, it is difficult to get 100% accurate user scribbles and even small errors in the input will degrade the conversion quality. This paper addresses the issue with scribble confidence that considers color differences between labeled pixels and their neighbors. First, it counts the number of neighbors which have similar and different color values for each labeled pixels, respectively. The ratio between these two numbers at each labeled pixel is regarded as its scribble confidence. Second, the sparse-to-dense depth conversion is formulated as a confident optimization problem by introducing a confident weighting data cost term and the local and k-nearest depth consistent regularization terms. Finally, the dense depth-map is obtained by solving sparse linear equations. The proposed approach is compared with existing methods on several representative images. The experimental results demonstrate that the proposed method can tolerate some errors from use input and can reduce depth-map artifacts caused by inaccurate user input.

1. Introduction

3D videos have attracted more and more attention, providing an immersive realism visual experience by exploiting depth information [1]. With rapid advances in 3D display technologies, 3D content shortage has become one of the bottlenecks which restrict the development of entire 3D industry [2]. To remedy this issue, many 2D-to-3D conversion methods have been developed to convert existing 2D images/videos into 3D format by creating depth-maps [3]. Semiautomatic 2D-to-3D conversion can produce high-quality depth-maps from sparse user scribbles by using sparse-to-dense depth propagation. However, current methods assume that user scribbles are perfectly accurate [4–6], and depth quality degrades significantly when inaccurate scribbles are present. Figure 1 shows an experimental result where scribbles are partly inaccurate. As shown in Figures 1(d) and 1(e), existing methods generate visual artifacts around inaccurate labeled regions. To handle the inaccurate input, a confident sparse-to-dense propagation algorithm is introduced in this paper that obtains accurate depth-maps even from erroneous user scribbles, as in Figure 1(f).

The proposed method is based on the observation that inaccurate input often occurs at or near object boundaries, and the number of correct scribbles is much larger than the number of incorrect ones. The rest of this paper is organized as follows. In Section 2, the related works about sparse-to-dense depth propagation for 2D-to-3D conversion are reviewed. The proposed method is described in Section 3. Experimental results are provided in Section 4. Finally, conclusion and future work are given in Section 5.

2. Related Work

2D-to-3D conversion algorithms can be categorized into manual methods, automatic methods, and semiautomatic methods. Manual methods can offer the highest quality conversion results but need per-pixel depth assignment precisely which is most time consuming and costly. Automatic methods infer depth information in image/video by

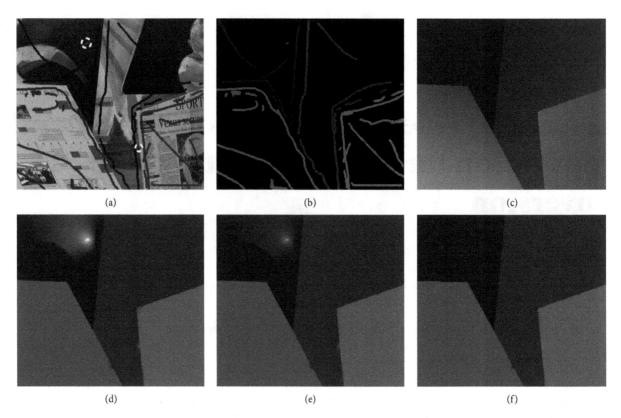

FIGURE 1: A sparse-to-dense depth propagation result with inaccurate input. (a) User scribbles (inaccurate scribbles are marked by the white circles). (b) Sparse depth-map extracted from user scribbles. (c) Groundtruth depth-map. (d) Depth-map generated by random walks [4]. (e) Depth-map generated by optimization method [6]. (f) Depth-map generated by the proposed method.

exploiting different depth perception cues such as motion, occlusion, vanishing points, defocus, and so on. Recently, with the popularity of deep learning, many neural networks have been proposed for automatic depth estimation [7–9]. However, existing automatic methods can generally provide a limited 3D effect due to ambiguities between depth and perception cues [2]. Semiautomatic methods are the most widely used schemes for 3D content creation, since they can balance conversion quality and production cost. The core step of semiautomatic methods is sparse-to-dense depth propagation on key frames, in which dense depth-maps are estimated from user-assigned sparse depth values. The conversion quality largely depends on the accuracy of depth-maps at key frames. Thus, this paper mainly focuses on sparse-to-dense depth propagation for semiautomatic 2D-to-3D conversion.

Phan and Androutsos [10] combine random walks (RW) with graph cuts (GC) for sparse-to-dense depth estimation, but incorrectly segmented object boundaries provided by GC may degrade depth quality. Rzeszutek and Androutsos [11] use the domain transform filter to propagate sparse labels throughout an image, but it may smooth out depth edges. Iizuka et al. [12] utilize superpixel-based geodesic distance weighting interpolation and optimization-based edge-preserving smooth to compute dense depth from user scribbles. Similarly, Wu et al. [13] apply superpixel-based optimization method to obtain dense depth-maps from sparse

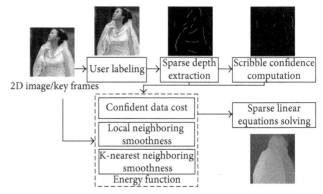

FIGURE 2: The flowchart of the proposed method.

input. However, these superpixel-based methods are affected by the performance of superpixel segmentation. Yuan et al. [14] propose a nonlocal RW algorithm to produce dense depth-map from user scribbles on single 2D image. Liang and Shen [15] further extend this scheme with the ability to process videos. However, RW-based methods cannot modify user-assigned labels, and erroneous input will degrade depth accuracy seriously. Lopez et al. [16] incorporate perspective and equality/inequality constraints into an optimization framework for dense depth estimation, but may add additional burden to user operations. Vosters and Haan [17]

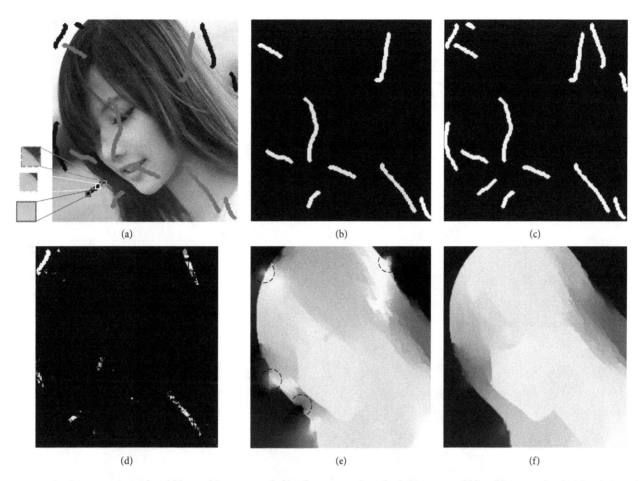

FIGURE 3: The demonstration of scribble confidence provided by the proposed method. (a) User scribbles. (b) Sparse depth. (c) Label mask. (d) Scribble confidence (the brighter the intensity, the higher the confidence of labeled pixels). (e) Depth-map of optimization method [6]. (f) Depth-map of confident optimization method.

propose a line scanning-based sparse-to-dense propagation method with low computation cost, but accuracy may be lost. Revaud et al. [18] use an edge-aware geodesic distance for sparse-to-dense optical flow interpolation, but the result is vulnerable to inaccurate input.

All of the above methods, however, do not account for the possibility of inaccurate scribbles. Thus, these methods can only give reliable results for accurate input. To address this issue, confidence of scribbles is calculated based on local color variation. There has been some recent works addressed on error-tolerant interactive image segmentation [19–21]. However, these methods are not well suited to 2D-to-3D conversion, since they mainly focus on foreground and background separation.

3. Method

As shown in Figure 2, the proposed method works as follows. Firstly, user draws sparse scribbles on 2D image/key frames, where brighter red marked regions are closer from the camera. Secondly, depth values at labeled pixels are extracted according to intensities of the scribbles. Thirdly, confidence of scribbles is calculated based on the color variation at labeled regions. Fourthly, an energy

function is built where scribble confidence is incorporated into the data cost. Finally, the energy function is minimized by solving a sparse linear system to obtain the dense depth-map.

3.1. Scribble Confidence. It can be found that pixels in accurate labeled regions often have similar color values, while erroneous input mainly appears at object boundaries with strong variations in color. Based on this observation, the scribble confidence is calculated using the following formula:

$$s_i = \begin{cases} \dfrac{\sum_{j \in N(i)} \delta\left(\left\|\mathbf{I}_i - \mathbf{I}_j\right\|_2\right)}{\sum_{j \in N(i)}\left\|\mathbf{I}_i - \mathbf{I}_j\right\|_0 + \varepsilon}, & \text{if } i \in \Omega, \\ \\ 0, & \text{if } i \notin \Omega, \end{cases} \tag{1}$$

where $\mathbf{I}_i$ denotes the Lab color values at pixel i. The reason for using Lab color space is that it takes into account human perception [22]. $\mathbf{N}(i)$ is the set of 8 neighbors of pixel i. $\delta(\cdot)$ is the Dirac delta function. $\|\|_0$ and $\|\|_2$ are L0 norm and L2 norm, respectively. ε is a small positive constant to prevent division by zero and set to 10^{-5}. Ω is the set of labeled pixels.

TABLE 1: SSIM comparison in the absence of inaccurate scribbles.

Image	Method					
	RW [4]	OPT [6]	HGR [10]	SOPT [13]	NRW [14]	Proposed
RGBZ_01	0.91	**0.92**	0.90	0.90	**0.92**	**0.92**
RGBZ_03	0.87	**0.88**	0.88	0.86	**0.88**	0.86
RGBZ_05	**0.93**	0.92	0.92	0.90	**0.93**	0.92
RGBZ_07	**0.91**	**0.91**	0.90	0.90	**0.91**	**0.91**
Average	**0.91**	**0.91**	0.90	0.89	**0.91**	**0.91**

The best SSIM at each row is shown in bold.

TABLE 2: PSNR comparison in the absence of inaccurate scribbles.

Image	Method					
	RW [4]	OPT [6]	HGR [10]	SOPT [13]	NRW [14]	Proposed
RGBZ_01	25.0	24.8	24.1	24.1	**25.7**	24.6
RGBZ_03	21.2	20.9	**22.4**	21.7	**22.4**	20.9
RGBZ_05	21.1	20.8	22.1	21.4	**23.7**	21.3
RGBZ_07	22.2	**22.3**	21.1	21.9	22.2	**22.3**
Average	22.4	22.2	22.4	22.3	**23.5**	22.3

The best PSNR (dB) at each row is shown in bold.

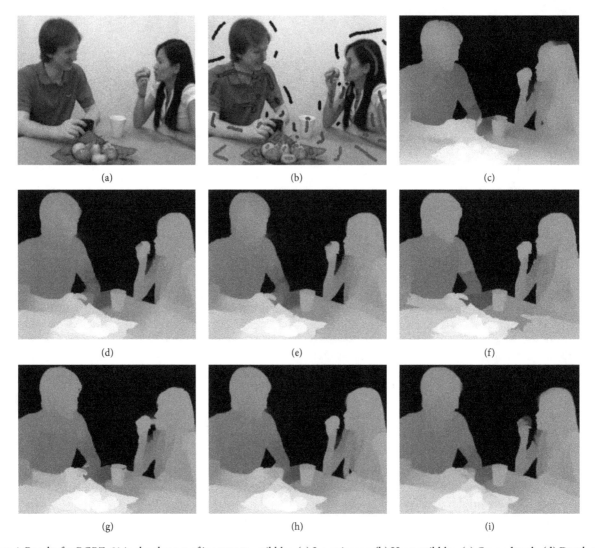

FIGURE 4: Results for RGBZ_01 in the absence of inaccurate scribbles. (a) Input image. (b) User scribbles. (c) Groundtruth. (d) Depth of RW [4]. (e) Depth of OPT [6]. (f) Depth of HGR [10]. (g) Depth of SOPT [13]. (h) Depth of NRW [14]. (i) Depth of proposed.

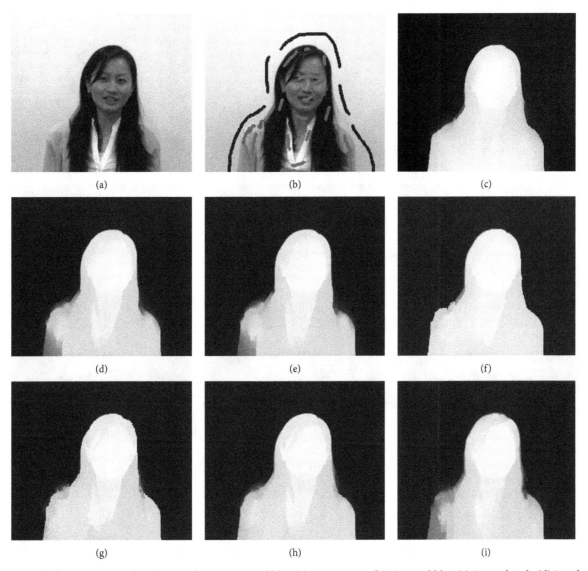

FIGURE 5: Results for RGBZ_03 in the absence of inaccurate scribbles. (a) Input image. (b) User scribbles. (c) Groundtruth. (d) Depth of RW [4]. (e) Depth of OPT [6]. (f) Depth of HGR [10]. (g) Depth of SOPT [13]. (h) Depth of NRW [14]. (i) Depth of proposed.

It can be seen from formula (1) that the confidence of a labeled pixel is lower when its color difference between neighboring pixels is larger. Since inaccurate input is mainly located at or near object boundaries around which the color changes significantly, the proposed method can penalize inaccurate scribbles. One may question whether or not the confidence of correct scribbles is high. The confidence of labeled pixels at texture regions is indeed low, and correct labels at these regions will be mistaken as incorrect ones. However, the number of correct scribbles is much larger than the number of incorrect ones. Therefore, the impact on the accurate scribbles can be tolerated.

Figure 3 gives an example on how scribble confidence works. The confidence of inaccurate scribbles which move across the object boundaries is low, as shown in Figure 3(d). Current optimization method [6] generates visual artifacts around inaccurate labeled regions, as can be seen from regions within the red circles in Figure 3(e). These artifacts can be removed if scribble confidence is

incorporated into the optimization method, as shown in Figure 3(f).

As shown as the blue square in Figure 3(a), when user scribbles are inside objects, the color variation at labeled pixel between its neighbors is small, in which case the scribble confidence of the pixel at the center of the blue square is 0.6. When user scribbles approach object boundaries, the color variation at labeled pixel between its neighbors becomes larger, as shown as the yellow and pink squares in Figure 3(a). The scribble confidence of the pixel at the center of the yellow square is 0.3, while confidence of the center pixel of the pink square is 0.0. Since erroneous scribbles mainly appears at object boundaries, the proposed method can remove erroneous input by using color differences between labeled pixels and their neighbors.

3.2. Energy Function. Let n be the total number of pixels and w and h the image width and height in pixels, that is,

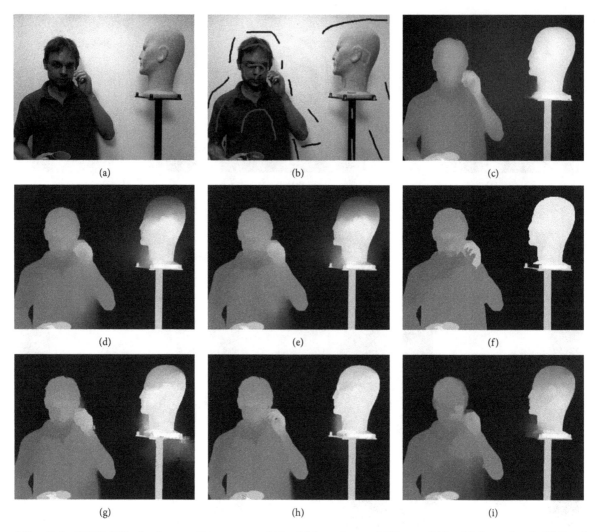

(a)   (b)   (c)

(d)   (e)   (f)

(g)   (h)   (i)

FIGURE 6: Results for RGBZ_05 in the absence of inaccurate scribbles. (a) Input image. (b) User scribbles. (c) Groundtruth. (d) Depth of RW [4]. (e) Depth of OPT [6]. (f) Depth of HGR [10]. (g) Depth of SOPT [13]. (h) Depth of NRW [14]. (i) Depth of proposed.

$n = w \times h$. For each pixel i, x_i, b_i, and $[r_i, c_i]^T$ denote, respectively, the estimated depth value, initial depth value, and spatial coordinate. Here, $b_i = 0$ if $i \in \Omega$; otherwise, b_i is user-assigned depth value. The $n \times 1$ lexicographically ordered column vectors $\mathbf{x}$ and $\mathbf{b}$ are the vector representation of the estimated dense depth-map and initial sparse depth-map, respectively. The objective of 2D-to-3D conversion is to recover $\mathbf{x}$ from $\mathbf{b}$. This is an ill-posed inverse problem. Local and k-nearest smoothness are introduced to regularize the problem and propose the following energy function:

$$E(x) = \sum_{i \in \Omega} s_i (x_i - b_i)^2 + \gamma \sum_{i=1}^{n} \sum_{j \in N(i)} w_{ij} (x_i - x_j)^2$$
$$+ \lambda \sum_{i=1}^{n} \sum_{j \in N^k(i)} w_{ij} (x_i - x_j)^2, \tag{2}$$

where the first term is data cost, the second term is local smoothness, and the last term is k-nearest smoothness. s_i is the scribble confidence at pixel i obtained from formula (1). $N^k(i)$ is the set of k-nearest neighbors of pixel i. Feature

vector $\mathbf{f}_i = [\mathbf{I}_i^T, \alpha r_i / \sqrt{h^2 + w^2}, \alpha c_i / \sqrt{h^2 + w^2}]^T$ is used to find k-nearest neighbors. Here, α is a parameter and set as 30 in all experiments. γ and λ in formula (2) are parameters to weigh the local smoothness term and k-nearest smoothness term, respectively. w_{ij} is the Gaussian weight to measure color similarity between pixels i and j and is defined as follows:

$$w_{ij} = \exp\left(-\frac{\left\|\mathbf{I}_i - \mathbf{I}_j\right\|_2^2}{2\sigma^2}\right), \tag{3}$$

where σ is the bandwidth parameter and fixed as 0.03 in all experiments.

In formula (2), the data cost is used to measure the consistency between the estimation and user-assigned depth values. Since scribble confidence is incorporated, the proposed method is robust to inaccurate use input. The local smoothness term makes the neighboring pixels with similar colors have similar depth values. To reduce the impact on correct scribbles at texture regions, the k-nearest smoothness term is introduced to make distant pixels with similar features also have similar depth values.

FIGURE 7: Results for RGBZ_07 in the absence of inaccurate scribbles. (a) Input image. (b) User scribbles. (c) Groundtruth. (d) Depth of RW [4]. (e) Depth of OPT [6]. (f) Depth of HGR [10]. (g) Depth of SOPT [13]. (h) Depth of NRW [14]. (i) Depth of proposed.

3.3. Solver. The energy function in formula (2) is minimized to obtain the dense depth-map $\mathbf{x}$ from the sparse depth-map $\mathbf{b}$. To facilitate computer implementation, formula (2) is rewritten in matrix form as follows:

$$E(\mathbf{x}) = (\mathbf{x} - \mathbf{b})^T \mathbf{S}(\mathbf{x} - \mathbf{b}) + \gamma \mathbf{x}^T \mathbf{L} \mathbf{x} + \lambda \mathbf{x}^T \mathbf{L}^k \mathbf{x}, \qquad (4)$$

where $\mathbf{S}$ is an $n \times n$ diagonal matrix whose i-th entry on the diagonal is s_i. $\mathbf{L}$ is the $n \times n$ Laplacian matrix for local neighbors and defined as $\mathbf{L} = \mathbf{D} - \mathbf{W}$, where $\mathbf{W} = [w_{ij}]_{n \times n}$ ($j \in \mathbf{N}(i)$) is the $n \times n$ affinity matrix for local neighbors and $\mathbf{D}$ is an $n \times n$ diagonal matrix whose i-th entry on the diagonal is $d_i = \sum_{j \in \mathbf{N}(i)} w_{ij}$. $\mathbf{L}^k$ is the $n \times n$ Laplacian matrix for k-nearest neighbors and defined as $\mathbf{L}^k = \mathbf{D}^k - \mathbf{W}^k$, where $\mathbf{W}^k = [w_{ij}]_{n \times n} (j \in \mathbf{N}^k(i))$ is the $n \times n$ affinity matrix for k-nearest neighbors and $\mathbf{D}^k$ is an $n \times n$ diagonal matrix whose i-th entry on the diagonal is $d_i^k = \sum_{j \in \mathbf{N}^k(i)} w_{ij}$.

The energy function in formula (4) to be minimized is convex and thus takes its derivative with respect to $\mathbf{x}$ and sets it equal to zero leading to the following system of linear equations:

$$\left(\mathbf{S} + \gamma \mathbf{L} + \lambda \mathbf{L}^k\right)\mathbf{x} = \mathbf{S}\mathbf{b}. \qquad (5)$$

The equation in formula (5) is sparse and positive definite which means the solution $\mathbf{x}$ can be obtained using the conjugate gradient method.

4. Experimental Results

4.1. Experimental Setup. Four representative test images, RGBZ_01, RGBZ_03, RGBZ_05, and RGBZ_07, from the RGBZ dataset [23] are used to evaluate the performance. The proposed method is compared with several state-of-the-art

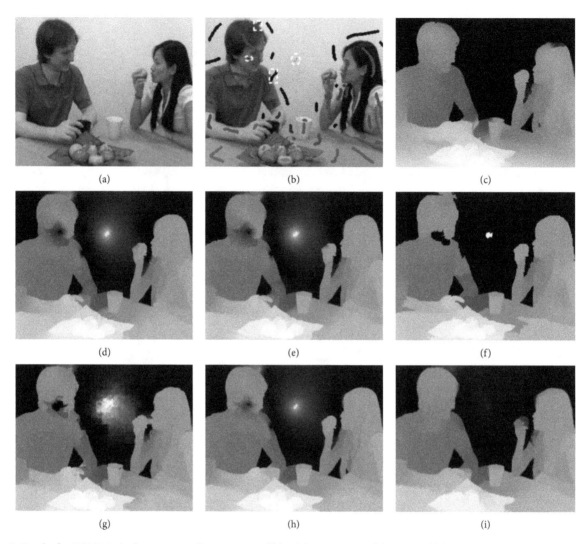

FIGURE 8: Results for RGBZ_01 in the presence of inaccurate scribbles. (a) Input image. (b) User scribbles. (c) Groundtruth. (d) Depth of RW [4]. (e) Depth of OPT [6]. (f) Depth of HGR [10]. (g) Depth of SOPT [13]. (h) Depth of NRW [14]. (i) Depth of proposed.

methods, including RW [4], optimization (OPT) [6], hybrid GC and RW (HGR) [10], superpixel-based optimization (SOPT) [13], and nonlocal RW (NRW) [14]. In the proposed method, the regularization weight parameters γ and λ are fixed to 1 and 10^{-5}, respectively. The local neighbors of formula (1) and (2) are empirically set to 3×3 size square windows centered at each pixel. The parameter k of k-nearest neighbors in (2) is set to 9. Structural similarity (SSIM) and PSNR are used as the quantitative measure for comparison, in which parameters of SSIM are set to default values as suggested by Wang et al. [24].

4.2. Experiments in the Absence of Inaccurate Scribbles.
In this section, user input is assumed to be perfectly accurate and show the performance of the proposed method in this case. The SSIM comparison is listed in Table 1. The PSNR comparison is shown in Table 2. As shown in Tables 1 and 2, the proposed method is comparable to current optimization method [6] when user input is accurate. Figures 4–7 show qualitative comparisons for different methods on the four test

images. It can be seen that the proposed method is superior in reducing depth bleeding artifacts compared with the previous optimization method [6]. The reason is that the k-nearest smoothness term in formula (2) is effective in preserving sharp depth boundaries [14]. In summary, the proposed method can be safely used in the case of accurate input.

4.3. Experiments in the Presence of Inaccurate Scribbles.
In this section, some inaccurate scribbles are added on the abovementioned experiments by roughly drawing labels across some randomly selected object boundaries (see regions within white squares of Figures 8(b)–11(b)) or wrongly drawing inside randomly selected regions (see regions within white circles of Figures 8(b)–11(b)).

The SSIM comparison in this case is listed in Table 3, and PSNR comparison is shown in Table 4. It can be seen that the proposed method is superior to other approaches when inaccurate input is present, and obtains the highest SSIM and PSNR values in average. This shows that scribble confidence can help resist inaccurate scribbles. The

FIGURE 9: Results for RGBZ_03 in the presence of inaccurate scribbles. (a) Input image. (b) User scribbles. (c) Groundtruth. (d) Depth of RW [4]. (e) Depth of OPT [6]. (f) Depth of HGR [10]. (g) Depth of SOPT [13]. (h) Depth of NRW [14]. (i) Depth of proposed.

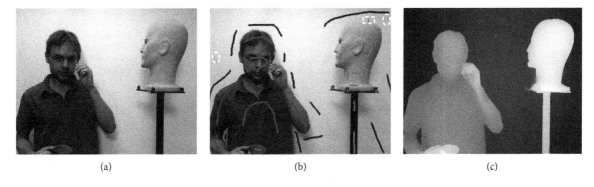

FIGURE 10: Continued.

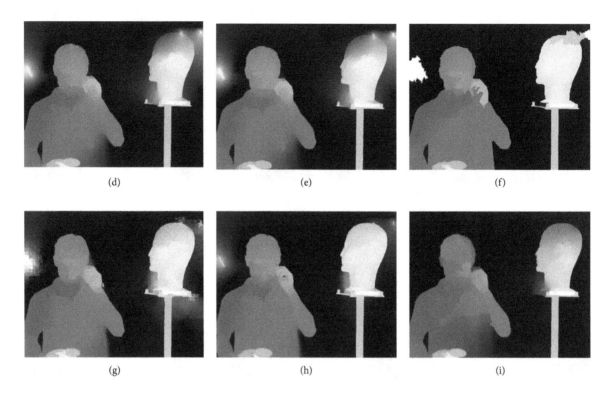

FIGURE 10: Results for RGBZ_05 in the presence of inaccurate scribbles. (a) Input image. (b) User scribbles. (c) Groundtruth. (d) Depth of RW [4]. (e) Depth of OPT [6]. (f) Depth of HGR [10]. (g) Depth of SOPT [13]. (h) Depth of NRW [14]. (i) Depth of proposed.

FIGURE 11: Continued.

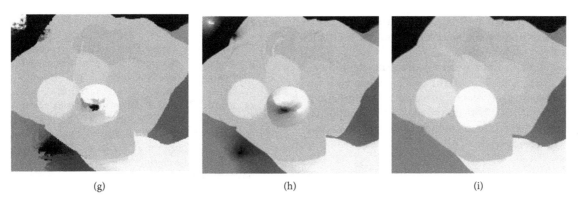

(g)   (h)   (i)

FIGURE 11: Results for RGBZ_07 in the presence of inaccurate scribbles. (a) Input image. (b) User scribbles. (c) Groundtruth. (d) Depth of RW [4]. (e) Depth of OPT [6]. (f) Depth of HGR [10]. (g) Depth of SOPT [13]. (h) Depth of NRW [14]. (i) Depth of proposed.

TABLE 3: SSIM comparison in the presence of inaccurate scribbles.

Image	Method					
	RW [4]	OPT [6]	HGR [10]	SOPT [13]	NRW [14]	Proposed
RGBZ_01	0.77	0.77	**0.88**	0.76	0.78	0.85
RGBZ_03	0.76	0.76	0.77	0.74	0.79	**0.83**
RGBZ_05	0.90	0.89	0.89	0.86	0.90	**0.92**
RGBZ_07	0.86	0.86	0.83	0.84	0.86	**0.91**
Average	0.82	0.82	0.84	0.80	0.83	**0.88**

The best SSIM at each row is shown in bold.

TABLE 4: PSNR comparison in the presence of inaccurate scribbles.

Image	Method					
	RW [4]	OPT [6]	HGR [10]	SOPT [13]	NRW [14]	Proposed
RGBZ_01	19.5	19.5	21.0	17.2	20.6	**24.1**
RGBZ_03	14.4	14.3	10.3	13.9	15.5	**19.0**
RGBZ_05	18.0	17.7	17.2	18.0	20.3	**21.3**
RGBZ_07	17.2	17.2	15.0	16.8	18.5	**22.3**
Average	17.3	17.2	15.9	16.5	18.7	**21.7**

The best SSIM at each row is shown in bold.

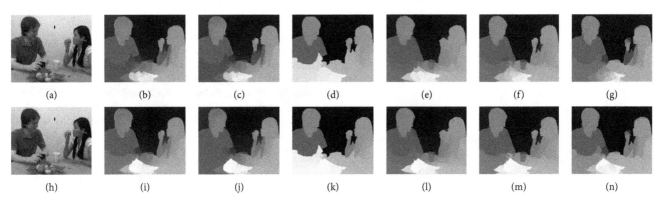

(a)   (b)   (c)   (d)   (e)   (f)   (g)

(h)   (i)   (j)   (k)   (l)   (m)   (n)

FIGURE 12: Results of depth for RGBZ_01 with sparse input. (a) User scribbles 1. (b) Depth of RW for scribbles 1. (c) Depth of OPT for scribbles 1. (d) Depth of HGR for scribbles 1. (e) Depth of SOPT for scribbles 1. (f) Depth of NRW for scribbles 1. (g) Depth of proposed for scribbles 1. (h) User scribbles 2. (i) Depth of RW for scribbles 2. (j) Depth of OPT for scribbles 2. (k) Depth of HGR for scribbles 2. (l) Depth of SOPT for scribbles 2. (m) Depth of NRW for scribbles 2. (n) Depth of proposed for scribbles 2.

performance of current methods degrades significantly in the case of inaccurate input, since they assume all scribbles are perfectly accurate.

The qualitative comparisons for different methods are shown in Figures 8–11. Current methods generate undesirable visual artifacts around inaccurate labeled regions, as shown in Figures 8–11. Thanks to the scribble confidence, the proposed method successfully reduces these artifacts caused by inaccurate input.

4.4. Experiments for Sparse Labeling. In this section, user input is assumed to be very sparse. In the first row of Figure 12, results are shown for a very sparse input which only contains seven strokes. In the second row, two strokes are added to the input image. It can be seen that the performance of all methods is improved as increase in the number of accurate scribbles. NRW and the proposed method are superior to others in preserving depth discontinuities since they both use nonlocal regularization. As analyzed in Section 3.1, although the proposed method may mistake correct labels for incorrect ones when they are located in texture regions, the proposed method can obtain acceptable results even with very sparse scribbles thanks to the k-nearest smoothness in formula (2), as shown in Figures 12(g) and 12(n).

5. Conclusion

Semiautomatic 2D-to-3D conversion has proven to be an effective solution for alleviating 3D content shortage. The key is sparse-to-dense depth conversion from user scribbles. Existing methods assume user input is entirely accurate, and even small errors may degrade the depth quality dramatically. To alleviate this problem, color difference between labeled pixels and neighbors is used to compute scribble confidence, and a confident optimization method is proposed for sparse-to-dense depth conversion. Furthermore, k-nearest smoothness is introduced to make the proposed method perform well even with very sparse input. The experiments demonstrate that the proposed method is superior to existing methods when inaccurate input is present, while at the same time competitive results are obtained when all scribbles are accurate.

Currently, the proposed method mainly focuses on 2D-to-3D conversion for images. In future, the proposed method will extend to videos.

Conflicts of Interest

The author declares that there are no conflicts of interest in the publication of this article.

Acknowledgments

This research was supported by the Zhejiang Provincial Natural Science Foundation of China (LY16F010014 and LY18F020025), the Ningbo City Natural Science Foundation of China (2017A610109), and the Educational Commission of Zhejiang Province of China (Y201533511).

References

[1] J. Chen and M. Huang, "2D-to-3D conversion system using depth map enhancement," *KSII Transactions on Internet and Information Systems*, vol. 10, no. 3, pp. 1159–1181, 2016.

[2] W. Huang, X. Cao, K. Lu, Q. Dai, and A. C. Bovik, "Toward naturalistic 2D-to-3D conversion," *IEEE Transactions on Image Processing*, vol. 24, no. 2, pp. 724–733, 2015.

[3] A. Kanchan and T. Mathur, "Recent trends in 2D to 3D image conversion: algorithm at a glance," *International Research Journal of Engineering and Technology*, vol. 4, no. 4, pp. 3480–3484, 2017.

[4] R. Rzeszutek, R. Phan, and D. Androutsos, "Semi-automatic synthetic depth map generation for video using random walks," in *Proceedings of IEEE International Conference on Multimedia and Expo*, pp. 1–6, Barcelona, Spain, July 2011.

[5] R. Rzeszutek and D. Androutsos, "Label propagation through edge-preserving filters," in *Proceedings of International Conference on Acoustics, Speech, and Signal Processing*, pp. 599–603, Florence, Italy, 2014.

[6] O. Wang, M. Lang, M. Frei, A. Hornung, A. Smolic, and M. Gross, "Stereobrush interactive 2D to 3D conversion using discontinuous warps," in *Proceedings of Eurographics Symposium on Sketch-Based Interfaces and Modeling*, pp. 47–54, Vancouver, Canada, 2011.

[7] F. Liu, C. Shen, G. Lin, and I. Reid, "Learning depth from single monocular images using deep convolutional neural fields," *IEEE Transactions on Pattern Analysis and Machine Intelligence*, vol. 38, no. 10, pp. 2024–2039, 2016.

[8] D. Eigen and R. Fergus, "Predicting depth, surface normals and semantic labels with a common multi-scale convolutional architecture," in *Proceedings of IEEE International Conference on Computer Vision*, pp. 2650–2658, Santiago, Chile, December 2015.

[9] J. Xie, R. Girshick, and A. Farhadi, "Deep3d: fully automatic 2D-to-3D video conversion with deep convolutional neural networks," in *Proceedings of European Conference on Computer Vision*, pp. 842–857, Amsterdam, Netherlands, October 2016.

[10] R. Phan and D. Androutsos, "Robust semi-automatic depth map generation in unconstrained images and video sequences for 2D to stereoscopic 3D conversion," *IEEE Transactions on Multimedia*, vol. 16, no. 1, pp. 122–136, 2014.

[11] R. Rzeszutek and D. Androutsos, "Propagating sparse labels through edge-aware filters," *Signal, Image and Video Processing*, vol. 9, no. 1, pp. 17–24, 2015.

[12] S. Iizuka, Y. Endo, Y. Kanamori, J. Mitani, and Y. Fukui, "Efficient depth propagation for constructing a layered depth image from a single image," *Computer Graphics Forum*, vol. 33, no. 7, pp. 279–288, 2014.

[13] S. Wu, H. Yuan, P. An, and P. Cheng, "Semi-automatic 2D-to-3D conversion using soft segmentation constrained edge-aware interpolation," *ACTA Electronica SINICA*, vol. 43, no. 11, pp. 2218–2224, 2015.

[14] H. Yuan, S. Wu, P. Cheng, P. An, and S. Bao, "Nonlocal random walks algorithm for semi-automatic 2D-to-3D image conversion," *IEEE Signal Processing Letters*, vol. 22, no. 3, pp. 371–374, 2015.

[15] Z. Liang and J. Shen, "Consistent 2D-to-3D video conversion using spatial-temporal nonlocal random walks," in *Proceedings of IEEE International Conference on Digital Signal Processing*, pp. 672–675, Beijing, China, October 2016.

[16] A. Lopez, E. Garces, and D. Gutierrez, "Depth from a single image through user interaction," in *Proceedings of Spanish*

Computer Graphics Conference, pp. 1–10, Zaragoza, Spain, 2014.

[17] L. Vosters and G. D. Haan, "Efficient and stable sparse-to-dense conversion for automatic 2-D to 3-D conversion," *IEEE Transactions on Circuits and Systems for Video Technology*, vol. 23, no. 3, pp. 373–386, 2013.

[18] J. Revaud, P. Weinzaepfel, Z. Harchaoui, and C. Schmid, "Epicflow: edge-preserving interpolation of correspondences for optical flow," in *Proceedings of IEEE Conference on Computer Vision and Pattern Recognition*, pp. 1164–1172, Boston, MA, USA, 2015.

[19] E. Zemene and M. Pelillo, "Interactive image segmentation using constrained dominant sets," in *Proceedings of European Conference on Computer Vision*, pp. 278–294, Amsterdam, Netherlands, October 2016.

[20] C. Oh, B. Ham, and K. Sohn, "Robust interactive image segmentation using structure-aware labeling," *Expert Systems with Applications*, vol. 79, pp. 90–100, 2017.

[21] K. Subr, S. Paris, C. Soler, and J. Kautz, "Accurate binary image selection from inaccurate user input," *Computer Graphics Forum*, vol. 32, no. 2, pp. 41–50, 2013.

[22] S. Hillaire, A. Lecuyer, T. Regiacorte, R. Cozot, J. Royan, and G. Breton, "Design and application of real-time visual attention model for the exploration of 3D virtual environments," *IEEE Transactions on Visualization and Computer Graphics*, vol. 18, no. 3, pp. 356–368, 2012.

[23] S. Lu, X. Ren, and F. Liu, "Depth enhancement via low-rank matrix completion," in *Proceedings of the IEEE Conference on Computer Vision and Pattern Recognition*, pp. 3390–3397, Columbus, OH, USA, 2014.

[24] Z. Wang, A. C. Bovik, H. R. Sheikh, and E. P. Simoncelli, "Image quality assessment: from error visibility to structural similarity," *IEEE Transactions on Image Processing*, vol. 13, no. 4, pp. 600–612, 2004.

16

A Zero-Watermarking Scheme for Vector Map based on Feature Vertex Distance Ratio

Yuwei Peng and Mingliang Yue

Computer School, Wuhan University, Wuhan 430072, China

Correspondence should be addressed to Yuwei Peng; ywpeng@whu.edu.cn

Academic Editor: D. I. Laurenson

With the rapid development of GIS and computer techniques, vector map data has been widely used in many fields. Since the production of map data is very costly, illegal copying will result in huge loss for data owners. In order to protect the copyright of vector data, digital watermarking has been employed in recent years. In this paper, a zero-watermarking scheme for vector map data is proposed. In the proposed scheme, FVDR (feature vertex distance ratio) is constructed based on the feature vertices of objects. The feature data, FVDR, is combined with watermark to generate the zero-watermark. Due to the specially designed cover data, the proposed scheme is robust to geometrical attacks, vertex attacks, and object attacks. The results of extensive experiments also demonstrate the robustness of the proposed scheme.

1. Introduction

The digital map is one type of important digital resources which has been widely used in navigation, urban planning, and many other areas. Due to high processing cost in the acquisition of digital map data, it becomes a valuable resource to its owner and has high price. Nevertheless, as one kind of digital data, a digital map could be easily copied. Therefore, copyright protection techniques for digital map have received extensive research attention in recent years.

As an effective approach for copyright protection, watermarking has been naturally introduced in the protection of digital map. Although many watermarking schemes have been proposed [1–7], most of them modify the map more or less to embed the watermark in it. For a vector map, which is sensitive to the precision, any form of distortion is insufferable. In order to make up for the shortage, zero-watermarking has been employed in digital map watermarking [8]. Like robust watermarking techniques, zero-watermarking comes from the area of image watermarking. The concept of zero-watermarking was first proposed in [9]. The main idea is generating a watermark from the characteristics of data without any modification on the host data. The generated watermark will be registered in an IPR (Intellectual Property Right) repository to facilitate future watermark detection.

However, the scheme proposed in [8] is only robust to geometrical attacks.

In this work, we focus on a watermarking scheme for a particular kind of object in digital map, polyline. Specifically, our goal is to generate a watermark from a set of polylines, without distortion of main characteristics and with resistance to malicious attacks. To summarize, the major contributions of this paper lie in the following aspects:

(1) We construct special cover data, called the feature vertex distance ratio (FVDR), from the characteristics of polylines and employ it to determine the watermark. Also, FVDR has been proven to be invariable against most of malicious attacks.

(2) Based on FVDR, we propose a method to map each bit of the watermark to a polyline in the host data. Due to FVDR's characteristics, the mapping relationship is robust to most of malicious attacks.

(3) A majority voting mechanism is adopted to generate watermark bits from corresponding groups of polylines, which provides robustness to both vertex and object attacks.

(4) Finally, we propose a zero-watermarking scheme for polylines. The scheme employs the aforementioned

mapping method to determine corresponding watermark bit for each polyline. Then FVDRs are calculated for generation of the corresponding bits. As shown by the experimental results, the proposed scheme is robust to geometrical attacks, vertex attacks, and object attacks.

The remainder of this paper is organized as follows. In Section 2, we present the proposed zero-watermarking scheme for polylines. Then, generation and detection algorithms are given in Section 3. In Section 4, we present experimental results and discuss their implications. Finally, the paper is concluded with final remarks and an outlook on future work in Section 5.

2. Proposed Zero-Watermarking Scheme

In the proposed zero-watermarking scheme, the watermark is a sequence of L bits. Each object in the vector map data, that is, a polyline, will be mapped to one bit of the watermark. Usually, since the number of objects is much bigger than L, some objects would be mapped to one same bit. To generate each bit of the watermark, the cover data of the objects mapped to it should be extracted first. Then the bit can be generated from the extracted cover data. Finally, the generated watermark will be registered in an IPR repository.

In this section, we detail three essential steps of the proposed scheme: (1) feature point selection; (2) cover data extraction; (3) watermark generation. Then, we present the watermark generation and detection algorithms based on the proposed scheme in the next section.

2.1. Feature Point Selection. In the proposed scheme, we employ cover data based on feature points. The feature points of a polyline are the vertices that are most likely to represent the objects structure and cannot be arbitrarily added or removed under interpolation or simplification [10, 11]. Methods that extract their cover data based on feature points take full advantage of this property to resist vertex attacks [12, 13]. As a result, the cover data can properly resist interpolation and simplification attacks under the assumption that a successful attack should not violate the map's validity. For a polyline, the most used simplification algorithm is Douglas-Peucker (DP) algorithm. However, an absolute threshold is employed in the DP algorithm to select feature points. While the map has been scaled, the feature points selected by the same threshold would not be the same with those selected before scaling.

To solve this problem, in this paper, we use a relative threshold instead of the absolute one. For a polyline $G_i = \{p_i^1, p_i^2, \ldots, p_i^j\}$, where p_i^k are the vertices of the object, given a relative threshold α, the feature point selection is described as follows.

Step 1. Find the first feature point f_i^1 that is farthest from the line segment (namely, reference line) between p_i^1 and p_i^j. The distance between f_i^1 and the reference line is denoted by $d(f_i^1)$.

Step 2. Apply $\alpha * d(f_i^1)$ as the absolute threshold and select the rest feature points by using DP algorithm.

In the DP algorithm with relative threshold, at least one feature point will be selected for each object. Then the product of its distance to the reference line and α is utilized as the threshold for selection of the other feature points. By this means, although the distances between vertices and their reference lines are scaled, the computed threshold is also scaled with the same magnitude. Thus, the exact same set of feature points can be properly found even when the vector map data has been scaled.

2.2. Cover Data Extraction. Since the set of feature points can always be found as long as the object exists legally, now we can construct our cover data based on the feature points set.

Angle and topological relation have been chosen as cover data for they are insensitive to geometrical attacks [1, 14]. However, a small vertex distortion will contribute to a large variation of the angle when the reference lines are short, while any object attacks will violate the correspondences of the objects used for topological relations extraction. Distance can be extracted from individual objects and is less sensitive to vertex distortion [13], but after scaling watermark covered by distance will inevitably be violated. For the fact that ratio between distances will not change under scaling, in this paper, we extract cover data based on distance ratio.

Given a polyline object G_i, suppose the set of feature points is $F_i = \{f_i^1, f_i^2, \ldots, f_i^n\}$; the cover data, FVDR, is constructed as follows:

$$x_i = \sum_{j=1}^{n} \frac{f_i^j(x)}{n},$$
$$y_i = \sum_{j=1}^{n} \frac{f_i^j(y)}{n}. \tag{1}$$

Step 1. Use all points in F_i to calculate the feature center $C_i(x_i, y_i)$ as shown in (1).

Step 2. Calculate the distance between every feature point f_i^k and C_i, denoted as feature distance d_i^k, and let $D_i = \{d_i^1, d_i^2, \ldots, d_i^n\}$ represent the set of feature distances.

Step 3. Calculate the feature vertex distance ratio (FVDR), R_i, as shown in

$$R_i = \sum_{j=1}^{\lfloor n/2 \rfloor} \frac{d_i^{2j-1}}{d_i^{2j} * \lfloor n/2 \rfloor}. \tag{2}$$

Clearly, FVDR has the property of geometrical invariability and vertex independence. That is, the watermarking scheme using FVDR as cover data can properly resist geometrical attacks as well as interpolation and simplification attacks.

2.3. Watermark Generation. Generally, in a zero-watermarking scheme, the watermark should be extracted from the most stable characteristics of the host data in order to ensure the robustness. In the proposed scheme, we employed FVDR extracted in previous subsections to generate the watermark. Basically, each FVDR is mapped to one bit of the watermark. Generally, the number of FVDRs is larger than the length of the watermark. Therefore, some FVDRs would be mapped to the same bit. After the mapping process, each bit could be generated from the FVDRs mapped to it.

2.3.1. Watermark Bit Mapping. The process of mapping FVDRs to bits in the watermark is called "watermark bit mapping." The kernel idea is a hash function, as shown in

$$S_i = H_m \left(H_b \left(R_i, h \right), L, K \right). \tag{3}$$

In (3), S_i is the index for the corresponding bit of FVDR, R_i; that is R_i is mapped to the S_ith bit in the watermark. H_m is the mapping function which produces S_i according to L, K (secret key), and the highest h bits of R_i. The highest h bits are calculated by function H_b. The reason of using $H_b(R_i, h)$ rather than R_i is the fact that the possible modification on the object G_i might result in slight difference between R_i obtained in watermark generation and detection. This difference would afterwards defeat the watermark detection. However, such difference only exists on the low bits of R_i. With this observation, we employ a truncation function H_b to eliminate the difference. With H_b, the highest h bits of R_i are obtained to ensure the same R_i could be regenerated in watermark detection. To guarantee the usability of the watermarked map, the impact of the modification would be controlled below the precision tolerance. With the precision tolerance λ of the map, the upper and lower bounds of R_i (denoted as R_i^u and R_i^l, resp.) can be calculated by (4). Therefore, h is the largest number by which $H_b(R_i, h)$, $H_b(R_i^u, h)$, and $H_b(R_i^l, h)$ have the same value:

$$
\begin{aligned}
R_i^u &= \sum_{j=1}^{\lfloor n/2 \rfloor} \frac{d_i^{2j-1} + \lambda}{\left(d_i^{2j} - \lambda \right) * \lfloor n/2 \rfloor}; \\
R_i^l &= \sum_{j=1}^{\lfloor n/2 \rfloor} \frac{d_i^{2j-1} - \lambda}{\left(d_i^{2j} + \lambda \right) * \lfloor n/2 \rfloor}.
\end{aligned}
\tag{4}
$$

The index of corresponding bit for each FVDR, R_i, can be obtained as follows.

(1) Calculate R_i^u and R_i^l based on R_i, and then the appropriate h can be determined with R_i, R_i^u, and R_i^l.

(2) Calculate the index of the corresponding bit by (3) and the h calculated above.

2.3.2. Watermark Bit Generation. For each group, we can extract one watermark bit from it. A majority voting mechanism is employed. The generation of watermark is described as follows.

Step 1. For each group, all hth position of FVDR is calculated.

Step 2. If there are more odd numbers than even numbers, the corresponding watermark bit is "1."

Step 3. If there are more even numbers than odd numbers, the corresponding watermark bit is "0."

After all watermark bits have been decided, they can be formed to the watermark according to their sequence number. And then the watermark can be registered into the IPR repository.

3. Generation and Detection Algorithms

Based on the steps described above, we can give the generation and detection algorithms in this section.

Let $G = \{G_1, G_2, \ldots, G_k\}$ be a set of polylines and let $W = \{w_1, w_2, \ldots, w_L\}$ be the watermark.

The generation algorithm includes the following steps.

Step 1. For every G_i in G, we calculate its FVDR, R_i.

Step 2. Use the highest h positions of R_i to map the object into a set of L mutually exclusive groups ($\{g_1, g_2, \ldots, g_L\}$); g_i corresponds to watermark bit, w_i.

Step 3. Generate the watermark bit, w_i, for group g_i and assemble watermark bits into the final watermark.

Step 4. Finally, the watermark generated is registered in an IPR repository.

The detection algorithm is similar to the generation algorithm.

Step 1. For every polyline, after division, a watermark bit is regenerated from each group. All regenerated watermark bits are assembled to a detected watermark.

Step 2. Compare the detected watermark with the one registered in IPR repository.

For every polyline, the algorithms need to invoke the DP algorithm for feature point selection. The time complexity of DP algorithm is $O(C)$, where C is the number of points of the polyline. So, the time complexity of both the generation and detection algorithm is $O(CN)$, where N is the number of polylines in the map.

4. Experiments and Analysis

To evaluate the performance of the proposed scheme, we performed experiments using a map of China which contains 3407 objects and 1128242 vertices.

In the experiments, attacks were applied to the watermarked map with different magnitudes. Then detection ratio was calculated by dividing the watermark length by the number of correct detected bits. Then the detection ratio was used for robust evaluation.

4.1. Geometrical Attacks. To assess the resilience of our algorithm to geometrical attacks, we apply a combination of translation, rotation, and scaling attacks to the watermarked map. Specifically, the magnitudes of the attacks are measured using (relative) coordinate offset, rotation angles, and scaling factors. And the ranges of the magnitudes were set to [−300%, 300%], [0, 360], and [0, 10], respectively. In this experiment, attack magnitudes were gradually increased with certain steps and all the detection ratios were the same and equal to 100%. The experiment result verifies the good performance of our method when facing geometrical attacks.

4.2. Vertex Attacks

4.2.1. Noise Distortion. In this experiment, we evaluate the influence of noise distortion. Attacks were applied by randomly modifying the coordinates with different magnitudes. Here we suppose the noise distortion satisfies uniform distribution and the range of the magnitudes was set to $[0, 1.2\tau]$, where τ is the positional accuracy. As shown in Figure 1, even when the attack magnitude exceeds the positional accuracy, the detection ratio remains acceptable. It verifies the robustness of the proposed method to noise distortion attack.

4.2.2. Interpolation and Simplification. In this experiment, interpolation and simplification were performed using Cubic Spline Algorithm [15] and Douglas-Peucker algorithm, respectively. Watermark data was generated using different relative thresholds. To evaluate the strength of the (interpolation and simplification) attack resistance, we gradually increased the attack magnitude and recorded the detection ratio of the corresponding thresholds. The results are presented in Figures 2 and 4, respectively. The attack magnitude was represented by the percentage of the vertices added or deleted due to interpolation or simplification. As we can see, the larger the relative threshold is, the more robust the algorithm is. And, given a properly selected relative threshold, the algorithms detection rate can remain 100% until the attack reaches a certain percentage of vertex addition or deletion (e.g., if the threshold is 0.06, the percentage of addition is 44% and the percentage of deletion is 36%).

4.3. Object Attacks

4.3.1. Reordering. Reordering of objects or their vertices is a special kind of attack; it only affects the artificially assigned identifiers of the objects and vertices. Figure 3 gives an example of reordering attack on vertices. However, neither the identifier of the object nor the one of the vertex is involved in the proposed scheme. Thus, the reordering attack could not affect the FVDR and the generated watermark. In this experiment, objects and their vertices in the watermarked map were reordered randomly for several times. For every reordering attack, the detection ratio is 100%. That is, the proposed scheme is robust to reordering attacks.

4.3.2. Deletion and Addition. The resistance for object deletion and addition relies on the number of objects in each group. Figures 5 and 6 present the experimental results of object deletion and addition, respectively. The results demonstrate that the more objects each group has, the more

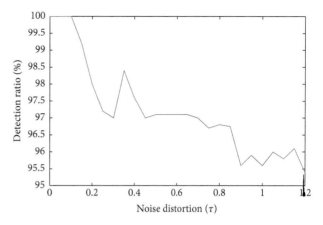

FIGURE 1: Resistance to noise distortion.

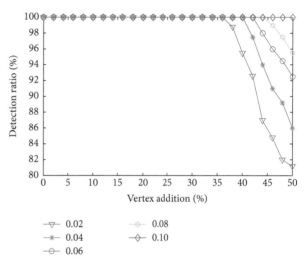

▽	0.02	⊹	0.08
✳	0.04	◇	0.10
⊖	0.06		

FIGURE 2: Resistance to interpolation.

robustness we get. And when the number of objects in each group is larger than six, the algorithm's detection ratio is as high as 98% even facing a magnitude of 50% object deletion or addition. That is, the proposed scheme is robust to object deletion and addition.

4.4. Assorted Attacks. We also designed an experiment to verify the robustness of the proposed schema against assorted attacks. In this experiment, all aforementioned attacks were applied on the watermarked map. The range of magnitude for every applied attack is listed in Table 1. The experiment has been performed for ten times with different random magnitude taken from the respective range. The detection ratio of these executions is illustrated in Figure 7. In Figure 7, the average and lowest detection ratios are 91.73% and 88.79%, respectively, which demonstrates that the proposed schema is robust against assorted attack.

5. Conclusion

Focusing on polyline objects in vector maps, the Douglas-Peucker algorithm with relative threshold is applied for

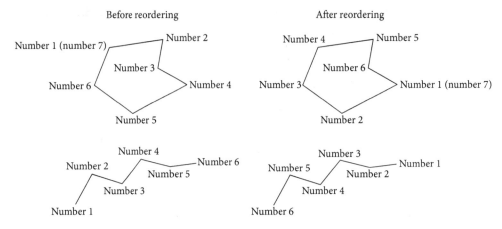

FIGURE 3: Examples of vertex reordering attack.

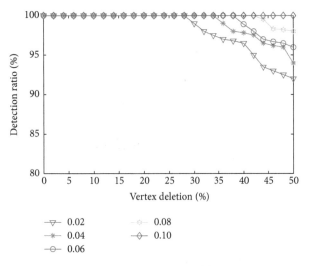

FIGURE 4: Resistance to simplification.

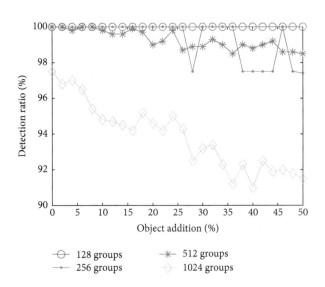

FIGURE 6: Resistance to object addition.

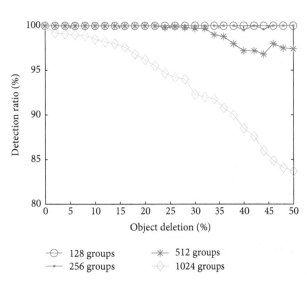

FIGURE 5: Resistance to object deletion.

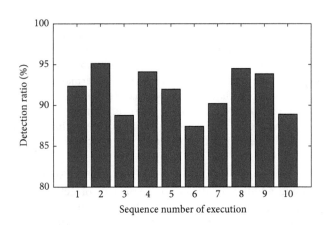

FIGURE 7: Resistance to assorted attack.

TABLE 1: Magnitudes of attacks.

Attack	Range of magnitude
Translation	-300%–300% on x-axis or y-axis
Rotation	$0°$–$360°$
Scaling	0–10
Object insertion	10%–20%
Object deletion	10%–20%
Noise distortion	0–1.2τ
Interpolation	10%–20%
Simplification	10%–20%

feature point extraction, and then cover data is defined based on the ratio between pairs of feature distances; finally, the objects are partitioned into groups according to the cover data and every bit of the watermark data is generated from objects of a corresponding group. The proposed scheme is robust to translation, rotation, scaling, simplification, interpolation, noise addition, object addition, deletion, and reordering attacks. In this paper, point and polygon objects are out of our consideration. Moreover, attacks like collusion attack that can only be resisted using protocols are not considered. These are planned for our future works.

Conflict of Interests

The authors declare that there is no conflict of interests regarding the publication of this paper.

Acknowledgment

The project was supported by the National Nature Science Foundation of China (nos. 61100019 and 61202033).

References

[1] C. J. Wang, Z. Y. Peng, Y. W. Peng, L. Yu, J. Z. Wang, and Q. Z. Zhao, "Watermarking geographical data on spatial topological relations," *Multimedia Tools and Applications*, vol. 57, no. 1, pp. 67–89, 2012.

[2] S.-H. Lee and K.-R. Kwon, "Vector watermarking scheme for GIS vector map management," *Multimedia Tools and Applications*, vol. 63, no. 3, pp. 757–790, 2013.

[3] B. Y. Wu and W. Wang, "Research on applied technology in blind and shape-preserving watermarking of vector map data using variable quantization step," *Advanced Materials Research*, vol. 886, pp. 706–710, 2014.

[4] H. Yang, L. Min, and X. Hou, "An asymmetrical watermarking algorithm for vector map data," *WIT Transactions on Information and Communication Technologies*, vol. 51, pp. 125–133, 2014.

[5] S. N. Neyman, I. N. P. Pradnyana, and B. Sitohang, "A new copyright protection for vector map using FFT-based watermarking," *Telecommunication Computing Electronics and Control*, vol. 12, no. 2, pp. 367–378, 2014.

[6] Y. Chen, L. Zhang, and X. Ji, "A new robust watermarking algorithm for small vector data set," *Applied Mechanics and Materials*, vol. 263–266, no. 1, pp. 2999–3004, 2013.

[7] J. Sun, G. Zhang, C. Men, Y. Wu, and X. Wang, "Lossless digital watermarking technology for vector maps," *Applied Mechanics and Materials*, vol. 241–244, pp. 2773–2778, 2013.

[8] X. Wang, D. J. Huang, and Z. Y. Zhang, "A robust zero-watermarking algorithm for 2D vector digital maps," in *Computer, Informatics, Cybernetics and Applications*, vol. 107 of *Lecture Notes in Electrical Engineering*, pp. 533–541, Springer, Amsterdam, The Netherlands, 2012.

[9] Q. Wen, T.-F. Sun, and S.-X. Wang, "Concept and application of zero-watermark," *Acta Electronica Sinica*, vol. 31, no. 2, pp. 214–216, 2003.

[10] D. H. Douglas and T. K. Peucker, "Algorithms for the reduction of the number of points required to represent a digitized line or its caricature," *Canadian Cartographer*, vol. 10, pp. 112–122, 1973.

[11] T. Gökgöz, "Generalization of contours using deviation angles and error bands," *The Cartographic Journal*, vol. 42, no. 2, pp. 145–156, 2005.

[12] Y.-C. Pu and I.-C. Jou, "Blind and robust watermarking for street-network vector maps," *Information Technology Journal*, vol. 8, no. 7, pp. 982–989, 2009.

[13] X.-M. Niu, C.-Y. Shao, and X.-T. Wang, "GIS watermarking: hiding data in 2D vector maps," *Studies in Computational Intelligence*, vol. 58, pp. 123–155, 2007.

[14] J. Kim, "Robust vector digital watermarking using angles and a random table," *Advances in Information Sciences and Service Sciences*, vol. 2, no. 4, pp. 79–90, 2010.

[15] H. S. Hou and H. C. Andrews, "Cubic splines for image interpolation and digital filtering," *IEEE Transactions on Acoustics, Speech and Signal Processing*, vol. 26, no. 6, pp. 508–517, 1978.

17

A DDoS Attack Detection Method based on Hybrid Heterogeneous Multiclassifier Ensemble Learning

Bin Jia,[1] Xiaohong Huang,[1] Rujun Liu,[2] and Yan Ma[1]

[1]*Information and Network Center, Institute of Network Technology, Beijing University of Posts and Telecommunications, Beijing 100876, China*
[2]*School of CyberSpace Security, Beijing University of Posts and Telecommunications, Beijing 100876, China*

Correspondence should be addressed to Bin Jia; jb_qd2010@bupt.edu.cn

Academic Editor: Jun Bi

The explosive growth of network traffic and its multitype on Internet have brought new and severe challenges to DDoS attack detection. To get the higher True Negative Rate (TNR), accuracy, and precision and to guarantee the robustness, stability, and universality of detection system, in this paper, we propose a DDoS attack detection method based on hybrid heterogeneous multiclassifier ensemble learning and design a heuristic detection algorithm based on Singular Value Decomposition (SVD) to construct our detection system. Experimental results show that our detection method is excellent in TNR, accuracy, and precision. Therefore, our algorithm has good detective performance for DDoS attack. Through the comparisons with Random Forest, k-Nearest Neighbor (k-NN), and Bagging comprising the component classifiers when the three algorithms are used alone by SVD and by un-SVD, it is shown that our model is superior to the state-of-the-art attack detection techniques in system generalization ability, detection stability, and overall detection performance.

1. Introduction

The explosive growth of network traffic and its multitype on Internet have brought new and severe challenges to network attack behavior detection. Some traditional detection methods and techniques have not met the needs of efficient and exact detection for the diversity and complexity of attack traffic in the high-speed network environment, especially such as DDoS attack.

Distributed Denial of Service (DDoS) attack is launched by some remote-controlled Zombies. It is implemented by forcing a kidnapped computer or consuming its resources, such as CPU cycle, memory, and network bandwidth. Moreover, Palmieri et al. [1] described the attack that exploits computing resources to waste energy and to increase costs. With the network migrating to cloud computing environments, the rate of DDoS attacks is growing substantially [2]. For DDoS attack detection, the previous researches in recent years mainly include the following.

In 2014, Luo et al. [3] developed a mathematical model to estimate the combined impact of DDoS attack pattern and network environment on attack effect by originally capturing the adjustment behaviors of victim TCPs congestion window. In 2015, Xiao et al. [4] presented an effective detection approach based on CKNN (K-nearest neighbor's traffic classification with correlation analysis) and a grid-based and named r-polling method to detect DDoS attack. The methods can reduce training data involved in the calculation and can exploit correlation information of training data to improve the classification accuracy and to reduce the overhead caused by the density of training data. In 2016, Saied et al. [5] designed a model to detect and mitigate the known and unknown DDoS attack in real-time environments. They chose an Artificial Neural Network (ANN) algorithm to detect DDoS attack based on specific characteristic features that separate DDoS attack traffic from normal traffic.

However, the existing detection methods still suffer from low True Negative Rate (TNR), accuracy, and precision. And their methods or models are homogeneous, so the robustness, stability, and universality are difficult to be guaranteed. To address the abovementioned problems, in this paper, we propose the DDoS attack detection method based on hybrid heterogeneous multiclassifier ensemble learning.

Ensemble learning finishes the learning task by structuring and combining multiple individual classifiers. It is homogeneous for the ensemble of the same type of individual classifiers, and this kind of individual classifier is known as "base classifier" or "weak classifier." Ensemble learning can also contain the different types of individual classifiers, and the ensemble is heterogeneous. In heterogeneous ensemble, the individual classifiers are generated by different learning algorithms. The classifiers are called as "component classifier." For the research of homogeneous base classifier, there is a key hypothesis that the errors of base classifier are independent of each other. However, for the actual attack traffic detection, they apparently are impossible. In addition, the accuracy and the diversity of individual classifiers conflict in nature. When the accuracy is very high, increasing the diversity becomes extremely difficult. Therefore, to generate the robust generalization ability, the individual classifiers ought to be excellent and different.

An overwhelming majority of classifier ensembles are currently constructed based on the homogeneous base classifier model. It was proved to obtain a relatively good classification performance. However, according to some theoretical analyses, while error correlation between every two individual classifiers is smaller, the error of ensemble system is smaller. Simultaneously, while the error of classifier is increased, the negative effect came into being. Therefore, the ensemble learning model for homogeneous individual classifiers cannot satisfy the needs of the higher ensemble performance [6].

According to the different measured standard in [7], while the value of diversity is larger, the difference is larger, and the classifying precision of classifier is higher. Through the abovementioned analysis, the heterogeneous multiclassifier ensemble learning owns more remarkable and more predominant generalization performance than the homogeneous multiclassifier ensemble learning.

This paper makes the following contributions. (i) To the best of our knowledge, this is the first attempt to apply the heterogeneous multiclassifier ensemble model to DDoS attack detection, and we provide the system model and its formulation. (ii) We design a heuristic detection algorithm based on Singular Value Decomposition (SVD) to construct the heterogeneous DDoS detection system, and we conduct thorough numerical comparisons between our method and several famous machine learning algorithms by SVD and by un-SVD.

The rest of this paper is organized as follows. Section 2 describes the system model and the related problem formulation. Section 3 presents DDoS detection algorithm in heterogeneous classification ensemble learning model. Our experimental results and analysis are discussed in Section 4. In Section 5, we conclude this paper.

2. System Model and Problem Formulation

2.1. System Model. The classification learning model based on Rotation Forest and SVD aims at building the accurate and diverse individual component classifiers. Here, the model is used for DDoS attack detection. Rodríguez et al. [8] applied Rotation Forest and Principal Component Analysis (PCA) algorithm to extract features subsets and to reconstruct a full feature set for each component classifier in the ensemble model. However, PCA has indeed some weaknesses. For instance, PCA sees all samples as a whole and searches an optimal linear map projection on the premise of minimum mean-square error. Nonetheless, categorical attributes are ignored. The ignored projection direction is likely to include some important divisible information. In order to overcome the abovementioned shortcomings, in this paper, we use SVD to substitute for PCA.

There are two key points to construct heterogeneous multiclassifier ensemble learning model [9]. The first one is the selection of individual classifiers. The second one is the assembly of individual classifiers. We discuss the two issues as follows.

(i) Firstly, classifiers in an ensemble should be different from each other; otherwise, there is no gain in combining them. These differences cover diversity, orthogonality, and complementarity [10]. Secondly, Kuncheva and Rodríguez [11] proposed static classifier selection and dynamic classifier selection. The difference of the two methods is whether or not evaluation of competence is implemented during the classification. Because of the characteristic of prejudged competence, the dynamic classifier selection approach is better than the static classifier selection. Last but not least, the powerful generalization ability is necessary in heterogeneous classification ensemble model. Irrelevance between every two individual classifiers is desired as much as possible, and the error of every individual classifier itself ought to be smaller. The interrelation between error rate of integrated system and correlation of individual classifiers is given [6] by

$$E = \left(\frac{1 + \rho (N - 1)}{N} \right) \overline{E} + E_{\text{Optimal Bayes}}, \qquad (1)$$

where E denotes Ensemble Generalization Error (EGE). $\overline{E}$ denotes the mean of these individual generalization errors. $E_{\text{Optimal Bayes}}$ denotes False Recognition Rate (FRR) that is got by using the Bayesian rules when all conditional probabilities are known. Therefore, the above formula shows that the ensemble error is smaller when individual differences are bigger and individual errors are smaller.

(ii) The majority voting method is chosen as our combined strategy of all component classifiers. For the prediction label of every record in testing data set, we choose those labels whose votes are more than half as final predicting outcomes. The majority voting is given by

$$H(x) = P_i, \quad \text{if } \sum_{i=1}^{t} h_i^j(x) > \frac{1}{2} \sum_{l=1}^{m} \sum_{i=1}^{t} h_i^l(x), \qquad (2)$$

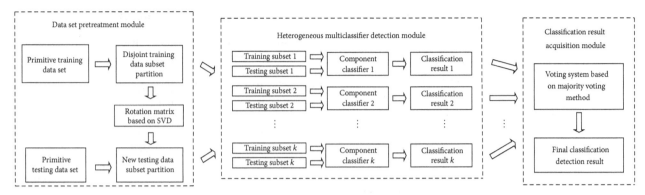

FIGURE 1: Hybrid heterogeneous multiclassifier ensemble classification model.

where the m-dimension vector $(h_i^1(x); h_i^2(x); \ldots; h_i^m(x))$ is denoted as prediction output. h_i is on the sample x, and $h_i^j(x)$ is the output on the class label P_i.

As shown in Figure 1, the proposed hybrid heterogeneous multiclassifier ensemble classification model includes three primary modules, and they are Data Set Pretreatment Module, Heterogeneous Multiclassifier Detection Module, and Classification Result Acquisition Module. In Data Set Pretreatment Module, the primitive training data set is split first into k disjoint training data subsets based on SVD. The new training data subset is generated by the linearly independent base transformation. Secondly, the primitive testing data sets are split also into k data subsets corresponding to the features of new training data subsets. Finally, the new testing data subsets are generated by Rotation Forest. In Heterogeneous Multiclassifier Detection Module, the k new training data subsets and testing data subsets are used as the input of k component classifiers. Next, the k classification detection results are got. In Classification Result Acquisition Module, the voting system votes on k results based on the majority voting method. Then, the final classification detection result is obtained.

2.2. Problem Formulation. We assume that the $m \times n$ matrix denotes a training data set, where m represents the number of network traffic records, and n represents the number of characteristic attributes in a record. In addition, D_i denotes the ith classifier in heterogeneous ensemble. Here, all component classifiers can be trained in parallel. The whole features of training data set are split into k disjoint data subsets. Each feature subset contains f ($f = [n/k]$) features. The SVD method is applied to every split subset.

Suppose that C is the $m \times f$ training subset matrix, U is the $m \times m$ square matrix, and V is the $f \times f$ square matrix. Here, the column of U is orthogonal eigenvector of CC^T and the column of V^T is orthogonal eigenvector of C^TC. In addition, r is rank of the matrix C. The SVD is shown by

$$C = U \sum V^T, \tag{3}$$

where $\sum$ is the $m \times f$ matrix. $\sum_{ii} = \sqrt{\lambda_i}$, and the different values of $\sum_{ii}$ are arranged by the descending order. The values on the other locations are zero.

Then, the computational formulae of the singular value and the eigenvectors are given by

$$\left(C^T C \right) v_i = \lambda_i v_i, \tag{4}$$

$$\sigma_i = \sqrt{\lambda_i}, \tag{5}$$

where v_i represents the eigenvector and σ_i represents the singular value.

The new training data subset C' whose all features are linearly independent is obtained by

$$C' = CV^T. \tag{6}$$

So far, the singular value and their eigenvectors of the corresponding eigenvalue by SVD for every subset are obtained. Next, the rotation matrix is got. It is denoted by

$$R_C = \begin{bmatrix} V_1 & [0] & \cdots & [0] \\ [0] & V_2 & \cdots & [0] \\ \vdots & \vdots & \ddots & \vdots \\ [0] & [0] & \cdots & V_k \end{bmatrix}, \tag{7}$$

where V_i ($i = 1, 2, \ldots, k$) represents the eigenvector set of C^TC for the ith training data subset C in the main diagonal position. And the null vectors are in the other positions.

The primitive testing data set C_p^T is split also into k data subsets corresponding to the features of new training data subsets. In order to get the new testing data set C^T, similarly, the linearly independent base transformation is operated by

$$C^T = C_p^T R_C. \tag{8}$$

One of the keys for good performance of ensembles is the diversity. There are several ways to inject diversity into an ensemble; the most common is the use of sampling [12]. To consider adequately the differentiation and complementarity between every different classification algorithm, in this paper, we select three typical machine learning algorithms as individual component classifiers, and they are Bagging [13], Random Forest [14], and k-Nearest Neighbor (k-NN) [15], respectively. Firstly, Bagging is the best famous representative of parallel ensemble learning methods. It employs "Random Sampling" in sampling data set. The algorithm focuses mainly on decreasing variance. Secondly, "Random Feature Selection" is farther introduced in the training process for Random Forest. In the constructing process of individual decision tree, Bagging uses "Deterministic Decision Tree" where all features in node are considered in choosing to divide property. However, "Stochastic Decision Tree" is used in Random Forest, where an attribute subset is considered. Thirdly, k-NN classifies by measuring distance between every two different feature values. It usually employs Euclidean distance by

$$d = \sqrt{(x_1 - y_1)^2 + (x_2 - y_2)^2 + \cdots + (x_n - y_n)^2}, \quad (9)$$

where $(x_1, x_2, \ldots, x_n)$ and $(y_1, y_2, \ldots, y_n)$ represent two different sample records which have n features, respectively.

In addition, a statistical test should be employed to eliminate the bias in the comparison of the tested algorithms. In our model, we use the statistical normalization [16] as a statistical testing method. The method's purpose is to convert data derived from any normal distribution to standard normal distribution. And 99.9% samples of the attribute are scaled into $[-3, 3]$ in the method. The statistical normalization is defined by

$$x_i = \frac{v_i - \mu}{\sigma}, \quad (10)$$

where μ is the mean of n values for a given attribute and σ is its standard deviation. The mean and the standard deviation are denoted by

$$\mu = \frac{1}{n} \sum_{i=1}^{n} v_i, \quad (11)$$

$$\sigma = \sqrt{\frac{1}{n} \sum_{i=1}^{n} (v_i - \mu)^2}. \quad (12)$$

3. A Detection Algorithm in Heterogeneous Classification Ensemble Model

In this section, we first describe DDoS attack detection process in heterogeneous multiclassifier ensemble model, and then the detection algorithm based on SVD is presented.

Firstly, all primitive training data set and all testing data set are split into k disjoint data subsets by the same feature fields, respectively. Secondly, the new training data subsets and the new testing data subsets are got by linearly independent base transformation based on SVD and Rotation Forest method. Thirdly, every new training data subset and every new testing data subset are normalized by the statistical normalization in a batch manner, and then they are input into every component classifier to classify and learn. The k classification detection results are acquired. Finally, the voting system votes on k results based on the majority voting method and outputs the final classification detection result.

Here, we propose a heuristics algorithm to keep the stronger generalization and sufficient complementarity.

The classification detection algorithm is shown as follows.

Input

C: a training data set: the $m \times n$ matrix

C_p^T: a testing data set: the $l \times n$ matrix

k: the number of data subsets and the number of component classifiers

Step 1. Split all features into k subsets: F_i ($i = 1, 2, \ldots, k$), and each feature subset contains f ($f = [n/k]$) features.

Step 2. **For** $i = 1$ to k **do.**

Step 3. Apply SVD on the training subset: the $m \times f$ matrix.

Step 4. Get the linearly independent column eigenvector matrix V^T.

Step 5. Get the new training data subset: C' ($C' = CV^T$).

Step 6. Get the new testing data subset: C_T' ($C_T' = C_T V^T$).

Step 7. C' and C_T' are normalized by the statistical normalization in a batch manner.

Step 8. C' and C_T' are input into the component classifier.

Step 9. Get the classification label.

Step 10. **End for.**

Step 11. Input the results of k component classifiers into the voting system based on the majority voting method.

Output

The final label of a testing data record, label = {Normal, DDoS}

In our algorithm, in order to select the component classifiers, we use the parallelization principle. The component classifiers have no strong dependencies by the principle. In addition, we select Bagging, Random Forest, and k-NN algorithms as the component classifiers. In Bagging, the CART algorithm is used as the base learner of our heterogeneous classification ensemble model.

4. Experimental Results and Analysis

In this section, we discuss how to apply the heterogeneous classification ensemble model in detecting DDoS attack traffic. We first present the data set and the data pretreatment method used in our experiments. Then, the experimental results are given, and we analyze and make comparisons with the homogeneous models based on three selected algorithms by SVD and by un-SVD. Here, the computer environment to run our experiments is listed in Table 1.

TABLE 1: Computer experimental condition.

CPU	Memory	Hard disk	OS	MATLAB
Intel® Xeon® CPU E5-2640 v2 @2.00 GHz 2.00 GHz (2 processors)	32 GB	2 TB	Windows Server 2008 R2 Enterprise	R2013a (8.1.0.604) 64-bit (win64)

In this paper, we use the famous Knowledge Discovery and Data mining (KDD) Cup 1999 dataset [17, 18] as the verification of our detection model. This data set has been widely applied to research and evaluate network intrusion detection methods [19, 20]. KDD CUP 1999 data set comprises about five million network traffic records, and it provides a training subset of 10 percent of network record and a testing subset. Every record of the data set is described by four types of features, and they are TCP connection basic features (9 features), TCP connective content features (13 features), time-based network traffic statistical characteristics (9 features), and host-based network traffic statistical characteristics (10 features), respectively. All 41 features in the four types are shown in Table 2.

In addition, KDD CUP 1999 data set covers four main categories of attack, and these are DoS, R2L, U2R, and Probing. Because the traffic records of "neptune" and "smurf" for DoS account for more than 99% and 96% in the abovementioned training subset and testing subset, we choose the two types for DoS as our algorithm evaluation and comparison with the three famous existing machine learning algorithms in this paper.

4.1. Data Pretreatment. Firstly, because the training subset of 10 percent and the "corrected" testing subset in KDD CUP 1999 data set include hundreds of thousands of network records, the hardware configuration of our sever cannot load the calculation to process the abovementioned data sets. Here, we use the built-in "random ()" method in MySQL to randomly select one in every ten records of the abovementioned training subset and testing subset as our data sets. The data sets used in our experiments are listed in Table 3.

Secondly, for each network traffic record, it includes the information that has been separated into 41 features plus 1 class label [21] in KDD CUP 1999, and there are 3 nonnumeric features in all features. In our experiments, we also transform the type of three features into the numeric type. The conversion process is listed as follows:

(i) TCP, UDP, and ICMP in the "protocol_type" feature are marked as 1, 2, and 3, respectively.

(ii) The 70 kinds of "service" for the destination host are sorted by the percentage in the training subset of 10 percent. We get the top three types, and they are ecr_i, private and http. The three types account for over 90%. The ecr_i, private, http, and all other types are marked as 1, 2, 3, and 0, respectively.

TABLE 2: All 41 features in the four types.

Number	
	TCP connection basic features
(1)	duration
(2)	protocol_type
(3)	service
(4)	flag
(5)	src_bytes
(6)	dst_bytes
(7)	land
(8)	wrong_fragment
(9)	urgent
	TCP connective content features
(10)	hot
(11)	num_failed_logins
(12)	logged_in
(13)	num_compromised
(14)	root_shell
(15)	su_attempted
(16)	num_root
(17)	num_file_creations
(18)	num_shells
(19)	num_access_files
(20)	num_outbound_cmds
(21)	is_hot_login
(22)	is_guest_login
	Time-based network traffic statistical characteristics
(23)	count
(24)	srv_count
(25)	serror_rate
(26)	srv_serror_rate
(27)	rerror_rate
(28)	srv_rerror_rate
(29)	same_srv_rate
(30)	diff_srv_rate
(31)	srv_diff_host_rate
	Host-based network traffic statistical characteristics
(32)	dst_host_count
(33)	dst_host_srv_count
(34)	dst_host_same_srv_rate
(35)	dst_host_diff_srv_rate
(36)	dst_host_same_src_port_rate
(37)	dst_host_srv_diff_host_rate
(38)	dst_host_serror_rate
(39)	dst_host_srv_serror_rate
(40)	dst_host_rerror_rate
(41)	dst_host_srv_rerror_rate

(iii) The "SF" is marked as 1, and the other ten false connection statuses are marked as 0 in the "flag" feature.

TABLE 3: Data sets used in our experiments.

Category	Training data set	Testing data set
Normal	9728	6059
DoS	38800	22209

TABLE 4: Confusion matrix.

	Predicted DoS	Predicted normal	Total
Original DoS	TP	FN	P
Original normal	FP	TN	N
Total	P'	N'	$P + N\ (P' + N')$

4.2. Fivefold Cross-Validation. Cross-validation is an effective statistical technique to ensure the robustness of a model. In this paper, to improve the reliability of the experimental data and to verify the availability of our model, a fivefold cross-validation approach is used in our experiments.

The training data set is randomly split into five parts. In turn, we take out one part as the actual training data set and the other four parts and testing data set as the final testing data set. The aforementioned statistical normalization method in Section 2.2 is employed as the data statistical test.

4.3. Evaluation Index. Whether normal or attack for the network traffic belongs to the category of the binary classification, we need some evaluation indexes to evaluate it. In this paper, we use three typical indexes to measure our detection model, and they are TNR, accuracy, and precision. Here, TNR denotes the proportion of normal samples that are correctly recognized as normal samples in the testing data set. It reflects the veracity that detection model discerns normal samples. Accuracy denotes the proportion between the number of correctly classified samples and the total number of samples in the testing data set. It reflects the distinguishing ability to differentiate normal samples from attack samples. Precision denotes the proportion of true attack samples in all attack samples recognized by detection model in the testing data set. TNR, accuracy, and precision are formulated as follows:

$$TNR = \frac{TN}{FP + TN}, \tag{13}$$

$$Accuracy = \frac{TP + TN}{TP + FP + TN + FN}, \tag{14}$$

$$Precision = \frac{TP}{TP + FP}. \tag{15}$$

The performance of a classification detection model is evaluated by the counts of records for the normal samples and the attack samples. The matrix is called as the confusion matrix [22] based on the abovementioned counts. The matrix is listed in Table 4, where

(1) TP (True Positive) is the number of attacks correctly classified as attacks;

(2) FP (False Positive) is the number of normal records incorrectly classified as attacks;

(3) TN (True Negative) is the number of normal records correctly classified as normal records;

(4) FN (False Negative) is the number of attacks incorrectly classified as normal records.

4.4. Experimental Results and Discussion. In this section, our heterogeneous detection model is compared with Random Forest, k-NN, and Bagging comprising the component classifiers when the three algorithms are used by themselves. Here, our comparisons are based on SVD and un-SVD, respectively.

We refer to the past experience threshold value along with conducting many experiments. In this paper, we finally select eight threshold values to evaluate the performance of our model. Experimental results demonstrate that TNR, accuracy, and precision of our model are excellent in the detection model, and the model is more stable than the previous three algorithms in TNR, accuracy, and precision.

In Figure 2(a), when Random Forest, k-NN, and Bagging are processed by SVD, respectively, our detection model is compared with them for TNR. It is shown that the TNRs of our model are about 99.4% for different threshold values. However, the TNRs of Random Forest, k-NN, and Bagging are about 99.8%, 99.1%, and 17.8%, respectively. Therefore, the TNR of our model is very close to the TNR of Random Forest, and it is superior to the TNRs of k-NN and Bagging.

In Figure 2(b), when Random Forest, k-NN, and Bagging construct alone their component classifiers by un-SVD, our detection model is compared with them for TNR. It is shown that the TNRs of Random Forest and Bagging are about 99.9% and 99.9%, respectively. The TNR of k-NN falls from 99.6% to 98.1% when the range of threshold value is from 25 to 200. The experimental results demonstrate that the TNR of our model is close to the TNRs of Random Forest and Bagging, and it is superior to the TNR of k-NN. In addition, the TNR of k-NN is relatively unstable with the change of different threshold values.

In Figure 3(a), when Random Forest, k-NN, and Bagging are processed by SVD, respectively, our detection model is compared with them for accuracy. It is shown that the accuracies of our model are about 99.8%. However, the accuracies of Random Forest, k-NN, and Bagging are about 99.9%, 21.2%, and 82.3%, respectively. Therefore, the accuracy of our model is very close to the accuracy of Random Forest, and it is superior to the accuracies of k-NN and Bagging.

In Figure 3(b), when Random Forest, k-NN, and Bagging construct alone their component classifiers by un-SVD, our detection model is compared with them for accuracy. It is shown that the accuracies of Random Forest and Bagging are about 99.9% and 99.9%, respectively. The accuracy of k-NN falls from 99.89% to 88.48% when the range of threshold value is from 25 to 75. The experimental results demonstrate that the accuracy of our model is close to the accuracies of Random Forest and Bagging, and it is superior to the accuracy of k-NN. In addition, the accuracy of k-NN is relatively unstable with the change of different threshold values.

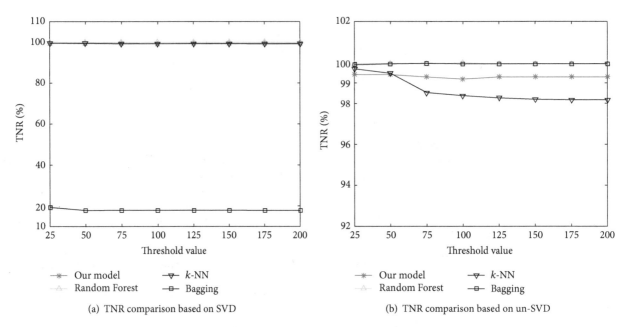

(a) TNR comparison based on SVD

(b) TNR comparison based on un-SVD

FIGURE 2: TNR for comparing our model with the other algorithms.

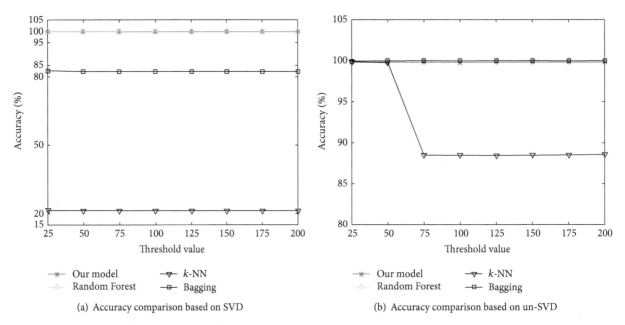

(a) Accuracy comparison based on SVD

(b) Accuracy comparison based on un-SVD

FIGURE 3: Accuracy for comparing our model with the other algorithms.

In Figure 4(a), when Random Forest, k-NN, and Bagging are processed by SVD, respectively, our detection model is compared with them for precision. It is shown that the precisions of our model are about 99.84%. However, the precisions of Random Forest, k-NN, and Bagging are about 99.9%, 0, and 81.6%, respectively. Therefore, the precision of our model is very close to the precision of Random Forest, and it is superior to the precisions of k-NN and Bagging.

In Figure 4(b), when Random Forest, k-NN, and Bagging construct alone their component classifiers by un-SVD, our

detection model is compared with them for precision. It is shown that the precisions of Random Forest and Bagging are about 99.98% and 99.98%, respectively. The precision of k-NN falls from 99.9% to 99.5% when the range of threshold value is from 25 to 75. The experimental results demonstrate that the precision of our model is close to the precisions of Random Forest and Bagging, and it is superior to the precision of k-NN. In addition, the precision of k-NN is relatively unstable with the change of different threshold values.

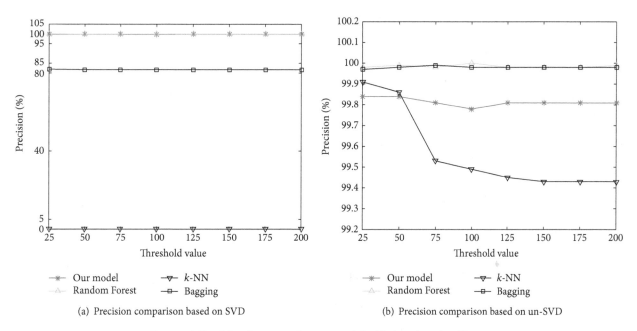

(a) Precision comparison based on SVD   (b) Precision comparison based on un-SVD

FIGURE 4: Precision for comparing our model with the other algorithms.

5. Conclusions

The efficient and exact DDoS attack detection is a key problem for diversity and complexity of attack traffic in high-speed Internet environment. In this paper, we study the problem from the perspective of hybrid heterogeneous multiclassifier ensemble learning. What is more, in order to get the stronger generalization and the more sufficient complementarity, we propose a heterogeneous detection system model, and we construct the component classifiers of the model based on Bagging, Random Forest, and k-NN algorithms. In addition, we design a detection algorithm based on SVD in heterogeneous classification ensemble model. Experimental results show that our detection method is excellent and is very stable in TNR, accuracy, and precision. Therefore, our algorithm and model have good detective performance for DDoS attack.

Competing Interests

The authors declare that they have no competing interests.

Acknowledgments

The work in this paper is supported by the Joint Funds of National Natural Science Foundation of China and Xinjiang (Project U1603261).

References

[1] F. Palmieri, S. Ricciardi, U. Fiore, M. Ficco, and A. Castiglione, "Energy-oriented denial of service attacks: an emerging menace for large cloud infrastructures," *The Journal of Supercomputing*, vol. 71, no. 5, pp. 1620–1641, 2015.

[2] Q. Yan, F. R. Yu, Q. X. Gong, and J. Q. Li, "Software-defined networking (SDN) and distributed denial of service (DDoS) attacks in cloud computing environments: a survey, some research issues, and challenges," *IEEE Communications Surveys & Tutorials*, vol. 18, no. 1, pp. 602–622, 2016.

[3] J. Luo, X. Yang, J. Wang, J. Xu, J. Sun, and K. Long, "On a mathematical model for low-rate shrew DDoS," *IEEE Transactions on Information Forensics and Security*, vol. 9, no. 7, pp. 1069–1083, 2014.

[4] P. Xiao, W. Y. Qu, H. Qi, and Z. Y. Li, "Detecting DDoS attacks against data center with correlation analysis," *Computer Communications*, vol. 67, pp. 66–74, 2015.

[5] A. Saied, R. E. Overill, and T. Radzik, "Detection of known and unknown DDoS attacks using artificial neural networks," *Neurocomputing*, vol. 172, pp. 385–393, 2016.

[6] S. S. Mao, L. Xiong, L. C. Jiao, S. Zhang, and B. Chen, "Isomerous multiple classifier ensemble via transformation of the rotating forest," *Journal of Xidian University*, vol. 41, no. 5, pp. 48–53, 2014.

[7] L. I. Kuncheva and C. J. Whitaker, "Measures of diversity in classifier ensembles and their relationship with the ensemble accuracy," *Machine Learning*, vol. 51, no. 2, pp. 181–207, 2003.

[8] J. J. Rodríguez, L. I. Kuncheva, and C. J. Alonso, "Rotation forest: a new classifier ensemble method," *IEEE Transactions on Pattern Analysis and Machine Intelligence*, vol. 28, no. 10, pp. 1619–1630, 2006.

[9] Z. L. Fu and X. H. Zhao, "Dynamic combination method of classifiers and ensemble learning algorithms based on classifiers Combination," *Journal of Sichuan University (Engineering Science Edition)*, vol. 43, no. 2, pp. 58–65, 2011.

[10] L. I. Kuncheva, "That elusive diversity in classifier ensembles," in *Proceedings of the 1st Iberian Conference on Pattern Recognition and Image Analysis (ibPRIA '03)*, pp. 1126–1138, Springer, Mallorca, Spain, June 2003.

[11] L. I. Kuncheva and J. J. Rodríguez, "Classifier ensembles with a random linear oracle," *IEEE Transactions on Knowledge and Data Engineering*, vol. 19, no. 4, pp. 500–508, 2007.

[12] J. F. Díez-Pastor, J. J. Rodríguez, C. García-Osorio, and L. I. Kuncheva, "Random balance: ensembles of variable priors classifiers for imbalanced data," *Knowledge-Based Systems*, vol. 85, pp. 96–111, 2015.

[13] L. Breiman, "Bagging predictors," *Machine Learning*, vol. 24, no. 2, pp. 123–140, 1996.

[14] L. Breiman, "Random forests," *Machine Learning*, vol. 45, no. 1, pp. 5–32, 2001.

[15] D. T. Larose, "*k*-nearest neighbor algorithm," in *Discovering Knowledge in Data: An Introduction to Data Mining*, pp. 90–106, 2nd edition, 2005.

[16] W. Wang, X. Zhang, S. Gombault, and S. J. Knapskog, "Attribute normalization in network intrusion detection," in *Proceedings of the 10th International Symposium on Pervasive Systems, Algorithms, and Networks (I-SPAN '09)*, pp. 448–453, IEEE, Kaohsiung, Taiwan, December 2009.

[17] R. Lippmann, J. W. Haines, D. J. Fried, J. Korba, and K. Das, "The 1999 DARPA off-line intrusion detection evaluation," *Computer Networks*, vol. 34, no. 4, pp. 579–595, 2000.

[18] J. McHugh, "Testing Intrusion detection systems: a critique of the 1998 and 1999 DARPA intrusion detection system evaluations as performed by Lincoln Laboratory," *ACM Transactions on Information and System Security (TISSEC)*, vol. 3, no. 4, pp. 262–294, 2000.

[19] K. C. Khor, C. Y. Ting, and S. Phon-Amnuaisuk, "A cascaded classifier approach for improving detection rates on rare attack categories in network intrusion detection," *Applied Intelligence*, vol. 36, no. 2, pp. 320–329, 2012.

[20] P. Prasenna, R. K. Kumar, A. V. T. R. Ramana, and A. Devanbu, "Network programming and mining classifier for intrusion detection using probability classification," in *Proceedings of the International Conference on Pattern Recognition, Informatics and Medical Engineering (PRIME '12)*, pp. 204–209, IEEE, Tamilnadu, India, March 2012.

[21] C. Bae, W. C. Yeh, M. A. M. Shukran, Y. Y. Chung, and T. J. Hsieh, "A novel anomaly-network intrusion detection system using ABC algorithms," *International Journal of Innovative Computing, Information and Control*, vol. 8, no. 12, pp. 8231–8248, 2012.

[22] C. Guo, Y. Zhou, Y. Ping, Z. Zhang, G. Liu, and Y. Yang, "A distance sum-based hybrid method for intrusion detection," *Applied Intelligence*, vol. 40, no. 1, pp. 178–188, 2014.

18

Algebraic Cryptanalysis Scheme of AES-256 using Gröbner Basis

Kaixin Zhao,[1] Jie Cui,[2] and Zhiqiang Xie[2]

[1]*Department of Computer Science and Technology, Henan Institute of Technology, Xinxiang 453003, China*
[2]*School of Computer Science and Technology, Anhui University, Hefei 230039, China*

Correspondence should be addressed to Jie Cui; cuijie@mail.ustc.edu.cn

Academic Editor: Jucheng Yang

The zero-dimensional Gröbner basis construction is a crucial step in Gröbner basis cryptanalysis on AES-256. In this paper, after performing an in-depth study on the linear transformation and the system of multivariate polynomial equations of AES-256, the zero-dimensional Gröbner basis construction method is proposed by choosing suitable term order and variable order. After giving a detailed construction process of the zero-dimensional Gröbner basis, the necessary theoretical proof is presented. Based on this, an algebraic cryptanalysis scheme of AES-256 using Gröbner basis is proposed. Analysis shows that the complexity of our scheme is lower than that of the exhaustive attack.

1. Introduction

On October 2, 2000, the Rijndael algorithm, which was designed by Daemen and Rijmen, was determined by the National Institute of Standards and Technology (NIST) for the Advanced Encryption Standard (AES) [1]. It has been of concern to the cryptographic community since the Rijndael algorithm was proposed, and there have been many attack methods. However, there is no successful attack on the full Rijndael algorithm up to now [2, 3].

Cryptanalysis and cryptography not only are mutually antagonistic, but also promote each other. Because of the great advantages of algebraic cryptanalysis technology, it has become a hot research topic in recent years. Algebraic attack is mainly composed of two steps: the first step is to establish a system of algebraic equations to describe the relationship among the plaintext, the ciphertext, and the key in cryptographic algorithm; the second step is to solve the system of equations to obtain the key by some of the known plaintext-ciphertext pairs. The first step has already obtained some research results, and many scholars have proposed many kinds of equation systems of AES algorithm [4, 5]. In the second step, the multivariate equation system is still a problem to be solved. Although solving the multivariate equation system is an NP-hard problem, the complexity of solving a sparse overdetermined system of equations is far lower than that of the NP-hard problem.

At present, the methods of solving the high order multivariate equation system mainly include XL, XSL, and Gröbner basis. Since the algebraic expression of AES algorithm is sparse and structured, it is inefficient to apply XL attacks directly. In 2002, Courtois et al. proposed an XSL attack method and claimed to break the key length of 256-bit AES algorithm in theory. However, the number of linear independent equations generated by XSL attacks in the academic field is disputed, and the validity of the attack is questioned [6, 7]. Gröbner basis is an effective method for solving the high order multivariate equation system, which is proposed by Buchberger. Its essence is to set up a set of arbitrary ideals in polynomial rings, describe and compute a set of generators with good properties, and then study the ideal structure and carry out the ideal computation [3].

Gröbner basis is a standard representation method of polynomial ideals, which has some useful properties [8]. Gröbner basis exists in any ideal, and the Gröbner basis of any ideal can be computed by the Buchberger algorithm or F4 or F5 algorithm [6]. Lexicographic order is a commonly used elimination order. The coefficient matrix of the basis is triangular when using lexicographical Gröbner basis in the computation, and the last row solves single-variable equations. This is the reason why lexicographical Gröbner basis can solve the equation system. But the direct computation of lexicographic Gröbner basis will produce excessive coefficients.

Common practice is to compute the total degree order Gröbner basis of the ideal firstly and then convert the total degree order Gröbner basis to lexicographical Gröbner basis using Gröbner basis conversion algorithm. Gröbner basis conversion algorithms include the Gröbner Walk [7] and the FGLM algorithm [6]. Compared with the Gröbner Walk, FGLM algorithm is simple and efficient, but the FGLM algorithm only works for zero-dimensional ideals [9, 10]. Therefore, constructing the zero-dimensional Gröbner basis of AES algorithm is crucial to implement Gröbner basis cryptanalysis. In 2013, the zero-dimensional Gröbner basis construction method of Rijndael-192 was proposed [11]. However, how to construct the zero-dimensional Gröbner basis of AES-256 and how to apply Gröbner basis cryptanalysis to AES-256 are still open questions. In this paper, the authors perform some particular studies on the linear transformation and the system of multivariate polynomial equations of AES-256 and propose its zero-dimensional Gröbner basis construction method through choosing suitable term order and variable order. After presenting the construction method of the Gröbner basis, the authors give the necessary theoretical proof. Moreover, the authors propose an algebraic cryptanalysis of AES-256 using Gröbner basis. Analysis suggests that the complexity of our scheme is lower than the exhaustive attack. The main contributions are given as follows:

(1) The zero-dimensional Gröbner basis construction method is proposed by choosing suitable term order and variable order.

(2) The necessary theoretical proof is given, and it shows that the set of polynomials is a zero-dimensional Gröbner basis.

(3) The effective algebraic cryptanalysis scheme of AES-256 using Gröbner basis is proposed.

The rest of this paper is formed as follows. The mathematical model of AES-256 is shown in Section 2. Section 3 demonstrates the Gröbner basis theory. The equation system of AES-256 is given in Section 4. In Section 5, the Gröbner basis construction method of AES-256 and the algebraic cryptanalysis scheme of AES-256 are proposed. Finally, the paper is concluded in Section 6.

2. Mathematical Model of AES-256

The block length and key length of AES can be specified independently as 128 bits, 192 bits, or 256 bits, and the corresponding round time is 10, 12, or 14. Each round consists of 4 transformations: the S-box substitution (ByteSub), ShiftRow, MixColumn, and AddRoundKey. With AES starting from the AddRoundKey, with 13 rounds of iteration, the final round is equal to the round with the MixColumn step removed. AES is an iterated block cipher with a variable block length and a variable key length. In this paper, both the block length and the key length are specified to 256 bits.

2.1. S-Box Substitution. The S-box transformation is a nonlinear byte substitution, operating on each of the state bytes independently. The S-box is invertible and is constructed by the composition of two transformations:

(1) Seeking the inverse operation of multiplication in $\mathrm{GF}(2^8) = Z_2[x]/(x^8 + x^4 + x^3 + x + 1)$ field, that is, input $\omega \in \mathrm{GF}(2^8)$ and output $v \in \mathrm{GF}(2^8)$, to meet

$$\omega * v = 1 \bmod \left(x^8 + x^4 + x^3 + x + 1\right), \tag{1}$$

then

$$v = \omega^{-1} = \begin{cases} \omega^{254}, & \omega \neq 0, \\ 0, & \omega = 0. \end{cases} \tag{2}$$

(2) Let element components of $x = v$ in $\mathrm{GF}(2)^8$ be $(x_7, x_6, x_5, x_4, x_3, x_2, x_1, x_0)$; the affine transformations are as follows:

$$y = \mathrm{La} \times x + \text{``}63\text{''}$$

$$= \begin{bmatrix} 1 & 1 & 1 & 1 & 1 & 0 & 0 & 0 \\ 0 & 1 & 1 & 1 & 1 & 1 & 0 & 0 \\ 0 & 0 & 1 & 1 & 1 & 1 & 1 & 0 \\ 0 & 0 & 0 & 1 & 1 & 1 & 1 & 1 \\ 1 & 0 & 0 & 0 & 1 & 1 & 1 & 1 \\ 1 & 1 & 0 & 0 & 0 & 1 & 1 & 1 \\ 1 & 1 & 1 & 0 & 0 & 0 & 1 & 1 \\ 1 & 1 & 1 & 1 & 0 & 0 & 0 & 1 \end{bmatrix} \begin{bmatrix} x_7 \\ x_6 \\ x_5 \\ x_4 \\ x_3 \\ x_2 \\ x_1 \\ x_0 \end{bmatrix} + \begin{bmatrix} 0 \\ 1 \\ 1 \\ 0 \\ 0 \\ 0 \\ 1 \\ 1 \end{bmatrix}. \tag{3}$$

The selection of constant "63" is to ensure the S-box is not a fixed point $S(a) = a$ and an opposite fixed point $S(a) = \overline{a}$. S-box has the ability to resist linear attacks and differential attacks [1].

2.2. ShiftRow and MixColumn Transformations. The 4×8-byte matrix is obtained by S-box substitution, where $S_{i,j}$ is the byte in the ith row and the jth column, $0 \leq i \leq 3, 0 \leq j \leq 7$. SR (ShiftRow) shift i bytes to the left for the ith row of the matrix:

$$\begin{bmatrix} s_{0,0} & s_{0,1} & s_{0,2} & s_{0,3} & s_{0,4} & s_{0,5} & s_{0,6} & s_{0,7} \\ s_{1,0} & s_{1,1} & s_{1,2} & s_{1,3} & s_{1,4} & s_{1,5} & s_{1,6} & s_{1,7} \\ s_{2,0} & s_{2,1} & s_{2,2} & s_{2,3} & s_{2,4} & s_{2,5} & s_{2,6} & s_{2,7} \\ s_{3,0} & s_{3,1} & s_{3,2} & s_{3,3} & s_{3,4} & s_{3,5} & s_{3,6} & s_{3,7} \end{bmatrix} \longrightarrow$$

$$\begin{bmatrix} s_{0,0} & s_{0,1} & s_{0,2} & s_{0,3} & s_{0,4} & s_{0,5} & s_{0,6} & s_{0,7} \\ s_{1,1} & s_{1,2} & s_{1,3} & s_{1,4} & s_{1,5} & s_{1,6} & s_{1,7} & s_{1,0} \\ s_{2,2} & s_{2,3} & s_{2,4} & s_{2,5} & s_{2,6} & s_{2,7} & s_{2,0} & s_{2,1} \\ s_{3,3} & s_{3,4} & s_{3,5} & s_{3,6} & s_{3,7} & s_{3,0} & s_{3,1} & s_{3,2} \end{bmatrix}. \tag{4}$$

MC (MixColumn) transforms the independent operation of each column for the purpose of causing confusion. Each byte in each column is mapped to the new value; this value is 4 bytes in the column with the function obtained. Transformation is as follows:

$$
\begin{bmatrix}
s'_{0,0} & s'_{0,1} & s'_{0,2} & s'_{0,3} & s'_{0,4} & s'_{0,5} & s'_{0,6} & s'_{0,7} \\
s'_{1,0} & s'_{1,1} & s'_{1,2} & s'_{1,3} & s'_{1,4} & s'_{1,5} & s'_{1,6} & s'_{1,7} \\
s'_{2,0} & s'_{2,1} & s'_{2,2} & s'_{2,3} & s'_{2,4} & s'_{2,5} & s'_{2,6} & s'_{2,7} \\
s'_{3,0} & s'_{3,1} & s'_{3,2} & s'_{3,3} & s'_{3,4} & s'_{3,5} & s'_{3,6} & s'_{3,7}
\end{bmatrix}
\tag{5}
$$

$$
= D \cdot
\begin{bmatrix}
s_{0,0} & s_{0,1} & s_{0,2} & s_{0,3} & s_{0,4} & s_{0,5} & s_{0,6} & s_{0,7} \\
s_{1,0} & s_{1,1} & s_{1,2} & s_{1,3} & s_{1,4} & s_{1,5} & s_{1,6} & s_{1,7} \\
s_{2,0} & s_{2,1} & s_{2,2} & s_{2,3} & s_{2,4} & s_{2,5} & s_{2,6} & s_{2,7} \\
s_{3,0} & s_{3,1} & s_{3,2} & s_{3,3} & s_{3,4} & s_{3,5} & s_{3,6} & s_{3,7}
\end{bmatrix},
$$

where

$$
D =
\begin{bmatrix}
02 & 03 & 01 & 01 \\
01 & 02 & 03 & 01 \\
01 & 01 & 02 & 03 \\
03 & 01 & 01 & 02
\end{bmatrix}.
\tag{6}
$$

For mathematical convenience, we use a column vector instead of the original matrix to represent intermediate states and keys. The mapping relationship between the elements in column vector and the elements in the original matrix is as follows:

$$
\varphi : F^{4 \times 8} \longrightarrow F^{32},
$$

$$
\begin{pmatrix}
s_{0,0} & s_{0,1} & s_{0,2} & s_{0,3} & s_{0,4} & s_{0,5} & s_{0,6} & s_{0,7} \\
s_{1,0} & s_{1,1} & s_{1,2} & s_{1,3} & s_{1,4} & s_{1,5} & s_{1,6} & s_{1,7} \\
s_{2,0} & s_{2,1} & s_{2,2} & s_{2,3} & s_{2,4} & s_{2,5} & s_{2,6} & s_{2,7} \\
s_{3,0} & s_{3,1} & s_{3,2} & s_{3,3} & s_{3,4} & s_{3,5} & s_{3,6} & s_{3,7}
\end{pmatrix}
\longmapsto
\tag{7}
$$

$$
(s_{0,0}, s_{1,0}, \ldots, s_{0,1}, s_{1,1}, \ldots)^T .
$$

The finite field $\mathrm{GF}(2^8)$ is denoted as F in this paper. Introducing a 32×32 0-1 transformation matrix M_{SR}, the SR transform is equivalent to left multiplication by the matrix M_{SR}. There is only one element in each column and each row of the matrix is 1 and all the others are 0. Similarly, by introducing a new transformation matrix M_{MC}, the MC transform is equivalent to left multiplication by the matrix M_{MC}. The construction principle of M_{MC} is $M_{\mathrm{MC}} = D \otimes I_8 \in F^{32 \times 32}$, where $\otimes$ denotes tensor product and I_8 denotes 8-order identity matrix. The composite transformation of the SR transform and the MC transform is denoted as M, and then $M = M_{\mathrm{MC}} \cdot M_{\mathrm{SR}}$. It is easy to get

$$
M = M_{\mathrm{MC}} \cdot M_{\mathrm{SR}}
$$

$$
=
\begin{bmatrix}
02 & 00 & 00 & 00 & 00 & 03 & 00 & 00 & 00 & 00 & 01 & 00 & 00 & 00 & 00 & 01 & 00 & 00 & 00 & 00 & 00 & 00 & 00 & 00 & 00 & 00 & 00 & 00 & 00 & 00 & 00 & 00 \\
01 & 00 & 00 & 00 & 00 & 02 & 00 & 00 & 00 & 00 & 03 & 00 & 00 & 00 & 00 & 01 & 00 & 00 & 00 & 00 & 00 & 00 & 00 & 00 & 00 & 00 & 00 & 00 & 00 & 00 & 00 & 00 \\
01 & 00 & 00 & 00 & 00 & 01 & 00 & 00 & 00 & 00 & 02 & 00 & 00 & 00 & 00 & 03 & 00 & 00 & 00 & 00 & 00 & 00 & 00 & 00 & 00 & 00 & 00 & 00 & 00 & 00 & 00 & 00 \\
03 & 00 & 00 & 00 & 00 & 01 & 00 & 00 & 00 & 00 & 01 & 00 & 00 & 00 & 00 & 02 & 00 & 00 & 00 & 00 & 00 & 00 & 00 & 00 & 00 & 00 & 00 & 00 & 00 & 00 & 00 & 00 \\
00 & 00 & 00 & 00 & 02 & 00 & 00 & 00 & 00 & 03 & 00 & 00 & 00 & 00 & 01 & 00 & 00 & 00 & 00 & 01 & 00 & 00 & 00 & 00 & 00 & 00 & 00 & 00 & 00 & 00 & 00 & 00 \\
00 & 00 & 00 & 00 & 01 & 00 & 00 & 00 & 00 & 02 & 00 & 00 & 00 & 00 & 03 & 00 & 00 & 00 & 00 & 01 & 00 & 00 & 00 & 00 & 00 & 00 & 00 & 00 & 00 & 00 & 00 & 00 \\
00 & 00 & 00 & 00 & 01 & 00 & 00 & 00 & 00 & 01 & 00 & 00 & 00 & 00 & 02 & 00 & 00 & 00 & 00 & 03 & 00 & 00 & 00 & 00 & 00 & 00 & 00 & 00 & 00 & 00 & 00 & 00 \\
00 & 00 & 00 & 00 & 03 & 00 & 00 & 00 & 00 & 01 & 00 & 00 & 00 & 00 & 01 & 00 & 00 & 00 & 00 & 02 & 00 & 00 & 00 & 00 & 00 & 00 & 00 & 00 & 00 & 00 & 00 & 00 \\
00 & 00 & 00 & 00 & 00 & 00 & 00 & 00 & 02 & 00 & 00 & 00 & 00 & 03 & 00 & 00 & 00 & 00 & 00 & 01 & 00 & 00 & 00 & 00 & 01 & 00 & 00 & 00 & 00 & 00 & 00 & 00 \\
00 & 00 & 00 & 00 & 00 & 00 & 00 & 00 & 01 & 00 & 00 & 00 & 00 & 02 & 00 & 00 & 00 & 00 & 00 & 03 & 00 & 00 & 00 & 00 & 01 & 00 & 00 & 00 & 00 & 00 & 00 & 00 \\
00 & 00 & 00 & 00 & 00 & 00 & 00 & 00 & 01 & 00 & 00 & 00 & 00 & 01 & 00 & 00 & 00 & 00 & 00 & 02 & 00 & 00 & 00 & 00 & 03 & 00 & 00 & 00 & 00 & 00 & 00 & 00 \\
00 & 00 & 00 & 00 & 00 & 00 & 00 & 00 & 03 & 00 & 00 & 00 & 00 & 01 & 00 & 00 & 00 & 00 & 00 & 01 & 00 & 00 & 00 & 00 & 02 & 00 & 00 & 00 & 00 & 00 & 00 & 00 \\
00 & 00 & 00 & 00 & 00 & 00 & 00 & 00 & 00 & 00 & 00 & 00 & 02 & 00 & 00 & 00 & 00 & 03 & 00 & 00 & 00 & 00 & 01 & 00 & 00 & 00 & 00 & 01 & 00 & 00 & 00 & 00 \\
00 & 00 & 00 & 00 & 00 & 00 & 00 & 00 & 00 & 00 & 00 & 00 & 01 & 00 & 00 & 00 & 00 & 02 & 00 & 00 & 00 & 00 & 03 & 00 & 00 & 00 & 00 & 01 & 00 & 00 & 00 & 00 \\
00 & 00 & 00 & 00 & 00 & 00 & 00 & 00 & 00 & 00 & 00 & 00 & 01 & 00 & 00 & 00 & 00 & 01 & 00 & 00 & 00 & 00 & 02 & 00 & 00 & 00 & 00 & 03 & 00 & 00 & 00 & 00 \\
00 & 00 & 00 & 00 & 00 & 00 & 00 & 00 & 00 & 00 & 00 & 00 & 03 & 00 & 00 & 00 & 00 & 01 & 00 & 00 & 00 & 00 & 01 & 00 & 00 & 00 & 00 & 02 & 00 & 00 & 00 & 00 \\
00 & 00 & 00 & 00 & 00 & 00 & 00 & 00 & 00 & 00 & 00 & 00 & 00 & 00 & 00 & 00 & 02 & 00 & 00 & 00 & 00 & 03 & 00 & 00 & 00 & 00 & 01 & 00 & 00 & 00 & 01 & 00 \\
00 & 00 & 00 & 00 & 00 & 00 & 00 & 00 & 00 & 00 & 00 & 00 & 00 & 00 & 00 & 00 & 01 & 00 & 00 & 00 & 00 & 02 & 00 & 00 & 00 & 00 & 03 & 00 & 00 & 00 & 01 & 00 \\
00 & 00 & 00 & 00 & 00 & 00 & 00 & 00 & 00 & 00 & 00 & 00 & 00 & 00 & 00 & 00 & 01 & 00 & 00 & 00 & 00 & 01 & 00 & 00 & 00 & 00 & 02 & 00 & 00 & 00 & 03 & 00 \\
00 & 00 & 00 & 00 & 00 & 00 & 00 & 00 & 00 & 00 & 00 & 00 & 00 & 00 & 00 & 00 & 03 & 00 & 00 & 00 & 00 & 01 & 00 & 00 & 00 & 00 & 01 & 00 & 00 & 00 & 02 & 00 \\
00 & 00 & 00 & 01 & 00 & 00 & 00 & 00 & 00 & 00 & 00 & 00 & 00 & 00 & 00 & 00 & 00 & 00 & 00 & 02 & 00 & 00 & 00 & 00 & 03 & 00 & 00 & 00 & 00 & 01 & 00 & 00 \\
00 & 00 & 00 & 01 & 00 & 00 & 00 & 00 & 00 & 00 & 00 & 00 & 00 & 00 & 00 & 00 & 00 & 00 & 00 & 01 & 00 & 00 & 00 & 00 & 02 & 00 & 00 & 00 & 00 & 03 & 00 & 00 \\
00 & 00 & 00 & 03 & 00 & 00 & 00 & 00 & 00 & 00 & 00 & 00 & 00 & 00 & 00 & 00 & 00 & 00 & 00 & 01 & 00 & 00 & 00 & 00 & 01 & 00 & 00 & 00 & 00 & 02 & 00 & 00 \\
00 & 00 & 00 & 02 & 00 & 00 & 00 & 00 & 00 & 00 & 00 & 00 & 00 & 00 & 00 & 00 & 00 & 00 & 00 & 03 & 00 & 00 & 00 & 00 & 01 & 00 & 00 & 00 & 00 & 01 & 00 & 00 \\
00 & 00 & 01 & 00 & 00 & 00 & 00 & 01 & 00 & 00 & 00 & 00 & 00 & 00 & 00 & 00 & 00 & 00 & 00 & 00 & 02 & 00 & 00 & 00 & 00 & 03 & 00 & 00 & 00 & 00 & 00 & 00 \\
00 & 00 & 03 & 00 & 00 & 00 & 00 & 01 & 00 & 00 & 00 & 00 & 00 & 00 & 00 & 00 & 00 & 00 & 00 & 00 & 01 & 00 & 00 & 00 & 00 & 02 & 00 & 00 & 00 & 00 & 00 & 00 \\
00 & 00 & 02 & 00 & 00 & 00 & 00 & 03 & 00 & 00 & 00 & 00 & 00 & 00 & 00 & 00 & 00 & 00 & 00 & 00 & 01 & 00 & 00 & 00 & 00 & 01 & 00 & 00 & 00 & 00 & 00 & 00 \\
00 & 00 & 01 & 00 & 00 & 00 & 00 & 02 & 00 & 00 & 00 & 00 & 00 & 00 & 00 & 00 & 00 & 00 & 00 & 00 & 03 & 00 & 00 & 00 & 00 & 01 & 00 & 00 & 00 & 00 & 00 & 00 \\
00 & 03 & 00 & 00 & 00 & 00 & 01 & 00 & 00 & 00 & 00 & 01 & 00 & 00 & 00 & 00 & 00 & 00 & 00 & 00 & 00 & 00 & 00 & 00 & 02 & 00 & 00 & 00 & 00 & 00 & 00 \\
00 & 02 & 00 & 00 & 00 & 00 & 03 & 00 & 00 & 00 & 00 & 01 & 00 & 00 & 00 & 00 & 00 & 00 & 00 & 00 & 00 & 00 & 00 & 00 & 01 & 00 & 00 & 00 & 00 \\
00 & 01 & 00 & 00 & 00 & 00 & 02 & 00 & 00 & 00 & 00 & 03 & 00 & 00 & 00 & 00 & 00 & 00 & 00 & 00 & 00 & 00 & 00 & 00 & 01 & 00 & 00 & 00 & 00 \\
00 & 01 & 00 & 00 & 00 & 00 & 01 & 00 & 00 & 00 & 00 & 02 & 00 & 00 & 00 & 00 & 00 & 00 & 00 & 00 & 00 & 00 & 00 & 00 & 03 & 00 & 00 & 00 \\
\end{bmatrix}.
\tag{8}
$$

Thus, the linear transformation consisting of the SR transform and the MC transform can be expressed as

$$\left(s''_{0,0}, s''_{1,0}, \ldots, s''_{0,1}, s''_{1,1}, \ldots\right)^T \\ = M \cdot \left(s_{0,0}, s_{1,0}, \ldots, s_{0,1}, s_{1,1}, \ldots\right)^T. \quad (9)$$

2.3. AddRoundKey. In this operation, a round key is applied to the state by a simple bitwise EXOR. The round key is derived from the cipher key by means of the key schedule. It can be denoted as $Y = X \oplus K$, where K is the round key.

2.4. Key Schedule Algorithm. Key schedule consists of two modules: key expansion and round key selection. The block length and key length are denoted as N_b and N_k, respectively, and the unit is a 4-byte word. That is, N_b = block length/32 and N_k = key length/32. The number of rounds is denoted by R.

For AES-256, $N_b = 8$, $N_k = 8$, and $R = 14$. The key expansion of AES-256 is to extend eight 4-byte key words into 90 4-byte words $W[\cdot]$, where $W[0], \ldots, W[7]$ is the cipher key. The expansion algorithm is as shown in Algorithm 1.

3. Gröbner Basis Theory

Let R be a ring; for a nonempty ideal $I \subset R$, its Gröbner basis is generally not unique [12, 13]. The Gröbner basis is related to the selection of term orders. Related definitions are given below.

Definition 1. Order $\leq$ on a set $T(R)$ is called term order, if and only if $\leq$ is a linear order, and satisfies two properties:

(1) For all $t \in T(R)$, $t \geq 1$.

(2) For any $s, t_1, t_2 \in T(R)$, if $t_1 \leq t_2$, then $st_1 \leq st_2$.

In a term order $\leq$, the largest element of a polynomial p is called the head term of p, denoted as $\mathrm{HT}(p)$.

The set of natural numbers is $\mathbb{N}$, and n is a given positive integer, and $x_1, x_2, \ldots, x_n$ are n variables in ring R. Let the set of terms be

$$T(R) = \left\{x_1^{\alpha_1} x_2^{\alpha_2} \cdots x_n^{\alpha_n} \mid \alpha_i \in \mathbb{N}, \; i = 1, 2, \ldots, n\right\}. \quad (10)$$

That is, $T(R)$ is the power product set of n variables. The degree of term $t = x_1^{\alpha_1} x_2^{\alpha_2} \cdots x_n^{\alpha_n} \in T(R)$ is denoted as $\deg(t) = \sum_{i=1}^n \alpha_i$. Let $X = (x_1, x_2, \ldots, x_n)$; then, the definitions of three common term orders will be given below.

Definition 2. $T(R)$ $x_1 > x_2 > \cdots > x_n$ on lexicographical order, denoted as lex, is defined as follows.

For $\alpha = (\alpha_1, \alpha_2, \ldots, \alpha_n)$, $\beta = (\beta_1, \beta_2, \ldots, \beta_n) \in \mathbb{N}^n$, then $X^\alpha <_{\text{lex}} X^\beta \Leftrightarrow$ let $\alpha_j = \beta_j, j = 0, 1, \ldots, k$, and $\alpha_{k+1} < \beta_{k+1}$ ($\alpha_0 = \beta_0$), where $0 \leq k \leq n - 1$.

Definition 3. $T(R)$ $x_1 > x_2 > \cdots > x_n$ on degree lexicographical order, denoted as deglex, is defined as follows.

For $\alpha = (\alpha_1, \alpha_2, \ldots, \alpha_n)$, $\beta = (\beta_1, \beta_2, \ldots, \beta_n) \in \mathbb{N}^n$, then

$$X^\alpha <_{\text{deglex}} X^\beta \Longleftrightarrow$$

$$\begin{cases} \sum_{i=1}^n \alpha_i < \sum_{i=1}^n \beta_i & \text{or} \\ \sum_{i=1}^n \alpha_i = \sum_{i=1}^n \beta_i, & \text{and according to the lexicographic order.} \\ X^\alpha <_{\text{lex}} X^\beta \end{cases} \quad (11)$$

Definition 4. $T(R)$ $x_1 > x_2 > \cdots > x_n$ on degree reverse lexicographical order, denoted as degrevlex, is defined as follows.

For $\alpha = (\alpha_1, \alpha_2, \ldots, \alpha_n)$, $\beta = (\beta_1, \beta_2, \ldots, \beta_n) \in \mathbb{N}^n$, then

$$X^\alpha <_{\text{degrevlex}} X^\beta \Longleftrightarrow$$

$$\sum_{i=1}^n \alpha_i < \sum_{i=1}^n \beta_i,$$

$$\text{or} \sum_{i=1}^n \alpha_i = \sum_{i=1}^n \beta_i, \quad (12)$$

$\alpha_n = \beta_n, \ldots, \alpha_{i+1} = \beta_{i+1}, \alpha_i \neq \beta_i, \alpha_i > \beta_i$, between α and β, the first different coords from right side, $\alpha_i > \beta_i$.

Definition 5. Let R be a ring and let I be one nonzero ideal in R, $G = \{g_1, \ldots, g_m\} \subset I$. G is called the Gröbner basis of ideal I if and only if

$$\langle \mathrm{HT}(g_1), \ldots, \mathrm{HT}(g_m) \rangle = \langle \{\mathrm{HT}(p) : p \in I\} \rangle. \quad (13)$$

The Gröbner basis of any nonzero ideal can be obtained by using the Buchberger algorithm [12]. In the implementation of the Buchberger algorithm, the Buchberger rule can be used to eliminate unnecessary polynomials [12, 14]. Based on the Buchberger rule, the following conclusions can be obtained.

Theorem 6. *Let G be a set of polynomials, $H = \{HT(f) : f \in G\}$; if all elements in H are pairwise prime, then G is a Gröbner basis.*

Proof. See [15]. □

A zero-dimensional ideal is an ideal that has a finite number of solutions over the closure of the field. It usually

```
(1)   for (i = 8; i < 90; i + +) do
(2)     if i %8 = 0 then
(3)       W[i] = W[i − 8] ⊕ BS(RotByte(W[i − 1])) ⊕const(i/8);
(4)     else
(5)       W[i] = W[i − 8] ⊕ W[i − 1];
(6)     end if
(7)   end for
(8)   return W[8], W[9], . . . , W[89];
```

ALGORITHM 1: Key expansion algorithm of AES-256.

is advantageous to have this property for Gröbner basis computations. By using Corollary 6.56 of [16], we can determine whether an ideal I is zero-dimensional. Below we state a reduced version of this corollary.

Theorem 7. *Let G be a Gröbner basis of the ideal I; then, $\dim(I) = 0$ if and only if, for any $1 \leq i \leq n$, there exists a polynomial $g \in G$, so that $HT(g) = x_i^{d_i}$.*

4. Equation System of AES-256

Let $((p_0, \ldots, p_{31}), (c_0, \ldots, c_{31})) \in F^{32} \times F^{32}$ be a known pair of plaintext and ciphertext in this paper. We call $x_{i,j}$ the jth element of the output of the AddRoundKey in the ith round transformation. We denote by $k_{i,j}$ the jth element of the ith round key. It is easy to see that $k_{0,j}$ denotes the cipher key, $0 \leq i \leq 14, 0 \leq j \leq 31$. The equation system on GF(2^8) consists of the following four parts:

(1) Initial round (round 0) equations and the cipher equations:

$$x_{0,0} + k_{0,0} + p_0 = 0 \qquad x_{14,0} + c_0 = 0$$
$$\vdots \qquad\qquad\qquad \vdots \qquad\qquad (14)$$
$$x_{0,31} + k_{0,31} + p_{31} = 0 \quad x_{14,31} + c_{31} = 0.$$

(2) The equations of intermediate rounds, that is, the encryption equation of the ith round, $1 \leq i \leq 13$:

$$\begin{pmatrix} x_{i,0} + k_{i,0} \\ x_{i,1} + k_{i,1} \\ \vdots \\ x_{i,31} + k_{i,31} \end{pmatrix} + M \cdot \begin{pmatrix} S(x_{i-1,0}) \\ S(x_{i-1,1}) \\ \vdots \\ S(x_{i-1,31}) \end{pmatrix} = 0. \qquad (15)$$

(3) The equations of the final round:

$$\begin{pmatrix} x_{14,0} + k_{14,0} \\ x_{14,1} + k_{14,1} \\ \vdots \\ x_{14,31} + k_{14,31} \end{pmatrix} + M_{SR} \cdot \begin{pmatrix} S(x_{13,0}) \\ S(x_{13,1}) \\ \vdots \\ S(x_{13,31}) \end{pmatrix} = 0. \qquad (16)$$

(4) Key scheduling equations:

$$\begin{pmatrix} k_{i,0} \\ k_{i,1} \\ k_{i,2} \\ k_{i,3} \\ k_{i,4} \\ k_{i,5} \\ \vdots \\ k_{i,31} \end{pmatrix} = \begin{pmatrix} k_{i-1,0} + S(k_{i-1,29}) + \xi^{i-1} \\ k_{i-1,1} + S(k_{i-1,30}) \\ k_{i-1,2} + S(k_{i-1,31}) \\ k_{i-1,3} + S(k_{i-1,28}) \\ k_{i-1,4} + k_{i,0} \\ k_{i-1,5} + k_{i,1} \\ \vdots \\ k_{i-1,31} + k_{i,27} \end{pmatrix}, \qquad (17)$$

where ξ^{i-1} ($1 \leq i \leq 14$) is a round constant.

5. Algebraic Cryptanalysis Scheme of AES-256

Definition 8. Denote the finite domain GF(2^8) as F; the multivariate polynomial ring on F, R is defined as

$$R := F\left[x_{i,j}, k_{i,j} : \{0 \leq i \leq 31, 0 \leq j \leq 14\}\right]. \qquad (18)$$

To construct AES-256 Gröbner basis, the multivariate equation system obtained in Section 4 must be improved to meet the requirements of Gröbner basis; that is, the head terms of the polynomial on the left-hand side of the equation are pairwise prime.

5.1. The Gröbner Basis Construction Method of AES-256. The Gröbner basis of AES-256 is constructed as follows.

Step 1. The purpose of this step is to construct the polynomial set of the S-box and the inverse S-box. In this step, we make use of the algebraic expression of the S-box and the inverse S-box.

AES S-box is constructed based on evident mathematical theory, so it can be written in the form of an algebraic expression. The sparse algebraic expression of the S-box in F is as follows:

$$S : F \longrightarrow F,$$
$$x \longmapsto \qquad (19)$$
$$05x^{FE} + 09x^{FD} + F9x^{FB} + 25x^{F7} + F4x^{EF} + B5x^{DF} + B9x^{BF} + 8Fx^{7F} + 63.$$

TABLE 1: Coefficients of algebraic expression of AES inverse S-box (Hex).

C (mn)	0	1	2	3	4	5	6	7	8	9	A	B	C	D	E	F
0	52	F3	7E	1E	90	BB	2C	8A	1C	85	6D	C0	B2	1B	40	23
1	F6	73	29	D9	39	21	CF	3D	9A	8A	2F	CF	7B	04	E8	C8
2	85	7B	7C	AF	86	2F	13	65	75	D3	6D	D4	89	8E	65	05
3	EA	77	50	A3	C5	01	0B	46	BF	A7	0C	C7	8E	F2	B1	CB
4	E5	E2	10	D1	05	B0	F5	86	E4	03	71	A6	56	03	9E	3E
5	19	18	52	16	B9	D3	38	D9	04	E3	72	6B	BA	E8	BF	9D
6	1D	5A	55	FF	71	E1	A8	8E	FE	A2	A7	1F	DF	B0	03	CB
7	08	53	6F	B0	7F	87	8B	02	B1	92	81	27	40	2E	1A	EE
8	10	CA	82	4F	09	AA	C7	55	24	6C	E2	58	BC	E0	26	37
9	ED	8D	2A	D5	ED	45	C3	EC	1C	3E	2A	B3	9E	B7	38	82
A	23	2D	87	EA	DA	45	24	03	E7	C9	E3	D3	4E	DD	11	4E
B	81	91	91	59	A3	80	92	7E	DB	C4	20	EC	DB	55	7F	A8
C	C1	64	AB	1B	FD	60	05	13	2C	A9	76	A5	1D	32	8E	1E
D	C0	65	CB	8B	93	E4	AE	BE	5F	2C	3B	D2	0F	9F	42	CC
E	6C	80	68	43	09	23	C5	6D	1D	18	BD	5E	1B	B4	85	49
F	BC	0D	1F	A6	6B	D8	22	01	7A	C0	55	16	B3	CF	05	00

The nonsparse algebraic expression of the inverse S-box contains 255 terms. The coefficients of the algebraic expression of AES inverse S-box are shown in Table 1. The abbreviated form of the algebraic expression of AES inverse S-box can be expressed as follows:

$$S^{-1} : F \longrightarrow F,$$
$$x \longmapsto \sum_{i=0}^{254} c_i x^i, \quad (20)$$

where c_i is the coefficient of the term with degree i.

Step 2. The purpose of this step is to construct the polynomial set of linear transformations (i.e., ShiftRow and MixColumn). In this step, we use the equation system given in Section 4.

By (14), the plaintext equations, that is, the initial round equation system, can be obtained as (21), and the ciphertext equations can be obtained as (22). Hence,

$$x_{0,i} + k_{0,i} + p_i = 0, \quad p_i \in F, 0 \le i \le 31, \quad (21)$$

$$x_{14,i} + c_i = 0, \quad c_i \in F, 0 \le i \le 31. \quad (22)$$

Since $x_{0,i}$ and $k_{0,i}$ have the same degree, the head term of polynomials in (21) is $x_{0,i}$ or $k_{0,i}$. If the selected term order is $x_{0,i} < k_{0,i}$, then the head term of polynomial is $k_{0,i}$, $0 \le i \le 31$. For (22), the head term of polynomial is $x_{14,i}$, $0 \le i \le 31$.

It is needed to improve (15) and (16) to meet the requirements of Gröbner basis. From (15), it is easy to get 24 polynomial equations of round i $(1 \le i \le 13)$ as shown in

$$\begin{pmatrix} S(x_{i-1,0}) \\ S(x_{i-1,1}) \\ \vdots \\ S(x_{i-1,31}) \end{pmatrix} + M^{-1} \cdot \begin{pmatrix} x_{i,0} + k_{i,0} \\ x_{i,1} + k_{i,1} \\ \vdots \\ x_{i,31} + k_{i,31} \end{pmatrix} = 0. \quad (23)$$

Similarly, from (16), the 32 polynomial equations of the final round can be obtained as shown in

$$\begin{pmatrix} S(x_{13,0}) \\ S(x_{13,1}) \\ \vdots \\ S(x_{13,31}) \end{pmatrix} + M_{SR}^{-1} \cdot \begin{pmatrix} x_{14,0} + k_{14,0} \\ x_{14,1} + k_{14,1} \\ \vdots \\ x_{14,31} + k_{14,31} \end{pmatrix} = 0. \quad (24)$$

For degree lexicographical order, the head term of polynomial in (23) and (24) is $x_{i,j}^{254}$, $0 \le i \le 13$, $0 \le j \le 31$. It is easy to see that the head term has no nontrivial common factor; that is, the greatest common factor is 1.

Step 3. The purpose of this step is to construct the polynomial set of the key schedule algorithm. In this step, we also use the equation system given in Section 4.

In order to get the polynomial Gröbner basis of the whole encryption algorithm, the equation system of the key schedule algorithm needs to be improved. It is easy to deduce (25) from (17). Hence,

$$\begin{pmatrix} k_{i,0} \\ k_{i,1} \\ k_{i,2} \\ k_{i,3} \\ k_{i,4} \\ k_{i,5} \\ \vdots \\ k_{i,31} \end{pmatrix} = \begin{pmatrix} k_{i-1,0} \\ k_{i-1,1} \\ k_{i-1,2} \\ k_{i-1,3} \\ k_{i-1,4} \\ k_{i-1,5} \\ \vdots \\ k_{i-1,31} \end{pmatrix} + \begin{pmatrix} S(k_{i-1,29}) \\ S(k_{i-1,30}) \\ S(k_{i-1,31}) \\ S(k_{i-1,28}) \\ k_{i,0} \\ k_{i,1} \\ \vdots \\ k_{i,27} \end{pmatrix}$$

$$+ \begin{pmatrix} \xi^{i-1} \\ 0 \\ 0 \\ 0 \\ 0 \\ 0 \\ \vdots \\ 0 \end{pmatrix} \cdot \qquad (25)$$

In order to ensure that the head terms of key schedule polynomials are pairwise prime, applying the inverse S-box transformation to (25) is needed. The transformation results are shown in

$$\begin{pmatrix} S^{-1}\left(k_{i,0}+k_{i-1,0}+\xi^{i-1}\right) \\ S^{-1}\left(k_{i,1}+k_{i-1,1}\right) \\ S^{-1}\left(k_{i,2}+k_{i-1,2}\right) \\ S^{-1}\left(k_{i,3}+k_{i-1,3}\right) \\ k_{i,4}+k_{i-1,4} \\ k_{i,5}+k_{i-1,5} \\ \vdots \\ k_{i,31}+k_{i-1,31} \end{pmatrix} + \begin{pmatrix} k_{i-1,29} \\ k_{i-1,30} \\ k_{i-1,31} \\ k_{i-1,28} \\ k_{i,0} \\ k_{i,1} \\ \vdots \\ k_{i,27} \end{pmatrix} = 0. \qquad (26)$$

According to the algebraic expression of the inverse S-box, all the equations included in (26) can be obtained. If the selected term order is

$$k_{i,31} > k_{i,30} > \cdots > k_{i,0} > k_{i-1,31} > \cdots > k_{i-1,1} \\ > k_{i-1,0}, \qquad (27)$$

where $1 \le i \le 14$, then the set of polynomial head terms of the key schedule equation (26) is

$$\left\{k_{i,j}^{254}, k_{i,h} : 1 \le i \le 14, 0 \le j \le 3, 4 \le h \le 31\right\}. \qquad (28)$$

It is easy to see that the elements of the head term set have no nontrivial common factor.

Step 4. The purpose of this step is the reasonable selection of term order and variable order. If we choose a degree lexicographical order over reasonable variable order, we can make the polynomial head terms of the whole encryption algorithm pairwise prime.

The left-hand sides of (21), (22), (23), (24), and (26) constitute a set of polynomials denoted as A, and the degree lexicographical order $<_A$ over the following variable order

makes the head terms of polynomials in A pairwise prime. Hence,

$$\underbrace{x_{0,0} < \cdots < x_{0,31}}_{\text{initial round state variables}} \underbrace{< k_{0,0} < \cdots < k_{0,31}}_{\text{initial key variable}}$$

$$\underbrace{< k_{1,0} < \cdots < k_{1,31}}_{\text{first round key variables}} < \cdots$$

$$\underbrace{< k_{14,0} < \cdots < k_{14,31}}_{\text{last round key variables}}$$

$$\underbrace{< \quad x_{1,0} < \cdots < x_{1,31}}_{\text{first round internal state variables}} < \cdots \qquad (29)$$

$$\underbrace{< \quad x_{13,0} < \cdots < x_{13,31}}_{\text{11th round internal state variables}}$$

$$\underbrace{< x_{14,0} < \cdots < x_{14,31}}_{\text{ciphertext variables}}.$$

After these four steps, the polynomial set A in the term order $<_A$ is a Gröbner basis of the ideal $\langle A \rangle$ in ring R. The following will give the relevant properties and their theoretical proof.

5.2. The Properties of AES-256 Gröbner Basis.
Gröbner basis is the standard notation of polynomial ideal, and there are two useful properties: (1) given a Gröbner basis of an ideal, it is effective to determine whether a polynomial belongs to the ideal; (2) for reasonable term order, the ideal type can be calculated effectively, and the polynomial equation systems deduced from these ideals can be solved. The polynomial set A contains 720 polynomials, where 384 polynomials are with the degree 254 and 336 are linear polynomials that contain 720 variables $x_{i,j}, k_{i,j}, 0 \le i \le 14, 0 \le j \le 31$. For polynomial set A, there are the following conclusions.

Theorem 9. *The set of polynomials A is a Gröbner basis relative to degree lexicographical order $<_A$.*

Proof. Relative to the term order $<_A$, the head term set of polynomials in (21) is $H_1 = \{k_{0,i} : 0 \le i \le 31\}$, the head term set of polynomials in (22) is $H_2 = \{x_{14,i} : 0 \le i \le 31\}$, the head term set of polynomials in (23) and (24) is $H_3 = \{x_{i,j}^{254} : 0 \le i \le 13, 0 \le j \le 31\}$, and the head term set of polynomials in (26) is $H_4 = \{k_{i,j}^{254}, k_{i,h} : 1 \le i \le 14, 0 \le j \le 3, 4 \le h \le 31\}$, so the head term set of polynomials A is $H = H_1 \cup H_2 \cup H_3 \cup H_4$. Since, $\forall a, b \in H, \gcd(a, b) = 1$, elements in H are pairwise prime. According to Theorem 6, it can be obtained that the set of polynomials A is a Gröbner basis relative to term order $<_A$. $\qquad \square$

Theorem 9 indicates that the set of polynomials A is a Gröbner basis of ideal $\langle A \rangle$ in ring R. This provides the possibility of carrying out the ideal calculation of AES-256.

Theorem 10. *The ideal $\langle A \rangle$ generated by Gröbner basis A of AES-256 is zero-dimensional.*

(1)   list the equation system of AES-256 algorithm;
(2)   select a known plaintext and ciphertext pair, and substitute it into the equation system;
(3)   construct Gröbner basis Ggrelex of the ideal relative to degree lexicographical order using the method in Section 5.1;
(4)   judge the solution structure of the Gröbner basis. Because the equation system contains the field equation, the equation
         is finite or no solution.
(5)   **if and only if** Ggrelex = (1) **then**
(6)   the equation system is no solution;
(7)   **if** it is no solution, **then**
(8)   select another plaintext and ciphertext pair to return to Step (3);
(9)   **else** continue;
(10)   **end if**
(11)   **end if**
(12)   convert degree lexicographical Gröbner basis Ggrelex to lexicographical Gröbner basis Glex by using FGLM algorithm;
(13)   solve the key variables;
(14)   verify the correctness of key by applying plaintext, ciphertext and key to AES-256 algorithm;
(15)   **return** the key value;

ALGORITHM 2: Algebraic cryptanalysis algorithm of AES-256.

Proof. The variable set of the AES-256 equation system is $V = \{x_{i,j}, k_{i,j} : 0 \leq i \leq 14, 0 \leq j \leq 31\}$, so the number of variables is $|V| = 720$. It can be seen from the proof process of Theorem 9 that the head term set of polynomials set A is H. $\forall x \in V$, there exists $1 \leq d \leq 254$ satisfying $x^d \in H$; that is, all variables are in the form of a certain number of times in H. Based on this, for any variable x, there exists a polynomial $g \in A$, so that $\mathrm{HT}(g) = x^d$. According to Theorem 7, it is obvious that $\dim(\langle A \rangle) = 0$; that is, the ideal $\langle A \rangle$ generated by the Gröbner basis A is zero-dimensional.

Theorem 10 points out that the Gröbner basis A constructed by this paper is zero-dimensional. Due to the term order conversion algorithm FGLM can convert any term order Gröbner basis of zero-dimensional ideal into lexicographical Gröbner basis, so the FGLM algorithm can convert degree lexicographical Gröbner basis A into lexicographical Gröbner basis. The construction of zero-dimensional Gröbner basis is helpful to simplify Gröbner basis calculation, which makes it possible to reduce the complexity of solving multivariate equation system.

5.3. The Algebraic Cryptanalysis Scheme and Its Complexity. The algebraic cryptanalysis algorithm of AES-256 is shown in Algorithm 2.

The maximum degree when computing the Gröbner basis is no more than N, where N is the number of the unknown variables in the equation system, so the upper bound of complexity of computing Gröbner basis is $O(2^N)$. Since the upper bound of the complexity of our scheme depends on the complexity of the Gröbner basis computation, the upper bound of the complexity of our scheme is $O(2^N)$. It can be seen from [17] that the complexity of exhaustively solving the equation system is $O(N2^N)$. It is obvious that the complexity of our scheme is less than the complexity of exhaustive attack, which indicates that our scheme is a successful attack scheme. Moreover, taking into account the sparse and overdefined features of AES-256 equation system, the actual complexity will be far less than the exhaustive attack.

Not all equations are always true in the equation system. For an S-box, there is an equation whose true probability is $255/256$. For the full AES-256, the true probability of this kind of equation is $1/9$. It needs 9 plaintext and ciphertext pairs to conduct computation 9 times in Step 3, and the equation system will have a finite set of solutions.

6. Conclusions

Based on the characteristics of the round transformation in AES-256, the ShiftRow and MixColumn transformations are merged into left multiplication by a matrix M, making it in the form of linear transformation. In further research on AES-256, the linear transformation and multivariate equation system of AES-256 are further studied. The Gröbner basis is proposed and constructed by choosing reasonable term order and variable order. At the same time, we point out and prove that the Gröbner basis is zero-dimensional. Based on this, the Gröbner basis attack scheme is proposed, and the attack complexity is far lower than the brute force attack. Taking into account the fact that the complexity of our scheme is very high, our research results have a theoretical value. However, the discovery of the zero-dimensional Gröbner basis of AES-256 has guiding significance for further study on efficient Gröbner based attack scheme. The complexity of FGLM and the effectiveness of Gröbner basis attack still need to be further studied.

Competing Interests

The authors declare that they have no competing interests.

Acknowledgments

This work was supported by the National Natural Science Foundation of China (no. 61502008), the Key Scientific Research Project of Henan Higher Education (no. 16A520084), the Natural Science Foundation of Anhui

Province (no. 1508085QF132), and the Doctoral Research Start-Up Funds Project of Anhui University.

References

[1] J. Daemen and V. Rijmen, *The Design of Rijndael: AES—The Advanced Encryption Standard*, Springer Science & Business Media, 2013.

[2] A. Hashemi and D. Lazard, "Sharper complexity bounds for zero-dimensional Gröbner bases and polynomial system solving," *International Journal of Algebra and Computation*, vol. 21, no. 5, pp. 703–713, 2011.

[3] M. Bardet, J.-C. Faugère, and B. Salvy, "On the complexity of the F_5 Gröbner basis algorithm," *Journal of Symbolic Computation*, vol. 70, pp. 49–70, 2015.

[4] A. Bogdanov and V. Rijmen, "Linear hulls with correlation zero and linear cryptanalysis of block ciphers," *Designs, Codes and Cryptography*, vol. 70, no. 3, pp. 369–383, 2014.

[5] Y. Sasaki, "Known-key attacks on rijndael with large blocks and strengthening shiftrow parameter," *IEICE Transactions on Fundamentals of Electronics, Communications and Computer Sciences*, vol. 95, no. 1, pp. 21–28, 2012.

[6] C. Cid and G. Leurent, "An Analysis of the XSL Algorithm," in *Advances in cryptology—ASIACRYPT 2005*, vol. 3788 of *Lecture Notes in Comput. Sci.*, pp. 333–352, Springer, Berlin, Germany, 2005.

[7] S. Murphy and M. Robshaw, "Comments on the security of the AES and the XSL technique," *Electronic Letters*, vol. 39, no. 1, pp. 36–38, 2003.

[8] J. Buchmann, A. Pyshkin, and R.-P. Weinmann, "A zero-dimensional Gröbner basis for AES-128," *Lecture Notes in Computer Science*, vol. 4047, pp. 78–88, 2006.

[9] S. Ghosh and A. Das, "An improvement of linearization-based algebraic attacks," in *Security Aspects in Information Technology*, vol. 7011 of *Lecture Notes in Computer Science*, pp. 157–167, Springer, 2011.

[10] M. R. Z'Aba, K. Wong, E. Dawson, and L. Simpson, "Algebraic analysis of small scale LEX-BES," in *Proceedings of the 2nd International Cryptology Conference: Curve is an Art, Cryptology is a Science (Cryptology '10)*, pp. 77–82, Universiti Teknikal Malaysia Melaka, Melaka, Malaysia, July 2010.

[11] J. Cui, L. Huang, H. Zhong, and W. Yang, "Algebraic attack on Rijndael-192 based on Grobner basis," *Acta Electronica Sinica*, vol. 41, no. 5, pp. 833–839, 2013.

[12] S. N. Ahmad and N. Aris, "The Gröbner package in Maple and computer algebra system for solving multivariate polynomial equations," *Academic Journal UiTM Johor*, vol. 10, pp. 156–174, 2011.

[13] M. Bardet, J. C. Faugere, and B. Salvy, "On the complexity of the F_5 Gröbner basis algorithm," *Journal of Symbolic Computation*, vol. 70, pp. 49–70, 2015.

[14] V. Gerdt and R. La Scala, "Noetherian quotients of the algebra of partial difference polynomials and Gröbner bases of symmetric ideals," *Journal of Algebra*, vol. 423, pp. 1233–1261, 2015.

[15] J. Buchmann, A. Pyshkin, and R.-P. Weinmann, "Block ciphers sensitive to Gröbner basis attacks," in *Topics in Cryptology—CT-RSA 2006*, vol. 3860 of *Lecture Notes in Comput. Sci.*, pp. 313–331, Springer, Berlin, Germany, 2006.

[16] D.-M. Li, J.-W. Liu, and W.-J. Liu, "W-Gröbner basis and monomial ideals under polynomial composition," *Applied Mathematics A*, vol. 26, no. 3, pp. 287–294, 2011.

[17] J.-C. Faugère and A. Joux, "Algebraic cryptanalysis of Hidden Field Equation (HFE) cryptosystems using Gröbner bases," in *Proceedings of the Annual International Cryptology Conference (CRYPTO '03)*, vol. 2729 of *Lecture Notes in Computer Science LNCS*, pp. 44–60, Springer, Santa Barbara, Calif, USA, 2003.

19

A Novel DBN Feature Fusion Model for Cross-Corpus Speech Emotion Recognition

Zou Cairong,[1,2] Zhang Xinran,[2] Zha Cheng,[2] and Zhao Li[2]

[1]*Department of Information and Communication Engineering, Guangzhou Maritime University, Guangzhou 510006, China*
[2]*Key Laboratory of Underwater Acoustic signal Processing of Ministry of Education, Southeast University, Nanjing 210096, China*

Correspondence should be addressed to Zhang Xinran; zxrzxr87324@126.com

Academic Editor: Alexey Karpov

The feature fusion from separate source is the current technical difficulties of cross-corpus speech emotion recognition. The purpose of this paper is to, based on Deep Belief Nets (DBN) in Deep Learning, use the emotional information hiding in speech spectrum diagram (spectrogram) as image features and then implement feature fusion with the traditional emotion features. First, based on the spectrogram analysis by STB/Itti model, the new spectrogram features are extracted from the color, the brightness, and the orientation, respectively; then using two alternative DBN models they fuse the traditional and the spectrogram features, which increase the scale of the feature subset and the characterization ability of emotion. Through the experiment on ABC database and Chinese corpora, the new feature subset compared with traditional speech emotion features, the recognition result on cross-corpus, distinctly advances by 8.8%. The method proposed provides a new idea for feature fusion of emotion recognition.

1. Introduction

In recent years, more attention is paid to the study of emotion recognition. Speech, as one of the most important ways of communication in human daily life, contains rich emotional information. Speech emotion recognition (SER), because of its wide application significance and research value in intelligence and naturalness of human-computer interaction aspects [1], gets more and more attention from the researchers in recent years. Emotion recognition system performance determines the quality of information feedback and the efficiency of human-computer interaction, while overall performance of SER depends on the matching degree between features and classifiers [2]. Although the earlier temporal features may not be suitable for the current corpus structures [3], the emotional information contained on the time domain still has good representation ability to be reserved. In order to research SER on the broader technology level, extending the database source and searching suitable fusion model for big emotional information data have become new focuses [3, 4].

Feature layer fusion is the integration of data after preprocessing and feature extraction, so many related researches are applied to this area. Through specific means such as fusion, the scale of feature sources is enhanced and the data sets are expanded. Further, some effective data analysis techniques are introduced and applied, such as Neural Network and Deep Learning. Common feature fusions are often used for single source data samples. Because the emotional properties of different features are various, the cross-corpus recognition effects of current fusion methods are not satisfactory. The development of Deep Learning technology brings a new orientation to SER. Using appropriate algorithm to train the deep neural network model, more valuable features can be derived from the vast amounts of original databases which are multiple sources [7]. Accordingly, Deep Belief Nets (DBN) model, which is a commonly used model in Deep Learning area [8], is introduced in our work. Through Restricted Boltzmann Machine (RBM) [9], DBN could constantly adjust the connection weight, which can realize effective fusion of features. Previous cross-corpus studies are dependent on traditional suprasegmental acoustic global features, which are often used in emotion recognition technology [10]. Since the emotional features have great significance to SER, exploring new features to promote the development of SER has an irreplaceable role in the cross-corpus research. Thus, this article introduces a new emotional feature category based on visual attention mechanism. The new feature space includes three kinds of image vectors: color, brightness, and orientation. Features extracted from spectrogram connect the time domain and frequency domain, so they have important significance for cross-corpus SER research. The new direction of the research which uses the spectrogram emotional features [4, 5] has advantages for its overall information. The integrated features with traditional acoustic traits could combine the global and temporal features, which supplement the original feature space.

This paper mainly studies the feature fusion method based on DBN which fuse spectrogram features and acoustic global features for SER. In Section 2, by selective attention mechanism, the features with time-frequency domain correlation traits are extracted while the emotion recognition abilities are analyzed. Then in Section 3, based on the DBN fusion method on feature level, an alternative DBN (so-called DBN21) feature fusion layer model is proposed for the extraction of spectrogram feature fusion. After that, the approximate optimal feature subset is obtained for overcoming the shortage of recognition ability differences between adjacent frames, which often appears in the traditional feature fusion method. Furthermore, as for the cross-corpus cases, a modified DBN network model (so-called DBN22) is designed for spectrogram features and acoustic features fusion. In Section 4, proven by simulation experiments on four databases, the features of proposed fusion method effectively improve the performance of SER system on cross-corpus.

2. Spectrogram Feature Extraction Based on Selective Attention

Spectrogram, namely, speech spectrum diagram, is based on the time domain signal processing, which has the horizontal axis representing time, the vertical axis representing the frequency, and the depth of the midpoint chart color representing the strength of the corresponding signal. Spectrogram is a communication between the time domain and frequency domain, which reflects the correlation of the two domains. Because spectrogram is the visual expression of the time-frequency distribution of the speech energy [11], it contains characteristic information, such as energy and formant. In our research, based on STB/Itti model [12], selective attention features on the orientation, color, and brightness of spectrogram are extracted as new characteristics for SER. Meanwhile, the dimension reduction and optimization for the features are conducted by proposed DBN model. And then an improved kernel learning K-nearest neighbor algorithm based on feature line centroid (kernel-KNNFLC) [13] classifier is carried on the experiment. The results show that the extracted features possess more powerful emotion recognition ability than their contrast. The spectrogram feature extraction process in SER with selective attention mechanism and DBN is shown in Figure 1.

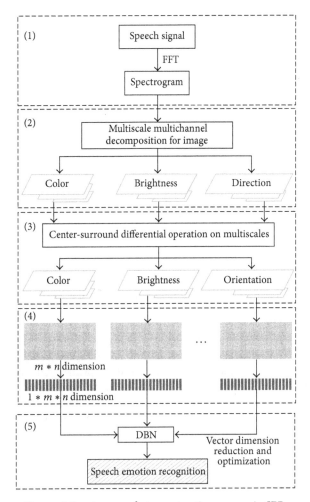

FIGURE 1: Spectrogram feature extraction process in SER.

2.1. Spectrogram Feature Extraction.
The computation formula of spectrogram is as follows:

$$L = |Y| = \left| \sum_{n=0}^{N-1} s(n)\, \omega(n)\, e^{-j(2\pi/N)kn} \right|, \quad k \in [0, N]. \quad (1)$$

$s(n)$ represents the input signal, $\omega(n)$ represents the hamming window function, and N is the window length. Figure 2 is the spectrogram extracted from a piece of the speech labeled "aggressive" emotion in ABC corpus.

2.2. Gaussian Pyramid Decomposition.
Based on the mechanism of selective attention, the area is easy to get the attention of people in a picture, which usually has strong difference compared to the surrounding area [14]. Multiscale multichannel filtering can be resolved by convolution operation with the linear Gaussian kernel. A 6×6 Gaussian kernel is used in this paper. The resulting image formula after Gaussian Pyramid Decomposition (GPD) is as follows:

$$I(\sigma + 1) = \frac{I(\sigma)}{2}, \quad \sigma = [0, 1, 2, 3, 4, 5, 6, 7, 8], \quad (2)$$

where σ represents the layer number and $I(\sigma)$ is the σ layer of the image after decomposition, in which $I(0)$ is the original

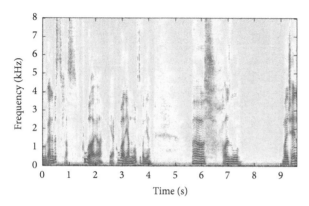

FIGURE 2: Spectrogram sample graph.

image. After the multiscale multichannel filtering, feature extractions are conducted of each scale image in orientation, color, and brightness, and then sequence images are formed, respectively.

In the retinal cone photoreceptors response level, the model is trichromatic mechanism. However, in the process of choosing messages for center selection in the brain, it changes into 4 primary mechanisms. As a result, 4 primary channels are defined in Itti model. Therefore, the antagonism of the R-G and B-Y colors could be used to simulate the saliency contribution which is made by the colors to images. And then the computation formula is

$$P_{R\text{-}G}(\sigma) = \frac{(r-g)}{\max(r,g,b)},$$
$$P_{B\text{-}Y}(\sigma) = \frac{(b-\min(r,g))}{\max(r,g,b)}. \tag{3}$$

In formula (3) r, g, and b, respectively, represent the three primary colors: red, green, and blue. Here are 16 GPD images based on the extracted color features of the different scale images.

The GPD images of brightness features are obtained after calculating the average of the normalized r, g, and b:

$$P_I(\sigma) = \frac{(r+g+b)}{3}. \tag{4}$$

Here are 8 GPD images of brightness.

The 2D Gabor directional filter could be used to simulate the directional selection mechanism of the retina [15]; therefore, we can use its convolution with the GPD of brightness feature to get the GPD images of local orientation feature. It has been proven that the angle $\theta \in (0°, 45°, 90°, 135°)$ can be used to represent the orientation feature:

$$P_\theta(\sigma) = \|P_I(\sigma) * G_0(\theta)\| + \|P_I(\sigma) * G_{\pi/2}(\theta)\|. \tag{5}$$

The corresponding formula is as follows:

$$G_\psi(\theta) = \exp\left(-\frac{x'^2 + \gamma^2 y'^2}{2\delta^2}\right)\cos\left(2\pi\frac{x'}{\lambda} + \psi\right). \tag{6}$$

γ is the orientation rate which has a value of 1; δ and λ, respectively, represent the standard deviation and the wavelength which have the value of 7/3 pixels and 7 pixels; ψ is the phase and $\psi \in \{0, \pi/2\}$. 32 GPD images of orientation feature could be obtained by using a total of 8 scales and 4 directions, 2D Gabor.

2.3. Features Obtaining and Matrix Reconstruction. Relying on the color and brightness features of GPD extracted previously, they cannot attract the selective attention insufficiently, which also needs the difference contrast of image characteristics. These features compared with the traditional acoustic global features, properties, have better characterization of different speech sample sources (language, speakers, including noise, etc.) in which emotional information is implied. In our research the center-surround is applied to the computing method of calculation [16]. Experimental results show that this center-surround method brings the model more reliable robustness in cross-corpus SER. After the calculation of contrastive feature vector, the gist feature images could be obtained based on the merger strategy (local iterative normalized).

$$FM_l(\sigma_c, \sigma_s) = N\left(\left|P_l(\sigma_c) - P_l(\sigma_s)\right|\right), \tag{7}$$

where $l \in \{R\text{-}G, B\text{-}Y, I, 0°, 45°, 90°, 135°\}$ represents the kinds of gist feature images which are a total of 7, including the R-G and B-Y 2 kinds of color features, one kind of brightness features, and four kinds of orientation features; $\sigma_c \in \{2, 3, 4\}$ is the central scale of Gaussian pyramid; and $\sigma_s = \sigma_c + d$ is the surrounding scale, among which $d = \{2, 3\}$. $N(\cdot)$ represents the merger strategy with local iterative normalized [17]. Finally we received 12 color-contrast, 6 brightness-contrast, and 24 orientation-contrast feature images. The extracted gist feature images based on the speech samples are shown in Figure 3.

A feature image is lot into m lines and n columns, forming total $m * n$ subregions. Then each subregion is replaced by its mean. Furthermore, the images are normalized to a $m * n$ feature matrix, so that a low resolution feature matrix of image is used to describe the whole spectrogram. The mathematical representation of the feature matrix is as follows:

$$FD_i(p,q) = \frac{mn}{vh}\sum_{g=pv/n}^{(p+1)v/n-1}\sum_{f=qh/m}^{(q+1)h/m-1} FM_i(g,f), \tag{8}$$
$$p \in [0, n-1], \quad q \in [0, m-1],$$

among which FM_i is feature image and FD_i is corresponding feature matrix, $i \in [1, 42]$. Here, m is 4 and n is 5. h and v represent the height and width of the feature image, respectively. And then, the characteristic matrix obtained is reconstructed to a $1 \times mn$ vector, in which the feature performance on the cross-corpus SER will be validated in the subsequent experiments.

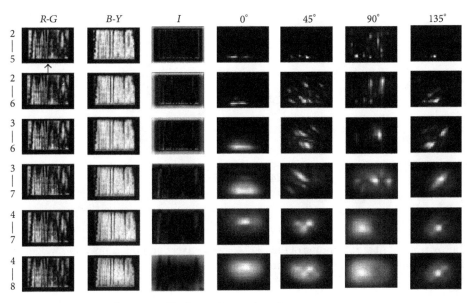

FIGURE 3: Gist feature images based on spectrogram.

3. DBN Feature Fusion Model for SER

The Deep Belief Nets model rooted in statistical mechanics, which is described through the energy function and probability distribution function. Energy function can reflect the stability of the system. When the system in an orderly state and the probability distribution are intense concentrated, the energy of the system is small. Conversely, if the system is in disorder and the probability distribution is uniform, the energy of system may be larger. DBN model is formed in a multilayer stack RBM, just like constructing a building. The RBM is accumulated in layers and is evaluated one by one from the bottom to the top. The training of each layer is independent while the top RBM has self-associative memory according to the information from the lower. Eventually the Error Back Propagation (BP) algorithm is applied to fine-tune weight. At the top of DBN, the kernel-KNNFLC classifier is connected for classification.

3.1. Restricted Boltzmann Machine in DBN. Boltzmann Machine (BM) is a kind of random neural network model, which is made up of two parts: visible and hidden layer. Although BM has strong unsupervised-learning ability and could learn the complex rules in the data, the training time is tremendous long. To solve this problem, Smolensky proposed the RBM, the structure of which is as shown in Figure 4.

The model figure reveals that it is inexistence of internal connection between the visible layer and hidden layer of RBM, which has the property: if the state of the hidden units is given, activated units in visible layer are conditionally independent, so that if the unit number of hidden and layers visible of RBM is m and n, respectively, which state vectors are h and v, according to a given state (v, h), the energy could be defined as follows:

$$E(v, h \mid \theta) = -\sum_{i=1}^{n} a_i v_i - \sum_{j=1}^{m} b_j h_j - \sum_{i=1}^{n} \sum_{j=1}^{m} v_i W_{ij} h_j, \quad (9)$$

in which a_i and b_j are the values of bias of visible unit i and hidden unit j, respectively, and W_{ij} represents the connection weight of j and i. Here $\theta = \{W_{ij}, a_i, b_j\}$ is used as the whole parameter set in RBM. When the parameter set is determined, the joint probability distribution of (v, h) could be obtained according to formula (10), as shown in the following formula:

$$P(v, h \mid \theta) = \frac{e^{-E(v,h|\theta)}}{Z(\theta)}, \quad Z(\theta) = \sum_{v,h} e^{-E(v,h|\theta)}. \quad (10)$$

Here $Z(\theta)$ is called the partition function. Because, with the unit being given by RBM, the activated states between each hidden unit are independent, if it is in a given unit state, the activation probability of j and i could be obtained as follows:

$$P\left(h_j = 1 \mid v, \theta\right) = \sigma\left(b_j + \sum_i v_i W_{ij}\right),$$

$$P\left(v_i = 1 \mid h, \theta\right) = \sigma\left(a_i + \sum_j h_j W_{ij}\right). \quad (11)$$

3.2. The Fast Learning Algorithm Based on Contrast Divergence. Gibbs Sampling algorithm is based on Markov Chain Monte Carlo (MCMC) strategy [18]. By getting a conditional probability distribution of the weight, which can begin from any state, the algorithm implements iteration sampling in turn for each component. Gibbs Sampling method is used to obtain the probability distribution, which is often necessary to employ a lot of sampling steps. In particular within the high-dimension data, the training efficiency of model may be greatly influenced. Therefore, Hinton proposed a fast learning algorithm of RMB called contrastive divergence (CD) [19]. Unlike Gibbs Sampling, this method (CD) uses the training data to initialize and just needs k steps (usually $k = 1$) to

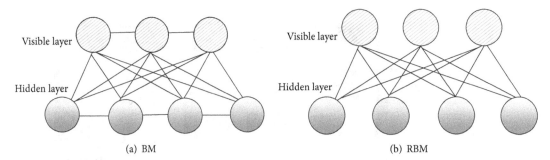

(a) BM

(b) RBM

FIGURE 4: BM and RBM model.

gain a satisfactory approximation. At the beginning of the CD algorithm, the visible unit state is set to a training sample, and then formula (12) is used to calculate the unit state of the hidden layer. After that, the probability of the ist unit hidden values equaling 1 could be calculated according to formula (12). Furthermore, refactoring of visible layer is obtained.

The task of training RBM is to get parameters θ. The logarithm likelihood function is obtained through the training set that is maximized for parameter set θ, which may fit the given training data. If the number of training samples is T, there are

$$\theta^* = \arg\max_{\theta} L(\theta) = \arg\max_{\theta} \sum_{t=1}^{T} \log P\left(v^{(t)} \mid \theta\right). \quad (12)$$

Then, the Stochastic Gradient Ascent method is used to find the optimal parameters maximizing equation (12):

$$\frac{\partial}{\partial\theta} L(\theta) = \frac{\partial}{\partial\theta} \sum_{t=1}^{T} \log \sum_{h} P\left(v^{(t)}, h \mid \theta\right) = \frac{\partial}{\partial\theta}$$

$$\cdot \sum_{t=1}^{T} \log \frac{\sum_{h} e^{[-E(v^{(t)}, h|\theta)]}}{\sum_{v} \sum_{h} e^{[-E(v^{(t)}, h|\theta)]}}$$

$$= \sum_{t=1}^{T} \left(\left\langle \frac{\partial}{\partial\theta} \left(-E\left(v^{(t)}, h \mid \theta\right)\right) \right\rangle_{P(h|v^{(t)}, \theta)} \right.$$

$$\left. - \left\langle \frac{\partial}{\partial\theta} \left(-E\left(v, h \mid \theta\right)\right) \right\rangle_{P(v, h|\theta)} \right). \quad (13)$$

In formula (13) $\langle\cdot\rangle_P$ is calculating mathematical expectation of the distribution P. The first item of the formula can be determined by the training sample, while $P(v, h \mid \theta)$ in the following item need to get the joint probability distribution of visible and hidden units first. And then, for calculating the distribution function $z(\theta)$, which cannot be directly calculated, the sampling method (such as Gibbs Sampling) is introduced to approximate the related value. When using "data" as the tag of $P(h \mid v^{(t)}, \theta)$ and "model" as $P(v, h|\theta)$, the offset on visible and hidden units of formula (13) is a_i and b_j,

respectively, and the connection weight is W_{ij}. Then a partial derivative is available:

$$\frac{\partial}{\partial a_i} \left[\log P(v \mid \theta)\right] = \langle v_i \rangle_{\text{data}} - \langle v_i \rangle_{\text{model}},$$

$$\frac{\partial}{\partial b_j} \left[\log P(v \mid \theta)\right] = \langle h_j \rangle_{\text{data}} - \langle h_j \rangle_{\text{model}}, \quad (14)$$

$$\frac{\partial}{\partial W_{ij}} \left[\log P(v \mid \theta)\right] = \langle v_i h_j \rangle_{\text{data}} - \langle v_i h_j \rangle_{\text{model}}.$$

Based on the criteria of formula (14), the method of Stochastic Gradient Rise is used to maximize the value of the logarithm likelihood function on the training data. Therefore, the updating criteria of parameters are

$$\Delta a_i = \varepsilon\left(\langle v_i \rangle_{\text{data}} - \langle v_i \rangle_{\text{recon}}\right),$$

$$\Delta b_j = \varepsilon\left(\langle h_j \rangle_{\text{data}} - \langle h_j \rangle_{\text{recon}}\right), \quad (15)$$

$$\Delta W_{ij} = \varepsilon\left(\langle v_i h_j \rangle_{\text{data}} - \langle v_i h_j \rangle_{\text{recon}}\right),$$

in which ε is the learning rate and $\langle\cdot\rangle_{\text{recon}}$ represents the distribution of model defined after one step refactoring.

From the above contents, the training procedure of RBM algorithm is divided into a few steps:

(1) Firstly, initialization of RBM is necessary. Thus, mainly the following contents are included: sample training set S; the number of neurons n_h contained in hidden layer, the number of visible layer neurons n_v; the connection weight W_{ij} of visible and hidden layer; the unit biases a_i and b_j of visible and hidden layer; the learning rate ε and the training cycle J; the number of the algorithm steps k.

(2) Rapid sampling is carried out based on the CD-k algorithm. Furthermore, according to the updates of each parameter, the value of parameter set is refreshed.

(3) The sampling process is repeated in the whole training period, until the convergence of formula (12).

3.3. DBN21 and DBN22 Models. According to the RBM, two kinds of DBN models, respectively, DBN21 and DBN22,

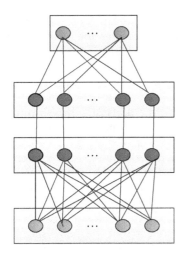

FIGURE 5: DBN21 model.

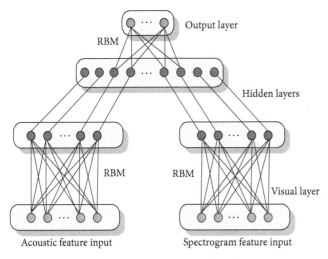

FIGURE 6: DBN22 model.

are structured for SER experiments on cross-database. As shown in Figures 5 and 6, (1) the DBN21 model is proposed for separate layer feature fusions with spectrogram features and traditional acoustic features (by the international general extracting method mentioned in Section 4.1.3); (2) the DBN22 model is constructed for integration of the spectrogram and traditional acoustic features in the feature layer. Because the speech emotion features extracted for SER experiments are real number data, it is not appropriate to apply the binary RBM for modeling. As a result, we chose the Gaussian-Bernoulli RBM (GRBM) [20] to build the bottom structure. The energy function of GRBM is

$$E(v, h \mid \theta) = -\sum_{i=1}^{V} \sum_{j=1}^{H} \frac{v_i}{\sigma_i} \omega_{ij} h_j + \sum_{i=1}^{V} \frac{(v_i - b_i)^2}{2\sigma_i^2} - \sum_{j=1}^{H} a_j h_j. \quad (16)$$

Formula (16) represents the Gaussian noise variance of the visible neurons. Due to the change of the energy function,

conditional probability is also changed, which should be amended as

$$p\left(h_j = 1 \mid v\right) = \text{logistic}\left(a_j + \sum_{i=1}^{V} \omega_{ij} \frac{v_i}{\sigma_i}\right), \quad (17)$$

$$p\left(v_i = 1 \mid h\right) = N\left(b_i + \sigma_i \sum_{j=1}^{H} \omega_{ij} h_j, \sigma_i^2\right). \quad (18)$$

As shown in Figure 6, the input visual, hidden, and output layers are represented as blue, red, and green colorized rounds, respectively. The restructures of models show that the DBN22 input has two representations (although in practice DBNN21 and DBN22 have the same structure once the feature vectors are combined). The training process of the DBN22 network model is conducted in accordance with the following steps.

(1) The initialization of unsupervised learning is needed at the beginning of training. The initialization process is step by step completed in each layer by multiple RBM in accordance with the order of the bottom-up.

First of all, the feature vector extracted from the traditional features is considered as the visual layer of the first left side in the RBM; the spectrogram feature vector is considered as the visual layer of the first right side in the RBM. Then, the CD-1 algorithm is applied to training for the weight of each layer, denoted by LW_1 and RW_1. According to the weights obtained and the input visible layers, the weighted summations are conducted on all the input nodes. Then, the hidden layers LH_1 and RH_1 could be obtained by mapping [21].

After that, LH_1 and RH_1 are the input of visual layer in the second RBM. Also after CD-1 training, connection weight W_2 can be obtained. Then, the hidden layer H_2 is gained according to the input visual layer and weight W_2.

(2) The Deep Belief Networks are constituted. The trained RBMs in top-bottom order are overlapped layer by layer as shown in Figure 6. The uppermost level of RBM is in the form of a two-way connection while the others are connected by top-bottom.

(3) The kernel-KNNFLC classifier is added to the top of the above for classification.

(4) The network weights are fine-tuned. Before the final network parameters being obtained, the fine-tuning is necessary by the training results and BP algorithm so that the weights may be more accurate.

The training process of DBN21 model is similar to DNB22, while the bottom layer RBM only has the left half of DBN22. The data generation process of DBN is through the top RBM with Gibbs Sampling and completed by transferring from top to bottom. The Gibbs Sampling of the top RBM is divided into multiple alternate processes, which makes the sample distribution obtained balanced. Then, the data are generated by top-bottom DBN network. This way effectively saves feature information of cross-corpus samples, so as to improve the robustness of the SER system. The operation of weights adjustment is conducted after the pretraining. Then, based on the method of Error Back Propagation, the tag data are used to fine-tune the weights. This strategy searches the weight space locally in the process of running, which could accelerate the training speed effectively.

4. Experimental Results and Analysis

4.1. Experimental Preparation

4.1.1. Settings of Experiments. In this section, the fusion experiments are divided into three parts. First of all, DBN21 model is used to carry out layer fusion for SER across the databases, in which features are traditional acoustic (see Section 4.1.3). Then, the results of the experiments are contrasted with the traditional features without DBN fusion and this experiment group is marked as *Fusion 1*. DBN21 model is then used to extract spectrogram features of layer fusion based on selective attention mechanism. Also the results are contrasted to the features without DBN fusion, which demonstrates the cross-corpus SER ability. This group of experiments is marked as *Fusion 2*. Finally the DNB22 model is proposed to fuse the traditional and spectrogram features. The experimental results are compared with Fusion 1 and Fusion 2. To prove that DBN22 possesses the significant improvement of performance on features fusion for SER, this group of experiments is marked as *Fusion 3*.

4.1.2. Database Settings. The selection of appropriate emotional databases is also an important part of speech emotion recognition. In our research, we chose one common speech emotion database: ABC (Airplane behaviors Corpus) which is recorded in German [22]. Moreover, the Deep Learning technology is suitable for the situation with a huge number of data sets, while the international classic databases usually have less samples. Meanwhile, in order to verify the effect of the fusion method proposed on Chinese speech databases, two Chinese corpora which are widely researched in China domestic are introduced and combined. The following are the brief introductions of the 3 databases, respectively.

ABC is obtained on a holiday aircraft flight in the background of prerecorded announcement played. The flight contains 13 upcoming trip scenarios and 10 return scenarios. Eight targeted passengers are chosen to get through the set condition: false meals, aircraft navigation turbulence, sleep, and conversation with the neighbors. During this process 11.5 hours of video and 431 voices with 8.4-second length are recorded. Finally the collected segments are independent analyzed by three professional researchers, and then the selected samples are labeled in accordance with the "aggressive," "amused," "excited," "strained," "neutral," and "tired" 6 kinds of emotional categories.

Chinese corpora used in our SER experiments consist of two databases which are recorded by induced and acted speech, respectively. One of them is the Chinese Database (CNDB) created by the Key Laboratory of Underwater Acoustic Signal Processing of in Southeast University. It consists of two parts: practical speech emotion database [23] and Whisper emotion database [24]. The statement materials of practical speech emotion database are recorded by performers with histrionic or broadcast experience (8 males and 8 females, aged between 20 to 30 years, without a recent cold,

standard Mandarin). The recording environment is indoors quiet. In order to guarantee the quality of the emotional corpora, the subjective listening evaluation is carried out. The statements selected with more than 85% confidence coefficient are in total 1410 from the male performers and 1429 from the female performers, including six basic emotional categories: "raged," "fear," "joy," "neutral," "sad," and "surprise." The Whisper database contains "happy," "angry," "surprise," "grieved," and "quiet" such five kinds of emotions. Then, the speech materials are divided into three types: word, phrase, and long sentence. The corpus contains 25 words, 20 phrases, and 6 long sentences for each emotion category. Each speaker repeats the whispers 3 times and with normal voice for 1 time (for later comparison), forming a total of 9600 statements. The research of whispered speech database has great significance: further improving the ability of human-computer interaction, combining with the semantic to judge the inner activities of speakers, and helping computers really understand the operators' thoughts, feelings, and attitudes. The analysis and processing of the emotional characteristics of whispered speech signals have important meaning of judgment and simulation of the emotion status from speakers in theory and application.

According to the recording criterion of corpora, the two Chinese databases are merged, ultimately forming 7839-statement CNDB Chinese corpora. The recording employs mono, 16-bit quantitative, and 11.025 kHz sampling rate. The selection of statements follows two principles: (1) the statements selected do not contain a particular emotional tendency; (2) the statements must have high emotional freedom, which could exert different emotions on the same statement.

Another Chinese corpus is the Speech Emotion Database of Institute of Automation Chinese Academy of Sciences (CASIA) [25]. The language of the database is Chinese, made by four actors. Database contains 1200 statements and is divided into 6 categories of emotions: "angry," "fear," "happy," "neutral," "surprise," and "sad."

In order to verify the effectiveness of the method proposed in this paper, in each group of experiments two kinds of schemes (*Case I and Case II*) are adopted, respectively, for testing. According to the theory of Emotion Wheel [26], mutual or similar 4 basic emotions in the three chosen databases, "angry (aggressive, raged)," "happy (joy, amused)," "surprise (excited, amazed)," and "neutral," are chosen for experimental evaluation. Because the DBN model could show the effectiveness of the fusion under the condition of large amount of data, we merge 3 Chinese speech emotion corpora into one called *Mandarin Database*. In *Case I*, Mandarin Database is as the training data set (known label), while ABC (unknown label) is as the testing set. The cross-corpus SER of this scheme adopts rotation experiment testing method: the data set is divided into 10 portions, in which the proportion of training/testing is 9 : 1. The set of this 10-fold cross-validation is intended to optimize the parameters within the source corpus [10]. After the cross-validation, the averages are obtained as the results for the cross-corpus experiments. In *Case II*, ABC corpus (known label) is as the training set, while Mandarin Database (unknown label) is as the testing set. Because the number of samples in German ABC corpus is less, for the sample balance of corpus in the process of SER evaluation, we join a part of the Mandarin samples (45% is the optimum by testing, known label) into ABC samples which are as the training set. Then the remaining Mandarin samples (55% corpora, unknown label) are as the testing set.

4.1.3. Settings of Feature Parameters and Classifier. With regard to the *traditional acoustic global features*, the common tool openSMILE is used for feature extraction whose tool number is set as 1 [27]. Then the feature set in the Interspeech 2010 SER competition [28], which contains a total of 1582 dimensions features, is introduced in our experiments. 38 acoustic low-level descriptors (LLDs) and their first-order differences are contained in the set. Through statistics of 21 class functions on the LLDs (16 features with 0 information are removed), we add the numbers and lengths of F0 to the feature set. In the contrast group without fusion, the feature sets extracted directly carried out the LDA dimension reduction, making its dimension match the fusion experimental group.

In this paper, the recognition experiment employs kernel-KNNFLC classifier, which may verify the SER ability of the fusion features. According to the gravity center criterion, Kernel-KNNFLC learns the sample distances and improves the K-neighbor with kernel learning method. The classifier optimizes the differentiation between kinds of the emotional feature vectors, which solves the problem about huge calculation caused by the features of prior samples. Based on the cross-corpus samples trained, the recognition model is established and then the different emotional categories are distinguished. The Gaussian Radial Basis kernel Function (RBF) is used in the classifier: $k(x, y) = \exp(-\|x - y\|^2/2\sigma^2)$, in which $\sigma = 4$. The KNNFLC classifier based on kernel has stable SER performance on high-dimensional data. In addition our experiments use 4 kinds of speech emotions, so the dimension dropped to 3 for achieving the best recognition rate. This is due to the solving of the generalized eigenvalue principle: the optimization is achieved when the minimum number of features is solved. With the K-nearest neighbor algorithm based on feature line centroid, the kernel function of RBF is improved and the optimum value is $K = 3$ [13].

4.2. Traditional Global Acoustic Feature Fusion Experiment (Fusion 1). The purpose of *Fusion 1* is comparing the fusion feature with DBN21 to features without DBN, so that the cross-corpus recognition performance of fusional traditional features could be revealed. The extracted acoustic features are as the input of DBN21 model. Then the optimization process is carried out by DBN. After that, combined with the kernel-KNNFLC classifier introduced before, the emotion recognition missions are proceeded on cross data sets.

The settings of RBM learning rate should be moderate, because too big or too small rates will both increase the reconstruction error. GRBM learning rate of bottom layer in *Fusion 1* is set as $\varepsilon = 0.001$ and training cycle is set as $J = 200$. The upper layer RBM is set as $\varepsilon = 0.01$ and $J = 70$. Since the numbers of visible layer unit and input

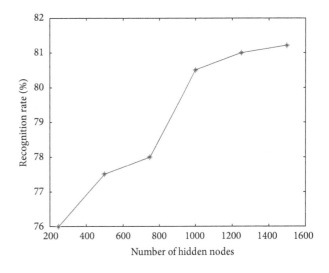

FIGURE 7: The influence of hidden node numbers to recognition rates *Fusion 1*.

dimension are the same, the input units number of visible layer in the experiment is $n_v = 60$ and the number of upper hidden units is set as $n_h = 20$. The weight is set according to the Gaussian random vector $N = (0, 0.01)$. The visible and hidden unit biases are $a_i = 0$ and $b_j = 0$. Because the number of hidden units in the middle layer may influence systemic performance, therefore we enumerate the 6 units' numbers of contrast experiments: 250, 500, 750, 1000, 1250, and 1500, in order to determine the optimal number of hidden units. The experimental comparison results are shown in Figure 7.

Figure 7 reveals that, along with the increase of the hidden nodes number, the recognition efficiency of system is growing. However, the increased number of nodes may cause the extra amount of calculation. It is clear that when the nodes number rises from 750 to 1000, the recognition rate has greatly improved, and then it is steady. Hereby considering the time consumed and accuracy, the number of hidden nodes in *Fusion 1* is set as 1000.

The speech emotion recognition experiments are carried out through the DBN21 model proposed. In our testing strategy, the ABC and Mandarin databases are cross-validated, which is to verify the robustness of algorithm proposed under the cross-corpus SER task. Toward each kind of emotion in two cross-database cases, recognition rates of the traditional features which are before and after fusion are shown in Table 1.

The experimental results indicate the traditional features after optimization by DBN. The emotion recognition ability has greatly ascended, which rises by 4.6% on the average recognition rate. It reveals that the DBN model proposed in feature layer is effective for SER feature fusion research. After training on ABC and Mandarin databases in *Case I*, SER rates of ABC testing set on Mandarin training set reach 52.2%. Among them "happy" and "neutral" reach over 63% as the highest, whose recognition effect is superior to *Case II*. It related to the many similar types of samples in

TABLE 1: Recognition results (%) of *Fusion 1* in two cross-corpus cases.

Cross-corpus scheme	Happy	Angry	Surprise	Neutral	Average
Case I					
DBN feature fusion	63.7	38.6	41.6	64.9	52.2
Without fusion	52.8	34.3	39.7	63.7	47.6
Case II					
DBN feature fusion	57.0	37.5	40.8	62.7	49.5
Without fusion	50.1	29.7	35.3	60.4	43.9

3 training corpora. Through the great amount of emotional data training in various categories by Deep Learning, the model becomes highly mature while the matching degrees of the traditional emotional categories with high inner-class discrimination ("happy," "neutral") are high. The comparison of two experiment schemes shows that the small amount of training samples in ABC gives rise to information insufficiently. Thus, further testing in large data corpus may cause undermatching with model.

4.3. Spectrogram Feature Fusion Experiment (Fusion 2).

Main aim of *Fusion 2* is to validate the feature effectiveness of spectrogram on cross-corpus. The feature sets abstracted are based on selective attention mechanism introduced in this paper. In order to reflect the promotional recognition performance on cross-databases, the experimental results after DBN21 fusion are compared with traditional features in *Fusion 1*.

The same as Fusion 1, GRBM learning rate of bottom layer in Fusion 2 is set as $\varepsilon = 0.001$ and training cycle is set as $J = 200$; the upper layer RBM is set as $\varepsilon = 0.01$ and $J = 70$. But the input units number of visible layer here is $n_v = 291$ and the number of upper hidden units is set as $n_h = 80$. The weight is set also as $N = (0, 0.01)$; meanwhile, the visible and hidden unit biases are $a_i = 0$ and $b_j = 0$. In consideration, the number of hidden nodes in layer RBM may cause the influence of system performance; this experiment still needs the discussion of the numbers of hidden nodes. The analysis of node numbers in traditional features is as in Figure 8.

As shown in the relationship in Figure 8, it is different from the traditional feature experiment; the recognition efficiency of spectrogram features has greatly promoted at 750 hidden nodes of point position. This is due to the traditional acoustic features compared to the spectrogram ones, which possess much higher input dimensions, so that, in the spectrogram feature fusion experiments, the number of hidden nodes in bottom RBM is set to 750.

According to the SER fusion model in feature layer, which is based on selective attention as shown in Figure 1, the cross-corpus experiments are carried out. In *Fusion 2*, ABC and Chinese databases are crossed training for cross-corpus testing. The SER confusion matrix in *Case I* by DBN21 fusion model is as shown in Figure 9.

It could be seen from the experimental results that the spectrogram features extracted integrally have strong ability of speech emotion recognition. When compared to traditional features, the spectrogram exhibits advantages in

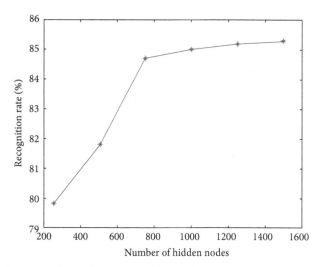

FIGURE 8: The influence of hidden node numbers to recognition rates in *Fusion 2*.

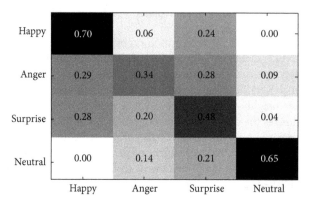

FIGURE 9: Cross-corpus SER confusion matrix in *Fusion 2* with *Case I*.

dealing with the cross data set tasks. This is because the traditional features contain only the local traits of common speech processing field, while the spectrogram, abstracted from the aspects of time and frequency domains, contains information between adjacent frames and the temporal features which can make up for a lack of global features. In spectrogram features, meanwhile, compared to traditional global features, the cascade vectors possess higher dimensions which contain more information for characterizing the emotions. Among them, the "happy," "angry," and experimental results improve significantly compared with the traditional fusion features. It reveals that spectrogram features have a relatively better distinction effect on the emotion category with high frequency domain correlation dependence.

4.4. DBN22 Feature Fusion Experiment on Cross-Corpus (Fusion 3).

In experiment *Fusion 3* with DBN22 model, we conduct feature layer fusion of traditional global acoustic features and spectrogram features based on selective attention. After that the kernel-KNNFLC is combined with SER system for cross-corpus experiments. This method integrates image characteristics and acoustic characteristics, which is a novel

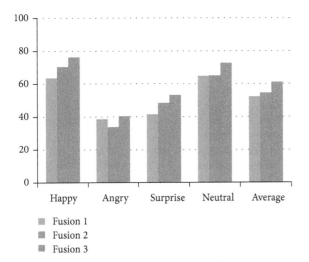

FIGURE 10: Recognition rates of 3 fusion models.

new attempt for data source extension in the field of speech emotion recognition. At the same time, the experiment may demonstrate that the features with thus fusion method have significant help for improving SER performance in cross-databases.

The settings of RBM in *Fusion 3* are as follow: GRBM learning rate of bottom layer is set as $\varepsilon = 0.001$ and training cycle is set as $J = 200$. The upper layer RBM is set as $\varepsilon = 0.01$ and $J = 70$. Since the numbers of visible layer unit and input dimension are the same, thus the input units numbers of visible layer in acoustic and spectrogram features are $Ln_v = 291$ and $Rn_v = 60$, respectively. The number of upper hidden units is set as $n_h = 100$. The weight is set according to the Gaussian random vector $N = (0, 0.01)$. The visible and hidden unit biases are $a_i = 0$ and $b_j = 0$. Because the number of hidden units in the middle layer may influence systemic performance, according to the two Fusion experiment advance, hidden units numbers in RBM of acoustic and spectrogram features are 1000 and 750, respectively.

After cross-database SER experiment, fusion features of traditional acoustic and spectrogram features are gained based on DBN22 network. Then the recognition results are compared with DBN21 groups in *Fusion 1* and *Fusion 2* by the bar plot (using *Case I* cross-corpus settings) (see Figure 10).

After the analysis of Figure 10, the cross-database recognition efficiency of the fused features in *Fusion 3* is the highest. Specifically "happy," "angry," "surprise," and "neutral" 4 emotional kinds compared with the traditional group rise by 12.6%, 1.8%, 11.6%, and 12.6%, respectively; the promotion of average recognition rate is 8.8%. Relative to the spectrogram features, the results increase by 5.8%, 5.8%, 6.6%, and 5.8%, respectively, and the elevation of average recognition rates up to 6.5%. The fusion by DBN22 of two kinds of features obtains excellent recognition effect in all of the emotion categories. The results benefit from the optimization of feature fusion layer in RBM stack of the DBN network, while there are also the factors of classifier and network parameters' settings. Experiments show that the DBN network model proposed successfully gains the fused features of traditional acoustic

characteristics and the information of spectrogram images, which meanwhile effectively improve the cross-corpus efficiency of the SER system.

5. Conclusion

This paper mainly researches the feature layer fusion model on the strength of DBN for speech emotion recognition. First of all, based on the mechanism of selective attention, the system extracts three kinds of spectrogram features with both temporal information and global information, which are used for cross-corpus SER. The spectrogram features introduced solve the problem of information loss by the traditional feature selection methods. Further, it is a supplement to the types of emotional information under the cross-database. Then, the modified DBN models are proposed to reasonably optimize the high-dimension spectral features, to retain the useful information and to improve the robustness of cross-corpus SER system. In the subsequent simulation experiments, the DBN21 and DBN22 models designed are used in the feature layer to fuse the spectrogram and traditional acoustic traits. Furthermore, the experimental results are compared with those of the benchmark models. Through experiments in cross-databases containing three Chinese ones and a general German one, DBN networks with multilayer RBM are proved as robust feature layer fusion models for cross-corpus. Spectrogram traits, at the same time, are validated conducive to boost emotional distinguish ability after feature fusion. In this paper, on the basis of Deep Learning thought, the DBN22 model proposed effectively fuses the spectrogram and traditional acoustic emotion features. This progress realizes the features fusion of various data sources and provides a new direction for further research of SER in cross-corpus.

Competing Interests

The authors declare that there is no conflict of interests regarding the publication of this paper.

Acknowledgments

This work has been supported by the national natural science foundation of china (NSFC) under Grants nos. 61231002 and 61375028.

References

[1] S. G. Koolagudi and K. S. Rao, "Emotion recognition from speech: a review," *International Journal of Speech Technology*, vol. 15, no. 2, pp. 99–117, 2012.

[2] S. Ramakrishnan and I. M. M. El Emary, "Speech emotion recognition approaches in human computer interaction," *Telecommunication Systems*, vol. 52, no. 3, pp. 1467–1478, 2013.

[3] E. Marchi, A. Batliner, B. Schuller et al., "Speech, emotion, age, language, task, and typicality: trying to disentangle performance and feature relevance," in *Proceedings of the International Conference on Privacy, Security, Risk and Trust (PASSAT '12) and International Conference on Social Computing (SocialCom '12)*, pp. 961–968, 2012.

[4] C. Parlak, B. Diri, and F. Gürgen, "A cross-corpus experiment in speech emotion recognition," in *Proceedings of the International Workshop on Speech, Language and Audio in Multimedia (SLAM '14)*, pp. 58–61, Penang, Malaysia, 2014.

[5] M. El Ayadi, M. S. Kamel, and F. Karray, "Survey on speech emotion recognition: features, classification schemes, and databases," *Pattern Recognition*, vol. 44, no. 3, pp. 572–587, 2011.

[6] S. Kim, P. G. Georgiou, S. Lee, and S. Narayanan, "Real-time emotion detection system using speech: Multi-modal fusion of different timescale features," in *Proceedings of the IEEE 9th International Workshop on Multimedia Signal Processing (MMSP '07)*, pp. 48–51, Crete, Greece, October 2007.

[7] K. Han, D. Yu, and I. Tashev, "Speech emotion recognition using deep neural network and extreme learning machine," in *Proceedings of the 15th Annual Conference of the International Speech Communication Association (Interspeech '14)*, pp. 223–227, Singapore, September 2014.

[8] H. Lee, C. Ekanadham, and Y. Ng A, "Sparse deep belief net model for visual area V2," in *Advances in Neural Information Processing Systems*, pp. 873–880, 2008.

[9] V. Nair and G. E. Hinton, "Rectified linear units improve Restricted Boltzmann machines," in *Proceedings of the 27th International Conference on Machine Learning (ICML '10)*, pp. 807–814, June 2010.

[10] B. Schuller, Z. Zhang, F. Weninger et al., "Selecting training data for cross-corpus speech emotion recognition: prototypicality vs. generalization," in *Proceedings of the 27th International Conference on Machine Learning (ICML-10 '11)*, pp. 807–814, 2011.

[11] T. A. Lampert and S. E. M. O'Keefe, "On the detection of tracks in spectrogram images," *Pattern Recognition*, vol. 46, no. 5, pp. 1396–1408, 2013.

[12] A. Borji, D. N. Sihite, and L. Itti, "Quantitative analysis of human-model agreement in visual saliency modeling: a comparative study," *IEEE Transactions on Image Processing*, vol. 22, no. 1, pp. 55–69, 2013.

[13] X. Zhang, C. Zha, X. Xu, P. Song, and L. Zhao, "Speech emotion recognition based on LDA+kernel-KNNFLC," *Journal of Southeast University (Natural Science Edition)*, vol. 45, no. 1, pp. 5–11, 2015.

[14] O. Kalinli and R. Chen, "Speech syllable/vowel/phone boundary detection using auditory attention cues," Google Patents, 2014.

[15] Y. Sun and R. Fisher, "Object-based visual attention for computer vision," *Artificial Intelligence*, vol. 146, no. 1, pp. 77–123, 2003.

[16] C. Stevens, B. Harn, D. J. Chard, J. Currin, D. Parisi, and H. Neville, "Examining the role of attention and instruction in at-risk kindergarteners: electrophysiological measures of selective auditory attention before and after an early literacy intervention," *Journal of Learning Disabilities*, vol. 46, no. 1, pp. 73–86, 2013.

[17] G. Evangelopoulos, A. Zlatintsi, A. Potamianos et al., "Multimodal saliency and fusion for movie summarization based on aural, visual, and textual attention," *IEEE Transactions on Multimedia*, vol. 15, no. 7, pp. 1553–1568, 2013.

[18] A. Smith, A. Doucet, N. de Freitas et al., *Sequential Monte Carlo Methods in Practice*, Springer Science & Business Media, 2013.

[19] G. E. Hinton, "Training products of experts by minimizing contrastive divergence," *Neural Computation*, vol. 14, no. 8, pp. 1771–1800, 2002.

[20] A.-R. Mohamed, T. N. Sainath, G. Dahl, B. Ramabhadran, G. E. Hinton, and M. A. Picheny, "Deep belief networks using discriminative features for phone recognition," in *Proceedings of the 36th IEEE International Conference on Acoustics, Speech, and Signal Processing (ICASSP 2011)*, pp. 5060–5063, Prague, Czech Republic, May 2011.

[21] Y. Tsao and Y.-H. Lai, "Generalized maximum a posteriori spectral amplitude estimation for speech enhancement," *Speech Communication*, vol. 76, pp. 112–126, 2016.

[22] B. Schuller, D. Arsic, G. Rigoll, M. Wimmer, and B. Radig, "Audiovisual behavior modeling by combined feature spaces," in *Proceedings of the IEEE International Conference on Acoustics, Speech and Signal Processing (ICASSP '07)*, pp. II-733–II-736, Honolulu, Hawaii, USA, April 2007.

[23] C. Huang, Y. Jin, Y. Zhao et al., "Design and establishment of practical speech emotion database," *Acoustic Technologies*, vol. 29, no. 4, pp. 396–399, 2010 (Chinese).

[24] Y. Jin, Y. Zhao, C. Huang et al., "The design and establishment of a Chinese whispered speech emotion database," *Technical Acoustics*, no. 1, pp. 63–68, 2010.

[25] Institute of Automation Chinese Academy of Sciences, The selected Speech Emotion Database of Institute of Automation Chinese Academy of Sciences (CASIA), 2010, http://www.chineseldc.org/resource_info.php?rid=76.

[26] T. Bänziger, V. Tran, and K. R. Scherer, "The Geneva Emotion Wheel: a tool for the verbal report of emotional reactions," in *Poster Presented at ISRE*, vol. 149, pp. 149–271, Bari, Italy, 2005.

[27] F. Eyben, M. Wöllmer, and B. Schuller, "Opensmile: the munich versatile and fast open-source audio feature extractor," in *Proceedings of the 18th ACM International Conference on Multimedia (MM '10)*, pp. 1459–1462, Firenze, Italy, October 2010.

[28] B. Schuller, S. Steidl, A. Batliner et al., "The INTERSPEECH 2010 paralinguistic challenge," in *Proceedings of the International Speech and Communication Association (INTERSPEECH '10)*, pp. 2794–2797, Makuhari, Japan, 2010.

20

Spatial Circular Granulation Method based on Multimodal Finger Feature

Jinfeng Yang, Zhen Zhong, Guimin Jia, and Yanan Li

Tianjin Key Lab for Advanced Signal Processing, Civil Aviation University of China, CAUC, Tianjin 300300, China

Correspondence should be addressed to Jinfeng Yang; jfyang@cauc.edu.cn

Academic Editor: Sook Yoon

Finger-based personal identification has become an active research topic in recent years because of its high user acceptance and convenience. How to reliably and effectively fuse the multimodal finger features together, however, has still been a challenging problem in practice. In this paper, viewing the finger trait as the combination of a fingerprint, finger vein, and finger-knuckle-print, a new multimodal finger feature recognition scheme is proposed based on granular computing. First, the ridge texture features of FP, FV, and FKP are extracted using Gabor Ordinal Measures (GOM). Second, combining the three-modal GOM feature maps in a color-based manner, we then constitute the original feature object set of a finger. To represent finger features effectively, they are granulated at three levels of feature granules (FGs) in a bottom-up manner based on spatial circular granulation. In order to test the performance of the multilevel FGs, a top-down matching method is proposed. Experimental results show that the proposed method achieves higher accuracy recognition rate in finger feature recognition.

1. Introduction

Biometrics based personal authentication is drawing increasing attention in both academic research and industrial applications. Among current biometric identifiers, finger-based biometrics is widely used because of its high user acceptance and convenience. Some commonly used finger-based biometrics, such as fingerprint [1, 2], finger vein [3–5], and finger-knuckle-print [6, 7], have been widely used in personal identification. However, many unimodal biometric-based systems have demonstrated that using a single finger-based biometric source for personal identification usually was far from perfect in many real applications. Compared with unimodal biometric approaches, multimodal biometrics always behave better in universality, accuracy, and security [8–10]. How to reliably and effectively fuse the multimodal features together, however, has still been a challenging problem in practice. In recent years, the research on granular computing (GrC) has attracted many researchers and practitioners. The basic idea of GrC is using information granules during complex problem solving, and granulation is one of key issues in GrC [11, 12]. Since Zadeh and Lin first proposed the concept of

GrC [11], many related applications have been proposed [13–16]. Firstly, Zheng et al. proposed a tolerance granular space model (TGSM) to study the problem of image segmentation [13, 14]. Then, Li and Meng proposed a method for MRI and MRA image fusion based on tolerance granular space modal [15]. Further, Bhatt et al. proposed face granulation scheme at multiple levels of granularity for face recognition [16]. These works imply that GrC is a new way to deal with the complex multimodal biometrics recognition problems.

In this paper, viewing fingerprint (FP), finger vein (FV), and finger-knuckle-print (FKP) as the constitutions of finger trait, we adopt a novel method to study the problems of multimodal finger feature recognition according to the spatial circular granulation. As we know, ridge texture information dominates over these three biometrics characteristics with a compatible feature space. Therefore, a finger itself can be viewed as a coarse granularity information granule with plenty of ridge texture, and each finger feature granule contains different discriminating information forming the finger image signature.

In the proposed method, we adopt the Gabor Ordinal Measures (GOM) [17, 18] for multimodal finger feature

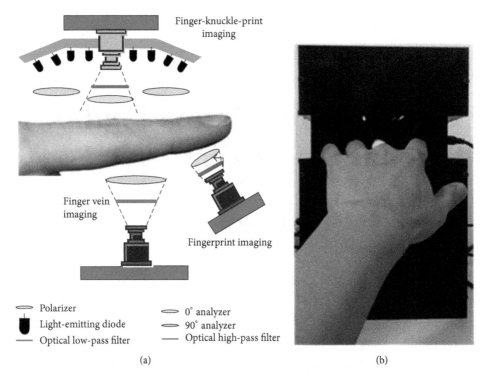

FIGURE 1: A homemade imaging system ((a) the proposed imaging principle and (b) an imaging device).

extraction. GOM integrates distinctiveness of Gabor features and robustness of ordinal measures to describe the image texture features. First, a bank of even-symmetric Gabor filters with 8 orientations [19] is used to exploit the magnitude features in FP, FV, and FKP images. Second, the ordinal filters [17] are conducted with the 8-orientation magnitude features to obtain the three-modal GOM feature maps. Third, combining the GOM feature maps into a color-feature map, we constitute the original feature object set of a finger. Forth, the original feature object set is granulated into nonoverlapping circular granules in a bottom-up manner based on spatial circular granulation to construct the multilevel feature granules (FGs). Finally, a top-down matching method is proposed to test the performance of multilevel FGs. Experimental results show that the proposed method yields high identification accuracy in finger feature recognition.

The rest of this paper is organized as follows. Section 2 introduces a homemade imaging system for the multimodal finger images acquisition. Section 3 presents a general framework of finger feature granulation based on spatial circular granulation. In Section 4, a self-built database with three modalities is used to validate the feasibility and effectiveness of the proposed algorithm; several experimental results are also reported in this section. Section 5 concludes this paper.

2. Multimodal Finger Image Acquisition

To obtain FP, FV, and FKP images, we have designed a homemade imaging system, which can capture these three modality images automatically and simultaneously when a finger is available, as shown in Figure 1. In the proposed imaging

system, a novel double-spectral polarized imaging system is proposed. Based on the physiological structure of fingers and its imaging property, the finger-knuckle-prints and fingerprints are imaged by reflected lights, and the finger veins are imaged using the near infrared light in a transillumination manner, as shown in Figure 1(a).

Connected to the imaging device with a computer, we can readily capture FP, FV, and FKP images using a specifically designed software, as shown in Figure 2(a). After the image is captured, it is sent to the data preprocessing module for preprocessing. To extract the ROIs of the three modality images, we, respectively, apply a method proposed in [7] for FKP ROI extraction, a method proposed in [20] for FP ROI extraction, and a method in [19] for FV ROI extraction. Then we obtain a group of 96 ∗ 208-pixel images of FV-ROI, 96 ∗ 208-pixel images of the FKP-ROI, and 160 ∗ 160-pixel images of the FP-ROI. The results are, respectively, shown in Figure 2(b).

3. Feature Extraction and Granulation

3.1. Feature Extraction. Feature extraction is essential for original feature domain construction and finger feature granulation. The three-modal finger features all bear special textures that can be viewed as signatures of finger. Therefore, the used feature extraction method should be powerful in describing the image texture feature.

First, all ROI images of FP, FV, and FKP are normalized to 162 ∗ 162 pixels, as shown in the top row of Figure 3, respectively. Due to different texture structure of the three modalities, we use Gabor filter [19] to enhance FV and Steerable filter [21] for FP and FKP enhancement to strengthen the

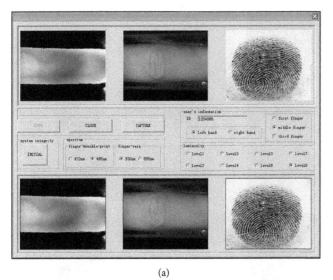

(a)

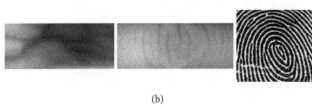

(b)

FIGURE 2: (a) A developed software interface of image acquisition. (b) The extracted ROI images (left: FV, middle: FKP, and right: FP).

blurred images, as shown in the middle row of Figure 3. Then, we use the Gabor filters with 8 orientations [19] to exploit Gabor magnitude features in the FP, FV, and FKP images:

$$
\begin{aligned}
&G(x, y) \\
&= \frac{\gamma}{2\pi\sigma^2} \exp\left\{-\frac{1}{2}\left(\frac{x_{\theta_k}^2 + \gamma^2 y_{\theta_k}^2}{\sigma^2}\right)\right\} \exp\left(\hat{j}2\pi f_k x_{\theta_k}\right). \quad (1)
\end{aligned}
$$

Here, $\begin{bmatrix} x_{\theta_k} \\ y_{\theta_k} \end{bmatrix} = \begin{bmatrix} \cos\theta_k & \sin\theta_k \\ -\sin\theta_k & \cos\theta_k \end{bmatrix} \begin{bmatrix} x \\ y \end{bmatrix}$, k is the number of orientations, σ and γ, respectively, represent the scale of Gabor filter and aspect ratio of the elliptical Gaussian envelope, and x_θ and y_θ are two rotated versions of the coordinates x and y.

Finally, the ordinal measures are conducted with the multichannel Gabor magnitude features to get the ordinal feature maps [17, 18], as shown in the last row of Figure 3. The difference filter is defined as

$$
\begin{aligned}
\text{MLDF} = {}&C_p \sum_{i=1}^{N_p} \frac{1}{\sqrt{2\pi}\delta_{pi}} \exp\left[\frac{-(X - \omega_{pi})^2}{2\delta_{pi}^2}\right] \\
&- C_n \sum_{j=1}^{N_n} \frac{1}{\sqrt{2\pi}\delta_{nj}} \exp\left[\frac{-(X - \omega_{nj})^2}{2\delta_{nj}^2}\right]. \quad (2)
\end{aligned}
$$

Here ω is the central position and δ is the scale of ordinal filter. N_p is the number of positive lobes and N_n is the number

of negative lobes. Constant coefficients C_n and C_p are used to keep the balance between positive and negative lobes. To satisfy $C_p N_p = C_n N_n$, we assume $C_p = 1$, $N_p = 2$ and $C_n = 2$, $N_n = 1$, since the difference filter with three lobes is more stable. The feature extraction scheme of GOM is capable of representing the distinctive and robust of texture features of finger images.

3.2. Feature Granulation.
Granulation is one of the key issues in GrC for complex problem solving. In order to effectively express the feature structure of the fingers, we firstly select the original feature object set on the basis of the feature analysis. Then, we adopt a bottom-up manner to construct the multilevel feature granules. Here, FGs are generated as the following procedure.

Step 1 (initializing). Based on feature-based registration of the three modalities, we combined FP, FV, and FKP feature maps in a color-based manner to form the RGB-GOM feature map, as shown in Figure 4. This map is used to constitute the original feature object set of a finger. Then we defined $O_0 = (x, y, R, G, B)$, where x, y are coordinate value and R, G, and B denote the FP, FV, and FKP feature maps, respectively.

O_1 represents the original feature object set, which is defined as

$$
O_1 = \left\{\bigcup_{\text{FP}}\{O_{i,j}\}\right\} \bigcap \left\{\bigcup_{\text{FV}}\{O_{i,j}\}\right\} \bigcap \left\{\bigcup_{\text{FKP}}\{O_{i,j}\}\right\}. \quad (3)
$$

Here, structure of 0-layer feature granules is constructed by a 2-tuple $G_0^1 = (IG_0^1, EG_0^1)$; the intension and extension of 0-layer feature granules are, respectively, defined as $IG_0^1 = (x, y, \text{map}R, \text{map}G, \text{map}B)$, $EG_0^1 = \{x \mid x \in O_1\}$. Here, IG_l^1 is the intension of granules in l-layer and EG_l^1 is the extension of granules in l-layer.

Step 2 (calculating 1-layer granule $G_1^1 = (IG_1^1, EG_1^1(\eta_1^1 \mid \text{tr}_1^1))$). According to the merger rules of the tolerance granularity grid, each 1-layer granule's extension can be generated by the definition $EG_1^1(\eta_1^1 \mid \text{tr}_1^1) = \{x \mid (x, \eta_1^1) \in \text{tr}_{1(\text{cp},w,\text{DIS},D)}\}$; here, cp, w, DIS, and D are the four elements of the compatible function, cp is the compound compatibility relation proposition, w is the weight coefficient of each component, DIS is distance function, and D is the vector of distance function. We use the circular granule as the shape of the FGs. In this way, FGs have the translation and rotation invariant characteristics. Let $\text{dis}(\alpha, \beta\omega) = \sum_{i=0}^{n-1} \omega_i(\alpha_i - \beta_i)^2$; $\text{cp}(\alpha, \beta\text{DIS}, D) = \text{dis}(\alpha, \beta\omega) \le d$, where $\omega = (1, 1, 0, 0, 0)$, DIS $= \{\text{dis}\}$, $D = \{d\}$, $\eta_1^1 \in \text{Grid}_1^1$, and Grid_1^1 is a grid point set, which includes all centers of granules G_1^1, $d = a^2$ ($a = 4$). The histogram of the ordinal code as the intension of FGs $IG_1^1 = (H_1, H_2, \ldots, H_L)$, and L is the bin number of the histograms. Thus, the original feature object set is granulated as circular granules with the radius of 4 pixels, denoted as 1-layer FGs:

$$
\text{radius} = \text{floor}\left(\frac{\text{pixels of the row}}{\text{the number of circular granules}}\right). \quad (4)
$$

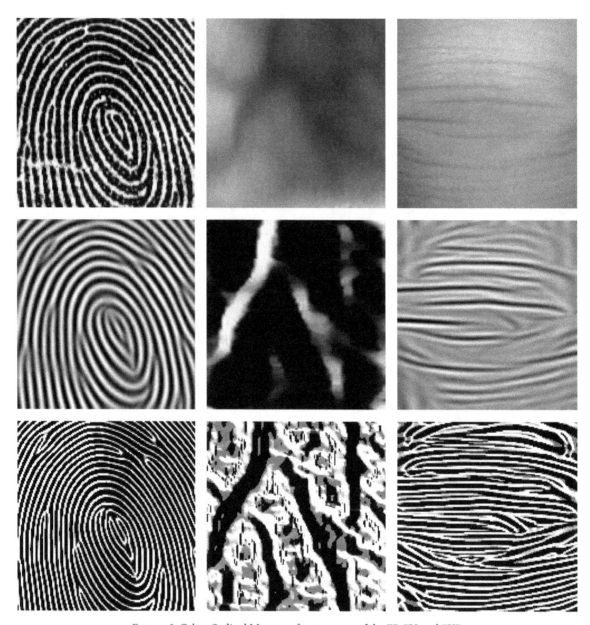

FIGURE 3: Gabor Ordinal Measures feature maps of the FP, FV, and FKP.

Step 3 (calculating $G_{i+1}^1 = (IG_{i+1}^1, EG_{i+1}^1(\eta_{i+1}^1 \mid \text{tr}_{i+1}^1)))$. Recursively, calculating the $i + 1$-layer feature granules, $G_{i+1}^1 = (IG_{i+1}^1, EG_{i+1}^1(\eta_{i+1}^1 \mid \text{tr}_{i+1}^1))$. Extension of feature granules on the layer $i + 1$ can be obtained by the following formula $EG_{i+1}^1(\eta_{i+1}^1 \mid \text{tr}_{i+1}^1) = \{x \mid (x, \eta_{i+1}^1) \in \text{tr}_{i+1(\text{cp}_{i+1}, w_{i+1}, \text{DIS}_{i+1}, D_{i+1})}^1 \wedge x \in EG_i^1\}$. If this step continues, the extension of the highest-level granules eventually contains only one original object. In this paper, FGs are generated considering three granularity levels, and the three-layer bottom-up granulation process is shown in Figure 5.

4. Experiments and Analysis

4.1. Recognition Analysis. As we know, statistical distribution of texture primitives has become a standard description of texture analysis. Since the ordinal codes are binary values and

8-orientation Gabor filters are used, we can obtain a binary number of 8 bits. This means that there is 256-bin histogram representation for each FG. To reduce the feature dimension, the histogram of each FG can be further reduced to contain only $B = 32$ bins by partitioning the histograms into uniform parts: $[0, \ldots, 256/B - 1], [256/B, \ldots, 2 * 256/B - 1], \ldots, [(B - 1) * 256/B, \ldots, B * 256/B - 1]$ [18]. To test the performance of the proposed method, the histograms computed for the FGs are concatenated here to represent different levels FGs. Here, we use the normalized histogram intersection $H(\text{FG}^1, \text{FG}^2)$ [22] as the similarity measurement of two FGs, then we defined the similarity between two finger images in the ith layer as

$$\text{Sim}_i\left(F^1, F^2\right) = \sum_{r=0}^{N_i-1} H\left(\text{FG}_r^1, \text{FG}_r^2\right). \tag{5}$$

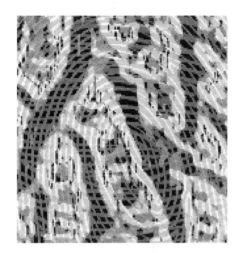

FIGURE 4: The original feature object set of a finger.

Here, N_i is the number of granules in the ith granularity level. If $\text{Sim}_i \geq T_i$ (T_i is the decision threshold of the ith layer), then the two finger images match in the ith layer granules. As the multimodal finger-based recognition can be addressed at multigranularity levels and the coarse granularity information is an abstract description of the finger feature, it is able to narrow the scope of problem solving and accelerate the calculating speed at the coarse granularity levels. In contrast, the fine granularity information represents a specific description of the finger feature. Hence, for the problems that cannot be solved at coarse granularity levels, we could address them in a fine granularity level. Thus, a top-down (coarse-to-fine) recognition method is proposed. Only when the two finger images matched in three granularity layers at the same time ($\text{Sim}_3 \geq T_3$, $\text{Sim}_2 \geq T_2$, and $\text{Sim}_1 \geq T_1$), the two finger images are similar.

4.2. Recognition Results. In this section, we carry out several experiments to prove the feasibility and effectiveness of the proposed algorithm. A self-constructed database which totally contains 3000 FP images, 3000 FV images, and 3000 FKP images from 300 individuals is used in these experiments. Firstly, the comparison between the three unimodal biometrics is shown in Figure 6. From these presented curves, we can see that FV achieves a lower EER than FP and FKP, which shows that FV has more robust and reliable texture feature information.

Also, Figure 7 shows the comparison between the multimodal biometric systems. From this we can see that fusion between features which performed better in single modal will get better results. As expected, FGs yields significantly better performance compared with any single modal or bimodal fusion of FP, FV, and FKP. The above comparison shows that the proposed method can effectively achieve information complementary between different finger features. This is beneficial for identification performance improvement.

Figure 8 shows the similarity distributions of genuine and imposter matching generated by the three granularity levels. From the curves we can see that the proposed algorithm is capable of differentiating finger images by setting appropriate

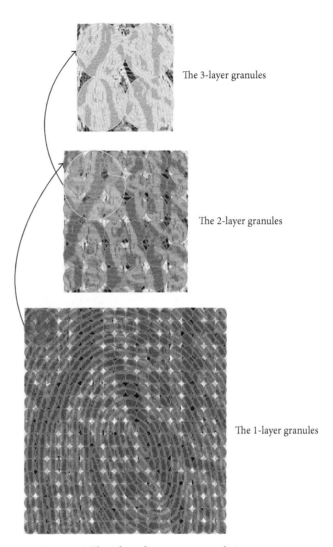

The 3-layer granules

The 2-layer granules

The 1-layer granules

FIGURE 5: The 3-layer bottom-up granulation process.

value of the threshold. This implies that the proposed algorithm can provide a good solution for handling both intraclass variations and interclass similarity of finger images. Moreover, from these curves we can also conclude that the discrimination of 1-layer FGs (fine-grained information) is better than the two other layers (coarse-grained information).

Figure 9 shows the ROC curves generated by the different granularity levels. Here the proposed algorithm is implemented using MATLAB R2010a on a standard desktop PC which is equipped with a Dual-Core CPU 2.5 GHz and 4 GB RAM. From these curves we can clearly see that the 1-layer FGs (1-FGs) make a lower EER compared with two other layers, indicating that the matching performance in fine-granularity space outperforms coarse granularity space. Further, Table 1 listed the matching results of three different granularity levels. From Table 1, we can draw the conclusion that the coarse-grained information has the higher matching efficiency and the fine-grained information has the higher matching accuracy. Therefore, the combination of coarse granularity information and fine-granularity information can keep the recognition efficiency in the premise of accuracy.

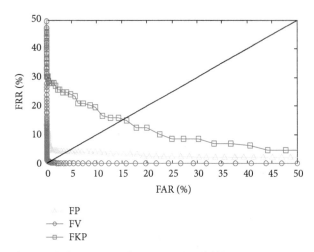

FIGURE 6: Comparisons between unimodal biometric systems.

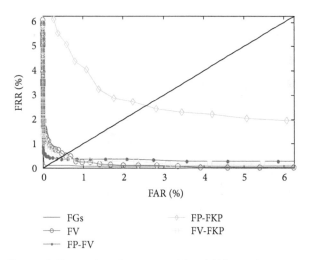

FIGURE 7: Comparisons between multimodal biometric systems.

TABLE 1: Matching results of different levels FGs.

Granular level	Matching performance		
	EER (%)	Matching time (s)	Recognition rate (%)
One-layer	0.853	0.257	99.15
Two-layer	2.230	0.074	97.77
Three-layer	3.408	0.028	96.59

Further, Table 2 listed the matching performance for the top-down matching method. From the data we can see that the coarse-to-fine matching method of 3-2-1-layer FGs achieves the best accuracy recognition results. According to T of 1-layer and 2-layer FGs when FAR is minimum and FRR = 0, the threshold of 3-layer and 2-layer FGs is, respectively, set as $T_3 = 0.738$ and $T_2 = 0.689$. The multilayer top-down matching method also reduces the matching time costs since the nonmatched granules are ignored in the high granularity level. Therefore, the top-down recognition method of multilayer FGs performs better in finger-based recognition in both efficiency and accuracy. And we should

TABLE 2: Matching results of the top-down matching method.

Granular level	Matching performance		
	EER (%)	Matching time (s)	Recognition rate (%)
3-2-layer	1.522	0.056	98.48
2-1-layer	0.627	0.096	99.37
3-2-1-layer	0.415	0.129	99.58

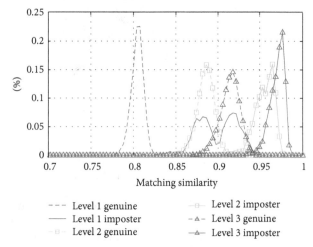

FIGURE 8: Similarity distributions of genuine and imposter matching at three granularity levels.

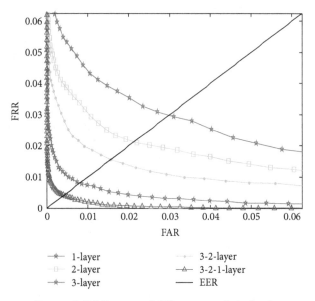

FIGURE 9: ROC curves of different granularity levels.

note that the matching time is related to the PC performance: when the run time is longer, the speed will slow down.

5. Conclusion

A new multimodal finger feature recognition scheme based on spatial circular granulation has been proposed in this paper. Firstly, the ridge texture features of the FP, FV, and FKP images were both extracted by the Gabor Ordinal Measures. Then, combining the GOM feature maps into a color-feature map, we then constitute the original feature object set of a finger. Finally, three-level FGs were constructed based on spatial circular granulation. Experimental results show that circular FGs are much more reliable and precise in multimodal finger feature recognition, and the top-down recognition method of multilevel FGs is helpful for identification performance and efficiency improvement.

Competing Interests

The authors declare that they have no competing interests.

Acknowledgments

This work is jointly supported by National Natural Science Foundation of China (no. 61379102) and the Fundamental Research Funds for the Central Universities (no. 3122014C003).

References

[1] A. Jain, L. Hong, and R. Bolle, "Online fingerprint verification," *IEEE Transactions on Pattern Analysis and Machine Intelligence*, vol. 19, no. 4, pp. 302–314, 1997.

[2] A. K. Jain, Y. Chen, and M. Demirkus, "Pores and ridges: high-resolution fingerprint matching using level 3 features," *IEEE Transactions on Pattern Analysis and Machine Intelligence*, vol. 29, no. 1, pp. 15–27, 2007.

[3] E. C. Lee, H. C. Lee, and K. R. Park, "Finger vein recognition using minutia-based alignment and local binary pattern-based feature extraction," *International Journal of Imaging Systems and Technology*, vol. 9, pp. 179–186, 2009.

[4] J. Yang, Y. Shi, and J. Yang, "Finger-vein recognition based on a bank of gabor filters," in *Proceedings of the Asian Conference on Computer Vision*, pp. 374–383, Xi'an, China, September 2009.

[5] J. Yang, Y. Shi, and J. Yang, "Personal identification based on finger-vein features," *Computers in Human Behavior*, vol. 27, no. 5, pp. 1565–1570, 2011.

[6] L. Zhang, L. Zhang, D. Zhang, and H. Zhu, "Ensemble of local and global information for fingerknuckle-print recognition," *Pattern Recognition*, vol. 44, no. 9, pp. 1990–1998, 2011.

[7] L. Zhang, L. Zhang, D. Zhang, and H. Zhu, "Online finger-knuckle-print verification for personal authentication," *Pattern Recognition*, vol. 43, no. 7, pp. 2560–2571, 2010.

[8] A. Ross and A. Jain, "Information fusion in biometrics," *Pattern Recognition Letters*, vol. 24, no. 13, pp. 2115–2125, 2003.

[9] A. Ross and A. K. Jain, "Multimodal biometrics: an overview," in *Proceedings of the 12th European Signal Processing Conference*, pp. 1221–1224, Vienna, Austria, September 2004.

[10] J. Yang and X. Zhang, "Feature-level fusion of fingerprint and finger-vein for personal identification," *Pattern Recognition Letters*, vol. 33, no. 5, pp. 623–628, 2012.

[11] D. Miao, G. Wang, and Q. Liu, *Granular Computing: Past, Present and Prospect*, Science Publishing House, Beijing, China, 2007 (Chinese).

[12] J. T. Yao, A. V. Vasilakos, and W. Pedrycz, "Granular computing: perspectives and challenges," *IEEE Transactions on Cybernetics*, vol. 43, no. 6, pp. 1977–1989, 2013.

[13] Z. Zheng, H. Hu, and Z. Z. Shi, "Tolerance granular space and its applications," in *Proceedings of the IEEE International Conference on Granular Computing*, pp. 367–372, Beijing, China, July 2005.

[14] Z. Shi, Z. Zheng, and Z. Meng, "Image segmentation-oriented tolerance granular computing model," in *Proceedings of the IEEE International Conference on Granular Computing*, pp. 566–571, IEEE, Hangzhou, China, August 2008.

[15] Z. Li and Z. Meng, "Technique of medical image fusion based on tolerance granular space," *Application Research of Computers*, vol. 27, pp. 1192–1194, 2010.

[16] H. S. Bhatt, S. Bharadwaj, R. Singh, and M. Vatsa, "Recognizing surgically altered face images using multiobjective evolutionary algorithm," *IEEE Transactions on Information Forensics and Security*, vol. 8, no. 1, pp. 89–100, 2013.

[17] Z. Sun, T. Tan, Y. Wang, and S. Z. Li, "Ordinal palmprint representation for personal identification," in *Proceedings of the IEEE Computer Society Conference on Computer Vision and Pattern Recognition (CVPR '05)*, vol. 1, pp. 279–284, San Diego, Calif, USA, June 2005.

[18] Z. Chai, Z. Sun, H. Mendez-Vazquez, R. He, and T. Tan, "Gabor ordinal measures for face recognition," *IEEE Transactions on Information Forensics and Security*, vol. 9, no. 1, pp. 14–26, 2014.

[19] J. Yang and Y. Shi, "Finger-vein ROI localization and vein ridge enhancement," *Pattern Recognition Letters*, vol. 33, no. 12, pp. 1569–1579, 2012.

[20] H. B. Kekre and V. A. Bharadi, "Fingerprint's core point detection using orientation field," in *Proceedings of the International Conference on Advances in Computing, Control and Telecommunication Technologies (ACT '09)*, pp. 150–152, IEEE, Kerala, India, December 2009.

[21] W. T. Freeman and E. H. Adelson, "The design and use of steerable filters," *IEEE Transactions on Pattern Analysis and Machine Intelligence*, vol. 13, no. 9, pp. 891–906, 1991.

[22] M. J. Swain and D. H. Ballard, "Color indexing," *International Journal of Computer Vision*, vol. 7, no. 1, pp. 11–32, 1991.

21

Multi-Input Convolutional Neural Network for Flower Grading

Yu Sun, Lin Zhu, Guan Wang, and Fang Zhao

School of Information Science and Technology, Beijing Forestry University, Beijing 100083, China

Correspondence should be addressed to Fang Zhao; fangzhao@bjfu.edu.cn

Academic Editor: Sos Agaian

Flower grading is a significant task because it is extremely convenient for managing the flowers in greenhouse and market. With the development of computer vision, flower grading has become an interdisciplinary focus in both botany and computer vision. A new dataset named BjfuGloxinia contains three quality grades; each grade consists of 107 samples and 321 images. A multi-input convolutional neural network is designed for large scale flower grading. Multi-input CNN achieves a satisfactory accuracy of 89.6% on the BjfuGloxinia after data augmentation. Compared with a single-input CNN, the accuracy of multi-input CNN is increased by 5% on average, demonstrating that multi-input convolutional neural network is a promising model for flower grading. Although data augmentation contributes to the model, the accuracy is still limited by lack of samples diversity. Majority of misclassification is derived from the medium class. The image processing based bud detection is useful for reducing the misclassification, increasing the accuracy of flower grading to approximately 93.9%.

1. Introduction

Flower grading means dividing flowers into several grades according to the quality based on the appearance. *Gloxinia* is a kind of flower which is beneficial for mental and physical health of humans. Our research is focused on the flower grading, taking the *Gloxinia* as an example. Quality grading of flowers is significant because it is extremely convenient for greenhouse and market. Flower grading has a very important effect in handling and marketing the flowers after cultivation. In addition, it can be used in our house to judge which grade the flowers belong to, making our daily life more intelligent. With the development of computer vision, flower grading becomes automatic and intelligent based on images identification.

Flower grading is considered as a challenging task because the differences between each grade are not obvious, as illustrated in Figure 1. In particular, the shape and color of medium grade flowers are very similar to high or low grade flowers. In addition, classifying quality of flowers is a challenging task also considering the lack of dataset which contains different quality grades of the flowers.

Many researchers pay attention to the quality grading. Arakeri and Lakshmana [1] proposed a computer vision based automatic system for tomato grading using ANN (artificial neural network). Wang et al. [2] also proposed an automatic grading system of diced potatoes based on computer vision and near-infrared lighting. Although these systems are successful, both of them focused on binary classification. In addition, these researches still need complex preprocessing such as extracting features from cleaned background. Al Ohali [3] proposed a date fruit grading system which classifies dates into three quality categories using back propagation neural network (BPNN) algorithm with only 80% accurately.

In computer vision, deep learning has made great breakthrough in the last few years, especially the convolutional neural networks (CNNs). CNNs are very successful in ImageNet Large Scale Visual Recognition Challenge (ILSVRC) [4]. Several researchers use CNNs to identify plant images. Lee et al. [5] presented system that utilizes CNN to automatically learn discriminative features from leaf images. Reyes et al. [6] fine-tuned a CNN model for plants identification achieving a great success. References [5, 6] are both based on the CNN where the architecture was firstly proposed by Krizhevsky [7].

This paper presents a deep learning model for flower grading. Each flower may not be fully described by one image.

Label	Number	Photo 1	Photo 2	Photo 3
Good	1			
	2			
	3			
Medium	4			
	5			
	6			
Bad	7			
	8			
	9			

FIGURE 1: Typical samples of the dataset.

FIGURE 2: Image acquisition and equipment setup.

At least, three images are requested. Plants should not be graded just based on partial regions. Thus, traditional CNN is not appropriate for our research. A new deep learning model named three-input convolutional neural network is proposed by us for flower grading. Differing from traditional CNN, three-input CNN takes three images as the input. Each sample which is inputted to three-input CNN model contains three images rather than single image. Empirically, our method achieves a satisfactory accuracy on the dataset. A new *Gloxinia* dataset named BjfuGloxinia consisting of 321 *Gloxinia* samples belonging to three grades is also proposed by us for training and validating our model.

The rest of the paper is organized as follows: Section 2 reviews the concept of CNN and then gives an overview of dataset and approach that we proposed. The experimental results are presented in Section 3. Section 4 introduces bud detection to improve the performance of flower grading. Section 5 draws the conclusions.

2. Proposed BjfuGloxinia Dataset and Multi-Input CNN Model

2.1. The Gloxinia Grade Dataset. The BjfuGloxinia (BG) dataset collected at a greenhouse in Beijing Forestry University, Beijing, China, is employed in the experiment. This is the first image dataset for flower grading. It can be downloaded from ftp://iot.bjfu.edu.cn/. The dataset containing 321 samples of *Gloxinia* is divided into three grades by expert according to the relevant rules. In these rules, the plant which has more than two high-quality flowers belongs to the good class. The plant which just has buds or only one flower belongs to the medium class. The plant with no flowers belongs to the bad class. Each grade contains 107 samples and each sample consists of three images. Typical samples of the BjfuGloxinia are illustrated in Figure 1. It is obvious that the dataset is

challenging because plants from different grades have very similar appearance, especially the samples in the medium class which are easily confused with the good or the bad class.

In order to obtain the training set and the testing set, some equipment and materials are needed, including a digital single lens reflex (DLSR) camera, a tripod, a timing switch, and an electric turntable disk. The datasets are collected by a series of processes as follows. Put each flower on the electric turntable disk and keep the vertical distance between the bottom of flowerpot and the ground at 49 cm. The electric turntable disk is connected to the timing switch. The horizontal distance between the center of the turntable and the center of the tripod is 70 cm. The DSLR camera is fixed on the tripod. The tilt angle is 25 degrees relative to the vertical direction. The vertical distance between the tripods to the ground is 92 cm. The image acquisition and equipment setup are depicted in Figure 2. Flowers are rotated by an electric turntable whose speed is fixed at 30 s a lap. The disk is set to rotate every 120 degrees and pause 5 seconds for image acquisition.

2.2. Three-Input Convolutional Neural Network. One image cannot cover the whole plant. Every sample in our research is described by taking at least three images. Therefore, traditional single-input CNN architecture is not suitable for our research. We designed a new CNN model to accept three images as input.

2.2.1. Convolutional Neural Network. Convolutional neural networks [8, 9], originally proposed by LeCun et al. for handwritten digit recognition, have been recently succeeded in image identification, detection, and segmentation tasks [10–15]. CNN is proved to have a strong ability in large scale image classification. It is mainly composed of three types of layers: convolutional layers, pooling layers, and full-connection layers. Convolutional and pooling layers are the most important layers. The convolutional layers are used to extract features by convolving image regions with multiple filters. As the layers increase, the CNN understands an image

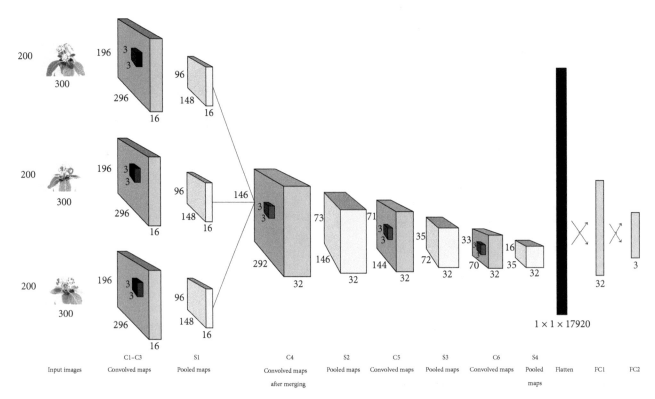

FIGURE 3: An architecture of 3-input CNN model for *Gloxinia* grading. This architecture has the best effect on testing set.

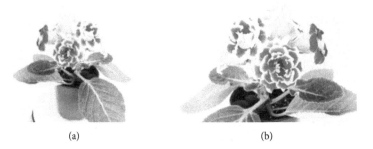

(a)   (b)

FIGURE 4: Extract features by cutting image. (a) The original image and (b) the cropped image.

progressively. The pooling layers reduce the size of output maps from convolutional layers and prevent overfitting. Through these two layers, numbers of neurons, parameters, and connections are much fewer in CNN models. Therefore, CNNs are more efficient than BP neural networks with similarly sized layers.

2.2.2. Architecture of Three-Input Convolutional Neural Networks. Based on the traditional CNN architecture, a new model named three-input CNN is proposed by us. The model is employed to perform *Gloxinia* grading and achieve a preferable result on the dataset. The full model of our CNN architecture is depicted in Figure 3. The convolutional layers C1–C3 filter three $300 \times 200 \times 3$ input images with 32 kernels of size $7 \times 7 \times 3$ with stride of 1 pixel. The stride of pooling layer S1 is 2 pixels. Then, the three convolutional layers are

merged into one. C4 has 16 kernels of size $3 \times 3 \times 3$ with stride of 1 pixel. S2 pools the merged features with a stride of 4. Both C5 and C6 have 32 kernels with size of $3 \times 3 \times 3$ with stride of 1 pixel. The dropout is applied to the output of S4 which has been flattened. The fully connected layer FC1 has 32 neurons and FC2 has 3 neurons. The activation of the output layer is softmax function.

3. Experiments and Results

3.1. Dataset Augmentation. The performance of models is limited by mini-scale dataset due to the lack of samples. To augment the dataset, images are flipped horizontally and vertically, shifted, and rotated. Besides these traditional methods for dataset augmentation, the main region which contains the important features is cut from the whole image. The operation is shown in Figure 4.

3.2. Implementation and Preprocess. 80% of BjfuGloxinia dataset is randomly selected for training and 20% of the dataset is for testing. The model is implemented in "Keras" which is a high-level neural networks API [16]. All the experiments were conducted on a Ubuntu Kylin 14.04 server with a 3.40 GHz i7-3770 CPU (16 GB memory) and a GTX 1070 GPU (8 GB memory). Our model is evaluated on Bjfu-Gloxinia dataset which is detailed in Section 2. The size of an original image is 4288×2848 pixels, which should be reduced to fit the GPU memory. All the original images are resized to 300×200 pixels and then per-pixel value is divided by 255. The images should also be normalized and standardized before being inputted to models for fast convergence. The inputted images are shuffled to avoid the model influenced by inputting order. Both the sequence of samples and the three images belonging to each sample should be shuffled.

3.3. Training Algorithm. Training algorithm of convolutional neural network is divided into two stages. The one is forward propagation and the other is backward propagation.

3.3.1. Forward Propagation. Data are transferred from the input layer to the output layer by a series of operations including convolution, pooling, and fully connected. Each convolutional layer uses trainable kernels to filter the result of previous layer followed by an activation function to form the output feature map. In generally, the operation is shown as follows:

$$x_j^\ell = f\left(\sum_{i \in M_j} x_i^{\ell-1} * k_{ij}^\ell + b_j^\ell\right), \tag{1}$$

where M_j represents the set of input maps that we selected, b is a bias added to every output map, k represents the kernels, and k_{ij}^ℓ is the weight of the row "i" and column "j" in each kernel. The operation of pooling layer is downsample which summarizes the outputs of surrounding neurons by a kernel map [7]

$$x_j^\ell = f\left(\beta_j^\ell \text{ down}\left(X_j^{\ell-1}\right) + b_j^\ell\right), \tag{2}$$

where β is the multiplicative bias and b is an additive bias and "down" is a subsampling function adopted max-pooling [17]. The reason why we select max-pooling rather than mean-pooling is because with the latter it is difficult to find the important information such as the edge of objects while the former selects the most active neuron of each region in feature maps [18]. Therefore, with max-pooling, it is easier to extract useful features. The fully connected layer is equal to hidden layer of multilayer perceptron. The activation of output layer is softmax function [19] applied for multiclassification, which is given by

$$\sigma(z)_j = \frac{e^{z_j}}{\sum_{k=1}^K e^{z_k}} \quad \text{for } j = 1, \ldots, K, \tag{3}$$

where Z is a K-dimensional vector and in the range $(0, 1)$. In this paper, K is 3.

3.3.2. Backward Propagation. Backward propagation updates parameters to minimize the discrepancy between the desired output and the actual output by stochastic gradient descent (SGD). The discrepancy is given by the categorical cross-entropy loss function:

$$\text{Loss}_i = -\log\left(\frac{e^{f_{yi}}}{\sum_j e^{f_j}}\right) \quad \text{for } j = 1, 2, 3, \tag{4}$$

where f_j is probability of sample i which is classified to class j. L_1 and L_2 regularization are adopted to prevent overfitting. L_1 is given by

$$C = C_0 + \frac{\lambda}{n} \sum_w |w|, \tag{5}$$

where C_0 is the loss in formula (4). L_2 is given by

$$C = C_0 + \frac{\lambda}{2n} \sum_w w^2. \tag{6}$$

In this paper, weight of L_1 and L_2 regularization is 0.0001. Dropout [20] is also adopted to prevent overfitting and it is set to 0.1. SGD algorithm computes the gradients and updates the coefficient or weights. It can be expressed as follows:

$$\delta_x = w_{x+1}\left(\sigma'\left(w_{x+1} \cdot c_x + b_{x+1}\right) \circ \text{up}\left(\delta_{x+1}\right)\right),$$

$$\Delta w_x = -\eta \cdot \sum_{i,j}\left(\delta_x \circ \text{down}\left(S_{x-1}\right)\right), \tag{7}$$

where δ_x denotes sensitivities of each unit with respect to perturbations of the bias b, $\circ$ denotes element-wise multiplication, up( ) represents an upsampling operation, down( ) represents subsampling operation, w is the updated weight, and η represents the learning rate.

3.4. Results and Failure Analysis. Large quantities of experiments are conducted to find the best-performing models for flower grading. The architectures of models varied by changing the size of filter kernels, number of feature maps, and convolutional layers. These models are depicted in Tables 1 and 2. As is shown in Table 1, when the number of convolutional layers after merging is in the range of one to two, change the number of layers before merging and observe the effect of models. As is shown in Table 2, the number and the size of filter kernels of the convolutional layers are varying when the number of convolutional layers in every branch before merging is fixed to one.

Top ten best-performing models are selected eventually. The accuracy evolution of 10 models on *Gloxinia* grading is shown in Figure 5.

The result of Table 1 shows that 1-2 layers before merging are better than more. Table 2 shows that 2-3 convolutional layers after merging is the best. As the number of layers increases, the accuracy tends to decline. The change of accuracy is not obvious when varying the size of kernels. The size of 5×5 is slightly better than 3×3. M4 is the best model with the highest accuracy of 0.89 on testing set.

TABLE 1: Architecture of models with different number of layers before merging.

Name of models	Convolutional layers								
	C1*	C2*	C3*	C4*	C5	C6	FC1	FC2	ACC
M1	3 × 3,16		—	—	3 × 3,32		32	3	76.2% ± 0.3
M2	3 × 3,16		—	—	3 × 3,32	3 × 3,32	32	3	81.6% ± 0.3
M3	3 × 3,16	3 × 3,16	—	—	3 × 3,32	—	32	3	85.5% ± 0.3
M4	3 × 3,16	3 × 3,16	—	—	5 × 5,64	5 × 5,32	32	3	84.6% ± 0.3
M5	3 × 3,16	3 × 3,32	—	—	3 × 3,64	3 × 3,64	32	3	88.8% ± 0.3
M6	5 × 5,16	5 × 5,16	—	—	5 × 5,32	5 × 5,32	32	3	84.7% ± 0.3
M7	3 × 3,16	3 × 3,32	—	—	5 × 5,32	5 × 5,32	32	3	80.6% ± 0.3
M8	3 × 3,16	3 × 3,32	3 × 3,32	—	3 × 3,64	—	64	3	82.7% ± 0.3
M9	3 × 3,16	3 × 3,16	3 × 3,32	—	3 × 3,64	3 × 3,64	64	3	82.1% ± 0.3
M10	5 × 5,16	3 × 3,16	3 × 3,32	3 × 3,32	3 × 3,32	—	32	3	81.6% ± 0.3
M11	5 × 5,16	5 × 5,16	3 × 3,32	3 × 3,32	3 × 3,32	3 × 3,32	32	3	80.6% ± 0.3

* represents the convolutional layers in each branch before merging. Each branch has only one convolutional layer. "3 × 3,32" represents the size of filter kernels which is 3 × 3 and the number of kernels is 32. All the strides of kernels are set to 1 × 1.

TABLE 2: Architecture of models with one convolutional layer before merging.

Name of models	Convolutional layers								
	C1–C3	C4	C5	C6	C7	C8	FC1	FC2	ACC
M12	3 × 3,32	3 × 3,32	3 × 3,32	3 × 3,64	3 × 3,64	3 × 3,64	32	3	33.3% ± 0.3
M13	3 × 3,32	3 × 3,32	3 × 3,32	3 × 3,64	3 × 3,64	—	32	3	68.4% ± 0.3
M14	3 × 3,32	3 × 3,32	3 × 3,32	3 × 3,64	—	—	32	3	87.8% ± 0.3
M15	5 × 5,16	3 × 3,32	3 × 3,32	3 × 3,32	—	—	32	3	89.6% ± 0.3
M16	7 × 7,16	3 × 3,32	3 × 3,32	3 × 3,32	—	—	32	3	83.7% ± 0.3
M17	3 × 3,32	3 × 3,48	3 × 3,48	3 × 3,48	—	—	32	3	85.7% ± 0.3
M18	3 × 3,16	3 × 3,32	3 × 3,32	—	—	—	32	3	81.6% ± 0.3
M19	3 × 3,16	3 × 3,32	3 × 3,16	—	—	—	16	3	81.6% ± 0.3
M20	5 × 5,16	3 × 3,32	3 × 3,16	—	—	—	16	3	84.7% ± 0.3
M21	5 × 5,16	3 × 3,64	3 × 3,32	—	—	—	32	3	87.8% ± 0.3
M22	7 × 7,16	3 × 3,32	3 × 3,16	—	—	—	16	3	87.8% ± 0.3
M23	3 × 3,16	5 × 5,32	3 × 3,32	—	—	—	32	3	87.8% ± 0.3

C1–C3 represent the layers in three branches before merging. Pooling layers are ignored in this table. Generally, every convolutional layer is followed by a pooling layer. All the sizes and strides of pooling layers are set to 2 × 2.

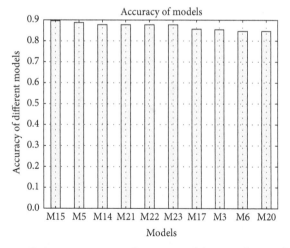

FIGURE 5: Average accuracy of top ten models on testing set. It is obvious that M15 is the best model with the highest accuracy 0.89 on testing set.

The process of flower grading by single-input CNN is divided into two steps. Firstly, each image of a sample is classified separately. Secondly, the majority of the categories are selected as a result of sample classification. As is shown in Table 3, comparing to the single-input CNN, multi-input CNN is much better than single-input CNN for flower grading. The single-input CNN cannot grade flowers well. The probable reason is that when the three image classification results are inconsistent, it is very difficult to draw the conclusion about which grades the sample is belonging to. For example, a sample contains three images. The first image is classified to the good class, the second image is classified to the medium class, and the third image is classified to the bad class. Therefore, the sample cannot be classified to any grades without additional rules. In this paper, the sample is considered to be misclassified in the case of inconsistent result. Comparing to the single-input CNN, multi-input CNN not only improves the accuracy, but also reduces the number of predictions. Multi-input CNN predicts a sample

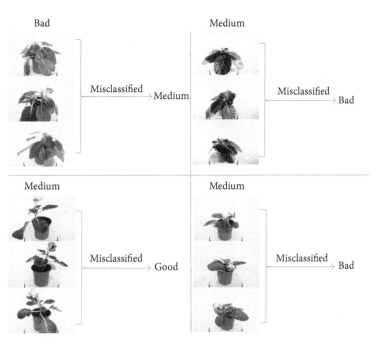

FIGURE 6: Examples of misclassified classes. This figure shows four misclassified samples. For example, the first sample in this figure which belongs to the bad class is misclassified to the medium class by our CNN model.

TABLE 3: Architecture of single-input models.

Name of models	Convolutional layers							
	C1	C2	C3	C4	C5	FC1	FC2	ACC
M24	$3 \times 3,32$	$3 \times 3,32$				32	3	$84.7\% \pm 0.3$
M25	$3 \times 3,32$	$3 \times 3,32$	$3 \times 3,32$	—	—	32	3	$77.6\% \pm 0.3$
M26	$3 \times 3,32$	$3 \times 3,32$	$3 \times 3,32$	$3 \times 3,64$	—	32	3	$75.5\% \pm 0.3$
M27	$3 \times 3,16$	$3 \times 3,32$	$3 \times 3,32$	$3 \times 3,64$	$3 \times 3,64$	32	3	$75.5\% \pm 0.3$

C1–C3 represent the layers in three branches before merging. Pooling layers are ignored in this table. Generally, every convolutional layer is followed by a pooling layer. All the sizes and strides of pooling layers are set to 2×2.

TABLE 4: Confusion matrix of our CNN model for flower grading.

Class		Predicted		
		Bad	Medium	Good
Actual class	Bad	30	2	0
	Medium	7	25	0
	Good	0	1	31

just once while single-input CNN needs to predict three images of a sample. The confusion matrix is depicted in Table 4. From the confusion matrix we can observe that with the model it is easier to classify the good class and the bad class. It is very difficult to classify the medium class (7 misclassified). The error rate of the medium class is near to 0.3.

From our investigation as illustrated in Figure 6, samples which were misclassified are probably caused by two reasons. One is that these plants have almost similar appearance to other classes. The other is that the proportion of features in the image is still very small, though the important region has been cut out from the whole image. For example, the bud is the most important feature which could distinguish the medium class from the bad class. But it is very small and difficult to be found in the image. It will be worse if the neurons which contain the bud information are thrown away after the dropout operation. Furthermore, due to the shortage of plants, although the dataset enlarged by several methods, it is still very small and lack samples diversity, limiting the accuracy of our models.

4. Bud Detection

Bud detection is based on PlantCV [21] which is an open source package. The buds were detected by image processing. The main idea of the detection is finding an appropriate threshold in training set which can separate the target region

 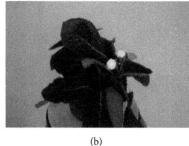

(a)   (b)

FIGURE 7: Example of bud detection. This figure shows the operation of bud detection. The buds in (b) are marked by aquamarine circle.

TABLE 5: Select samples for bud detection.

Number	Bad class	Medium class	Good class	Selected
1	$9.16e - 01$	$8.08e - 02$	$2.46e - 03$	False
2	$9.88e - 01$	$3.86e - 03$	$7.65e - 03$	False
3	$6.92e - 01$	$3.02e - 01$	$4.63e - 03$	True
4	$9.46e - 01$	$1.39e - 02$	$3.96e - 02$	False
5	$4.53e - 01$	$4.34e - 01$	$1.10e - 01$	True

Number 3 and number 5 are selected for bud detection because $6.92e - 01$ is close to $3.02e - 01$ and $4.53e - 01$ is close to $4.34e - 01$.

of image from others. The binary threshold is expressed as follows:

$$\text{dst}(x, y) = \begin{cases} \text{max value} & \text{if src}(x, y) > \text{threshold} \\ 0 & \text{otherwise,} \end{cases} \quad (8)$$

where the max value is set to 256 and threshold is 190 and $\text{src}(x, y)$ is the g channel value of (x, y) in the image using RGB color space.

The result shows that almost all of the errors derived from the medium class are misclassified to the bad class. The most problem probably is difficulty to extract the small important feature. In order to solve this problem and improve the accuracy of classifying the medium class, we focus on bud detection. At first, our model is used to predict the probability that every sample belongs to each class. The samples whose probability belonging to the bad class is close to the medium class are selected for bud detection. Sample selection is shown in Table 5. A sample is classified to the medium class if it contains buds. The accuracy of our model on testing set is lifted to 93.9% after detection. Bud detection is shown in Figure 7.

5. Conclusion

This paper presents a three-input convolutional neural model for grading every three images of a flower. This paper also presents a new *Gloxinia* dataset named BjfuGloxinia which consists of three grades, containing 107 samples and 321 images of each quality grade. After dataset augmentation, the number of plants in dataset are increased to 760 samples and 2780 images in training set. The experimental results

show that learning the features through three-input CNN can make good performance on *Gloxinia* grading with the highest accuracy of 89.6% on the testing set after dataset augmentation. This accuracy is increased by 8 percentage points compared to using the original dataset. The result demonstrates that the method of dataset augmentation is effective and three-input CNN is the promising model for large scale flower grading. Bud detection is proposed to improve the accuracy of classifying the medium class. It lifts the accuracy on testing set to 93.9%.

In the future work, BjfuGloxinia will be enlarged by more quality grades and more plants. The performance of the model should also be improved. Application of the model will be extended from flower grading to more plant species grading even to other fields, such as plant disease detection and segmentation.

Conflicts of Interest

The authors declare that they have no conflicts of interest.

Authors' Contributions

Yu Sun and Lin Zhu contributed equally to this work.

Acknowledgments

This work was supported by the Fundamental Research Funds for the Central Universities: 2017JC02 and TD2014-01. The authors thank Jie Chen, Ying Liu, Ke Ma, and YingJie Liu for collecting dataset with them.

References

[1] M. P. Arakeri and Lakshmana, "Computer vision based fruit grading system for quality evaluation of tomato in agriculture industry," *Procedia Computer Science*, vol. 79, pp. 426–433, 2016.

[2] C. Wang, W. Huang, B. Zhang et al., "Design and Implementation of an Automatic Grading System of Diced Potatoes Based on Machine Vision," in *Computer and Computing Technologies in Agriculture IX*, vol. 479 of *IFIP Advances in Information and Communication Technology*, pp. 202–216, Springer, Cham, 2016.

[3] Y. Al Ohali, "Computer vision based date fruit grading system: Design and implementation," *Journal of King Saud University - Computer and Information Sciences*, vol. 23, no. 1, pp. 29–36, 2011.

[4] A. Berg, J. Deng, and L. Fei-Fei, Large scale visual recognition challenge 2010, http://www.image-net.org/challenges/LSVRC.

[5] S. H. Lee, C. S. Chan, P. Wilkin, and P. Remagnino, "Deep-Plant: Plant Identification with convolutional neural networks," *Computer Science*, 2015.

[6] A. K. Reyes, J. C. Caicedo, and J. E. Camargo, Fine-tuning Deep Convolutional Networks for Plant Recognition,.

[7] A. Krizhevsky, Convolutional Deep Belief Networks on CIFAR-10.

[8] Y. LeCun, L. Bottou, Y. Bengio, and P. Haffner, "Gradient-based learning applied to document recognition," *Proceedings of the IEEE*, vol. 86, no. 11, pp. 2278–2323, 1998.

[9] Y. LeCun, B. Boser, J. S. Denker et al., "Handwritten digit recognition with a back-propagation network," *in Advances in Neural Information Processing Systems*, pp. 396–404, 1990.

[10] R. Vaillant, C. Monrocq, and Y. L. Cun, "An original approach for the localization of objects in images," in *Proceedings of the in International Conference on Artificial Neural Networks*, pp. 26–30, 1993.

[11] P. Sermanet, D. Eigen, X. Zhang, M. Mathieu, R. Fergus, and Y. Lecun, *OverFeat: Integrated Recognition, Localization and Detection using Convolutional Networks, Eprint Arxiv*, 2013.

[12] S. J. Nowlan and J. C. Platt, "A Convolutional Neural Network Hand Tracker," *in Advances in Neural Information Processing Systems 7*, pp. 901–908, 1995.

[13] S. Lawrence, C. L. Giles, A. C. Tsoi, and A. D. Back, "Face recognition: a convolutional neural-network approach," *IEEE Transactions on Neural Networks*, vol. 8, no. 1, pp. 98–113, 1997.

[14] B. Hariharan, P. Arbelaez, R. Girshick, and J. Malik, "Object Instance Segmentation and Fine-Grained Localization Using Hypercolumns," *IEEE Transactions on Pattern Analysis and Machine Intelligence*, vol. 39, no. 4, pp. 627–639, 2017.

[15] C. Garcia and M. Delakis, "Convolutional face finder: A neural architecture for fast and robust face detection," *IEEE Transactions on Pattern Analysis and Machine Intelligence*, vol. 26, no. 11, pp. 1408–1423, 2004.

[16] Google, François Chollet, keras, 2015, https://github.com/fchollet/keras.

[17] M. Riesenhuber and T. Poggio, "Hierarchical models of object recognition in cortex," *Nature Neuroscience*, vol. 2, no. 11, pp. 1019–1025, 1999.

[18] D. Ciregan, U. Meier, and J. Schmidhuber, "Multi-column deep neural networks for image classification," in *Proceedings of the IEEE Conference on Computer Vision and Pattern Recognition (CVPR '12)*, pp. 3642–3649, June 2012.

[19] C. M. Bishop, *Pattern Recognition and Machine Learning*, Springer, New York, NY, USA, 2006.

[20] N. Srivastava, G. Hinton, A. Krizhevsky, I. Sutskever, and R. Salakhutdinov, "Dropout: a simple way to prevent neural networks from overfitting," *The Journal of Machine Learning Research*, vol. 15, no. 1, pp. 1929–1958, 2014.

[21] N. Fahlgren, M. Feldman, M. A. Gehan et al., "A versatile phenotyping system and analytics platform reveals diverse temporal responses to water availability in Setaria," *Molecular Plant*, vol. 8, no. 10, pp. 1520–1535, 2015.

22

Research on Fault Diagnosis for Pumping Station based on T-S Fuzzy Fault Tree and Bayesian Network

Zhuqing Bi, Chenming Li, Xujie Li, and Hongmin Gao

College of Computer and Information Engineering, Hohai University, Nanjing 211100, China

Correspondence should be addressed to Chenming Li; lcm@hhu.edu.cn

Academic Editor: Lei Zhang

According to the characteristics of fault diagnosis for pumping station, such as the complex structure, multiple mappings, and numerous uncertainties, a new approach combining T-S fuzzy gate fault tree and Bayesian network (BN) is proposed. On the one hand, traditional fault tree method needs the logical relationship between events and probability value of events and can only represent the events with two states. T-S fuzzy gate fault tree method can solve these disadvantages but still has weaknesses in complex reasoning and only one-way reasoning. On the other hand, the BN is suitable for fault diagnosis of pumping station because of its powerful ability to deal with uncertain information. However, it is difficult to determine the structure and conditional probability tables of the BN. Therefore, the proposed method integrates the advantages of the two methods. Finally, the feasibility of the method is verified through a fault diagnosis model of the rotor in the pumping unit, the accuracy of the method is verified by comparing with the methods based on traditional Bayesian network and BP neural network, respectively, when the historical data is sufficient, and the results are more superior to the above two when the historical data is insufficient.

1. Introduction

With the operation of the first phase of the South-to-North Water Diversion Project, the reliability and ability to achieve preset functions of the pumping stations and units at every level will affect the effectiveness of the whole project, while the faults of each pumping station may cause major issues about engineering safety, significant economic losses, and serious social impact if expanded further. Therefore, it is of great significance to monitor, evaluate, predict, and diagnose the running state of the pumping stations and units.

The operating state of the large-scale pumping station is affected by the coupling of hydraulic, mechanical, and electromagnetic factors. And the factors that affect its efficiency or failure are often multiple. At the same time, there is different steady status or transition status corresponding to different conditions like starting and stopping and blade adjustment in the course of operating. Therefore, the fault diagnosis of pumping station (group) can be divided into conventional fault diagnosis and uncertain fault diagnosis. The former such as electrical equipment has been solved because it is possessed

in its computer monitoring system. However, these uncertain fault diagnoses under the coupling of mechanical, hydraulic, and electromagnetic factors are difficult [1–3].

Bayesian network is an intelligent method combining probability theory, graph theory, and decision theory. Recently, many researchers focus on the field of fault diagnosis, especially in the complex systems with large amount of uncertain information [4–6]. But its application in large pumping and drainage pumps is very little. In paper [7], Bayesian network is firstly applied to the fault diagnosis of the hydrogenerator by constructing a simple fault diagnosis system for the hydrogenerator set, SmartHydro, which uses vibration of different frequency as the fault features to realize the diagnosis of several major faults caused by factors that are mechanical, hydraulic, electromagnetic, etc. This method makes full use of the advantage of Bayesian network to solve the problem of uncertain fault diagnosis in pumping unit. However, the fault mechanism of a real pumping unit is far more complicated. A large number of nodes and conditional probability tables are required to construct a complete Bayesian network. So Bayesian network is combined with the Noisy Or model in paper [8] to calculate the connection probability between a single node and the result in the whole system with formula only by determining the probability relationship between every node and the result. It is verified that this model greatly reduces the amount of conditional probabilities that need to be determined and advances the application of Bayesian network in fault diagnosis in pumping units. However, it is difficult to understand the fault mechanism and build a Bayesian network accurately in large complex systems such as pumping stations. That needs the assistance of experienced experts and learning based on a large number of historical data, especially historical fault data. As a newly developed large-scale complex system, the number of historical fault data of pumping station (group) in the South-to-North Water Diversion Project is very little. In addition, the number of nodes in constructed Bayesian network is very large. Therefore, it is more difficult to determine the structure and conditional probability tables.

Some researchers have combined the traditional fault tree theory with the Bayesian network to solve the problem of constructing a Bayesian network. However, there are many shortcomings in the traditional fault tree: (1) the logical relationships and probability between events need to be known exactly. (2) Compatibility is not strong. That means the existing data is not applicable when the system conditions are changed. (3) Every event can be described only with two states: $\{0, 1\}$. The T-S fuzzy gate fault tree analysis method proposed by Song et al. [9] integrates the fuzzy theory into the fault tree, which can not only overcome shortcoming (1) through describing the connection between events as an uncertain item but also describe multiple states of the system conveniently. But there are still some disadvantages, such as poor compatibility, complex reasoning process, and only one-way reasoning.

Therefore, this paper combines T-S fuzzy gate fault tree method and Bayesian network method [10] that can convert the fuzzy gate rule of T-S fuzzy gate fault tree into the conditional probability table of Bayesian network and make full use of the efficient parallel two-way reasoning ability of Bayesian network to realize the uncertain fault diagnosis of pumping station. Finally, the Bayesian network is constructed according to the above method, and the fault diagnosis of the rotor, which is one of the most important and most faulty components of the pump unit, proves the correctness and superiority of the network.

The remainder of this paper is outlined as follows: first, the T-S fuzzy gate fault tree and Bayesian network are briefly reviewed. Then, the concrete steps of transforming the T-S fuzzy gate fault tree to Bayesian network are described. Finally, the effectiveness and superiority of the proposed approach are illustrated by taking the rotor which is one of the most important and most prone to fault in the pump unit.

2. T-S Fuzzy Gate Fault Tree

Compared with the traditional fault tree method, T-S fuzzy gate fault tree method combines the fuzzy theory with the fault tree method, provides the relationships between upper and lower events with uncertainties, and expresses

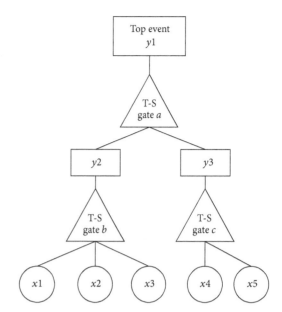

FIGURE 1: T-S fuzzy fault tree.

TABLE 1: Rules for T-S gate b.

Rules	x_1	x_2	x_3	y_2
R_b	$x_1^{k_{1i}}$	$x_1^{k_{2i}}$	$x_3^{k_{3i}}$	$P^{R_b}(y_2^{b_{2j}})$

fault probabilities with fuzzy numbers. These events between layers are connected through the fuzzy gate, which is a production rule defining the probability of different states of the top event caused by different combinations of bottom events. A typical T-S fuzzy gate fault tree model is depicted in this section. Figure 1 shows a T-S fuzzy fault tree model.

In Figure 1, $x1, x2, \ldots, x5$ are five bottom events, each with k_i $(i = 1, 2, \ldots, 5)$ values of state described as $x_1^{k_{1i}}, x_2^{k_{2i}}$, $\ldots, x_5^{k_{5i}}$, respectively. b_j $(j = 1, 2, 3)$ is the number of fault states for the top event y_1, and the intermediate events y_2, y_3 can be described as $y_1^{b_{1j}}$, $y_2^{b_{2j}}$, and $y_3^{b_{3j}}$. R_a, R_b, and R_c represent fuzzy rules of T-S gates a, b, and c, respectively. The fuzzy rules of the local T-S fuzzy gate fault tree composed of y_2, T-S gates b, and x_1, x_2, and x_3 can be represented in Table 1.

T-S gate has the following rule or formula, which is also the conditional probability of the corresponding nodes in BN:

$$P^{R_b}\left(y_2^{b_{21}}\right) = P\left(y_2 = y_2^{b_{21}} \mid x_1 = x_1^{k_{1i}}, \ldots, x_3 = x_3^{k_{3i}}\right)$$

$$P^{R_b}\left(y_2^{b_{22}}\right) = P\left(y_2 = y_2^{b_{22}} \mid x_1 = x_1^{k_{1i}}, \ldots, x_3 = x_3^{k_{3i}}\right)$$

$$\vdots \tag{1}$$

$$P^{R_b}\left(y_2^{b_{2j}}\right) = P\left(y_2 = y_2^{b_{2j}} \mid x_1 = x_1^{k_{1i}}, \ldots, x_3 = x_3^{k_{3i}}\right).$$

3. BN

3.1. Overview of Bayesian Network. The Bayesian network uses a graphical mode to express the joint probability of

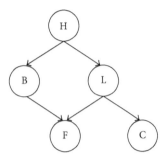

FIGURE 2: A typical Bayesian network structure.

multiple variables, and the causality between variables is represented by directional connection lines. Give each root node a prior probability, and each child node takes the conditional probability Table 9. A Bayesian network can be represented by a multiple tuple $\langle V, D, P \rangle$ where V is the node variable, D is the directional connection line between nodes, P is the conditional probability table representing the connection strength between nodes. It combines directional acyclic graph with probability theory. It is more objective and scientific with the formal probability theory foundation, and its knowledge representation form is also more intuitive. The Bayesian network is more objective with the combination of the prior knowledge of experts and the posterior data. The prior knowledge dominates when the posterior data is less, while the posterior knowledge dominates when the posterior knowledge is abundant. A typical Bayesian network structure is depicted in Figure 2.

3.2. Construction of Bayesian Network. Three parts should be determined when building a complete Bayesian network: the node variables, the structure of the network, and the conditional probability table for every node. There are three main methods to determine the latter two.

(1) Through Experts' Experience Completely. This method is affected by the limitation of human's knowledge, and the bias of a network can be found easily in practical application.

(2) Learning through Historical Data Completely. When the historical data is sufficient, this method has strong adaptability by reasoning the structure and parameters of BN scientifically.

(3) Combining the above Two. The historical data is often insufficient, so the nodes and structure of BN can be determined by experts, and the parameters can be determined through learning from data. This method is applied more in practice because it can reduce the difficulty of determining parameters of the network and the structural learning error caused by insufficient data.

Parameter learning methods of data-driven BN are mainly the following two:

(1) Maximum-likelihood estimation method and Bayesian method can be used when data is sufficient. They are shown, respectively, in

$$L(\theta \mid D) = P(D \mid \theta) = \prod_{i=1}^{m} P(D_i \mid \theta) \quad (2)$$

$$p(\theta \mid D) \propto p(\theta) L(\theta \mid D), \quad (3)$$

where θ is a random variable, $D = (D_1, D_2, D_3, \ldots, D_m)$ is a data set, and $L(\theta \mid D)$ is the maximum-likelihood function of θ.

(2) When data is insufficient, if the topology of the network is known, EM (expectation maximization) can be used to calculate the parameters. If the structure of network is unknown, the structure maximum expectation method can be used. Specific steps are not detailed here, which can be found in related literature.

3.3. Bayesian Network Inference. There are three kinds of inference in Bayesian network: support inference, causal inference, and diagnostic inference. This section focuses on the last one, which determines the cause according to the measured characteristic node with abnormal phenomenon when the fault occurs. Steps are as follows:

(1) Obtain the state fact of the feature node, and let its probability value be 1.

(2) Let the obtained fact node be e, and then the marginal probability of any node A is

$$P(Ae) = \frac{P(A, e)}{P(e)}. \quad (4)$$

(3) According to the given $P(e)$, $P(A, e)$ can be calculated by marginalizing the joint probability density of all nodes.

The formula used in the process of fault diagnosis include the following:

Bayesian formula is

$$P(B_i A) = \frac{P(B_i) P(A \mid B_i)}{\sum_{j=1}^{n} P(B_j) P(A \mid B_j)}. \quad (5)$$

Chain rules are

$$P(X_1 X_2, \ldots, X_n) = \prod_{i=1}^{n} P(X_i \mid \pi(X_i)). \quad (6)$$

4. Transformation from T-S Fuzzy Tree to BN

In the process of transforming T-S fuzzy fault tree to BN, the top event, middle event, and bottom event of the T-S fuzzy fault tree correspond to the leaf node, the intermediate node, and the root node of the Bayesian network. For the fuzzy rules between events, they correspond to the conditional probability tables between nodes. According to the relationship between the top events and the middle events and the relationship between the middle events and the bottom events, the root nodes, the intermediate nodes, and the leaf nodes are connected with the directed connection lines to form a complete BN [10, 11]. The flow chart is depicted in Figure 3.

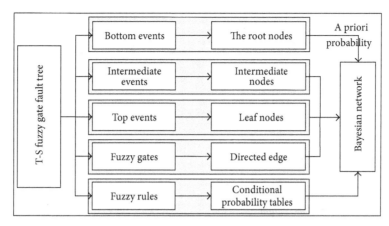

FIGURE 3: T-S fuzzy tree converted into BN.

Given the leaf node's fault state T_q, the posterior probability $P(x_i = x_i^{k_i} \mid T = T_q)$ of the root node x_i with fault state $x_i^{k_i}$ can be obtained by Bayesian conditional probability formula:

$$P\left(x_i = x_i^{k_i} \mid T = T_q\right) = E\left[\frac{\widetilde{P}\left(x_i = x_i^{k_i}, T = T_q\right)}{\widetilde{P}\left(T = T_q\right)}\right], \quad (7)$$

where $E[\widetilde{P}(x_i = x_i^{k_i}, T = T_q)/\widetilde{P}(T = T_q)]$ is the center of gravity of the fuzzy subset, which converts the fuzzy subset into an exact value.

If the fault probability fuzzy subset of all the root nodes is known, then the fault probability fuzzy subset of the leaf node $T = T_q$ can be obtained through the conditional independence of Bayesian networks and chain rules. It is expressed by the following formula:

$$\widetilde{P}\left(T = T_q\right)$$
$$= \sum_{\substack{x_1, x_2, \ldots, x_n \\ y_1, y_2, \ldots, y_m}} \widetilde{P}\left(x_1, x_2, \ldots, x_n; y_1, y_2, \ldots, y_m; T = T_q\right)$$
$$= \sum_{\pi(T)} \widetilde{P}\left(T = T_q \mid \pi(T)\right) \times \sum_{\pi(y_1)} \widetilde{P}\left(y_1 \mid \pi(y_1)\right) \quad (8)$$
$$\times \cdots \times \sum_{\pi(y_m)} \widetilde{P}\left(y_1 \mid \pi(y_m)\right) \widetilde{P}\left(x_1^{k_1}\right) \cdots \widetilde{P}\left(x_n^{k_n}\right),$$

where $\pi(T)$ represents the set of all parent nodes of the leaf node T and $\widetilde{P}(x_i^{k_i})$ is the fault probability fuzzy subset if fault state of the root node x_i is denoted as $x_i^{k_i}$.

5. Fault Diagnosis of Rotor Based on T-S Fuzzy Gate Fault Tree and BN

5.1. Rotor Fault Diagnosis of Water Pump. Buildings, electrical and mechanical equipment, and auxiliary equipment are the main components of the pump station. The mechanical and electrical equipment mainly includes the main water pump, the power machine, the electrical equipment, and the metal structure [12]. As the direct work part of the operation of the unit, the main water pump and motor are the most prone to failure of the pumping station, whether they can operate safely affects the function and efficiency of the pumping unit directly. Studies have shown that more than half of faults of rotating machinery are caused by the fault of the rotor, which is a major component of a pump unit [13]. Therefore, the fault diagnosis of rotor is the most important part of the fault diagnosis of the whole pump unit. When there is a fault in the rotor, it not only does great harm to the whole pump unit but also affects the task of watering and drainage of pump unit seriously so as to result in immeasurable losses. So it is necessary to implement fault diagnosis for rotor. Vibration is the main form of faults in the rotor and abnormal increase in amplitude of power frequency is the most common phenomenon. In the following, the effectiveness of the proposed method in fault diagnosis is illustrated through the phenomenon that the amplitude of power frequency of the rotor increases.

The common faults that cause the abnormal increase in amplitude of the rotor's power frequency are the mass imbalance and thermal bending of the rotor. And the reasons for the mass imbalance are the fouling, breakage, or shedding of components and initial eccentricity, while the causes of the thermal bending are the inappropriate parking of unit and uneven heat in movement. The T-S fuzzy gate fault tree constructed with this method is depicted in Figure 1. Table 2 represents the corresponding modes or causes and states of faults of each node. There are two states (yes, no) in the events of an abnormal increase in amplitude of the rotor's power frequency and a breakage or shedding of the component and three states (severe, general, and none) for the other fault events. Then, the T-S fuzzy gate fault tree is transformed into a Bayesian network depicted in Figure 4 according to the method depicted in Figure 3.

Table 3 shows the fault data of some root nodes. This data comes from some large pumping stations in Jiangsu Province in recent years and is sorted out by using statistics. When the fault state of fundamental frequency is 1, combine these data and consultations with experts, and the possible fault probability fuzzy subset of the rotor system are shown in

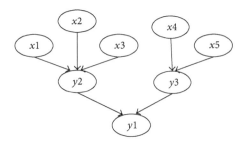

FIGURE 4: Bayesian network for fault diagnosis when the amplitude of the rotor's power frequency increased.

TABLE 2: The fault modes and cause for increased amplitude of the rotor's power frequency.

Symbol	Node events	State (1, 0.5, 0)
$y1$	Abnormal increase in fundamental frequency	(Yes, No)
$y2$	Quality imbalance	(Serious, General, No)
$y3$	Rotor thermal bending	(Serious, General, No)
$x1$	Fouling	(Serious, General, No)
$x2$	Parts break or fall off	(Yes, No)
$x3$	Initial eccentricity	(Serious, General, No)
$x4$	Improper starting and stopping	(Serious, General, No)
$x5$	Uneven heat in the movement	(Serious, General, No)

TABLE 3: Partial characteristic data of fault state of rotor system of some large pumping stations in Jiangsu Province.

Node	$y1$	$y2$	$y3$	$x1$	$x2$	$x3$	$x4$	$x5$
	1	1	0	1	0	0.5	0	0
	1	0	1	0	0	0	0.5	0.5
State	0	0	0	0	0	0.5	0	0
	0	0.5	0	0.5	0	0	0	0
	0	0	0.5	0	0	0	0.5	0
	...	...	...	...	...	...	...	...

TABLE 4: Fault probability fuzzy subset of root node with fault state 1.

Rules x_i	x_i fault probability fuzzy subset of x_i (/h)
x_1	$\{3.95 \times 10^{-6},\ 4.0 \times 10^{-6},\ 4.05 \times 10^{-6}\}$
x_2	$\{0.98 \times 10^{-6},\ 1.0 \times 10^{-6},\ 1.02 \times 10^{-6}\}$
x_3	$\{2.47 \times 10^{-6},\ 2.5 \times 10^{-6},\ 2.53 \times 10^{-6}\}$
x_4	$\{2.47 \times 10^{-6},\ 2.5 \times 10^{-6},\ 2.53 \times 10^{-6}\}$
x_5	$\{2.96 \times 10^{-6},\ 3.0 \times 10^{-6},\ 3.04 \times 10^{-6}\}$

Table 4, where the central value of every fuzzy probability subset is the maximum possible value of probability of fault, and the left is the lower limit, and right is the upper limit.

TABLE 5: The fuzzy gate rules for imbalance of rotor's quality.

Rules	$x1$	$x2$	$x3$	$y2$ 0	0.5	1
1	0	0	0	1	0	0
2	0	0	0.5	0.55	0.25	0.2
3	0	0	1	0.1	0.35	0.55
⋮		...			...	
16	1	1	0	0.05	0.05	0.9
17	1	1	0.5	0	0.05	0.95
18	1	1	1	0	0	1

TABLE 6: The fuzzy gate rules for thermal bending of rotor's quality.

Rules	$x4$	$x5$	$y3$ 0	0.5	1
1	0	0	1	0	0
2	0	0.5	0.5	0.3	0.2
3	0	1	0.1	0.3	0.6
4	0.5	0	0.5	0.3	0.2
5	0.5	0.5	0.2	0.3	0.5
6	0.5	1	0.05	0.15	0.8
7	1	0	0.1	0.3	0.6
8	1	0.5	0.05	0.15	0.8
9	1	1	0	0	1

TABLE 7: The fuzzy gate rules for increased amplitude of the rotor's power frequency.

Rules	$y2$	$y3$	$y1$ 0	1
1	0	0	1	0
2	0	0.5	0.6	0.4
3	0	1	0.4	0.6
4	0.5	0	0.65	0.35
5	0.5	0.5	0.3	0.7
6	0.5	1	0.2	0.8
7	1	0	0.3	0.7
8	1	0.5	0.2	0.8
9	1	1	0	1

Tables 5~7 are the fuzzy gate rule corresponding to the constructed T-S fuzzy gate fault tree. For example, rule 1 in Table 5 indicates that when the state of (x_1, x_2, x_3) is (0,0,0), the probability that the upper event takes 0, 0.5, and 1 is 1, 0, and 0, respectively.

The fault probability fuzzy subsets of y_1, y_2, and y_3 can be obtained in Table 8 by (1) and (8).

When the fault state of the leaf node y_1 is 1, the fault probability of the root node $x_1 = 1$ can be obtained by (7).

$$P(x_1 = 1 \mid y_1 = 1) = E\left[\frac{\widetilde{P}(x_1 = 1, y_1 = 1)}{\widetilde{P}(y_1 = 1)}\right] \quad (9)$$

$$= 0.11649.$$

TABLE 8: Probabilities fuzzy subsets of leaf nodes and intermediate nodes.

Node state	Fault probability fuzzy subset
$\tilde{P}(y_1 = 1)$	$\{9.264 \times 10^{-6},\ 9.385 \times 10^{-6},\ 9.507 \times 10^{-6}\}$
$\tilde{P}(y_2 = 0.5)$	$\{4.195 \times 10^{-6},\ 4.250 \times 10^{-6},\ 4.305 \times 10^{-6}\}$
$\tilde{P}(y_2 = 1)$	$\{5.552 \times 10^{-6},\ 5.625 \times 10^{-6},\ 5.699 \times 10^{-6}\}$
$\tilde{P}(y_3 = 0.5)$	$\{3.258 \times 10^{-6},\ 3.300 \times 10^{-6},\ 3.342 \times 10^{-6}\}$
$\tilde{P}(y_3 = 1)$	$\{4.344 \times 10^{-6},\ 4.400 \times 10^{-6},\ 4.456 \times 10^{-6}\}$

TABLE 9: Conditional probability table of root nodes.

Unit x_i	The probability of failure of x_i (/h)
x_1	0.11649
x_2	0.43342
x_3	0.42758
x_4	0.22761
x_5	0.22421

Similarly, the fault probability of the remaining root nodes is shown in Table 9.

In the case where the amplitude of the acquired rotor's power frequency increased abnormally, the probability of fault of each root node is obtained through the above reasoning. From Table 9, the order from large to small is $x_2 > x_3 > x_4 > x_5 > x_1$. So the most likely cause of the abnormal increase in the amplitude of the rotor's power frequency is breakage or shedding of components and then is eccentric.

5.2. Algorithm Comparison and Analysis. In the case of complete historical data, the structure of BN is constructed by experts' experience, and the conditional probability table of every node is obtained through learning from the data. When the leaf nodes are abnormal, the traditional fault diagnosis method based on BN is built through this method, and it calculates the fault probability of leaf nodes shown in Table 10. In addition, the BP neural network is trained for the same data, and the results of fault diagnosis are also shown in Table 10. Considering the incomplete data, the states of some nodes are set as unknown, and the results of fault diagnosis through the method this paper mentions, traditional BN, and BP neural network are also shown in Table 10.

For ease of analysis, the results in Table 10 are converted into the line chart shown in Figure 5. It can be seen from the figure that when the historical data is complete, the results of the method proposed in this paper are similar to that of traditional fault diagnosis method based on BN, so the effectiveness of the method proposed in this paper is demonstrated. But the results of the method based on BP neural network have errors with both, because fault diagnosis based on BP neural network requires a lot of effective historical data, which is not available in reality. When the historical data is incomplete, the results obtained by the three methods are all in error with that obtained when the data is complete. But the diagnosis results of the method in this paper are closer to that with complete data. The reason is

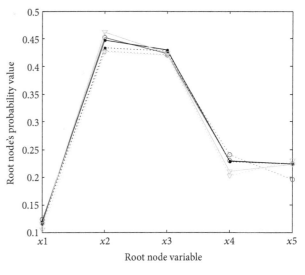

FIGURE 5: The fault probability of root nodes when the leaf nodes state is 1.

that when the data is incomplete, the accuracy of diagnosis result through traditional BN is affected by the increasing error in parameter learning, and the diagnosis result of BP neural network is more inaccurate because of the incomplete data. The method in this paper can reduce the impact of data loss effectively for the integration of experts' experience and T-S fuzzy fault tree.

In this paper, T-S fuzzy fault tree is used in construction, and the advantage of BN is used in reasoning. At present, the reasoning algorithm based on joint tree is the fastest in calculation and the most widely used in BN. The computational complexity of the method is exponentially increasing with the increase of the largest agglomeration in the joint tree. In dealing with general BN, the computing speed of current computers can meet the requirements.

6. Conclusions

This paper combines the T-S fuzzy fault tree method with Bayesian network method to solve the problem of fault diagnosis of pumping unit. This method overcomes not only the complex reasoning of T-S fuzzy fault tree method but also the difficulty of determining the structure and conditional probability table of Bayesian network. The effectiveness of the method is verified by fault diagnosis of the rotor, which is one of the most prone parts in the pump unit. The results are superior to the simple Bayesian network method when the data is insufficient. This method can be applied to the fault diagnosis of pumping station with complex structure, many uncertainties, and multiple mapping.

TABLE 10: Fault probability of root node when the state of leaf nodes is 1.

Root node x_i	Complete data			Incomplete data		
	BN	FFTA&BN	BPNN	BN	FFTA&BN	BPNN
x_1	0.11721	0.11649	0.11525	0.12412	0.12018	0.10525
x_2	0.45258	0.43342	0.46220	0.42775	0.44785	0.42550
x_3	0.42334	0.42758	0.42353	0.42123	0.43002	0.42023
x_4	0.23002	0.22761	0.21002	0.24024	0.22886	0.20236
x_5	0.22358	0.22421	0.22350	0.19583	0.22410	0.22965

Conflicts of Interest

The authors declare that there are no conflicts of interest regarding the publication of this paper.

Acknowledgments

This work was supported in part by "Key Technology Integration and Demonstration of Optimum Dispatching of Pumping Stations of East Route of South-to-North Water Diversion Project" of the National Key Technology R&D Program in the 12th Five-Year Plan of China (2015BAB07B01).

References

[1] B. Qiu, Y. Yang, T. Yan et al., "Main failure modes and their discriminant criteria of large low-lift pump units," *Fluid Machinery*, vol. 43, no. 11, pp. 51–56, 2015.

[2] Z. Zhu and H. Tang, "Study on condition monitoring and cooperative fault diagnosis of pump station in south-to-north water diversion project," *Water Resources Informatization*, vol. 3, pp. 46–49, 2015.

[3] Q. Jiang, B. Huang, S. X. Ding, and X. Yan, "Bayesian fault diagnosis with asynchronous measurements and its application in networked distributed monitoring," *IEEE Transactions on Industrial Electronics*, vol. 63, no. 10, pp. 6316–6324, 2016.

[4] S. Minn, S. Fu, and T. Lv, "Algorithm for exact recovery of Bayesian network for classification," *Application Research of Computers*, vol. 33, no. 05, pp. 1327–1334, 2016.

[5] B. Cai, H. Liu, and M. Xie, "A real-time fault diagnosis methodology of complex systems using object-oriented Bayesian networks," *Mechanical Systems and Signal Processing*, vol. 80, pp. 31–44, 2016.

[6] Z. Zhang, J. Zhu, and F. Pan, "Fault detection and diagnosis for data incomplete industrial systems with new Bayesian network approach," *Journal of Systems Engineering and Electronics*, vol. 24, no. 3, Article ID 6550961, pp. 500–511, 2013.

[7] B. Hua, J. Zhou, and J. Yu, "Application of Bayesian Networks in faults diagnosis of hydroelectric unit," *Journal of North China Electric Power University*, vol. 31, no. 05, pp. 33–36, 2004.

[8] Y. Hu, Z. Xiao, Y. Zhou et al., "Study of hydropower units fault diagnosis based on Bayesian network Noisy or model," in *Proceedings of the 6th International Symposium on Fluid Machinery and Fluid Engineering ISFMFE '14*, pp. 1–6, October 2014.

[9] H. Song, H.-Y. Zhang, and C. W. Chan, "Fuzzy fault tree analysis based on T-S model with application to INS/GPS navigation system," *Soft Computing*, vol. 13, no. 1, pp. 31–40, 2009.

[10] C. Yao, D. Chen, and B. Wang, "Fuzzy reliability assessment method based on T-S fault tree and Bayesian network," *Journal of Mechanical Engineering*, vol. 50, no. 2, pp. 193–201, 2014.

[11] Y. F. Wang, M. Xie, K. M. Ng, and Y. F. Meng, "Quantitative risk analysis model of integrating fuzzy fault tree with Bayesian network," in *Proceedings of the 2011 IEEE International Conference on Intelligence and Security Informatics, ISI '11*, pp. 267–271, July 2011.

[12] Code of practice for technical management of pumping station GB/T 30948-2014, General Administration of quality supervision, inspection and Quarantine of People's Republic of China and China National Standardization Administration, 2014.

[13] China Irrigation and Drainage Development Center, *Research on Key Technology of Large Pumping Station Renewal*, Water and Power Press, Beijing, China, 2011.

Permissions

The contributors of this book come from diverse backgrounds, making this book a truly international effort. This book will bring forth new frontiers with its revolutionizing research information and detailed analysis of the nascent developments around the world.

We would like to thank all the contributing authors for lending their expertise to make the book truly unique. They have played a crucial role in the development of this book. Without their invaluable contributions this book wouldn't have been possible. They have made vital efforts to compile up to date information on the varied aspects of this subject to make this book a valuable addition to the collection of many professionals and students.

This book was conceptualized with the vision of imparting up-to-date information and advanced data in this field. To ensure the same, a matchless editorial board was set up. Every individual on the board went through rigorous rounds of assessment to prove their worth. After which they invested a large part of their time researching and compiling the most relevant data for our readers.

The editorial board has been involved in producing this book since its inception. They have spent rigorous hours researching and exploring the diverse topics which have resulted in the successful publishing of this book. They have passed on their knowledge of decades through this book. To expedite this challenging task, the publisher supported the team at every step. A small team of assistant editors was also appointed to further simplify the editing procedure and attain best results for the readers.

Apart from the editorial board, the designing team has also invested a significant amount of their time in understanding the subject and creating the most relevant covers. They scrutinized every image to scout for the most suitable representation of the subject and create an appropriate cover for the book.

The publishing team has been an ardent support to the editorial, designing and production team. Their endless efforts to recruit the best for this project, has resulted in the accomplishment of this book. They are a veteran in the field of academics and their pool of knowledge is as vast as their experience in printing. Their expertise and guidance has proved useful at every step. Their uncompromising quality standards have made this book an exceptional effort. Their encouragement from time to time has been an inspiration for everyone.

The publisher and the editorial board hope that this book will prove to be a valuable piece of knowledge for researchers, students, practitioners and scholars across the globe.

List of Contributors

Bin Zhou and JiaHao Tan
College of Computer Science, South-Central University for Nationalities, Wuhan, Hubei 430074, China

ShuDao Zhang
School of Information Engineering, Wuhan Technology and Business University, Wuhan, Hubei 430065, China

Ying Zhang
School of Foreign Languages, Huazhong University of Science and Technology, Wuhan, Hubei 430074, China

Xinyue Cao
School of Computer and Software, Nanjing University of Information Science and Technology, Nanjing 210044, China

Zhangjie Fu and Xingming Sun
School of Computer and Software, Nanjing University of Information Science and Technology, Nanjing 210044, China
Jiangsu Engineering Centre of Network Monitor, Nanjing University of Information Science and Technology, Nanjing 210044, China

Ibrahim Delibalta and Lemi Baruh
Koc University, Istanbul, Turkey

Suleyman Serdar Kozat
Bilkent University, Ankara, Turkey

Yujia Jiang and Xin Liu
College of Architecture and Artistic Design, Hunan Institute of Technology, Hengyang 421001, China

K. C. Okafor and Gordon C. Ononiwu
Department of Mechatronics Engineering, Federal University of Technology Owerri, Ihiagwa, Nigeria

Ifeyinwa E. Achumba and Gloria A. Chukwudebe
Department of Electrical and Electronic Engineering, Federal University of Technology Owerri, Ihiagwa, Nigeria

Ge Zhou
School of Information Engineering, Chongqing Youth Vocational & Technical College, Chongqing 400712, China

Yong-feng Dong
School of Computer Science and Engineering, Big Data Computing Key Laboratory of Hebei Province, Hebei University of Technology, No. 5340 Xiping Road, Shuangkou, Beichen District, Tianjin 300401, China

Hong-mei Xia
School of Computer Science and Engineering, Hebei University of Technology, No. 5340 Xiping Road, Shuangkou, Beichen District, Tianjin 300401, China

Yan-cong Zhou
School of Information Engineering, Tianjin University of Commerce, Tianjin, China

Uma R. Salunkhe
Smt. Kashibai Navale College of Engineering, Savitribai Phule Pune University, Pune, India

Suresh N. Mali
Sinhgad Institute of Technology and Science, Savitribai Phule Pune University, Narhe, Pune, India

Shengcheng Ma, Xin Chen and Yingjie Yang
School of Computer Science, Beijing Information Science and Technology University, Beijing, China

Zhuo Li
Beijing Key Laboratory of Internet Culture and Digital Dissemination Research, School of Computer Science, Beijing Information Science and Technology University, Beijing, China

Özge Cepheli and Güneş Karabulut Kurt
Department of Electronics and Communication Engineering, Istanbul Technical University, 34469 Istanbul, Turkey

Saliha Büyükçorak
Department of Electronics and Communication Engineering, Istanbul Technical University, 34469 Istanbul, Turkey
Gebze Technical University, 41400 Kocaeli, Turkey

Zhe Zhang and Ying Li
Institute of Software, Nanyang Normal University, Nanyang, Henan 473061, China

Li Li
College of Communication Engineering, Xidian University, Xi'an 710071, China
Department of Electronic and Information Engineering, Beijing Electronics Science and Technology Institute, Beijing 100070, China

Kui Geng
State Key Laboratory of Information Security, Institute of Information Engineering, CAS, Beijing 100093, China

Fenghua Li
State Key Laboratory of Information Security, Institute of Information Engineering, CAS, Beijing 100093, China
School of Cyber Security, University of Chinese Academy of Sciences, Beijing 100049, China

Guozhen Shi
Department of Information Security, Beijing Electronic Science and Technology Institute, Beijing 100070, China

Yunyu Shi, Xiang Liu and Yongxiang Xia
School of Electronic and Electrical Engineering, Shanghai University of Engineering Science, Shanghai, China

Haisheng Yang and Ming Gong
Shanghai Media Group, Shanghai, China

Weihang Shi
College of Software Technology, Zhengzhou University, Zhengzhou, Henan 450002, China

Hongxing Yuan
School of Electronics and Information Engineering, Ningbo University of Technology, Ningbo 315211, China

Yuwei Peng and Mingliang Yue
Computer School, Wuhan University, Wuhan 430072, China

Bin Jia, Xiaohong Huang and Yan Ma
Information and Network Center, Institute of Network Technology, Beijing University of Posts and Telecommunications, Beijing 100876, China

Rujun Liu
School of CyberSpace Security, Beijing University of Posts and Telecommunications, Beijing 100876, China

Kaixin Zhao
Department of Computer Science and Technology, Henan Institute of Technology, Xinxiang 453003, China

Jie Cui and Zhiqiang Xie
School of Computer Science and Technology, Anhui University, Hefei 230039, China

Zou Cairong
Department of Information and Communication Engineering, Guangzhou Maritime University, Guangzhou 510006, China
Key Laboratory of Underwater Acoustic signal Processing of Ministry of Education, Southeast University, Nanjing 210096, China

Zhang Xinran, Zha Cheng and Zhao Li
Key Laboratory of Underwater Acoustic signal Processing of Ministry of Education, Southeast University, Nanjing 210096, China

Jinfeng Yang, Zhen Zhong, Guimin Jia and Yanan Li
Tianjin Key Lab for Advanced Signal Processing, Civil Aviation University of China, CAUC, Tianjin 300300, China

Yu Sun, Lin Zhu, Guan Wang and Fang Zhao
School of Information Science and Technology, Beijing Forestry University, Beijing 100083, China

Zhuqing Bi, Chenming Li, Xujie Li and Hongmin Gao
College of Computer and Information Engineering, Hohai University, Nanjing 211100, China

Index

CPSIA information can be obtained
at www.ICGtesting.com
Printed in the USA
LVHW061951020920
664884LV00007B/292